SECOND EDITION

# ADVANCED
# READING POWER 4

*Extensive Reading • Vocabulary Building • Comprehension Skills • Reading Fluency*

Linda Jeffries

Beatrice S. Mikulecky

PEARSON
Longman

**Advanced Reading Power 4, Second Edition**

Pearson Education, 10 Bank Street, White Plains, NY 10606

**Staff credits:** The people who made up the *Advanced Reading Power 4, Second Edition* team, representing editorial, production, design, and manufacturing, are Tracey Munz Cataldo, Rosa Chapinal, Aerin Csigay, Nancy Flaggman, Ann France, Barry Katzen, Amy McCormick, Lise Minovitz, Liza Pleva, Joan L. Poole, and Jane Townsend.

**Project Management:** Jennifer Stem/JTS Studio, Inc.
**Development:** Jaimie Scanlon, Waterstone Editorial Services, LLC.
**Text composition:** ElectraGraphics, Inc.
**Text font:** Adobe Caslon Pro
**Illustration and tech art:** ElectraGraphics, Inc.
**Photo credits:** Cover: (left) lichtmeister/Fotolia, (middle left) Jeffrey Coolidge/Corbis, (middle right) 2happy/Shutterstock, (right) Mike Flippo/Shutterstock; Page 1 lichtmeister/Fotolia; p. 20 Rechitan Sorin/Shutterstock; p. 22 ra2studio/Shutterstock; p. 37 Jeffrey Coolidge/Corbis; p. 101 2happy/Shutterstock; p. 255 Mike Flippo/Shutterstock.

**Library of Congress Cataloging-in-Publication Data**

Jeffries, Linda.
  Advanced Reading Power 4 / Linda Jeffries, Beatrice S. Mikulecky.—Second edition.
    pages cm
  ISBN 978-0-13-304717-2
  1. English language—Textbooks for foreign speakers. 2. Reading comprehension—Problems, exercises, etc. 3. Vocabulary—Study and teaching. 4. Reading (Higher education) I. Mikulecky, Beatrice S. II. Title. III. Title: Advanced Reading Power four.
  PE1128.J3474 2014
  428.6'4—dc23

ISBN-10: 0-13-304717-2
ISBN-13: 978-0-13-304717-2

Printed in the United States of America
      31 2020

# Contents

**Introduction**                                                                    v

| Part 1 | **Extensive Reading** |
|---|---|

Unit 1:  An Introduction to Extensive Reading                    2
Unit 2:  Fiction and Nonfiction                                           9
Unit 3:  Books for Extensive Reading                                 19

| Part 2 | **Vocabulary Building** |
|---|---|

Unit 1:  Learning New Vocabulary from Your Reading       38
Unit 2:  Inferring Meaning from Context                          54
Unit 3:  Word Parts                                                           66
Unit 4:  Phrases                                                                83

| Part 3 | **Comprehension Skills** |
|---|---|

Unit 1:  Scanning and Previewing                                   103
Unit 2:  Making Inferences and Predictions                    123
Unit 3:  Paragraphs: Structure and Reference                146
Unit 4:  Identifying Patterns                                          165
Unit 5:  Reading for Study                                             189
Unit 6:  Genres of Writing                                             206
Unit 7:  Skimming                                                         220
Unit 8:  Critical Reading                                                237

| Part 4 | **Reading Fluency** |
|---|---|

Unit 1:  An Introduction to Reading Fluency                  256
Unit 2:  People Who Have Made a Difference                 265
Unit 3:  The Impact of Modern Technology                    280
Unit 4:  Issues and Ideas                                               295

**Appendix**                                                                        310

# Acknowledgments

Many thanks in particular to Joan Chamberlin and Lindsey Gutt, who, as reviewers, gave invaluable feedback, offered suggestions on various aspects of the book, and enlightened me about their teaching concerns.

I am grateful to my friend and colleague in Modena, Anna Masetti, for her suggestions and support, and to my husband for his infinite patience.

Finally, I am enormously indebted, once again, to the development editor, Jaimie Scanlon, for her insight, encouragement, and sense of humor, which kept me going on many occasions.

## *Advanced Reading Power 4* Reviewers

The publisher and authors would like to extend special thanks to the following individuals who reviewed *Advanced Reading Power 4*, and whose comments were instrumental in developing this edition.

Thanks,
Linda

**Sung Yung Bae,** University of San Francisco, Department of Rhetoric and Language/ESL, San Francisco, CA; **Joan Chamberlin** Iowa State University, Intensive English and Orientation Program, Ames, IA; **Sukyun Lee,** Pace University, English Language Institute, New York, NY; **Lindsey Gutt,** York University, English Language Institute, Toronto, Canada

# About the Authors

**Linda Jeffries** holds a master's degree in TESOL from Boston University. She has taught reading, writing and ESL/EFL at Boston College, Boston University, the Harvard University Summer ESL Program, the University of Opole, Poland, and the University of Bologna, Italy. She lives in Italy, near Bologna, and teaches academic reading and writing at the University of Modena.

**Bea Mikulecky** holds a master's degree in TESOL and a doctorate in Applied Psycholinguistics from Boston University. In addition to teaching reading, writing, and ESL, she has worked as a teacher trainer in the Harvard University Summer ESL Program, in the Simmons College MATESL Program, and in Moscow, Russia. Bea Mikulecky is the author of *A Short Course in Teaching Reading Skills*.

# Introduction

## To the Teacher

*Advanced Reading Power 4* is unlike most other reading textbooks. First, the book is organized in a different way. It has four separate parts that correspond to four important aspects of proficient reading, and, therefore, it is like four books in one.

**Teachers should assign work in all four parts of the book every week.**

The four parts of *Advanced Reading Power 4* are:

- **Part 1: Extensive Reading**
- **Part 2: Vocabulary Building**
- **Part 3: Comprehension Skills**
- **Part 4: Reading Fluency**

The focus of *Advanced Reading Power 4* is also different. While most books focus on content, this book directs students' attention to their own reading processes. The aim is for students to develop a strategic approach to reading, so that they learn to view reading in English as a problem-solving activity rather than a translation exercise. This will enable them to acquire good reading habits and skills and build confidence for dealing with college- or university-level reading requirements.

*Advanced Reading Power 4* is designed to meet the needs of students who are enrolled in pre-college or university programs, or upper-intermediate to advanced classes at the post-secondary level (Common European Framework of Reference for Languages: B2–C1). Emphasis has been placed on the development of skills necessary for academic success, including building academic vocabulary.

To encourage awareness of reading and thinking processes, students are often asked to work in pairs or small groups. Discussion with others not only provides students with opportunities to practice speaking and consolidate vocabulary learning, but it can also help them formulate and articulate their ideas more precisely and acquire new ways of talking and thinking about a text. Furthermore, including pair and group work enlivens the reading class and helps dispel views of reading as a tedious and solitary activity.

In this second edition of *Advanced Reading Power 4*, the approach remains the same as in the first edition, with updated content and exercise types in response to recent research and feedback from teachers. The major changes in this edition include:

**Part 1: Extensive Reading**—new fiction and nonfiction passages; more guidance for dealing with new vocabulary in extensive reading; additional activities for evaluating and sharing reading experiences

**Part 2: Vocabulary Building**—more guidance in vocabulary learning methods and students' own selection of useful vocabulary; additional dictionary work; new collocations exercises; a new word list that includes both academic and general vocabulary

**Part 3: Comprehension Skills**—new activities in many units; a genre-based approach to reading longer passages and a new approach to skimming; new content with related themes and more passages from authentic academic texts

**Part 4: Reading Fluency**—new and updated content and new question types

Note: A separate *Teacher's Guide* contains the Answer Key, a rationale for the approach taken in *Advanced Reading Power 4*, specific suggestions for using it in the classroom, a sample syllabus to aid teachers in planning their courses, and the Pearson Academic Collocations List.

A test booklet is also available separately. It includes tests of vocabulary presented in the Student Book, as well as additional skills exercises for evaluation or additional practice.

## To the Student

Reading is an essential skill for study at school, college, or university. Improving your reading ability in English will benefit your academic performance in many ways.

1) You will be able to complete reading assignments and deal with reading comprehension tasks more efficiently and effectively.

2) Improving your reading ability will allow you to read more in English.

3) Reading more in English will help you expand your knowledge of vocabulary, develop the thinking skills necessary for study in English, and improve your writing skills in English.

In *Advanced Reading Power 4*, you will work on reading in four ways in the four parts of the book:

**Part 1: Extensive Reading**—reading a lot in books that you choose
**Part 2: Vocabulary Building**—learning how to study vocabulary
**Part 3: Comprehension Skills**—understanding and following ideas in English
**Part 4: Reading Fluency**—learning to read faster with understanding

Work on **all four parts** of the book every week to improve your reading ability in English.

# Extensive Reading

# UNIT 1

# An Introduction to Extensive Reading

## Reading in Your Life

**A.** *Complete this questionnaire about reading in your life.*

### Reading Questionnaire

1. Looking back at your childhood, what do you remember about your early reading experiences?

2. What kinds of reading material did your parents have in the house when you were young?

3. Do your parents enjoy reading? Your friends?

4. What do you read in your first language? (books, magazines, newspapers, comics, graphic novels, web articles, blog posts)

5. If you read books in your language, what types of books do you enjoy most? (novels, mysteries, thrillers, fantasy, history, biography, science, etc.)

6. If you have a favorite book or writer (in any language), what or who is it?

7. What kind of reading is important in your life today? Why? In what language(s)?

8. About how many hours a week do you usually read for interest or pleasure (in any language)?

9. Have you ever read a whole book in English? If so, what book?

10. If you could easily read anything in English, what would you like to read?

**B.** *Talk about your answers with two or three other students.*

**C.** *Discuss these questions with your group:*

1. Who has enjoyable memories of reading as a child?

2. Who enjoys reading in his or her own language?

3. Who reads the most for interest and pleasure?

4. Who has the same favorite books and/or writers?

5. Who has read a book in English?

## What Is Extensive Reading?

Basically, extensive reading means *reading a lot*. In this part of the reading course, you will

- read whole books.
- choose books that interest **you**.
- read at **your** own pace.
- **not** be tested on comprehension or vocabulary (in these books).

## Why Should You Read Extensively?

Extensive reading is the first and most important part of this reading course. Research has shown that it is the best way to improve your reading. If you read a lot, you become a faster reader, and your comprehension improves. In fact, the best readers are usually people who **love to read** and who **read extensively**.

Furthermore, studies have shown that extensive reading can also help improve your English language skills in various ways that are important for academic success, including:

- expanded vocabulary (new words and a deeper understanding of known words)
- a better sense of how words and phrases are used
- a better understanding of sentence structure
- the ability to write more natural-sounding English
- more confidence in speaking and writing

All this is possible for a very simple reason: When you read extensively, your brain gets a lot of practice processing written language. You have to recognize and make sense of thousands of words, phrases, and sentences in English. Not surprisingly, you become better at this kind of processing.

As you become more comfortable with the way words, phrases, and sentences are put together in English, you will probably also develop a better sense of how to use the language yourself in speaking and writing. You may even begin to *think* in English. (But remember, this only happens if you read *a lot*.)

# New Vocabulary in Your Reading

When you read extensively, you will encounter many words that are new to you. What should you do about them?

There are a number of strategies you can use with new words. Which of these strategies do you use when you read?

1. Look up the words in the dictionary.
2. Skip over the new words and continue to read.
3. Look at the context for clues to their meanings.

In fact, good readers use all of these strategies at different times, depending on the word, the text, and the reason for reading the text. However, keep in mind that your goal with this kind of reading is to *read as much as possible*. If you stop often to look up words when you are reading in your extensive reading book, you will have trouble following the story, you will enjoy it less, and, as a result, you will read less.

## Unknown Words and Comprehension

> **Strategy 1**  When you read extensively, *do not look up every unfamiliar word in the dictionary*. Look up only the words you need to know to follow the story.

You may be wondering if you will be able to understand what you are reading without looking up the new words and phrases. In fact, if there are too many unknown words, you may have trouble understanding. That is why it is important to choose an extensive reading book that is not too difficult for you. In general, there should not be more than 3 percent unknown words (for example, nine unknown words on a page of 300 words).

In extensive reading, it is usually not necessary to know the exact meaning of every word. For example, novels often contain descriptions full of nouns and adjectives that are not very common. You may never see some of those words again and never need to use them. Also, you may not need to know the precise meaning of all the words in order to follow the story; a general understanding of the description or situation may be enough.

> **Strategy 2**  When you encounter a new word in your extensive reading, try skipping over it and reading ahead. You may be able to follow the story or ideas without it.

In the following exercises, some words in the story have been replaced with *xxxxxx*, as though they were unknown to you.

**A.** *This passage is from the beginning of a short story, "The Use of Force," by William Carlos Williams. Read the passage and answer the questions at the end. Do not try to guess the missing words.*

They were new patients to me, all I had was the name, Olson. Please come down as soon as you can, my daughter is very sick.

When I arrived I was met by the mother, a big xxxxxx woman, very clean and xxxxxx, who merely said, Is this the doctor? and let me in. In the back, she added. You must excuse us, doctor, we have her in the kitchen where it is warm. It is very xxxxxx here sometimes.

The child was fully dressed and sitting on her father's xxxxxx near the kitchen table. He tried to get up, but I xxxxxx for him not to bother, took off my overcoat and started to look things over. I could see that they were all very nervous, eyeing me up and down xxxxxx. As often, in such cases, they weren't telling me more than they had to, it was up to me to tell them; that's why they were spending three dollars on me.

The child was fairly eating me up with her cold, xxxxxx eyes, and no expression to her face whatever. She did not move and seemed, inwardly, quiet; an unusually attractive little thing, and as strong as a xxxxxx in appearance. But her face was xxxxxx, she was breathing rapidly, and I realized that she had a high fever. She had xxxxxx blonde hair . . . like one of those pictures of children often reproduced in advertising leaflets and the photogravure sections of the Sunday papers.

1. When and where do you think this story takes place?
2. Who is the narrator? (The narrator is "I" in the story.)
3. Why is the narrator at the Olson's house?
4. Why are the mother and father very nervous?
5. What have you learned about the child?

**B.** *Discuss your answers with another student. Give evidence from the text to support your answers.*

**A.** *The story continues below. Read the passage and answer the questions at the end. Do not try to guess the missing words.*

She's had a fever for three days, began the father, and we don't know what it comes from. My wife has given her xxxxxx, you know, like people do, but it don't do no good. And there's been a lot of sickness around. So we thought you'd better look her over and tell us what is the matter.

. . . Has she had a sore throat?

Both parents answered me together, No . . . No, she says her throat don't hurt her.

Does your throat hurt you? xxxxxx the mother to the child. But the little girl's expression didn't change nor did she move her xxxxxx from my face.

Have you looked?

I tried to, said the mother, but I couldn't see.

As it happens we had been having a number of cases of xxxxxx in the school to which this child went during that month and we were all, quite xxxxxx, thinking of that, though no one had as yet spoken of the thing.

Well, I said, suppose we take a look at the throat first. I smiled in my best xxxxxx manner and asking for the child's first name I said, come on, Mathilda, open your mouth and let's take a look at your throat.

Nothing doing.

Aw, come on, I xxxxxx, just open your mouth wide and let me take a look. Look, I said opening both hands wide, I haven't anything in my hands. Just open up and let me see.

Such a nice man, put in the mother. Look how kind he is to you. Come on, do what he tells you to. He won't hurt you.

At that I ground my teeth in xxxxxx. If only they wouldn't use the word "hurt" I might be able to get somewhere. But I did not allow myself to be hurried or xxxxxx but speaking quietly and slowly I xxxxxx the child again.

As I moved my chair a little nearer suddenly with one catlike movement both her hands xxxxxx instinctively for my eyes and she almost reached them too. In fact she xxxxxx my glasses flying and they fell, though unbroken, several feet away from me on the kitchen floor.

1. What is wrong with the child?
2. Why does the narrator want to look at the girl's throat?
3. What does the narrator think about the mother?
4. What does the child do at the end? Why?

B. *Discuss your answers with another student. Give evidence from the text to support your answers.*

C. *Discuss Exercises 1 and 2 with the class. How many questions could you answer in each exercise? How well do you think you understood the passages in spite of the missing words? What does this tell you about unfamiliar words in your reading?*

## Making Use of the Context

When you encounter a word that seems important in the story, don't reach immediately for your dictionary. This will take your mind off the story and slow you down.

Instead, you should look for clues to meaning in the context—the words and sentences around the word. You may not be able to guess the precise meaning, but you may be able to get a general idea, and that may be enough to follow the story.

**Example:** During the storm, a large branch from the old sycamore came down right beside the house, just missing the car and the garage.

From the context, you learn that a *sycamore* has branches that can fall down during a storm. You can guess it must be a kind of tree, probably a large one. You don't need to know any more than that in order to understand what happened.

| |
|---|
| **Strategy 3** Before you look up an unfamiliar word, look at the context—the words and sentences around the word. Figure out the part of speech and try to guess the general meaning. |

In the next exercises, you will try to guess missing words in a passage using the context around a word or phrase. This is like guessing the meaning of unknown words.

**A.** *Read the passage. This time, try to guess a word or phrase for each blank.*

They were new patients to me, all I had was the name, Olson. Please come down as soon as you can, my daughter is very sick.

When I arrived I was met by the mother, a big _____ woman, very clean
                                                                    1
and _____ who merely said, Is this the doctor? and let me in. In the back,
            2
she added. You must excuse us, doctor, we have her in the kitchen where it is warm. It is
very _____ here sometimes.
            3
The child was fully dressed and sitting on her father's _____ near the
                                                                          4
kitchen table. He tried to get up, but I _____ for him not to bother, took
                                                      5
off my overcoat and started to look things over. I could see that they were all very nervous,
eyeing me up and down _____. As often, in such cases, they weren't telling
                                      6
me more than they had to, it was up to me to tell them; that's why they were spending
three dollars on me.

The child was fairly eating me up with her cold, _____ eyes, and
                                                                  7
no expression to her face whatever. She did not move and seemed, inwardly, quiet; an
unusually attractive little thing, and as strong as a _____ in appearance.
                                                                    8
But her face was _____, she was breathing rapidly, and I realized that she
                          9
had a high fever. She had _____ blonde hair . . . one of those pictures of
                                      10
children often reproduced in advertising leaflets and the photogravure sections of the
Sunday papers.

**B.** *Discuss your answers with another student. Give evidence from the text to support your answers.*

**A.** *Read the passage from Exercise 2 again. Try to guess a word or phrase for each blank.*

She's had a fever for three days, began the father and we don't know what it comes
from. My wife has given her _____, you know, like people do, but it don't
                                          1

do no good. And there's been a lot of sickness around. So we thought you'd better look her over and tell us what is the matter.

. . . Has she had a sore throat?

Both parents answered me together, No . . . No, she says her throat don't hurt her.

Does your throat hurt you? _____ 2 the mother to the child. But the little girl's expression didn't change nor did she move her _____ 3 from my face.

Have you looked?

I tried to, said the mother, but I couldn't see.

As it happens we had been having a number of cases of _____ 4 in the school to which this child went during that month and we were all, quite _____ 5, thinking of that, though no one had as yet spoken of the thing.

Well, I said, suppose we take a look at the throat first. I smiled in my best _____ 6 manner and asking for the child's first name I said, come on, Mathilda, open your mouth and let's take a look at your throat.

Nothing doing.

Aw, come on, I _____ 7, just open your mouth wide and let me take a look. Look, I said opening both hands wide, I haven't anything in my hands. Just open up and let me see.

Such a nice man, put in the mother. Look how kind he is to you. Come on, do what he tells you to. He won't hurt you.

At that I ground my teeth in _____ 8. If only they wouldn't use the word "hurt" I might be able to get somewhere. But I did not allow myself to be hurried or _____ 9 but speaking quietly and slowly I _____ 10 the child again.

As I moved my chair a little nearer suddenly with one catlike movement both her hands _____ 11 instinctively for my eyes and she almost reached them too. In fact she _____ 12 my glasses flying and they fell, though unbroken, several feet away from me on the kitchen floor.

B. *Talk about your answers with another student. Give evidence from the text to support your answers.*

# UNIT 2

# Fiction and Nonfiction

In this unit, you will read a short story (fiction) and an article (nonfiction) and practice steps for understanding both fiction and nonfiction.

## Fiction

Works of fiction include short stories, novels, science fiction, fantasy, mysteries, and thrillers. They usually deal with imaginary people and events, though they can also be based on real people and events (historical novels, for example).

The first three exercises focus on a short story by Jeremy Glazer, a writer who lives in Florida.

## EXERCISE 1

**A.** *Discuss these questions with a group of students:*

1. How common is it for young people in your country to attend college or university?
2. Who makes the decision about whether to attend—the young person, the parents, both?
3. How common is it for someone to stop their studies to work for a year or two between high school and college? Do you know anyone who has done that?
4. Do you think it's a good idea?
5. What do you know about Miami, Florida?

**B.** *Read the title of the story on the next page. Discuss these questions with your group:*

1. What are dolphins? Oysters? Crabs?
2. What do you think of when you hear these words?
3. Based on the title, what do you think this story might be about?

**C.** *Preview Part 1 of the story for the answers to these questions. When you preview, do not read many words or lines. Move your eyes through the text very quickly–for about one minute. Then discuss these questions with another student:*

1. How long is this part of the story?
2. Are there many characters?
3. How much dialogue is there?
4. What can you tell about the setting of the story?
5. Will the story be easy or difficult for you to read? Why?

## Dolphins, Oysters and Crabs (Part 1)

by Jeremy Glazer

"The world is your oyster."

My principal actually said that at graduation. And she said it like it was original, like she had come up with the line herself and was so proud. Sitting there, in the auditorium, I felt sorry for her.

But I don't feel sorry for her anymore. Lately, I've been feeling sorry for me because so far—the world hasn't been my oyster.

It's more like a crab. When I grab it wrong, it hurts.

That graduation speech was a year ago. And maybe that's why I started thinking about the whole oyster thing again. And maybe that's what depressed me, because I felt stuck.

See, I was supposed to go to college last year. I got in to FIU [Florida International University]. For engineering. But I didn't like school much, and, with this ocean of possibilities in front of me, I wasn't sure I should keep doing the one thing I knew I didn't like. So when I showed up for orientation in July and couldn't find a place to park, and couldn't find the room where I was supposed to go, and then couldn't find anyone who even looked halfway nice enough to ask, I figured it was a sign. I got in the car and drove home.

"You have to go to college," my mom said. "You can't even get a real job with a college degree these days."

I said "Ma, it won't be forever." My dad was silent, which was worse. He just shook his head, slowly.

Then he called his friend Stan and asked for a favor. And the following Saturday we went to meet Stan for lunch at a barbecue shack in Hialeah.

On the way, my dad said, "You don't work, you don't stay in our house. Get it?"

Stan and my dad talked for most of the meal about how the world is going to hell in a handbasket, and after Stan sucked the meat off his last rib, he pointed it at me and said:

"You're hired. Be there Monday. Front gate." Then, he handed me his card. It said Miamiquarium with a picture of a killer whale.

So now I welcome visitors to the Miamiquarium. I scan their tickets with this wand that lights up and makes a screeching dolphin sound.

Turns out, it's worse than school. I sit in this birdcage-looking shed. It feels like a prison cell—with bars and everything. The only perk is that during breaks, I get to peek in on the shows. There's a huge whale that dances, a bunch of dolphins that jump and play catch, a tank full of stingrays with their tails chopped off so you can pet them, and, of course, the big sea lion show.

There is something amazing about watching those animals. It almost makes the job bearable.

**E.** *Discuss these questions with another pair of students:*

1. Where does the story take place?
2. What is the meaning of "the world is your oyster"?
3. How old do you think the narrator is?
4. What do you know about him? His personality? His family?
5. Why did he decide not to go to college?
6. Why did he have lunch with his father and Stan?
7. What does the narrator do at his job and what does he think about it?

**A.** *Preview Part 2 of the story quickly—about one minute—for the answers to these questions. Discuss them with another student.*

1. How long is this part?
2. Are there any new characters?
3. How much dialogue is there?
4. Does the setting change?

**B.** *Read Part 2. Do not stop reading to look up words in the dictionary. Skip the unfamiliar words, or try to guess their meaning from the context.*

### Dolphins, Oysters and Crabs (Part 2)

by Jeremy Glazer

But it wasn't just knowing it's been a year since graduation and remembering the oyster thing that was depressing me.

A month or so ago, a bunch of protestors showed up. They had signs about a whale in a bathtub and dolphins in slave chains and they were wearing these 'Free Ferdinand' t-shirts. He's our famous sea lion–or at least, Miami famous.

I left the birdcage to come out and watch. There were TV cameras and everything.

"Slaveowner! Get off the plantation!" one of the protestors yelled at me when I walked over. She looked a little like my elementary school music teacher.

I said "I only take tickets." She said, "You're a foot soldier. Defect!"

After a while, the protestors lost steam. They seemed to be withering in the sun. I don't think they were from here.

But it got me thinking. They're right. The animals must hate this. All us humans who work here hate it. And the animals work harder than we do.

It started to really bother me.

Then, one morning on my way to work I was early so I stopped and parked on the causeway out to Key Biscayne. Downtown Miami looks like Atlantis rising out of the sea, especially on hazy summer mornings. I was standing there looking at the buildings and I caught a little black out of the corner of my eye. A fin. A dolphin. Then there was another. And a third.

They were a dark shiny black rather than prison grey, like the ones in the tank at the park. They were swimming together, playing around. They looked so happy. No one had to throw them any cut up fish to get them to jump.

I watched for so long I was late to work, but all I got was a stern look from my boss. It was worth it, and I stopped the next day to watch too, and the day after that. The next week they were gone. I thought I caught sight of a tail one day, but I wasn't sure. After that, I still stopped, but I would just sit there. I wouldn't get out and look. It was too disappointing. I was getting to work later and later, and I guess Stan called my house because, one morning, when I was sitting there, paralyzed in my car, I heard a tap on the window. It was my dad. He must have followed me. I was screwed.

He tilted his head to tell me to get out of the car, and then he turned and walked toward the water. I followed him, and we stopped on a ridge of dry seaweed. Neither of us said anything. We just stared at the pastel skyline coming more into focus as the haze burned off.

"What are you waiting for?" he asked.

"Dolphins," I said.

He looked at me.

I told him about the world not being my oyster. About seeing dolphins. About not seeing them. About it driving me crazy.

I said, "If I knew the dolphins were there every day, that would be one thing. I'd just have to be patient, look long enough. But they aren't. Some days, I just won't be able to see them no matter how long I wait. It's out of my hands."

"You know where they are when you don't see them?" my dad asked. I squinted at him, not sure of the right answer. He pointed to the horizon with his chin. "They're out there. Free. They don't need you to worry about them. Worry about you."

We stood there, staring out at the water. After a few minutes, he reached over and squeezed my shoulder—gently, but I could feel the power in his hand. He walked back to his car and drove off. I went back to my car and drove to work.

That was two weeks ago and I haven't been late since. I leave really early for work now, in case I want to stop on the causeway.

Now, if I see any dolphins, I get happy. If I don't, I get happy too because I know they're out there in the ocean, far away from some big bathtub and frozen fish scraps.

Just knowing that makes it a little easier to sit in my cage and use that wand for eight hours. And, to plot my own escape.

**C.** *Discuss these questions with another student:*

1. Why were there protesters at the aquarium?
2. What was the narrator's reaction to the protesters?
3. Why did the narrator stop on his way to work?
4. How would you describe the narrator's relationship with his father?
5. What do you think the narrator will do after this?

## EXERCISE 3

**A.** *Read the story again (Exercises 1 and 2), and underline the unfamiliar words or phrases. Use the context to guess their meanings. For words and phrases you can't guess, look them up if they are necessary for understanding the story. Then write their definitions in the margins.*

**B.** *Compare work with another student. Did you look up the same words or phrases? Then, with a partner, retell the story from beginning to end.*

**C.** *Join another pair of students and discuss these questions:*

1. Are the characters in this story believable? Sympathetic [likeable]? Why or why not?
2. What is the climax [high point or key moment] of the story, in your opinion?
3. How would you describe the ending of this story—happy, sad, open-ended? Can you think of an alternative ending?
4. Did you ever have any doubts about attending college/university, like the narrator?
5. Have you ever worked at a job like the narrator's or at any service job, such as waiter/waitress, salesperson, etc.? If so, describe your experience.
6. Have you ever been to an aquarium? If so, where? How was the experience?
7. What are your views about animal rights? Have you ever met any animal activists?

# Nonfiction

Nonfiction writing is about real people, places, events, or things, and contains information that the writer believes or says is true, though others may disagree.

There are many kinds of nonfiction, including biography, history, "how-to" books about gardening, cooking, running a business, etc., and books about science, politics, health, travel, and so on. Some nonfiction–especially biography and history–may be appropriate for extensive reading, but other nonfiction may require more intensive reading because it contains complex ideas or technical vocabulary.

The following exercises focus on an article published in the *Wall Street Journal* and written by Amy Chua, professor of law at Yale University.

## EXERCISE 4

**A.** *Discuss these questions with a group of students:*

1. When you were a child, how much free time did you have?
2. What did you do in your free time?
3. Did you have "playdates" [scheduled play time] with friends at your house or their houses? Did you ever sleep over at a friend's house?
4. What kinds of activities were you involved in outside of school?
5. How much time were you allowed to watch TV? Be on the computer? Play video games?
6. Who in your family made decisions about your education? Your free time activities?

**B.** *Read the title, subtitle, and information about the author for the article below. Discuss these questions with your group:*

1. What do you think is the purpose or main point of the article?
2. What do you know about Chinese families? Chinese mothers?
3. What do you think is meant by a "Tiger Mother"?
4. What does the phrase "Battle Hymn" refer to?
5. Based on the title of the article (and the book), what do you think the article might be about?

**C.** *Preview Part 1 of the article for the answers to these questions. Then discuss them with another student:*

1. How long is this part of the article?
2. Are there a lot of names of people or places?
3. Are there a lot of numbers or dates?
4. Are there any quotations?
5. Will the article be easy or difficult for you to read? Why?

**D.** *Read Part 1 of the article. Do not stop reading to look up words in the dictionary. Skip the unfamiliar words, or try to guess their meaning from the context.*

# Why Chinese Mothers Are Superior (Part 1)

**Can a regimen of no playdates, no TV, no computer games, and hours of music practice create happy kids? And what happens when they fight back?**

by Amy Chua, professor of law at Yale University and author of *Battle Hymn of a Tiger Mother*

A lot of people wonder how Chinese parents raise such stereotypically successful kids. They wonder what these parents do to produce so many math whizzes and music prodigies, what it's like inside the family, and whether they could do it too. Well, I can tell them, because I've done it. Here are some things my daughters, Sophia and Louisa, were never allowed to do:

- attend a sleepover
- have a playdate
- be in a school play
- complain about not being in a school play
- watch TV or play computer games
- choose their own extracurricular activities
- get any grade less than an A
- not be the No. 1 student in every subject except gym and drama
- play any instrument other than the piano or violin
- not play the piano or violin.

I'm using the term "Chinese mother" loosely. I know some Korean, Indian, Jamaican, Irish and Ghanaian parents who qualify too. Conversely, I know some mothers of Chinese heritage, almost always born in the West, who are not Chinese mothers, by choice or otherwise. I'm also using the term "Western parents" loosely. Western parents come in all varieties.

All the same, even when Western parents think they're being strict, they usually don't come close to being Chinese mothers. For example, my Western friends who consider themselves strict make their children practice their instruments 30 minutes every day. An hour at most. For a Chinese mother, the first hour is the easy part. It's hours two and three that get tough.

Despite our squeamishness about cultural stereotypes, there are tons of studies out there showing marked and quantifiable differences between Chinese and Westerners when it comes to parenting. In one study of 50 Western American mothers and 48 Chinese immigrant mothers, almost 70% of the Western mothers said either that "stressing academic success is not good for children" or that "parents need to foster the idea that learning is fun." By contrast, roughly 0% of the Chinese mothers felt the same way.

Instead, the vast majority of the Chinese mothers said that they believe their children can be "the best" students, that "academic achievement reflects successful parenting," and that if children did not excel at school then there was "a problem" and parents "were not doing their job." Other studies indicate that compared to Western parents, Chinese parents spend approximately 10 times as long every day drilling academic activities with their children. By contrast, Western kids are more likely to participate in sports teams.

What Chinese parents understand is that nothing is fun until you're good at it. To get good at anything you have to work, and children on their own never want to work, which is why it is crucial to override their preferences. This often requires fortitude on the part of the parents because the child will resist; things are always hardest at the beginning, which is where Western parents tend to give up. But if done properly, the Chinese strategy produces a virtuous circle. Tenacious practice, practice, practice is crucial for excellence; rote repetition is underrated in America. Once a child starts to excel at something—whether it's math, piano, pitching or ballet—he or she gets praise, admiration and satisfaction. This builds confidence and makes the once not-fun activity fun. This in turn makes it easier for the parent to get the child to work even more.

Chinese parents can get away with things that Western parents can't. Once when I was young—maybe more than once—when I was extremely disrespectful to my mother, my father angrily called me "garbage" in our native Hokkien dialect. It worked really well. I felt terrible and deeply ashamed of what I had done. But it didn't damage my self-esteem or anything like that. I knew exactly how highly he thought of me. I didn't actually think I was worthless or feel like a piece of garbage.

As an adult, I once did the same thing to Sophia, calling her garbage in English when she acted extremely disrespectfully toward me. When I mentioned that I had done this at a dinner party, I was immediately ostracized. One guest named Marcy got so upset she broke down in tears and had to leave early. My friend Susan, the host, tried to rehabilitate me with the remaining guests.

The fact is that Chinese parents can do things that would seem unimaginable—even legally actionable—to Westerners. Chinese mothers can say to their daughters, "Hey fatty—lose some weight." By contrast, Western parents have to tiptoe around the issue, talking in terms of "health" and never ever mentioning the f-word, and their kids still end up in therapy for eating disorders and negative self-image. (I also once heard a Western father toast his adult daughter by calling her "beautiful and incredibly competent." She later told me that made her feel like garbage.)

Chinese parents can order their kids to get straight A's. Western parents can only ask their kids to try their best. Chinese parents can say, "You're lazy. All your classmates are getting ahead of you." By contrast, Western parents have to struggle with their own conflicted feelings about achievement, and try to persuade themselves that they're not disappointed about how their kids turned out.

**E.** *Discuss these questions with your partner:*

1. What members of her family has Chua mentioned so far?
2. What is the stereotype of Chinese children that Chua refers to?
3. According to Chua, what is different about the way Western parents and Chinese parents view academic success?
4. Why does Chua say a parent should not let a child give up practicing "math, piano, pitching or ballet"?
5. What is different about the way Chinese and Western parents speak to their children?

## EXERCISE 5

**A.** *Preview Part 2 of the article quickly—about two minutes—for the answers to these questions. Discuss them with another student.*

1. How long is this part?
2. Does the style and content seem similar to the first part?
3. What do you notice about the way it is organized?

**B.** *Read Part 2. Do not stop reading to look up words in the dictionary.*

### Why Chinese Mothers Are Superior (Part 2)

I've thought long and hard about how Chinese parents can get away with what they do. I think there are three big differences between the Chinese and Western parental mind-sets.

First, I've noticed that Western parents are extremely anxious about their children's self-esteem. They worry about how their children will feel if they fail at something, and they constantly try to reassure their children about how good they are notwithstanding a mediocre performance on a test or at a recital. In other words, Western parents are concerned about their children's psyches. Chinese parents aren't. They assume strength, not fragility, and as a result they behave very differently.

For example, if a child comes home with an A-minus on a test, a Western parent will most likely praise the child. The Chinese mother will gasp in horror and ask what went wrong. If the child comes home with a B on the test, some Western parents will still praise the child. Other Western parents will sit their child down and express disapproval, but they will be careful not to make their child feel inadequate or insecure, and they will not call their child "stupid," "worthless" or "a disgrace." Privately, the Western parents may worry that their child does not test well or have aptitude in the subject or that there is something wrong with the curriculum and possibly the whole school. If the child's grades do not improve, they may eventually schedule a meeting with the school principal to challenge the way the subject is being taught or to call into question the teacher's credentials.

If a Chinese child gets a B—which would never happen—there would first be a screaming, hair-tearing explosion. The devastated Chinese mother would then get dozens, maybe hundreds of practice tests and work through them with her child for as long as it takes to get the grade up to an A.

Chinese parents demand perfect grades because they believe that their child can get them. If their child doesn't get them, the Chinese parent assumes it's because the child didn't work hard enough. That's why the solution to substandard performance is always to excoriate, punish and shame the child. The Chinese parent believes that their child will be strong enough to take the shaming and to improve from it. (And when Chinese kids do excel, there is plenty of ego-inflating parental praise lavished in the privacy of the home.)

Second, Chinese parents believe that their kids owe them everything. The reason for this is a little unclear, but it's probably a combination of Confucian filial piety and the fact that the parents have sacrificed and done so much for their children. (And it's true that Chinese mothers get in the trenches, putting in long grueling hours personally tutoring, training, interrogating and spying on their kids.) Anyway, the understanding is that Chinese children must spend their lives repaying their parents by obeying them and making them proud.

By contrast, I don't think most Westerners have the same view of children being permanently indebted to their parents. My husband, Jed, actually has the opposite view. "Children don't choose their parents," he once said to me. "They don't even choose to be born. It's parents who foist life on their kids, so it's the parents' responsibility to provide for them. Kids don't owe their parents anything. Their duty will be to their own kids." This strikes me as a terrible deal for the Western parent.

Third, Chinese parents believe that they know what is best for their children and therefore override all of their children's own desires and preferences. That's why Chinese daughters can't have boyfriends in high school and why Chinese kids can't go to sleepaway camp. It's also why no Chinese kid would ever dare say to their mother, "I got a part in the school play! I'm Villager Number Six. I'll have to stay after school for rehearsal every day from 3:00 to 7:00, and I'll also need a ride on weekends." God help any Chinese kid who tried that one.

Don't get me wrong: It's not that Chinese parents don't care about their children. Just the opposite. They would give up anything for their children. It's just an entirely different parenting model.

C.  *Discuss these questions with your partner:*

1. What is the first difference between Chinese and Western parents that Chua discusses?
2. What is the second?
3. What is the third?
4. What does Chua's husband Jed seem to think about Chinese mothers?
5. What can you infer about the grades that Chua's daughters got in school?

**A.** *Preview Part 3 of the article—about two minutes—for the answers to these questions. Discuss them with another student.*

1. How long is this part?
2. Does the style and content seem similar to the first part?
3. What do you notice about the way it is organized?

**B.** *Read Part 3. Do not stop reading to look up words in the dictionary.*

## Why Chinese Mothers Are Superior (Part 3)

Here's a story in favor of coercion, Chinese-style. Lulu was about 7, still playing two instruments, and working on a piano piece called "The Little White Donkey" by the French composer Jacques Ibert. The piece is really cute—you can just imagine a little donkey ambling along a country road with its master—but it's also incredibly difficult for young players because the two hands have to keep schizophrenically different rhythms.

Lulu couldn't do it. We worked on it nonstop for a week, drilling each of her hands separately, over and over. But whenever we tried putting the hands together, one always morphed into the other, and everything fell apart. Finally, the day before her lesson, Lulu announced in exasperation that she was giving up and stomped off.

"Get back to the piano now," I ordered.

"You can't make me."

"Oh yes, I can."

Back at the piano, Lulu made me pay. She punched, thrashed and kicked. She grabbed the music score and tore it to shreds. I taped the score back together and encased it in a plastic shield so that it could never be destroyed again. Then I hauled Lulu's dollhouse to the car and told her I'd donate it to the Salvation Army piece by piece if she didn't have "The Little White Donkey" perfect by the next day. When Lulu said, "I thought you were going to the Salvation Army, why are you still here?" I threatened her with no lunch, no dinner, no Christmas or Hanukkah presents, no birthday parties for two, three, four years. When she still kept playing it wrong, I told her she was purposely working herself into a frenzy because she was secretly afraid she couldn't do it. I told her to stop being lazy, cowardly, self-indulgent and pathetic.

Jed took me aside. He told me to stop insulting Lulu—which I wasn't even doing, I was just motivating her—and that he didn't think threatening Lulu was helpful. Also, he said, maybe Lulu really just couldn't do the technique—perhaps she didn't have the coordination yet—had I considered that possibility?

"You just don't believe in her," I accused.

"That's ridiculous," Jed said scornfully. "Of course I do."

"Sophia could play the piece when she was this age."

"But Lulu and Sophia are different people," Jed pointed out.

"Oh no, not this," I said, rolling my eyes. "Everyone is special in their special own way," I mimicked sarcastically. "Even losers are special in their own special way. Well don't worry, you don't have to lift a finger. I'm willing to put in as long as it takes, and I'm happy to be the one hated. And you can be the one they adore because you make them pancakes and take them to Yankees games."

I rolled up my sleeves and went back to Lulu. I used every weapon and tactic I could think of. We worked right through dinner into the night, and I wouldn't let Lulu get up, not for water, not even to go to the bathroom. The house became a war zone, and I lost my voice yelling, but still there seemed to be only negative progress, and even I began to have doubts.

Then, out of the blue, Lulu did it. Her hands suddenly came together—her right and left hands each doing their own imperturbable thing—just like that.

Lulu realized it the same time I did. I held my breath. She tried it tentatively again. Then she played it more confidently and faster, and still the rhythm held. A moment later, she was beaming.

"Mommy, look—it's easy!" After that, she wanted to play the piece over and over and wouldn't leave the piano. That night, she came to sleep in my bed, and we snuggled and hugged, cracking each other up. When she performed "The Little White Donkey" at a recital a few weeks later, parents came up to me and said, "What a perfect piece for Lulu—it's so spunky and so *her*."

Even Jed gave me credit for that one. Western parents worry a lot about their children's self-esteem. But as a parent, one of the worst things you can do for your child's self-esteem is to let them give up. On the other hand, there's nothing better for building confidence than learning you can do something you thought you couldn't.

There are all these new books out there portraying Asian mothers as scheming, callous, overdriven people indifferent to their kids' true interests. For their part, many Chinese secretly believe that they care more about their children and are willing to sacrifice much more for them than Westerners, who seem perfectly content to let their children turn out badly. I think it's a misunderstanding on both sides. All decent parents want to do what's best for their children. The Chinese just have a totally different idea of how to do that.

Western parents try to respect their children's individuality, encouraging them to pursue their true passions, supporting their choices, and providing positive reinforcement and a nurturing environment. By contrast, the Chinese believe that the best way to protect their children is by preparing them for the future, letting them see what they're capable of, and arming them with skills, work habits and inner confidence that no one can ever take away.

**C.** *Discuss these questions with your partner:*

1. What was challenging about the piano piece that Lulu was working on?
2. What did Chua do when Lulu said she wanted to give up?
3. What did Jed think about the situation?
4. What happened in the end?
5. How do Western parents handle their children's interests, according to Chua?
6. How do Chinese parents handle their children's interests?

## EXERCISE 7

**A.** *Read the story again (Exercises 4–6), and underline the unfamiliar words or phrases. Use the context to guess their meanings. For words and phrases you can't guess, look them up if they are necessary for understanding the story. Then write their definitions in the margins.*

**B.** *Compare work with another student. Did you look up the same words or phrases? Then, with your partner, retell the story from beginning to end.*

**C.** *Join another pair of students and discuss these questions:*

1. What do you think about Chua as a mother? About Jed as a father?
2. Did you study a musical instrument when you were young? If so, what was your parents' role?
3. Did your parents ever put pressure on you in school? In other ways? Give examples.
4. Have you ever known any "Chinese" mothers, as Chua describes them?
5. Think about yourself as a parent. Do you think your parenting style would be more "Western" or "Chinese"? In what ways?
6. How do you think Chua's work as a lawyer and professor of law might have influenced her ideas?

# Books for Extensive Reading

## Choosing Books for Extensive Reading

Since the goal of extensive reading is to read a lot, it is very important to choose books that you will enjoy. If you choose books about topics and stories that interest you, you will enjoy reading them, and you will finish them.

## Which Books Are Best for You?

*Books that interest you*—Ideas for books may come from teachers and friends, but keep in mind that people can have very different tastes in books. Choose books that interest you and that you think you will enjoy reading.

*Books that are not too difficult*—Do not choose books with a lot of unfamiliar words. Some students think they may learn more vocabulary this way, but that is not what usually happens. If there are too many unknown words, you will probably read slowly and have trouble understanding. As a result, you won't enjoy your reading, will read little, and won't learn much. (You will learn how to check the difficulty of a book on page 23.)

*Books written for English learners*—If you do not feel confident enough to read books written for native speakers, you can choose one of the many good novels and books of nonfiction that are written especially for learners at all levels.

*Books written for native speakers*—If you are confident reading in English, you will have a wider choice among these books. Books for young people and children may be easier than those for adults, but they are not always easy. Check the level of difficulty as with other books. (See pages 23 and 24.)

### Remember

- Any book that interests you and that is not too difficult is appropriate for extensive reading.
- If you find that you are not enjoying a book for any reason, you do not have to finish it. Look for another book. The important thing is to *read*.

At the end of this unit is a short list of books that are popular with students, but you do not need to limit your choice to these. Your teacher or students in your class may be able to suggest other books. If there is a bookstore or library near you, you can browse the books there for something that appeals to you. You can also look for recommendations and reviews online on websites, such as Amazon.com or http://www.ala.org.

# Previewing

Wherever you go for books—a library, a bookstore, or online–preview them before you make your choice.

When you preview:
- Read the front and back covers and the first page (often viewable on bookselling websites). What kind of book is it? What is it about? Is it something you would enjoy?
- Read reviews by your classmates or online (Amazon.com or other sites). What do people say about the book? Do they recommend it?

## EXERCISE 1

A. *Look at the front and back covers and read the first page and review of* Going It Alone, *by Hilda Christenson. Then discuss the questions with another student.*

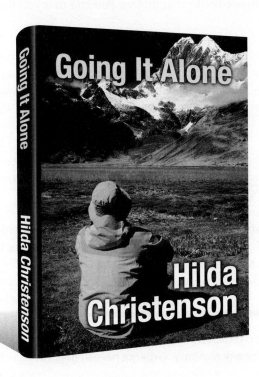

"Terrifying . . . eloquent . . . A soul-wrenching drama of human yearning. A must read for every young person." —*The New York Tribune*

"Compelling and tragic . . . Hard to put down."—*San Francisco Star*

"Haunting . . . few writers of the day can match Christenson for bringing outside adventure to life on the page." —*Portland Journal*

"Though it's a true story, *Going It Alone* also gives us the thrills of mystery." —*Women's Weekly*

"Sensational . . . Christenson is such a good writer that we seem to be looking into another person's heart and soul."—*The Pacific Review*

# Preface

The story made a big media splash in June 2010. On a high Andean plateau, a group of American hikers found the body of Sally Harkness, a 23-year-old American who had been missing for two years.

At last, the months of searching were over. She had left her hometown of Shipton, Oregon, without a word to anyone and simply walked off the map. Neither her family nor her friends heard from her again.

People who had met her in Huarez spoke of a quiet, serious young woman, small and slim with long fair hair and green eyes. She never volunteered any information about herself or her motives for being in Peru and deflected questions asked of her. She volunteered at an aid organization in Lima and then she taught English in a private school in Huarez, a city that attracted mountaineers from around the world on their way to or from the peaks of the Cordillera Blanca.

Finding her body answered the question of where she had gone, but, in the months afterward, I found myself wondering why. The news stories hinted at a mystical crisis. They also mentioned a homicide investigation.

I couldn't get her out of my mind. I too had traveled to South America soon after college, living and working for six months in Bolivia. In my case, those months had led to a future. I wrote an article about the village where I lived and then returned to the States to become a journalist.

For Sally, it all came to an end in the Andes. I had to find out why. Who was she? What was she doing in Peru? What happened on the mountain?

This is what I set out to understand—the story I try to tell in this book.

**Review:** Brilliant and unforgettable          By Meg M          (Tampa, Florida)

★★★★

*Going It Alone* is not a mystery story. It's a true story about a young woman named Sally Harkness, and you find out right away that she went off on an expedition into the Andes alone and died there. But there is a different kind of suspense in this book. Why did this young woman leave her family and boyfriend, quit her job, and head off alone to South America? She didn't speak Spanish, had no money, and had never traveled much, not even in the U.S. Why did she head off into the mountains? How long did she survive?

As the book tries to answer these questions, it gives an unforgettable portrait of a young woman seeking meaning in her life. Of all the books I've read in recent years, this one may have left the strongest impression on me. Some reviewers have criticized it because they say it gives an unsympathetic and unrealistic portrait of Harkness. It's true that her actions are hard to explain and may seem selfish. But haven't many of us at some point in our lives dreamed of a solitary adventure? In the end, I was moved by her fate. The last scenes are emotionally devastating. You don't need to know anything about the mountains to appreciate this book, which I think is destined to become a classic.

**B.**  *Discuss these questions with another student:*

1. What kind of book is this?
2. What is it about?
3. What is the reviewer's opinion of the book?
4. Based on the covers and the review, would you choose to read the book? Why or why not?

**A.** *Look at the front and back covers. Then read the first page and review of* **Denny Carson** *by* **Jason Knight.**

"Gory and horrifying . . . only for those with a strong stomach."
*Miami Sun*

"Sheer terror . . . you won't be able to put it down, and you won't sleep afterwards."
*Entertainment Monthly*

"Gripping. The best to come along in many years. This young writer has the sure touch of a master, and we look forward to more."
*Chicago Post*

"Don't miss this debut novel. A dark and chilling tale . . . "
*U.S. Daily News*

## Chapter 1

Nobody was really surprised when it happened. Some of the girls claimed surprise, but of course it wasn't true. They had known Denny Carson since the first day of first grade at Trenton Elementary School. Known her and despised her. And ever since, this feeling had been growing in them. They no longer bothered with the kind of tricks they'd played on her in elementary school or junior high school. They were ready for something bigger and better. Something that would teach her once and for all that she didn't belong at Trenton High.

They didn't know, of course, about the powers of certain rare individuals who have the ability to move objects through willpower alone.

That May afternoon they were waiting for her outside the school—Cynthia, Lana, Billie and Janet. It was prom season, and the talk was about dresses, hair, boys, music, and more. Denny walked out of the school a few minutes late, as usual, hoping they'd have dispersed. Small, thin, frail, with mousy shoulder-length hair with bangs, and a small mousy face that looked ready to be hurt.

"Hey, Denny!" said Cynthia, always the leader.

Denny walked faster and tried to get by the group quickly without saying a word. She was afraid, and they could read it on her face.

**Review:** Terrific coming-of-age story    By Molly (Milwaukee, Wisconsin)

★★★★

A great debut novel by a young author. The reviewers have called it "gory and horrifying" and "sheer terror," but they must be exaggerating for the promotional value. Yes, it does have elements of horror—the supernatural powers, the black suspense—but this is really an old-fashioned coming of age tale about a girl who goes through suffering and gets her revenge. Anyone who reads this book will be caught in its spell. It's fast-moving and reads easily, but most of all, it's a terrific story.

It all happens in a small town like any other, at a high school like any other. Denny is a shy sixteen-year-old who all her life has been the target of her schoolmates' bullying, mainly because of her family. Her mother disappeared or died long ago—we never learn and Denny herself doesn't know what happened to her. Her father has taken up with a strange woman and a strange religion and forces Denny to wear strange clothes that naturally attract teasing and worse. Quiet little Denny pretends not to notice and hides away when she can, but by the time she gets to high school, she's tired of being tormented. The way she gets her revenge is a bit violent, I'll admit, but that's not the main point of the book. Anyway, I think that anyone who has suffered from being different would understand why she does what she does, even if a lot of innocent young people end up paying the price along with the guilty ones.

**B.** *Discuss these questions with another student:*

1. What kind of book is this?
2. What is it about?
3. What is the reviewer's opinion of the book?
4. Would you choose to read the book? Why or why not?

**C.** *Of the books in Exercises 1 and 2, which is more interesting to you? Ask at least four other students which book they would prefer to read and why. Which one is more popular? What are some of your classmates' reasons for their choices?*

## Assessing the Difficulty

If the book is written for English language learners, you should probably start at Level 4 (intermediate/upper-intermediate, with about a 1000-word vocabulary). If that seems easy, your next book can be at a higher level.

If the book is for native speakers, read the first page. Can you understand it easily? If not, try reading another page. Sometimes the beginning of a story may seem harder, but it will get easier soon. But if you cannot understand what you are reading after two or three pages, the book may not be right for you.

Try this method to check the difficulty for you of a book in another language.

---

### *A Quick Method for Assessing a Book's Difficulty*

1. Calculate the number of words on a full page: Count the number of words in three full lines; divide that by three; multiply that by the number of lines on the page. _____

2. Calculate the average number of words on a page. Find two full pages—one near the beginning and one in the middle. Count the number of unfamiliar words on both pages and divide by two. _____

3. Calculate the percentage of unfamiliar words per page. (For example, nine unfamiliar words on a 300-word page is 3 percent.) _____

---

If the book contains more than 3 percent unfamiliar words, it may not be appropriate for you. However, that depends partly on you. If you read a lot in your first language, and/or do not have particular difficulties reading in English, then you may still enjoy a book with more unknown words. It also depends on the book. If the topic or story is very interesting or engaging, you may be able to tolerate more unknown words. If you are not sure, ask your teacher for advice.

## Guidelines for Extensive Reading

1. Read for at least 30 minutes every day. If possible, find a regular time in your day for reading. When you stop reading each time, write the date in pencil in the margin. Your teacher will check on your progress.

2. Do not stop to look up new words unless they are necessary to follow the story or ideas.

3. If you want to learn vocabulary from your book, use a pencil to underline the words you think might be useful. Later, when you have finished reading, or on another day, you can look them up. If you think they will be useful, write them in your vocabulary notebook.

4. When you finish a book:
   • Tell your teacher.
   • Write the title of the book on your Reading Log on page 33.
   • Fill in a Book Report form like the one on pages 31 and 32.
   • Tell your classmates about the book, if you liked it.

# Learning to Read Faster

If you can read faster—with a faster reading rate [speed]—you will enjoy your extensive reading more. You will probably also read more books, which will help you improve your comprehension, learn to read even faster, and so on.

Many students read slowly in English. This is often the result of habit. Their eyes are used to moving across the page at a certain rate, so they continue to read that way.

Reading faster is not the same as "speed reading"—reading whole books in an hour, as sometimes advertised. It means reading somewhat faster than you do now. Not all your reading should be faster. There are times when slow reading is appropriate, for example, when reading poetry, technical material, or instructions. However, it is very useful to be able to read faster when you want to, especially in extensive reading. (See the Introduction to Part 4 for more about reading faster.)

## Reading Rate Practice

The first step in learning to read faster is to find out how fast you read now–your reading rate.

---

### *How to Calculate Your Reading Rate*

1. Calculate the number of words on a full page: Count the number of words in three full lines and divide by three to get the average number of words per line. Multiply that by the number of lines on a full page.

   _____ × _____ = _____.
   (lines)                  (average words per line)          (words per page)

2. Time your reading: Open your book to the page you are now reading. With a pencil, mark your place on the page. Before you start reading, write the exact time in the margin. Read at a comfortable speed for 10 or 15 minutes. Write the exact time you finish.

3. Calculate the number of minutes you read:

   _____ min. – _____ min. = _____ min.
   (finishing time)                  (starting time)                  (words per page)

4. Calculate the number of words you read: Count the number of pages you read (including parts of pages); multiply that by the number of words per page.

   _____ × _____ = _____.
   (pages read)                  (words per page)          (words you read)

5. Calculate your reading rate: Divide the number of words you read by the number of minutes.

   _____ ÷ _____ = _____.
   (words read)                  (minutes)          (reading rate-words per minute)

6. Write the date and your reading rate on the Extensive Reading Rate Progress Log on page 26.

---

Reading rates for students may vary widely. To be able to deal with reading assignments at the college or university level, you need a reading rate of at least 250 words per minute for texts of average difficulty (not textbooks or technical texts). However, you should be able to read some kinds of texts faster than that—extensive reading books, for example.

## Checking Your Progress

Follow the steps above to check your reading rate regularly (about once a week). Each time you check it, write the date and your rate in the chart.

When you start a new book, use a new chart. When you have completed the charts here, ask your teacher for new blank charts.

**Extensive Reading Rate Progress Log**

Book Title _____     Book Title _____

Author _____     Author _____

RATE (words per minute—WPM)

| 520 |
| 500 |
| 480 |
| 460 |
| 440 |
| 420 |
| 400 |
| 380 |
| 360 |
| 340 |
| 320 |
| 300 |
| 280 |
| 260 |
| 240 |
| 220 |
| 200 |
| 180 |
| 160 |
| 140 |
| 120 |
| 100 |
| 80 |

Date

RATE (words per minute—WPM)

| 520 |
| 500 |
| 480 |
| 460 |
| 440 |
| 420 |
| 400 |
| 380 |
| 360 |
| 340 |
| 320 |
| 300 |
| 280 |
| 260 |
| 240 |
| 220 |
| 200 |
| 180 |
| 160 |
| 140 |
| 120 |
| 100 |
| 80 |

Date

## Remember

- The best way to improve your reading rate and your reading ability in general is to read as much as possible! Try to read at least 30 minutes a day.
- Don't stop to look up new words when you are reading unless you can't follow the story without them. Mark the words you'd like to know (but are not necessary while reading) and look them up later.

## Reading Sprints

One way you can improve your reading rate is by doing reading sprints, which are just like the sprints that athletes do to improve their running speed. They force themselves to run much faster for short periods, and this helps them run a bit faster all the time.

Regular practice with reading sprints (about twice a month) will help you increase your reading rate and help you become a more flexible reader, so you can speed up or slow down as you need.

To do reading sprints, you will need:

- your extensive reading book (preferably a book that you have already started)
- a clock or watch if you are at home (Your teacher will time you if you are in the classroom.)

### How to Do Reading Sprints

Read through all the instructions before you begin.

1. With a pencil, mark the place where you are now in your book. Write the exact starting time in the margin. Then read for *five* minutes. (Your teacher will time you the first time.)

2. Make a mark (X) in the margin where you stopped reading. Count the number of pages you just read: _____.

3. Starting at the X, count ahead the same number pages you read in step 2. (For example, if you just read two and a quarter pages, count ahead two and a quarter pages.) Make a new mark in the margin (*).

4. Now try to read from the X to the * in only *four* minutes. Time yourself, or your teacher will time you. You will need to force your eyes to move faster along the page, skipping words or even whole lines of text.

5. If you do not succeed the first time, try again until you do. Each time you try, start from where you finished the last time and count ahead the same number of pages in new text. Mark the place (△) where you stop reading. (Do not worry about understanding everything you read now.)

6. When you are able to read the pages in four minutes, count ahead and try to read the same number of pages in *three* minutes. (You can read these pages again later if you feel you are missing a lot.) Keep trying until you succeed.

7. Now try for *two* minutes. At this speed, you may be able to catch just a few words from each page. This does not matter. The important thing is to make your eyes move quickly and understand *something*.

8. When you can "read" the pages in two minutes (or close to that), mark the place where you stopped. You do not need to count ahead this time. Start reading from that place at a comfortable speed for five minutes. Time yourself, or your teacher will time you.

9. Count the number of pages you read during these five minutes. _____ How does this compare with the number of pages you read the first time? Many students find that their comfortable reading speed is faster than it was before the sprints.

## Discussing Your Books

There are several reasons why talking about your reading is useful:

- It can help you understand your reading better. In order to tell others about your book, you need to think about it more, organize your thoughts, and communicate them to others. This, along with comments from your classmates or teacher, may help you gain new insight.
- Talking about your books will give you practice expressing your thoughts in English about something you have read—an important academic skill. In the activities in this section, you will learn about the ways good readers in English think and talk about their reading.
- It also allows you to share your reading experiences with others. In fact, reading does not have to be a solitary experience. In English-speaking countries, many people enjoy discussing books with friends, or they join book clubs to have regular opportunities to talk about their reading.
- Finally, in discussions about books, you may also get ideas about what you might like to read next.

## Book Conferences

A book conference is not a test and does not require studying. It is simply a conversation with your teacher about your book. Each time you finish a book, you should tell your teacher and make a date for a conference. Below are some questions your teacher might ask you.

---

*Possible Questions for Book Conferences*

General questions:

- Why did you choose this book?
- Would you recommend it to others? Explain your opinion.
- Does the book relate to your own life? If so, how?
- Has this book changed your thinking in any way?

---

For fiction:

- Where does the story take place? When?
- What did you already know about the setting?
- Who are the main characters (people in the story)?
- Is there a character you particularly like? Dislike?
- Did any character remind you of someone you know?
- Would this book be a good movie? Why or why not?
- Would you recommend it to others? Explain your opinion.

For nonfiction:

- Would you recommend this book to others? Explain your opinion.
- What is it about?
- What did you already know about this topic?
- What have you learned from reading this book?
- Is the topic especially interesting to you? Why or why not?
- Does the author explain it well?

## Reading Circles

A reading circle is a small group of students (four to five) that meets to talk about the books they are reading. There are two ways they can be organized:

1. Each student in the group reads a different book. When the group meets, the group members take turns telling the others about their books.
2. The group chooses one book to read. Group members read the same chapters at the same time and meet regularly to discuss what they read.

Your teacher will tell you how the reading circles will be organized, how the groups will be formed, and when you will meet (about once a week).

### Instructions for Reading Circles

1. At each meeting, group members take turns talking about their books. Each student should speak for no more than four minutes.

2. Group members who are not talking must listen to each speaker and then ask at least one question. The student to the right of the speaker keeps track of the time and says when four minutes are up.

3. Suggested talking points:
   - where you are in the book
   - difficulties or challenges with vocabulary, dialogue, plot, or background
   - (fiction) the setting, characters and/or plot (But do not try to retell the whole plot!)
   - (nonfiction) the subject, the author's ideas, the content
   - your reaction to a part of the book that was exciting, scary, sad, interesting, etc.
   - your opinion about the style, characters, plot, topic, etc.

## Book Presentations

A book presentation is a short (four–five minutes) oral report to the class about a book you have read.

---

### *How to Prepare for a Book Presentation*

1. Write notes (not whole sentences). Include the following points:

   a. Information about the book:
   - the title and author
   - any aspects that were difficult (vocabulary, dialogue, plot, etc.)
   - if fiction: the setting, main characters, and a *brief* summary of the plot
   - if nonfiction: the subject and a *brief* summary of the content

   b. Your comments about one or two aspects of the book that struck you:
   - a part of the book that especially interests you
   - a character you like or identify with
   - a situation, scene, or event that relates to your personal experience
   - an issue dealt with in the book (family trauma, racism, poverty, war, etc.)

   c. Your opinion: Would you recommend it? Why or why not?

2. Prepare your presentation:

   a. Go through it many times using your notes—by yourself and with a friend. Keep practicing until you can complete the whole talk smoothly.

   b. When you practice, don't look down at your notes all the time. Look up as much as possible. Try to speak slowly and clearly, without stopping or saying "um" or "uh" too often.

   c. Time your talk before you give it in class. If it takes less than four minutes, you need to expand it. If it takes more than five minutes, you need to cut something out.

   d. Record yourself and listen to the recording. Is your speech clear enough? Loud enough? Smooth enough?

---

## Writing about Your Books

Writing about your reading gives you opportunities to practice putting your thoughts down in written form. This forces you to further clarify your thinking and to find ways of expressing yourself that are appropriate in writing. What you write can then be consulted (as a book file, report, or review) by other students who are looking for something to read.

## Book Files

When you finish a book, ask your teacher for a book file card and fill it in. (Or fill in the appropriate form on a class website.) You and your classmates can consult these files or forms when you are looking for your next book.

Title: *Going it Alone*

Author: *Hilda Christenson*     Total pages: *203*

Fiction:          Nonfiction: *X*     Difficulty: *7*     (1 = very easy, 10 = very difficult)

Summary: *The true story of a young woman who left her parents and boyfriend, quit her job, and traveled to South America on her own. She had hoped for adventure in the Andes and she found it. But her lack of her experience and bad weather in the mountains was too much for her and she died. She was probably selfish to go off like that alone and stupid not to be better prepared. But I can understand her dream of a more exciting life. I really felt bad for her and thought it was an amazing story. Sometimes it was not easy to read, but I couldn't put it down!*

Rate the book: * * * *

## Book Reviews

Write a book review, like those for *Going It Along* and *Denny Carson,* on pages 21 and 23. Tell briefly about the story, characters, setting, or subject of the book, and give your opinion. Mention any aspect of the book that you especially liked or disliked.

Remember that this should be *your* writing, not a review you found on the Internet. Your teacher can easily find out if you have downloaded or copied it.

## Book Reports

Write one of these types of book reports for each book you finish.

## Complete a book report form.

Ask your teacher for another form when you have filled in the one on the next page. Possible book genres include: novel, mystery, thriller, adventure, fantasy, science-fiction, history, biography, science/technology, nature, and travel.

## BOOK REPORT

Title: _____

Author: _____

No. pages: _____ Difficulty: _____ (1 = very easy, 10 = very difficult)

Genre (type of book): _____

Setting (fiction) *or* subject (nonfiction): _____

_____

_____

Characters and plot (fiction) *or* ideas/explanation (nonfiction):

_____

_____

_____

_____

Your general opinion: _____

_____

What did you like best about this book?

_____

_____

What did you like least?

_____

_____

Rate this book: _____

★ ★ ★ ★ = a great book!        ★ = not very interesting
★ ★ ★ = a good book             x = a terrible book!
★ ★ = some good parts

## Write a book report using your notes.

Use your book report form and the instructions for giving book presentations on pages 30–31 to guide you in writing a report on your book. Include the same information and ideas as you would in a presentation. The report should not be longer than one page (about 200 words).

## Reading Log

Fill in the log every time you finish a book.

---

### Reading Log

**1.** Title: _____ No. pages: _____

Author: _____ Date: _____

**2.** Title: _____ No. pages: _____

Author: _____ Date: _____

**3.** Title: _____ No. pages: _____

Author: _____ Date: _____

**4.** Title: _____ No. pages: _____

Author: _____ Date: _____

**5.** Title: _____ No. pages: _____

Author: _____ Date: _____

**6.** Title: _____ No. pages: _____

Author: _____ Date: _____

**7.** Title: _____ No. pages: _____

Author: _____ Date: _____

**8.** Title: _____ No. pages: _____

Author: _____ Date: _____

**9.** Title: _____ No. pages: _____

Author: _____ Date: _____

**10.** Title: _____ No. pages: _____

Author: _____ Date: _____

**11.** Title: _____ No. pages: _____

Author: _____ Date: _____

**12.** Title: _____ No. pages: _____

Author: _____ Date: _____

---

# A Short List of Suggested Reading

Some of the books on the list were written for young adults (YA) and are generally easier to read, but you should always preview a book before making your choice. (See pages 20–24 about previewing.)

Note that the books marked with 🎧 have audio versions.

## Book List

**Key:**

\*    This author has written other books that are popular with students.

🎧    Audiobook available

YA    Young Adult

## Fiction

*A is for Alibi.* Grafton, Sue. Nikki served a jail sentence for a crime she didn't commit. Then she hired Detective Kinsey Mulhone to find her husband's real killer. (214 pages)

🎧 *The Alchemist.* Coelho, Paulo\*. The story of a Spanish shepherd boy who dreams of treasure, goes on a journey, and meets many people who teach him about life. (208 pages)

🎧 *Absolutely True Diary of a Part-time Indian.* Alexie, Sherman. A young American Indian draws cartoons to deal with the family disasters and racism in his life. (288 pages) YA

*And Then There Were None.* Christie, Agatha\*. Ten strangers meet on a weekend trip to a private island. They have one thing in common: a secret, evil past. (275 pages)

*Animal Farm.* Orwell, George. What happens when mistreated animals take over the farm? This story reflects any situation where one's rights to freedom is attacked. (139 pages)

*Bridget Jones' Diary.* Fielding, Helen. A humorous and realistic novel written in diary form about a young single woman in search of her inner self. (267 pages)

*The Call of the Wild.* London, Jack. The classic story of life in the Alaskan wilderness. Buck, the family dog, is kidnapped and put to work as a sled dog. (143 pages)

🎧 *Code Orange.* Cooney, Caroline. When a New York teenager discovers a hundred-year-old sample of smallpox, he and his friends are in danger. (208 pages) YA

🎧 *Confessions of a Shopaholic.* Kinsella, Sophie\*. International best-seller about a young woman who is addicted to shopping. Colorful and funny. (320 pages)

🎧 *Curious Incident of the Dog in the Night-time.* Haddon, Mark. A funny, original, and moving story told from the point of view of an autistic teenager. (226 pages)

*The Daydreamer.* McKewan, Ian. A boy dreams of becoming a cat. Then the dreams seem to become real. (137 pages)

🎧 *Double Helix.* Werlin, Nancy. A suspenseful novel about love and the genetic-engineering experiments of Dr. Wyatt. (252 pages)

🎧 *Flush.* Hiassen, Carl\*. Serious personal and environmental issues dealt with in a humorous way and in a colorful Florida setting. (272 pages) YA

🎧 *The Giver.* Lowry, Lois\*. Jonas lives in a perfect society: no pain, no crime, no unhappiness. But then he becomes the receiver of memories, and he learns about some terrible choices. (192 pages) YA

🎧 *Harry Potter and the Sorcerer's Stone (Original U.K. title: Harry Potter and the Philosopher's Stone).* Rowling, J. K.* In these famous adventures, Harry discovers that he's a wizard. (312 pages) YA

*Hitchhiker's Guide to the Galaxy, A.* Adams, Douglas. This book is science fiction, fantasy, and lots of fun—a best-seller for many years. (224 pages)

🎧 *The House on Mango Street.* Cisneros, Sandra. Growing up in the poor Hispanic part of Chicago, Esperanza learns to make a happy life in the midst of difficulties. (110 pages)

🎧 *The Hunger Games.* Susanne Collins*. The famous fantasy about the not-too-distant future, when young people must compete in a brutal game. (384) YA

🎧 *I Know What You Did Last Summer.* Duncan, Lois. A horror story full of suspense about a group of young people and their secret. (198 pages) YA

🎧 *Hatchet.* Paulson, Gary. Brian is on the way to visit his father when the airplane crashes, and Brian finds himself alone in the Canadian wilderness. (195 pages) YA

🎧 *The Island of the Blue Dolphins.* O'Dell, Scott*. This beautiful book tells the story of a Native American girl left alone for years on an island. (192 pages) YA

🎧 *Lord of the Flies.* Golding, William. A classic—their plane crashes into the sea and a group of English schoolboys find themselves alone on an island. (208 pages)

🎧 *The Lucky One.* Sparks, Nicholas*. Near death leads a soldier to the love of his life. (336 pages)

🎧 *No. 1 Ladies Detective Agency.* McCall Smith, Alexander*. Madame Ramotswe decides to open a detective agency in Botswana (Africa). Delightful and revealing. (272 pages)

🎧 *The Outsiders.* Hinton, S. E. An intensely realistic and dark tale about youth gangs, written when the author was 16 years old. A classic. (208 pages) YA

🎧 *The Pigman.* Zindel, Paul. Funny and serious, moving and perceptive, this is a classic story about two young people's search for meaning in life. (192 pages) YA

🎧 *The Redheaded Princess.* Rinaldi, Anne. The dramatic story of the beautiful young princess who became Queen Elizabeth I. (224 pages) YA

*The Secret Life of Bees.* Monk, Sue Ellen. 14-year-old Lily Owens, a white girl runs away with Rosaleen, her family's black housekeeper. The two are taken in by a family of beekeepers. (302 pages)

🎧 *Speak.* Anderson, Laurie Halse*. Why is Melinda no longer speaking to anyone? It's not because of the usual problems at home or at school. (208 pages) YA

🎧 *Witness.* Hesse, Karen*. When the Klu Klux Klan arrives in a small town in Vermont, the people in the town react in many different ways. (288 pages) YA

## Nonfiction

*A Long Way Gone: Memoirs of a Boy Soldier.* Beah, Ishmael. The experiences of a boy growing up in Sierra Leone and how he was forced to take part in the civil war. (229 pages)

*A Really Short History of Nearly Everything.* Bryson, Bill. A very entertaining and complete explanation of key scientific concepts. Enjoyable for both scientific and non-scientific readers. (176 pages) YA

🎧 *Boy.* Dahl, Roald. The firsthand account of the silly and surprising childhood and school experiences of the famous English writer. (176 pages) YA

*The Chimpanzees I Love: Saving Their World and Ours.* Goodall, Jane. The world-famous expert tells of her experiences with chimpanzees. (268 pages)

*China's Son.* Chen, Da. How the author survived the Cultural Revolution in China and went on to study at Beijing University. (213 pages)

*The Diary of a Young Girl.* Frank, Anne. This well-known book tells the true story of a Jewish girl hiding from the Nazis in World War II Holland. (368 pages) YA

🎧 *Escape: The Story of the Great Houdini.* Fleischman, Sid. The rags-to-riches story of a poor Jewish boy who became a great magician and escape artist. (210 pages) YA

*Farewell to Manzanar: A True Story of Japanese-American Experience During and After the World War II Internment.* Houston, Jeanne Wakatsuki and James D. A girl from a Japanese American family grows up behind barbed wire in California. (146) YA

*Go Ask Alice.* Anonymous. The realistic diary of a fifteen-year-old girl who became addicted to drugs. (188 pages) YA

*J. K. Rowling: The Wizard Behind Harry Potter.* Shapiro, Marc. This biography of one today's most successful writers. (163 pages)

*Hiroshima.* Hersey, John. What Hersey learned when he went to Japan and interviewed survivors after the United States dropped an atomic bomb on Hiroshima. (117 pages)

*Into the Wild.* Krakauer, Jon. Why a young man chose to walk into the Alaskan wilderness alone and what happened to him there. (207 pages)

🎧 *Letters to a Young Brother: Manifest Your Destiny.* Harper, Hill. The author's personal story as a young black man in America and his responses to letters from other young men. (192 pages) YA

🎧 *Marley: A Dog Like No Other.* Grogan, John. As a family dog, Marley is 90 pounds of trouble, fun, and love. (208 pages)

🎧 *Night.* Wiesel, Elie. Taken from his Hungarian village as a boy, the author survived the Nazi death camps. This book asks fundamental questions about life and faith. A masterpiece. (120 pages)

*Only the Names Remain: The Cherokees and the Trail of Tears.* Bealen, Alex W. The sad history of the Cherokee Indians, from the sixteenth century up to their removal from Georgia in 1837. (80 pages) YA

*The Perilous Journey of the Donner Party.* Calabro, Marian. In 1846, ninety people traveling to California were trapped for the winter—a story of survival and cannibalism. (192 pages) YA

*Red Scarf Girl.* Jiang, Ji-Li. This Chinese writer tells about her difficult childhood in China during the Cultural Revolution. (285 pages) YA

*Rosa Parks: My Story.* Parks, Rosa with Jim Haskins. Rosa Parks tells of her life and her role in the civil rights movement in 1950s America. (188 pages)

*Strength in What Remains.* Kidder, Tracy. A young man escapes from violence in Burundi, Africa, and arrives in New York City. An absorbing and stirring story of survival. (259 pages)

*Traveling with Che Guevara.* Grenado, Albert. Two young medical students from Buenos Aires tell of their travels through South America by motorcycle. (204 pages)

*When I was a Soldier: A Memoir.* Zenatti, Valerie. The author writes about her two years in the Israeli army, the difficulties, dangers, and lessons. (240 pages)

🎧 *Zlata's Diary: A Child's Life in Wartime Sarajevo.* Filipovish, Zlata. Ten-year-old Zlata tells in her diary about the bombings and hardship of life in Sarajevo. (240 pages) YA

# Vocabulary Building

# UNIT 1 Learning Vocabulary from Your Reading

In this unit you will learn how to use your reading to expand your vocabulary. This includes selecting words and phrases that are useful for you to learn and developing an effective study method.

## Selecting Words and Phrases to Learn

It would be very difficult and frustrating to try to learn *all* the new words and phrases you find in your reading. Instead, you can make your vocabulary learning more effective by selecting the words and phrases that will be the most useful to you.

## Which Words and Phrases Are Most Useful to You?

In general, you should focus on words and phrases that you will encounter most often in your academic career.

Learn words that are used frequently, for example,

1. the most common words in general and academic English, which can be found in textbooks, articles, seminars, lectures, discussions, and course catalogs. These are listed in the Appendix on page 310.
2. words used in academic English to present, explain, analyze information, refer to examples, or compare ideas. These are marked with an asterisk (*) in the Appendix.
3. the specialized or technical words you may need in order to comprehend lectures and readings in your subject of study or professional interest.
4. the phrases that are common in general English. You can find most frequent phrases in learner dictionaries. If you do not find a particular phrase, check with your teacher or look it up in a collocations dictionary or an online dictionary. (You will learn more about them in Part 2, Unit 4.)
5. the phrases that are most frequently used in academic English. Several phrase lists are available, including the Phrasal Expressions List (Martinez and Schmitt).

### Examples:

a. While reading an assignment in your economics textbook, you find the new word *outcome*. You find it on the word list in the Appendix, and it is followed by an asterisk. You should look it up in your dictionary and learn it.
b. Later in the same paragraph you find the term *turnover*. It's not on the word list, but it is mentioned a number of times in the chapter. You should look it up and learn it.
c. You also find the new word *subsist*. It is used only once and is not on the word list. From the context, you can understand generally what it means *(to live or survive)*. You do not need to look it up or learn it. Keep reading.
d. You find the phrase *by trial and error* in your reading. It is listed in your dictionary. This is a common phrase, and you should learn it.

e. You also find *He's in the hot seat.* You can guess the general meaning of the phrase from the sentences around it (*He's feeling a lot of pressure*). You don't need to stop and look it up. Keep reading. You may want to look it up later and learn it. (It is included in most dictionaries.)

## Guidelines for Choosing Words and Phrases to Learn from a Reading Passage*

1. Read to the end of the passage without stopping to look up new words or phrases.

2. Read the passage again and underline new words and phrases.

3. Look for them on the list in the Appendix on page 310 or in the dictionary, and circle (in the passage) the ones you find. Mark the academic words with a star.

4. For a phrase or a word that is not on the list, ask yourself: *Is it necessary for understanding the passage? Have I seen or heard it before? Is it related to my academic subjects or interests?* If the answer is yes to any of these questions, circle the word or phrase.

5. If the answer is no, try to understand the meaning of the sentence and passage without looking up the word or phrase.

6. Look up your circled words and phrases in the dictionary. Write them in your vocabulary notebook.

* These guidelines should not be used with extensive reading books unless you want to do extra vocabulary work on parts of a book you have already read.

In the next section, you will practice selecting useful words and phrases from your reading. The passages in the exercises are taken from the introduction to *Fast Food Nation: The Dark Side of the All-American Meal*, by investigative journalist Eric Schlosser. This book examines the local and global influence of the U.S. fast-food industry.

**Note:** A word in your reading may appear in a different form on the list in the appendix.
**Examples:** *revolutionary → revolution; unexceptional → exceptional; reissue → issue*
Include both forms in your vocabulary notebook. (You will learn more about word forms in Part 2, Unit 4.)

A.  *Read the title of the book and the title of the introduction. What do you think the passage will be about? Then preview the passage—look through it quickly to get the general idea (not more than one minute).*

## Fast Food Nation: The Dark Side of the All-American Meal

**What We Eat**

Over the last three decades, fast food has infiltrated every nook and cranny of American society. An industry that began with a handful of modest hot dog and hamburger stands in southern California has spread to every corner of the nation, selling a broad range of foods wherever paying customers may be found. Fast food is now served at restaurants and drive-throughs, at stadiums, airports, zoos, high schools, elementary schools, and universities . . . In 1970, Americans spent about $6 billion on fast food; in 2000, they spent more than $110 billion. Americans now spend more money on fast food than on higher education, personal computers, computer software, or new cars. They spend more on fast food than on movies, books, magazines, newspapers, videos, and recorded music—combined.

Pull open the glass door, feel the rush of cool air, walk in, get in line, study the color photographs above the counter, place your order, hand over a few dollars, watch teenagers in uniforms pushing various buttons, and moments later take hold of a plastic tray full of food wrapped in colored paper and cardboard. The whole experience of buying fast food has become so routine, so thoroughly unexceptional and mundane, that it is now taken for granted, like brushing your teeth or stopping for a red light . . .

This is a book about fast food, the values it embodies, and the world it has made. Fast food has proven to be a revolutionary force in American life; I am interested in it both as a commodity and as a metaphor. What people eat (or don't eat) has always been determined by a complex interplay of social, economic, and technological forces. The early Roman Republic was fed by its citizen-farmers; the Roman Empire, by its slaves. A nation's diet can be more revealing than its art or literature. On any given day in the United States about one-quarter of the adult population visits a fast food restaurant. During a relatively brief period of time, the fast food industry has helped to transform not only the American diet, but also our landscape, economy, workforce, and popular culture. Fast food and its consequences have become inescapable, regardless of whether you eat it twice a day, try to avoid it, or have never taken a single bite.

B.  *Now read the passage carefully. Do not stop reading to look up unfamiliar words or phrases.*

C.  *Read the passage again and underline unfamiliar words or phrases. Look for the underlined words on the word list in the Appendix (page 310). If you find a word on the list, circle it in the passage. Mark the academic words with a star.*

D.  *Look up all the words and phrases you circled. On a separate piece of paper, make a vocabulary list. Include the part of speech, the sentence where you found the word or phrase, and the definition. (Keep this list. You will use it later.)*

E.  *Look at the underlined words and phrases in the passage that you did not circle. Make a box around the ones you think will be useful. Look them up and add them to your list.*

**A.** *Preview the next part of the introduction to* **Fast Food Nation**—*not more than one minute.*

The extraordinary growth of the fast food industry has been driven by fundamental changes in American society. Adjusted for inflation, the hourly wage of the average U.S. worker peaked in 1973 and then steadily declined for the next twenty-five years. During that period, women entered the workforce in record numbers, often motivated less by a feminist perspective than by a need to pay the bills. In 1975, about one-third of American mothers with young children worked outside the home; today almost two-thirds of such mothers are employed. As the sociologists Cameron Lynne Macdonald and Carmen Sirianni have noted, the entry of so many women into the workforce has greatly increased demand for the types of services that housewives traditionally perform: cooking, cleaning, and child care. A generation ago, three-quarters of the money used to buy food in the United States was spent to prepare meals at home. Today about half of the money used to buy food is spent at restaurants—mainly at fast food restaurants.

The McDonald's Corporation has become a powerful symbol of America's service economy, which is now responsible for 90 percent of the country's new jobs. In 1968, McDonald's operated about one thousand restaurants. Today it has about twenty-eight thousand* restaurants worldwide and opens almost two thousand new ones each year. An estimated one out of every eight workers in the United States has at some point been employed by McDonald's. The company annually hires about one million people, more than any other American organization, public or private. McDonald's is the nation's largest purchaser of beef, pork, and potatoes—and the second largest purchaser of chicken. The McDonald's Corporation is the largest owner of retail property in the world. Indeed, the company earns the majority of its profits not from selling food but from collecting rent. McDonald's spends more money on advertising and marketing than any other brand. As a result it has replaced Coca-Cola as the world's most famous brand. McDonald's operates more playgrounds than any other private entity in the United States. It is one of the nation's largest distributors of toys. A survey of American schoolchildren found that 96 percent could identify Ronald McDonald. The only fictional character with a higher degree of recognition was Santa Claus. The impact of McDonald's on the way we live today is hard to overstate. The Golden Arches are now more widely recognized than the Christian cross.

*As of 2013, there were more than 33,000 McDonald's restaurants worldwide.

**B.** *Now read the passage carefully. Do not stop reading to look up unfamiliar words or phrases.*

**C.** *Read the passage again and underline unfamiliar words or phrases. Look for the underlined words on the word list in the Appendix (page 310). If you find a word on the list, circle it in the passage. Mark the academic words with a star.*

**D.** *Look up all the words and phrases you circled. Add them to your vocabulary list. Include the part of speech, the sentence where you found the word or phrase, and the definition.*

**E.** *Look at the underlined words and phrases in the passage that you did not circle. Make a box around the ones you think will be useful. Look them up and add them to your list.*

**A.** *Preview the next part of the introduction to* Fast Food Nation—*not more than one minute.*

In the early 1970s, the farm activist Jim Hightower warned of the McDonaldization of America. He viewed the emerging fast food industry as a threat to independent businesses, as a step toward a food economy dominated by giant corporations, and as a homogenizing influence on American life. In *Eat Your Heart Out* (1975), he argued that "bigger is *not* better." Much of what Hightower feared has come to pass. The centralized purchasing decisions of the large restaurant chains and their demand for standardized products have given a handful of corporations an unprecedented degree of power over the nation's food supply. Moreover, the tremendous success of the fast food industry has encouraged other industries to adopt similar business methods. The basic thinking behind fast food has become the operating system of today's retail economy, wiping out small businesses, obliterating regional differences, and spreading identical stores throughout the country . . .

America's main streets and malls now boast the same Pizza Huts and Taco Bells, Gaps and Banana Republics, Starbucks, and Jiffy Lubes, Food Lockers, Snip N'Clips, Sunglass Huts, and Hobbytown USAs. Almost every facet of American life has now been franchised or chained, from the maternity ward at a Columbia/HCA hospital to an embalming room owned by Service Corporation International—the world's largest provider of death care services, based in Houston, Texas, which since 1968 has grown to include 3,823 funeral homes, 523 cemeteries, and 198 crematoriums, and which today handles the final remains of one out of every nine Americans—a person can now go from the cradle to the grave without spending a nickel at an independently owned business.

The key to a successful franchise, according to many texts on the subject, can be expressed in one word: uniformity. Franchises and chain stores strive to offer exactly the same product or service at numerous locations. Customers are drawn to familiar brands by an instinct to avoid the unknown. A brand offers a feeling of reassurance when its products are always and everywhere the same. "We have found out . . . that we cannot trust some people who are nonconformists," declared Ray Kroc, one of the founders of McDonald's, angered by some of his franchisees. "We will make conformists out of them in a hurry . . . The organization cannot trust the individual; the individual must trust the organization."

**B.** *Now read the passage carefully. Do not stop reading to look up unfamiliar words or phrases.*

**C.** *Read the passage again and underline unfamiliar words or phrases. Look for the underlined words on the word list in the Appendix (page 310). If you find a word on the list, circle it in the passage. Mark the academic words with a star.*

**D.** *Look up all the words and phrases you circled. Add them to your vocabulary list. Include the part of speech, the sentence where you found the word or phrase, and the definition.*

**E.** *Look at the underlined words and phrases in the passage that you did not circle. Make a box around the ones you think will be useful. Look them up and add them to your list.*

**A.** *Preview the next part of the introduction to* **Fast Food Nation**—*not more than one minute.*

One of the ironies of America's fast food industry is that a business so dedicated to conformity was founded by iconoclasts and self-made men, by entrepreneurs willing to defy conventional opinion. Few of the people who built fast food empires ever attended college, let alone business school. They worked hard, took risks, and followed their own paths. In many respects, the fast food industry embodies the best and the worst of American capitalism at the start of the twenty-first century—its constant stream of new products and innovations, its widening gulf between rich and poor.

The industrialization of the restaurant kitchen has enabled the fast food chains to rely upon a low-paid and unskilled workforce. While a handful of workers manage to rise up the corporate ladder, the vast majority lack full-time employment, receive no benefits, learn few skills, exercise little control over their workplace, quit after a few months, and float from job to job. The restaurant industry is now America's largest private employer, and it pays some of the lowest wages. During the economic boom of the 1990s, when many American workers enjoyed their first pay raises in a generation, the real value of wages in the restaurant industry continued to fall. The roughly 3.5 million fast food workers are by far the largest group of minimum wage earners in the United States. The only Americans who consistently earn a lower hourly wage are migrant farm workers.

A hamburger and french fries became the quintessential American meal in the 1950s, thanks to the promotional efforts of the fast food chains. The typical American now consumes approximately three hamburgers and four orders of french fries every week. But the steady barrage of fast food ads, full of thick juicy burgers and long golden fries, rarely mentions where these foods come from nowadays or what ingredients they contain. The birth of the fast food industry coincided with Eisenhower-era glorifications of technology, with optimistic slogans like Better Living through Chemistry and Our Friend the Atom. The sort of technological wizardry that Walt Disney promoted on television and at Disneyland eventually reached its fulfillment in the kitchens of fast food restaurants . . . The leading fast food chains still embrace a boundless faith in science—and as a result have changed not just what Americans eat, but also how their food is made.

(Source: Eric Schlosser, *Fast Food Nation*, Mariner Books, Houghton Mifflin, 2001)

**B.** *Now read the passage carefully. Do not stop reading to look up unfamiliar words or phrases.*

**C.** *Read the passage again and underline unfamiliar words or phrases. Look for the underlined words on the word list in the Appendix (page 310). If you find a word on the list, circle it in the passage. Mark the academic words with a star.*

**D.** *Look up all the words and phrases you circled. Add them to your vocabulary list. Include the part of speech, the sentence where you found the word or phrase, and the definition.*

**E.** *Look at the underlined words and phrases in the passage that you did not circle. Make a box around the ones you think will be useful. Look them up and add them to your list.*

# Studying Vocabulary

> **Note:** To complete the exercises in this section, you will need a small notebook that you use only for vocabulary.

## Check What You Know

According to research:

- learning a word means a lot more than memorizing a definition. It includes other aspects of word knowledge, such as pronunciation, spelling, variations in meaning, and how words are used together.
- your memory is not a computer. It cannot automatically take in and hold onto every word you encounter. If you want to remember a new word six days or six months from now, you must help your memory. That means taking the time and making an effort to study.
- repetition is essential in vocabulary learning. Experts say you need to encounter a word at least 7–10 times before you will remember it in the long term. Reading is one way to have repetition of new words. A good study method (including a vocabulary notebook and the use of word study cards) will also result in a lot of repetition and will help you remember.
- it's difficult to remember a word if you cannot say it to yourself. For this reason, it's important to learn the pronunciation of new words and to say them aloud when you review. The sound of words reinforces them in your memory.
- you are much more likely to remember a word if you focus on it and use it in various ways in speaking or writing. The more your brain has to process it, the more it will "stick" in your memory.

How many of these facts did you know already?

If you want to expand your vocabulary, you need to follow the recommendations in the list above. When you write down words or phrases for study, you also need to include essential information about them, including the part of speech and example sentences, so you can understand how they are used.

# Vocabulary Study Tools

## Dictionaries and Definitions

### *Choosing a Dictionary*

Dictionaries may be either paper or electronic. What matters is the information they give you, including:

- spelling. Learning the spelling allows you to recognize words faster and, therefore, to read faster.
- pronunciation. Knowing the pronunciation gives you better access to the word in your memory and makes it much more likely to stick.
- part of speech. This is essential information for understanding how to use the word.

- definition(s). When there is more than one, they are listed by part of speech.
- usage. Example sentences help you understand when and how to use a word. Frequently used collocations and idioms are listed and defined.
- common phrases. These are listed and defined with examples.

A *bilingual dictionary* (English and your language) may be more useful when you need to get a quick idea of the meaning of a word or phrase. An *advanced learner dictionary* has more information and examples of usage. Ideally, you should have one of each.

## *Finding the Best Definition*

When there are multiple definitions for a word in the dictionary:

1. Look at the way the word fits into the sentence where you found it and decide on the part of speech. Then look for the entry under that part of speech.
2. Look through the definitions for the one that makes the most sense in the original sentence. Read the example phrases or sentences for each definition to help you decide on the best one.
3. Multiple definitions for a word often have a common underlying meaning. Look for this underlying meaning and write it in your notebook entry. It will help you understand and remember the word.

### EXAMPLE

In each of these sentences, the context and definition for the word *rough* is different.

| Sentences | Definitions |
|---|---|
| The tree bark was very *rough*. | not smooth |
| He gave us a *rough* idea of the cost. | not exact, not in final form |
| Ice hockey can be a very *rough* sport. | violent |
| Don't say anything to her—she's had a *rough* week. | difficult |
| The school was in a *rough* part of town. | area with violence and crime |
| The sea was *rough* this morning, so the boats didn't go out. | with strong winds and big waves |

Underlying meaning for all the definitions: the idea that something is not smooth, easy, exact, or gentle.

**Notes:**

- Multiple definitions are numbered according to how common they are, starting with the most common.
- For common meanings, dictionaries often give synonyms SYN or opposites OPP.

**A.** *Write the part of speech and definition for each underlined word as it is used in the sentence.*

1. The elderly woman at the back of the room <u>bid</u> $15,000 for the painting.

   Part of speech: _____

   Definition: _____

   _____

2. After his failed <u>bid</u> for election to the city council, he retired from politics.

   Part of speech: _____

   Definition: _____

   _____

3. Thank you all again for coming! And now, I <u>bid</u> you good night and Happy New Year!

   Part of speech: _____

   Definition: _____

   _____

4. Not surprisingly, the lowest <u>bid</u> for the new sports center came from a friend of the mayor.

   Part of speech: _____

   Definition: _____

   _____

---

**bid¹** /bɪd/ W3 *n.* [C] **1** an offer to do work or provide services for a specific price: **+for/on** *the lowest bid for the bridge-building project* **2** an attempt to achieve or obtain something: **+for** *Wilson's successful bid for the senate* | **bid to do sth** *a desperate bid to escape* **3** an offer to pay a particular price for something, especially at an AUCTION: **+for** *Walter made a bid for the painting.* **4** a statement of how many points you hope to win in a card game

**bid²** *v. past tense and past participle* **bid, bidding 1** [I] to offer to do work or provide services for a specific price, in competition with other offers: **+for/on** *Four companies were invited to bid for the contract.* **2** [I,T] to offer to pay a particular price for goods, especially in an AUCTION: **bid (sb) sth for** *Jill bid $20,000 for an antique desk.* | **bid against sb** *The two men ended up bidding against each other* **3** [I,T] to say how many points you think you will win in a game of cards—**bidder** *n.* [C]

**bid³** *v. past tense* **bade** /bæd, beɪd/ *or* **bid**, *past participle* **bid** *or* **bidden** /ˈbɪdn/, **bidding** OLD USE OR LITERARY **1 bid sb good afternoon/good morning etc.** to say good morning, good afternoon etc. to someone **2** [T] to order or tell someone what to do: **bid sb (to) do sth** *The queen bade us to enter.* **3 bid fair to do sth** to seem likely to do something

---

**B.** *Compare answers with another student. Three of the definitions have a common underlying meaning, and one is different. Which three are similar and why?*

**A.** *Write the part of speech and definition for each underlined word as it is used in the sentence.*

1. In fifth grade, he had a huge <u>crush</u> on his music teacher.

   Part of speech: _____

   Definition: _____

   _____

2. She couldn't swallow the pills whole, so she <u>crushed</u> them and put them in a glass of water.

   Part of speech: _____

   Definition: _____

   _____

3. After their <u>crushing</u> defeat, the Spanish team didn't do well again for years.

   Part of speech: _____

   Definition: _____

   _____

4. In the <u>crush</u> of fans leaving the concert, Joan lost sight of her friends.

   Part of speech: _____

   Definition: _____

   _____

5. Her hopes of getting the job were <u>crushed</u> when she learned that it had already been filled.

   Part of speech: _____

   Definition: _____

   _____

---

**crush¹** /krʌʃ/ v. [T]
**1** PRESS HARD to press someone or something so hard that it breaks or is damaged: *Joe crushed his cigarette into an ashtray.* | *A zookeeper was* **crushed to death** *by a hippopotamus.* ▶see THESAURUS box at **press¹**
**2** BREAK INTO PIECES to press something in order to break it into very small pieces, or into a powder: *Crush two cloves of garlic* | *crushed ice* ▶see THESAURUS box at **cooking¹** → see picture on page A32
**3** DEFEAT to completely defeat someone or something that is fighting against you or opposes you: *Seles crushed her opponent in yesterday's match.* | **crush resistance/opposition/a revolt etc.** *The military is determined to crush the student-led uprising.*
**4** **crush sb's hopes/enthusiasm/confidence etc.** to make someone lose all hope, confidence etc.: *Not getting their bonus checks has crushed the staff's morale.*
**5** SHOCK/UPSET to make someone feel extremely upset or shocked: *He was crushed by his sister's death.*
**6** **crush sb to/against you** LITERARY to hold someone in your arms very tightly
[**Origin:** 1300–1400 Old French *cruisir*]

**crush²** *n.* **1** [C] a feeling of romantic love for someone, especially someone you do not know very well, used especially about feelings that young people have: *Actually, I* **had a** big **crush on** *Mel Gibson.* | *a silly* **schoolgirl crush** **2** [singular] a crowd of people pressed so close together that it is difficult to move: *the crush of holiday shoppers* **3** [singular] a great amount or number of something: *the crush of media attention*

**crush•ing** /ˈkrʌʃɪŋ/ *adj.* **1** very hard to deal with, and making you lose hope and confidence: *a crushing blow* **2** a crushing win or loss is very easy and complete: *a crushing defeat* **3** a crushing remark, reply etc. expresses very strong criticism —**crushingly** *adv.*

---

**B.** *Compare answers with another student. What underlying meaning do the definitions have in common?*

## Vocabulary Notebooks

When you write words or phrases in your notebook, you should organize them so you can find them again. You can organize them alphabetically, by topic, by the source where you found them, by the date, or by any other system. Do not just write words in the order you find them, or you will have trouble finding them later.

You should also say each new word or phrase aloud when you write it. If you are unsure about the pronunciation, check the dictionary or ask your teacher. You are much more likely to remember a word if you can pronounce it.

Many students find it useful to organize their notebooks like the example below so they can easily test themselves on words or meanings.

- On the left-hand page, write the new word or phrase and the part of speech or grammatical function.
- Below the word or phrase, write the sentence(s) where you found it.
- Write the dictionary definition on the right-hand page. Include synonyms or helpful notes about the usage.

*EXAMPLE*
..............

crush (verb)
    She couldn't swallow the pills whole, so she crushed them and put them in water.

to press something in order to break it into very small pieces (synonyms: press, squash)

mere (adjective)
    No one could believe how well Gina sang; after all she was a mere child.

only, just—used to describe how small something is [used only with a noun, no comparative, adv: merely]

take for granted (verb phrase)
    The whole experience of buying fast food has become so routine that it is now taken for granted, like brushing your teeth.

not considered special or interesting, so you don't think about it much

## Guidelines for Reviewing with Your Vocabulary Notebook

1. Cover the words/phrases. Read the definitions and try to remember the words/phrases. Say aloud the ones you remember.

2. Cover the definitions. Read the words/phrases and try to remember the definitions. Say aloud the ones you remember.

3. With a pencil, circle words/phrases you had trouble remembering. Review them again.

4. Ask another student to test you:

- Give the other student your notebook.
- Tell him or her to ask you for words/phrases or definitions.
- Write the answers and say them aloud. Did you remember them and write them correctly? Did you pronounce them correctly?

5. Circle any words or phrases in your notebook that you did not remember this time and review them again.

## EXERCISE 7

A. *Look back at the vocabulary list you created from the exercises in this unit. Write the words or phrases in your vocabulary notebook with the part of speech, the sentence(s) where you found each one, and the definitions. Include synonyms or helpful notes about the usage.*

B. *Compare notebooks with another student. Did you choose any of the same words and phrases?*

C. *Review on your own. Follow steps 1–3 in the guidelines on page 48.*

D. *Review with another student. Follow step 4 in the guidelines. Then change roles.*

E. *Circle any words or phrases in your notebook that you did not remember and review them again later.*

## Word Study Cards

Use word study cards in addition to your vocabulary notebook. You will need small cards (3 × 5 inches or 7 × 12 cm).

Follow this system for writing words or phrases on the cards:

1. On one side of the card, write the new word or phrase, with the part of speech.
2. Below the word or phrase, write the sentence(s) where you found it.
3. On the other side of the card, write the definition.

### EXAMPLE
· · · · · · · · · · ·

*Side A*

crush (verb)
     She couldn't swallow the pills whole, so she crushed them and put them in water.

*Side B*

> to press something in order to break it into very small pieces (synonyms: press, squash)

Update your cards regularly.

- Keep about 15–20 cards at a time.
- Take out a card when you have learned the word or phrase on it well—when you can immediately give the definition for the word/phrase and the word/phrase for the definition.
- Add a new card for each one you remove.

**Note: Electronic alternatives** are available to students who feel more comfortable using their smartphone or tablet for vocabulary study.

- Be sure to include the sentence where you found the word or phrase, the part of speech, the definition (synonyms), and any helpful notes about the usage.
- Organize the information so that you can test yourself by covering either the word/phrase or the definition.

## Guidelines for Reviewing with Word Study Cards

Word study cards can be used in a variety of ways. Experiment with them and find ways that work well for you.

- Use the cards for the words or phrases you have trouble remembering. At the end of each week, choose words or phrases from your vocabulary notebook to write on your cards.
- Carry your cards with you all the time. Review them while you are waiting for class, while you are on a bus, before dinner, etc.
- When you are not at home, put your cards in a pocket of your bag or jacket. Whenever you have a free moment, pull out a card and test yourself. If you remember the word/phrase and definition, move the card to another pocket. If you don't remember the word/phrase or definition, put it back in the first pocket. When all the cards are in the "done" pocket, go through them again. If you know them all well this second time, make new cards.
- Instead of cards, you can use sticky notes, putting the word/phrase, part of speech, and sentence on the front, and the definition on the back. Stick the notes on your desk, refrigerator, bathroom mirror, or any place you pass by often. Test yourself whenever you have a few moments. Continue removing and replacing words as you learn them.
- You can also use your smartphone or tablet instead of cards. Make sure you can't see both the words and the meanings at the same time. Replace the old words with new ones as soon as you know them well.

A. *Review the words in your vocabulary notebook.*

B. *On word study cards, write 15 words or phrases from your notebook that you have trouble remembering. Follow the example on pages 49 and 50.*

C. *Review your cards until you can remember both the words/phrases and the definitions/synonyms immediately.*

D. *Exchange 10 cards with another student and test each other. Write your answers on a separate piece of paper.*

E. *Check your answers, including the spelling. How many were correct?*

F. *Practice saying the words and phrases aloud. Check your pronunciation if you are not sure.*

G. *If there are more words or phrases in your notebook that you have trouble remembering, make new sets of cards and review them as you did above.*

## Remember

To learn words or phrases well, you need to review them often in your notebook or on study cards. You should review them:
• a day later
• a week later
• at the end of the month
• at the end of the semester

## Keyword Technique

You may have heard stories about people who have exceptional powers of memory. For example, there are people who can take one look at a deck of playing cards and memorize the order of the cards. Some of these people were born with this special skill, but many others have trained their memories by using techniques like the one below.

Like most other memorizing techniques, this one helps you remember a certain fact by linking it to other kinds of information—especially images—that are already stored in your memory. It can be used for all vocabulary study, or just for words that cause particular difficulty.

*Examples:*

• An Italian student wants to learn the meaning of the word *available*. He thinks of the Italian phrase *a vela* (with sails). He imagines a beautiful big sailboat with sails up and ready to be taken out.
• A Tanzanian student wants to learn the meaning of the word *twist*. She thinks of the Swahili word *twiga* (giraffe). She imagines a giraffe's long neck and the way it can bend and twist in all directions.

## Using the Keyword Technique

1. Choose a word in your vocabulary notebook or on your study cards that you want to learn (the target word).
2. Think of a word in your language that sounds like the target word (It can sound like the whole word or just the beginning). This is your *keyword*.
3. Now create an image in your mind that connects the meaning of both the target word and the keyword. Concentrate for a moment on this image. It is important to actually see it as a picture in your mind.

*This idea was taken from *Teaching Vocabulary: Strategies and Techniques,* I.S.P. Nation, Heinle Cengage Learning, 2008.

## EXERCISE 9

A.  *Write five words from your vocabulary notebook or study cards that you have trouble remembering.*

**Target words**

1. _____        4. _____

2. _____        5. _____

3. _____

B.  *For each target word, think of a keyword in your language—a word that sounds similar. Write the keywords below. Then think of an image that includes the meaning of both the target word and the keyword. Give a short description of the image.*

**Keywords**               **Images**

1. _____    _____

_____

2. _____    _____

_____

3. _____    _____

_____

4. _____    _____

_____

5. _____    _____

_____

**C.**   *Compare work with another student. Did you choose any of the same target words? If so, do you have the same keywords and images?*

## Reflecting on Your Learning

*At the beginning of this unit (page 38), you read some facts about learning vocabulary, especially the importance of repetition and of working with the words and phrases. Now take a few minutes to reflect on your work in this unit.*

**1.** Look at all the words and phrases in your vocabulary notebook. How well do you know each of them now?

**2.** Which words or phrases do you still have trouble remembering? Why?
   • Have you seen/used/reviewed them enough?
   • Are they difficult to pronounce?
   • Are the meanings complex or unclear to you?

**3.** Think about the techniques and strategies in this unit. Which ones do you think will be most helpful?

**4.** Do you know about or use any other techniques or strategies for learning vocabulary?

# Inferring Meaning from Context

As you have seen in earlier units, you can learn a lot about a new word or phrase from the context—the other words and sentences around it. The context allows you to:

- figure out the part of speech. Then you can find the correct dictionary entry if you look it up.
- choose the best dictionary definition when there is more than one.
- get a general idea of the meaning. This may be enough so you can continue reading and understanding the ideas in a passage or story without stopping to look up the word.

The exercises in this unit will give you practice in inferring meaning from context. This is particularly useful when reading in your extensive reading books or other kinds of material where you only need to follow the story or the general ideas.

It is also useful for some course reading when you encounter words or phrases that are not central to the main ideas. If you can infer at least a general meaning, you do not have to stop to use the dictionary, so you can stay focused on the ideas.

**Notes:**

- Sometimes it is not possible to guess even a general meaning because there are not enough clues in the context. In this case, if the word or phrase is necessary for understanding the passage, you need to look it up.
- In some kinds of reading, it may not be appropriate to infer meaning from context because you need a more exact understanding of the meaning. When reading a textbook, instructions, or a poem, for example, you should look up the words you don't know.

## Inferring Meaning from the Sentence

For a single word, the first step in inferring meaning is to figure out the part of speech. Then you can look for clues to the meaning.

The examples come from the short story, "Dolphins, Oysters and Crabs", in Part 1, Unit 2, page 10.

### EXAMPLES

1. I sit in this birdcage-looking <u>shed</u>. It feels like a prison cell—with bars and everything. The only perk is that during breaks, I get to peek in on the shows.

   Part of speech: _noun_

   General meaning: _a small building_

**2.** I watched for so long I was late to work, but all I got was a <u>stern</u> look from my boss.

Part of speech: _adjective_

General meaning: _not pleased, but not too angry_

Inferring the meaning of a phrase is very similar. First think about the way the phrase functions grammatically in the sentence. Does it function like a verb, noun, adverb, etc.?) Then look for clues to the meaning.

## EXAMPLES

**1.** And she said it like it was original, like she had <u>come up with</u> the line herself and was so proud.

Function: _verb phrase_

General meaning: _invented_

**2.** After a while, the protestors <u>lost steam</u>. They seemed to be withering in the sun. I don't think they were from here.

Function: _verb phrase_

General meaning: _lost energy, became quieter_

---

### Guidelines for Inferring Meaning from the Sentence

1. For a single word, decide on the part of speech. For a phrase, decide on its grammatical function in the sentence.

2. Look at the other words in the sentence for clues (information) about the meaning.

3. Think about the meaning and the structure of the sentence.

4. Make a guess about the meaning of the word or phrase.

5. Read the sentence again with your guessed meaning in place of the word or phrase. Does it make sense?

---

## PRACTICE

**A.** *For each underlined word, use the context to figure out the part of speech or the grammatical function, and infer the general meaning.*

**1.** Just as the match started, the weather began to change. Dark clouds appeared, covered the whole sky, and then the storm broke. It took a few minutes for everyone to leave the stands and run to the clubhouse. By then they were all <u>drenched</u>.

Part of speech: _____

General meaning: _____

2. Not all women love going to the shops and spending money. Some truly <u>dread</u> it, especially shopping for clothes. It seems to bring out all their anxieties. Sukey was one of these. She needed to find something to wear to the reception, but she hated the thought of trying things on.

Part of speech: _____

General meaning: _____

B. *Compare answers with another student and explain your inferences to each other. Then look up the words and phrases in the dictionary. How well did you guess the meanings?*

## EXERCISE 1

A. *For each underlined word or phrase, use the context to figure out the part of speech or the grammatical function, and infer the general meaning.*

1. The stranger never said a word, but <u>thrust</u> a folded piece of paper into Pilar's hand. Before she could say anything to him, he had disappeared into the crowd. Had he been sent by Salvatore? She slipped the paper quickly into her pocket. It would have to wait until she was alone.

Part of speech: __*verb*__

General meaning: _____

2. When the train pulled out and the crowd had thinned, he could see the small, <u>forlorn</u> figure of a girl sitting on a suitcase. She sat very still, not looking around—her face serious, waiting to see what would happen next.

Part of speech: __*adj*__

General meaning: __*sad*_____

3. It was clear that if they continued living in their big house, their financial <u>woes</u> would get worse when they retired and had even less income. They would have to sell the house, move to a much smaller place, and cut way back on all their expenses.

Part of speech: __*noun*__

General meaning: _____

4. Media coverage of the recent disappearance of a boy on his way home from school has led many parents to worry unnecessarily about the possibility of their child being <u>abducted</u>. Statistically, it is far less likely than being hit by a car crossing the street, and even less likely than being struck by lightning.

Part of speech: _____

General meaning: _____

5. Harold held tight to Maggie's wrist. She looked around the crowded street. Should she scream? She didn't want everyone looking at her, so she made a last desperate effort, managed to <u>wrench</u> herself free, and ran into a shop.

   Part of speech: _____

   General meaning: _____

6. I was ten when my father took me on the train to Chicago. I sat there for hours, reading my book and, from time to time, looking out the window to see the outside world going by <u>in a flash</u>. The trip took many hours, but in those days it would have taken all day or more by car, so the speed seemed magical to me.

   Function: _____

   General meaning: _____

B. *Compare answers with another student and explain your inferences to each other. Then look up the words and phrases in the dictionary. How well did you guess the meanings?*

## EXERCISE 2

A. *For each underlined word or phrase, use the context to figure out the part of speech or the grammatical function, and infer the general meaning.*

1. No matter how thirsty it is, a horse that has been used to drinking out of a pond or stream will often refuse water out of a <u>trough</u>. This is especially true if other animals have drunk from it or if the water has been sitting there for some hours or days.

   Part of speech: _____

   General meaning: container for food or water for animals

2. It was their job to buy horses for the army and to <u>scour</u> the countryside for food and supplies. These soldiers cared little about keeping up good relations with the local people. They had a job to do and they did it, sometimes brutally.

   Function: verb

   General meaning: look carefully or search

3. After seven years on the TV series *Hot Spot*, Hugh Carey has announced he is leaving. It was a great experience, he says, but it was a real <u>grind</u> producing those shows every week. He'd like to have time and energy for new projects.

   Part of speech: noun

   General meaning: _____

4. To make the perfect crêpe, first put some butter in a pan and <u>tilt</u> it in every direction so the butter covers the bottom. Then pour in a small amount of the batter made of flour and water, and tilt the pan again until the batter is evenly spread.

Function: _____

General meaning: _____

5. Working the late <u>shift</u> can create problems for some employees, especially women with young children. Some women have the support of husbands or grandparents who can take care of their children while they are working, but others are on their own.

Part of speech: _____noun_____

General meaning: _____late work / work at night / period of time_____

6. With her extra income from babysitting, they managed to <u>scrape by</u>, but they had to cut down on everything, even her visits home to her mother. Still, at the end of the month they found themselves with no food in the fridge and no money to buy any.

Function: _____

General meaning: _____

B. *Compare answers with another student and explain your inferences to each other. Then look up the words and phrases in the dictionary. How well did you guess the meanings?*

## EXERCISE 3

A. *For each underlined word or phrase, use the context to figure out the part of speech or the grammatical function, and infer the general meaning.*

1. Mr. Troy is usually very serious, but he's also got a <u>witty</u> side. I expect he'd be good fun to sit next to at a dinner party, and in his speeches, he really knows how to get the audience laughing.

Part of speech: _____adj_____

General meaning: _____Funny_____

2. When archeologists were digging at a new site in Turkey, they made some interesting new discoveries. For example, at one spot near a ten-thousand-year-old fireplace, small round stones were found grouped in small <u>heaps</u>, forming a circle.

Part of speech: _____noun_____

General meaning: _____steps, level, pile_____

3. The young man's story was very moving. When the fighting started, he managed to <u>flee</u> Rwanda for Burundi to the south, but he had to leave his parents, three brothers, and a sister—all of whom were later killed. Now he had returned and started a new life, but he sometimes suffered from depression, like other survivors.

Part of speech: _____verb_____

General meaning: _____run away_____

4. With his academic and business experience, Mr. Kibaki had an impressive <u>track record</u> when he came into power in 2002. His failure was thus a great disappointment to all those who had voted for him and believed he could turn around the depressed economy.

Function: _____noun_____

General meaning: _____story / history_____

5. When Peter fell and broke his kneecap, the doctors said they had to put it in a <u>cast</u> for three weeks. He thought that when it was taken off, he'd be back on the playing fields the next day, but of course it was another week before he could walk well, and several weeks before he could run.

Part of speech: _____n_____

General meaning: _____box_____

*→ yes*

6. There is a serious lack of activities at the retirement home: no library and no musical or creative activities. There isn't even a television. Some residents spend hours walking slowly up and down the corridors. Others just sit in the lounge, completely <u>idle</u>, waiting for visitors.

*→ inactive*

Part of speech: _____adj,_____

General meaning: _____alone / boring / lazy / inactive_____

**B.** Compare answers with another student and explain your inferences to each other. Then look up the words and phrases in the dictionary. How well did you guess the meanings?

## EXERCISE 4

**A.** For each underlined word or phrase, use the context to figure out the part of speech or the grammatical function, and infer the general meaning.

1. Anyone who goes before the prince is expected to show respect. The men have to take off their hats and bow; the women are supposed to make a deep <u>curtsy</u>. Since many women these days don't know how to curtsy, they have to be shown the proper way to do it.

Part of speech: _____noun_____

General meaning: _____respect_____

2. In England during World War I, certain war experiences <u>cut across</u> social boundaries and removed some of the deepest class divisions. When there was an air raid, everyone ran to the shelters—lords together with cabbies (taxi drivers) and cooks.

Function: _ignore_

General meaning: _do not care_

3. My mother had very beautiful, thick long hair when she was young. In those days, they thought that long thick hair would <u>sap</u> a child's strength. So when she came down with a bad flu, her hair was cut very short. Afterwards, she refused to leave her room.

Part of speech: _____

General meaning: _____

4. Growing up during the hard times of the 1930s, my parents' generation learned not to waste a <u>morsel</u>. "Remember the starving Armenians," my mother would say when I left food on my plate. I doubted that anyone—starving or not—would want to eat her cooking.

Function: _noun_

General meaning: _small crap of food_

5. The men who worked in the fields picking tomatoes had to labor very long hours and were paid a <u>pittance</u>. They were also forced to live in horrible conditions. But since they were illegal immigrants, they didn't dare go to the police to complain.

Part of speech: _noun_

General meaning: _small amount of money_

6. I would not advise taking any action right now. Certain political forces are likely to <u>play themselves out</u> sooner rather than later, given the global economic crisis. The best strategy is probably to wait for the situation to calm down.

Function: _verb — phrase_

General meaning: _take place_

**B.** *Compare answers with another student and explain your inferences to each other. Then look up the words and phrases in the dictionary. How well did you guess the meanings?*

**A.** *For each underlined word or phrase, use the context to figure out the part of speech or the grammatical function, and infer the general meaning.*

1. The failure to contain HIV and AIDS has not been caused by a lack of scientific knowledge; we argue that application of this knowledge has been <u>thwarted</u> by other forces, especially political and economic ones.

   Part of speech: _____

   General meaning: _____

2. Ending dependence on foreign oil and promoting economic freedom will lead to a more efficient distribution of resources, create greater wealth, <u>curb</u> corruption and waste, and contribute significantly to the reduction of poverty.

   Part of speech: _____

   General meaning: _____

3. In contemporary society, tolerance has taken on a more general significance, according to the broad democratic principle of equality of opportunity, <u>regardless of</u> race, color, sexual orientation, or beliefs.

   Function: _____

   General meaning: _____

4. It was not Rupert's knowledge of literary history that made him a poet; rather, he became a poet <u>by virtue of</u> a poetic intelligence and awareness, which he arrived at through practice and experimentation.

   Function: _____

   General meaning: _____

5. During the World War I years, when most northern cities experienced large <u>increments</u> in their black populations, San Francisco's remained comparatively small, mainly because of the lack of economic opportunity in the city.

   Part of speech: _____

   General meaning: _____

6. It is an offense to <u>tamper with</u> any piece of fire or safety equipment on campus. Guilty persons will be charged the cost of replacement or repair and will also be subject to a fixed fine.

   Function: _____

   General meaning: _____

**B.** *Compare answers with another student and explain your inferences to each other. Then look up the words and phrases in the dictionary. How well did you guess the meanings?*

# Inferring Meaning from a Passage

When you are reading, you sometimes need to look at larger pieces of text for clues to the meaning of a word or phrase. In this section, you will find exercises for practice finding clues in the context of a longer passage.

## Guidelines for Inferring Meaning from a Passage

1. Decide on the part of speech or grammatical function of the word or phrase.

2. Look at the words close to it.

3. Think about the meaning of the sentence and the topic of the passage.

4. Look to see if the word or phrase is repeated in the passage.

5. Look for synonyms or opposites.

6. Look for an explanation or definition of the word or phrase (especially in a textbook).

7. Make an inference about the meaning.

8. Read the sentence again with your inferred meaning in place of the word or phrase. Does it make sense?

## EXERCISE 6

**A.** *Preview the passage for the gist [the general idea]: Read the title and look very quickly through the passage—not more than one minute. What is it about? Compare ideas with another student.*

**B.** *Read the passage without stopping to look up unfamiliar words or phrases.*

### Food Technology

The current methods for preparing fast food are less likely to be found in cookbooks than in trade journals such as *Food Technologist* and *Food Engineering*. Aside from the salad greens and tomatoes, most fast food is delivered to the restaurant already frozen, canned, dehydrated, or freeze-dried. A fast food kitchen is merely the final stage in a vast and highly complex system of mass production. Foods that may look familiar have in fact been completely reformulated. What we eat has changed more in the last forty years than in the previous forty thousand. Today's fast food conceals remarkable technological advances behind an ordinary-looking façade. Much of the taste and aroma of American fast food, for example, is now manufactured at a series of large chemical plants off the New Jersey Turnpike.

In the fast food restaurants of Colorado Springs, behind the counters, amid the plastic seats, in the changing landscape outside the window, you can see all the virtues and destructiveness of our fast food nation. I chose Colorado Springs as a focal point for this book because the changes that have recently swept through the city are emblematic of those that fast food—and the fast food mentality—have encouraged throughout the United States. Countless other suburban communities, in every part of the country, could have been used to illustrate the same points. The extraordinary growth of Colorado Springs neatly parallels that of the fast food industry: during the last few decades, the city's population has more than doubled. Subdivisions, shopping malls, and chain restaurants are appearing in the foothills of Cheyenne Mountain and the plains rolling to the east. The Rocky Mountain region as a whole has the fastest-growing economy in the United States, mixing high-tech and service industries in a way that may define America's workforce for years to come. And new restaurants are opening there at a faster pace than anywhere else in the nation.

(Source: Eric Schlosser, *Fast Food Nation,* Mariner Books, Houghton Mifflin, 2001)

**C.** *Find each of these words and phrases in the passage. Look at the context and write the part of speech or grammatical function. Then write the general meaning.*

1. dehydrated     Part of speech: _____

          General meaning: _____

2. façade     Part of speech: _____

          General meaning: _____

3. aroma     Part of speech: _____

          General meaning: _____

4. plants     Part of speech: _____

          General meaning: _____

5. swept through     Function: _____

          General meaning: _____

6. emblematic     Part of speech: _____

          General meaning: _____

7. countless     Part of speech: _____

          General meaning: _____

8. subdivisions     Part of speech: _____

          General meaning: _____

9. foothills     Part of speech: _____

          General meaning: _____

10. plains     Part of speech: _____

          General meaning: _____

**D.** *Compare answers with another student and explain your inferences.*

**E.** *Underline other words you are not familiar with. Look in the Appendix on page 310 for the words in Part C. Look up the words and phrases you want to learn from the passage and write them in your vocabulary notebook (with the sentence where you found each, the part of speech, and the meaning or a synonym).*

## EXERCISE 7

**A.** *Preview the passage for the gist: Read the title, and look very quickly through the passage—not more than one minute. What is it about? Compare ideas with another student.*

**B.** *Read the passage without stopping to look up unfamiliar words or phrases.*

### Why Write About Fast Food?

Elitists have always looked down at fast food, criticizing how it tastes and regarding it as another tacky manifestation of American popular culture. The aesthetics of fast food are of much less concern to me than its impact upon the lives of ordinary Americans, both as workers and consumers. Most of all, I am concerned about its impact on the nation's children. Fast food is heavily marketed to children and prepared by people who are barely older than children. This is an industry that both feeds and feeds off the young. During the two years spent researching this book, I ate an enormous amount of fast food. Most of it tasted pretty good. That is one of the main reasons people buy fast food; it has been carefully designed to taste good. It's also inexpensive and convenient. But the value meals, two-for-one deals, and free refills of soda give a distorted sense of how much fast food actually costs. The real price never appears on the menu.

The sociologist George Ritzer has attacked the fast food industry for celebrating a narrow measure of efficiency over every other human value . . . Others consider the fast food industry proof of the nation's great economic vitality, a beloved American institution that appeals overseas to millions who admire our way of life. Indeed, the values, the culture, and the industrial arrangements of our fast food nation are now being exported to the rest of the world. Fast food has joined Hollywood movies, blue jeans, and pop music as one of America's most prominent cultural exports. Unlike other commodities, however, fast food isn't viewed, read, played, or worn. It enters the body and becomes part of the consumer. No other industry offers, both literally and figuratively, so much insight into the nature of mass consumption.

Hundreds of millions of people buy fast food every day without giving it much thought . . . They rarely consider where this food came from, how it was made, what it is doing to the community around them. They just grab their tray off the counter, find a table, take a seat, unwrap the paper, and dig in. The whole experience is transitory and soon forgotten. I've written this book out of a belief that people should know what lies behind the shiny, happy surface of every fast food transaction. They should know what really lurks between those sesame-seed buns. As the old saying goes: You are what you eat.

(Source: Eric Schlosser, *Fast Food Nation*, Mariner Books, Houghton Mifflin, 2001)

**C.** *Find each of these words and phrases in the passage. Look at the context and write the part of speech or grammatical function. Then write the general meaning.*

1. elitist

   Part of speech: _____

   General meaning: _____

2. look down at

   Function: _____

   General meaning: _____

3. tacky

   Part of speech: _____

   General meaning: _____

4. aesthetics

   Part of speech: _____

   General meaning: _____

5. most of all

   Function: _____

   General meaning: _____

6. feeds off

   Function: _____

   General meaning: _____

7. figuratively

   Part of speech: _____

   General meaning: _____

8. dig in

   Function: _____

   General meaning: _____

9. transitory

   Part of speech: _____

   General meaning: _____

10. lurk

    Part of speech: _____

    General meaning: _____

**D.** *Compare answers with another student and explain your inferences.*

**E.** *Underline other words you are not familiar with. Look in the Appendix on page 310 for the words in Part C. Look up the words and phrases you want to learn from the passage and write them in your vocabulary notebook (with the sentence where you found each, the part of speech, and the meaning or a synonym).*

## Remember

- Review the words and phrases in your vocabulary notebook every day.
- Ask another student to test your knowledge of the words from the meanings and the meanings of the words.
- At the end of every week, choose 10–20 words that you have trouble remembering and put them on word study cards (see Part 2, Unit 1). Review them until you know them well.
- Ask another student to test your knowledge of the words on the cards.

Many words in English are made up of several parts. Adding or taking away different word parts can change the word's meaning, part of speech, or grammar.

You will learn vocabulary better if you can recognize word parts and understand how they can change a word. There are two reasons for this:

1. You will have a more complete understanding of the words.
2. You will remember the words better because you can connect them to something you already know (the parts or other words with the same parts).

In this unit, you will practice dividing words into parts, and you will learn about some parts that are found in many words.

## Parts of Words

The root is the most important part of a word. It gives the basic meaning.

> **Example:** agree

A prefix is a part added before the root.

> **Example:** *dis* + agree = disagree

A suffix is a part added after the root.

> **Example:** agree + *ment* = agreement

Some words contain both a prefix and a suffix.

> **Example:** *dis* + agree + *ment* = disagreement

## Roots

There are two kinds of roots in English.

- Roots that can stand alone as words: These are usually not difficult to recognize. They may be used with a prefix and/or a suffix.

    **Examples:**

    | Root | Prefix | / | Root | / | Suffix |
    |------|--------|---|------|---|--------|
    | agree | dis | + | agree | + | ment |
    | break | un | + | break | + | able |
    | view | re | + | view | + | er |

- Roots that cannot stand alone: These may be harder to recognize because they usually come from other languages, especially Latin and Greek.

### Examples

| Root | Source | Prefix / Root / Suffix |
|------|--------|------------------------|
| natio | Latin *natus:* born | *multi* + *nation* + *al* |
| athl | Greek *athlos:* contest | *tri* + *athl* + *on* |

**Note:** The spelling of a root may change in the English word.

**Example:** *nunc* (from Latin *nuntius* meaning *messenger*) → pro**nunc**iation

## EXERCISE 1

A. **Work with another student. Find a root from the box in each of the words below and circle it. Then write the meaning of the root.**

> ann, enn (Latin *annus:* year)
> cogno, gnosi (Latin *cognoscere:* to know)
> cycle (Greek *kyklos:* circle)
> dict (Latin *dicere:* to say)
> duc (Latin *ducere:* to lead)
> fact (Latin *factum:* something done)
> form (Latin *forma:* shape)
> func (Latin *fungere:* to perform)
> gener (Latin *genus:* kind, type)
> labor (Latin *labor:* to work)
> lit (Latin *littera:* writing)
> loc (Latin *locus:* place)
> log (Greek *logos:* word, reason)
> nunc (Latin *nuntiare:* to announce)
> path (Greek *pathos:* suffering)
> poli (Greek *polis:* city)
> port (Latin *portare:* to carry)
> scrib, script (Latin *scribere:* to write)
> sid, sed (Latin *sedere:* to sit)
> vers, vert (Latin *vertere:* to turn)

| Word with Root | Meaning of Root | Word with Root | Meaning of Root |
|----------------|-----------------|----------------|-----------------|
| 1. (path)etic | suffering | 9. literally | _____ |
| 2. annual | _____ | 10. prescription | _____ |
| 3. diagnosis | _____ | 11. generalize | _____ |
| 4. cyclical | _____ | 12. relocate | _____ |
| 5. laboratory | _____ | 13. factor | _____ |
| 6. formulate | _____ | 14. denounce | _____ |
| 7. dictator | _____ | 15. vertical | _____ |
| 8. reduction | _____ | 16. logical | _____ |

17. portable     _____     19. functional     _____

18. politician     _____     20. sedentary     _____

B.   *Compare answers with another pair of students. Look up any unfamiliar words in the dictionary. Then add any useful new words to your vocabulary notebook.*

## EXERCISE 2

A.   *Work with another student. Find a root from the box in each of the words below and circle it. Then write the meaning of the root.*

astr (Greek *astron:* star)
aut, auto (Greek *autos:* self, same)
ben (Latin *bene:* good, well)
bio (Greek *bios:* life)
cad, cas, cid (Latin *cadere:* to fall)
ced, cess (Latin *cedere:* to go)
cred (Latin *credere:* to believe)
dur (Latin *durus:* hard)
fen, fend (Latin *fendere:* to strike)
fid (Latin *fides:* faith, loyalty)

gram, graph (Greek *gramma:* writing)
man, manu (Latin *manus:* hand)
meter (Greek *metron:* measure)
pass, pati (Latin *passus:* to suffer, permit)
pon, posit (Latin *ponere:* to put)
rump, rupt (Latin *rumpere:* to break)
senti, sents (Latin *sentire:* to feel)
spec, spic (Latin *specere:* to look)
struct (Latin *struere:* to build)
tele (Greek *telos:* far, end)

| Word with Root | Meaning of Root | Word with Root | Meaning of Root |
|---|---|---|---|
| 1. autonomy | _____ | 11. offending | _____ |
| 2. beneficial | _____ | 12. telegram | _____ |
| 3. biology | _____ | 13. fidelity | _____ |
| 4. specimen | _____ | 14. asterisk | _____ |
| 5. rupture | _____ | 15. destruction | _____ |
| 6. durable | _____ | 16. passive | _____ |
| 7. accidental | _____ | 17. grammatical | _____ |
| 8. recession | _____ | 18. manual | _____ |
| 9. creditor | _____ | 19. position | _____ |
| 10. thermometer | _____ | 20. sensation | _____ |

B.   *Compare answers with another pair of students. Look up any unfamiliar words in the dictionary. Then add any useful new words to your vocabulary notebook.*

## Prefixes

Adding a prefix before the root changes the meaning of the word in some way.

    ***Examples:*** *re* + read = read again

                   *il* + logical = not logical

A few prefixes change the part of speech.

    ***Examples:*** *a* + side (noun) = aside (adverb)

                   *en* + courage (noun) = encourage (verb)

> **Notes:**
>
> - Sometimes a hyphen is put between the prefix and the root. (The use of hyphens may be different in British English and North American English.)
>
>   **Examples:** non-native, pre-existing
>
> - Some word parts can function as roots or prefixes.
>
>   **Examples:** *manu* + *fact* + ure = manufacture
>
>                       *bio* + *log* + y = biology

## EXERCISE 3

**A.** *Work with another student. For each word, find the root from the boxes in Exercises 1 and 2 and circle it. Then write the prefix.*

| Word | Prefix | Word | Prefix |
|------|--------|------|--------|
| 1. president | _____ | 9. illiterate | _____ |
| 2. centennial | _____ | 10. conductor | _____ |
| 3. recycling | _____ | 11. subscription | _____ |
| 4. monopoly | _____ | 12. sympathize | _____ |
| 5. collaboration | _____ | 13. dislocate | _____ |
| 6. prediction | _____ | 14. manufacture | _____ |
| 7. pronunciation | _____ | 15. reversible | _____ |
| 8. regenerate | _____ | 16. recognize | _____ |

|  | Word | Prefix |  | Word | Prefix |
|---|---|---|---|---|---|
| 17. | deformation | _____ | 19. | dialogue | _____ |
| 18. | imported | _____ | 20. | malfunction | _____ |

**B.** *Compare answers with another pair of students. Look up any unfamiliar words in the dictionary. Then add them to your vocabulary notebook.*

**C.** *Look again at the prefixes. Do you know or can you guess the meaning of any of them? Write the prefixes below with their meanings. (Some prefixes are repeated.)*

pre = before, early _____      _____

_____      _____

_____      _____

_____      _____

_____      _____

_____      _____

_____      _____

**D.** *Check your guesses in the dictionary and change them if necessary. Look up the ones you did not know and add them above. (Dictionaries list prefixes as words.)*

**E.** *Write any useful new words in your vocabulary notebook.*

## EXERCISE 4

**A.** *Work with another student. For each word, find a root from the boxes in Exercises 1 and 2 and circle it. Then write the prefix.*

|  | Word | Prefix |  | Word | Prefix |
|---|---|---|---|---|---|
| 1. | disaster | _____ | 7. | diameter | _____ |
| 2. | autobiography | _____ | 8. | defender | _____ |
| 3. | manuscript | _____ | 9. | endurance | _____ |
| 4. | indicate | _____ | 10. | confidence | _____ |
| 5. | propose | _____ | 11. | telegraphic | _____ |
| 6. | incredible | _____ | 12. | impatient | _____ |

| Word | Prefix | | Word | Prefix |
|------|--------|---|------|--------|
| 13. postpone | _____ | | 17. construct | _____ |
| 14. insensitive | _____ | | 18. astrology | _____ |
| 15. inspection | _____ | | 19. telepathy | _____ |
| 16. interrupt | _____ | | 20. monologue | _____ |

**B.** *Compare answers with another pair of students. Look up any unfamiliar words in the dictionary. Then add them to your vocabulary notebook.*

**C.** *Look again at the prefixes. Do you know or can you guess the meaning of any of them? Write the prefixes with their meanings.*

_____    _____

_____    _____

_____    _____

_____    _____

_____    _____

_____    _____

_____    _____

**D.** *Check your guesses in the dictionary and change them if necessary. Look up the ones you did not know and add them above. Write any useful new words in your vocabulary notebook.*

## Identifying Prefixes

**Note:** The first letters of a word may look like a prefix, but may not actually be a prefix. The pronunciation is sometimes, though not always, a clue. (See the second example below.)

**EXAMPLE:**
. . . . . . . . . . . .

In each group of words, all except one start with the same prefix. Find the word that is different and cross it out. Then write the prefix and its meaning.

1. retrain      revise      ~~result~~      reform      refund

   Prefix: _re-_      Meaning: _again, back, as before_

2. unable      ~~uniform~~      unemployed      unfortunate      uncertain

   Prefix: _un-_      Meaning: _not_

**A.** *In each group of words, all <u>except one</u> start with the same prefix. Find the word that is different and cross it out. Then write the prefix (from the other words) and its meaning.*

1. procedure    problem    program    proposal    prospect

   Prefix: _____    Meaning: _____

2. precious    prejudice    previously    preparation    prescription

   Prefix: _____    Meaning: _____

3. immobile    impatient    impersonal    impression    impractical

   Prefix: _____    Meaning: _____

4. companion    command    commission    combination    comedy

   Prefix: _____    Meaning: _____

5. collection    collateral    collocation    collar    colleague

   Prefix: _____    Meaning: _____

6. misadventure    misplace    mission    miscalculate    misconduct

   Prefix: _____    Meaning: _____

7. disapprove    discipline    disappointment    discomfort    disgust

   Prefix: _____    Meaning: _____

8. industry    inappropriate    ineffective    incomprehensible    inconvenient

   Prefix: _____    Meaning: _____

9. bifocal    bilateral    binary    binoculars    billion

   Prefix: _____    Meaning: _____

10. illustrate    illiterate    illogical    illegal    illegible

    Prefix: _____    Meaning: _____

**B.** *Look up any useful new words. Write them in your vocabulary notebook.*

**A.** *Work with another student. Look through Exercises 1–5 and write all the prefixes (seven) that make words negative or change the meaning of the word to the opposite. Make a note if you find a pattern in the use of the negative prefixes.*

1. *il- used before words or roots that start with the letter l*

2. _____

3. _____

4. _____

5. _____

6. _____

7. _____

**B.** *Look back at Exercises 1 and 3. For each root listed in Exercise 1, find the words in both exercises that contain it. Talk with your partner about the connection between the meaning of the root and the meaning of the words, for example:*

- Root: *cycle* = circle: *cyclical, recycling, bicycle*—all relate to some kind of circle
- Root: *astr* = star: *astronomy* = the study of the stars (and planets); *asterisk* = a mark that looks like a star; *disaster* = a sudden, terrible event, from the idea of bad luck coming from the stars

**C.** *Look back at Exercises 2 and 4. For each root listed in Exercise 2, find the words in both exercises that contain it. Talk with your partner about the connection between the meaning of the root and the meanings of the words.*

## Suffixes

A suffix at the end of a word can:

- indicate the part of speech.

    ***Examples:*** sedi + *ment* (noun), annu + *al* (adjective)

- change the part of speech.

    ***Example:*** creative (adjective) + *ly* = creatively (adverb)

- influence the meaning of the word.

    ***Example:*** young (adjective) + *est* = youngest (superlative form of adjective)

- change the part of speech and also influence the meaning.

    ***Example:*** help (noun or verb + *less* = helpless (negative adjective)

- change the verb tense.

    ***Example:*** realize (present tense verb) + *d* = realized (past tense verb)

**Notes:**

- Sometimes the spelling of the root changes when you add a suffix.

    **Examples:** simple + *ly* = simply (the letter *e* is dropped)
    wealthy + *est* = wealthiest (y → i)
    succeed + *ss* = success (the letters *ed* are dropped)

- More than one suffix can be added to a root.

    **Examples:** intent + *ion* + *ally* = intentionally
    revolve + *ution* + *ize* = revolutionize
    simple + *ify* + *cation* = simplification

## EXERCISE 7

A. *Follow these steps for each word:*
   - *Find and circle the suffix or suffixes.*
   - *Write the part of speech of the word <u>with</u> the suffix.*
   - *Write the root or roots alone (without prefix or suffix). It (They) may or may not stand alone.*
   - *If the root(s) can stand alone, write the part of speech. If the root cannot stand alone, write X.*

| Word | Part of Speech (with suffix) | Root(s) Alone | Part of Speech of Root |
|---|---|---|---|
| 1. form(al) | adjective | form | noun, verb |
| 2. annivers(ary) | noun | anni + vers | X |
| 3. diagnosis | | | |
| 4. cyclical | | | |
| 5. laboratory | | | |
| 6. pathetic | | | |
| 7. dictionary | | | |
| 8. reduction | | | |
| 9. literally | | | |
| 10. scripture | | | |
| 11. generalize | | | |
| 12. locally | | | |
| 13. factory | | | |

| Word | Part of Speech (with suffix) | Root(s) Alone | Part of Speech of Root |
|------|------------------------------|---------------|------------------------|
| 14. vertical | _____ | _____ | _____ |
| 15. portable | _____ | _____ | _____ |
| 16. telegraphic | _____ | _____ | _____ |
| 17. sentimental | _____ | _____ | _____ |
| 18. destruction | _____ | _____ | _____ |

B. *Look at the parts of speech in the left column in Part A. Write the suffixes that are used to form the following parts of speech.*

1. Suffixes that form nouns: _____

2. Suffixes that form verbs: _____

3. Suffixes that form adjectives: _____

4. Suffixes that form adverbs: _____

C. *Compare work with another student. Write any useful new words in your vocabulary notebook.*

## EXERCISE 8

A. *Follow these steps for each word:*
   - *Find and circle the suffix or suffixes.*
   - *Write the part of speech of the word <u>with</u> the suffix.*
   - *Write the root or roots alone (without prefix or suffix). It (They) may or may not stand alone.*
   - *If the root(s) can stand alone, write the part of speech. If the root(s) cannot stand alone, write X.*

| Word | Part of Speech (with suffix) | Root(s) Alone | Part of Speech of Root |
|------|------------------------------|---------------|------------------------|
| 1. autonomy | _____ | _____ | _____ |
| 2. beneficial | _____ | _____ | _____ |
| 3. biology | _____ | _____ | _____ |
| 4. accident | _____ | _____ | _____ |
| 5. recession | _____ | _____ | _____ |
| 6. creditor | _____ | _____ | _____ |
| 7. constructive | _____ | _____ | _____ |

| Word | Part of Speech (with suffix) | Root(s) Alone | Part of Speech of Root |
|---|---|---|---|
| 8. durable | _____ | _____ | _____ |
| 9. offensive | _____ | _____ | _____ |
| 10. fidelity | _____ | _____ | _____ |
| 11. grammatically | _____ | _____ | _____ |
| 12. manual | _____ | _____ | _____ |
| 13. patience | _____ | _____ | _____ |
| 14. position | _____ | _____ | _____ |
| 15. sympathize | _____ | _____ | _____ |
| 16. politician | _____ | _____ | _____ |
| 17. functional | _____ | _____ | _____ |
| 18. sedentary | _____ | _____ | _____ |

B. *Look at the parts of speech in the left column in Part A. Write the suffixes that are used to form the following parts of speech.*

1. Suffixes that form nouns: _____

2. Suffixes that form verbs: _____

3. Suffixes that form adjectives: _____

4. Suffixes that form adverbs: _____

C. *Compare work with another student. Write any useful new words in your vocabulary notebook.*

# Word Families

A word family is a group of different forms of a word that all have the same root. The word forms in a word family are closely related in meaning, but are different parts of speech. It is important to learn the various forms of a word so that you can recognize them quickly in your reading and use them correctly in your writing.

---

**Notes:**

- There may be more than one form for a part of speech. Each form usually has a somewhat different meaning.

  ***Examples:*** *careful, caring (adjectives)*
  
  *careful* = trying hard not to make mistakes, damage something, or cause problems
  
  *caring* = someone who is caring is kind to other people and tries to help them

- The same form may sometimes be used for more than one part of speech.

  ***Examples:***

  | Noun | Verb | Adjective |
  |---|---|---|
  | direction | direct | direct |
  | limit | limit | limited |

- Some words do not have a form for every part of speech.

  ***Examples:***

  | Noun | Verb | Adjective | Negative Adjective | Adverb |
  |---|---|---|---|---|
  | cold | X | cold | X | coldly |
  | youth | X | young, youthful | X | youthfully |

- When there is no negative adjective, the negative may be expressed with an opposite or with *not*.

  ***Examples:*** *young/old, youthful/not youthful*

---

## Guidelines for Studying Word Families

Work on word families is a useful way to build your vocabulary.

- Continue adding word families to your vocabulary notebook.
- When you encounter a new form of a word you have studied, write the new form on that page in your vocabulary notebook.
- Include word forms whenever you review vocabulary in your notebook and when you write words on study cards.

A. *Work with another student. Write the missing forms for each word in the chart. Do not use the dictionary. If you do not know a form, make a guess. Sometimes more than one form exists for a part of speech. An "X" means the form is rare or does not exist.*

| | Noun | Verb | Adjective | Negative adjective | Adverb |
|---|---|---|---|---|---|
| 1. | agreement disagreement | agree, disagree | agreeable | disagreeable | agreeably, disagreeably |
| 2. | | | high | X | |
| 3. | contest | | | | X |
| 4. | program | | | | X |
| 5. | | diagnose | | | X |
| 6. | | | political | | |
| 7. | defense | | | | |
| 8. | | | endurance | | |
| 9. | confidence | | | X | |
| 10. | | | | X | generally |
| 11. | | describe | | | |
| 12. | construction | | | | |
| 13. | | X | responsible | | |
| 14. | | X | selfish | | |
| 15. | effort | X | X | | |

B. *Check your work in the dictionary. Correct the forms if necessary. Write any useful new words in your vocabulary notebook.*

A.  Work with another student. Write the missing forms for each word in the chart. Do not use the dictionary. If you do not know a form, make a guess. Sometimes more than one form exists for a part of speech. An "X" means the form is rare or does not exist.

| | Noun | Verb | Adjective | Negative adjective | Adverb |
|---|---|---|---|---|---|
| 1. | | | | X | locally |
| 2. | logic | X | | | |
| 3. | | | | insensitive | |
| 4. | | employ | | | X |
| 5. | problem | X | | | |
| 6. | courage | | | | |
| 7. | | | endurable | | |
| 8. | grammar | X | | | |
| 9. | | destroy | | | |
| 10. | | benefit | | X | |
| 11. | autonomy | X | | X | |
| 12. | | prescribe | | X | |
| 13. | meaning | | | | |
| 14. | | | foolish | X | |
| 15. | recession | | | X | X |

B.  Check your work in the dictionary. Correct the forms if necessary. Write any useful new words in your vocabulary notebook.

**A.** *Work with another student. Write the missing forms for each word in the chart. Do not use the dictionary. If you do not know a form, make a guess. Sometimes more than one form exists for a part of speech. An "X" means the form is rare or does not exist.*

|  | Noun | Verb | Adjective | Negative adjective | Adverb |
|---|---|---|---|---|---|
| 1. |  | prepare |  |  | X |
| 2. |  |  | mobile |  | X |
| 3. |  |  | sympathetic |  |  |
| 4. | collection |  |  | X |  |
| 5. | commission |  |  |  | X |
| 6. |  | calculate |  | X | X |
| 7. |  | approve |  |  |  |
| 8. | illustration |  |  | X | X |
| 9. | comprehension |  |  |  |  |
| 10. |  |  | convenient |  |  |
| 11. |  | cycle |  | X |  |
| 12. |  | function |  |  |  |
| 13. | generation |  |  | X |  |
| 14. | crisis | X |  |  |  |
| 15. |  | suffer |  |  |  |

**B.** *Check your work in the dictionary. Correct the forms if necessary. Write any useful new words in your vocabulary notebook.*

**A.** *Work with another student. Write the missing forms for each word in the chart. Do not use the dictionary. If you do not know a form, make a guess. Sometimes more than one form exists for a part of speech. An "X" means the form is rare or does not exist.*

| | Noun | Verb | Adjective | Negative adjective | Adverb |
|---|---|---|---|---|---|
| **1.** | creditor | | | | |
| **2.** | | collaborate | | | |
| **3.** | prediction | | | | |
| **4.** | | X | | illiterate | |
| **5.** | reduction | | | | X |
| **6.** | incident | X | | X | |
| **7.** | | | legal | | |
| **8.** | impression | | | | |
| **9.** | | | appropriate | | |
| **10.** | reward | | | | |
| **11.** | | | final | X | |
| **12.** | master | | | X | |
| **13.** | | | extensive | X | |
| **14.** | effect | | | | |
| **15.** | | X | vulnerable | | |

**B.** *Check your work in the dictionary. Correct the forms if necessary. Write any new useful words in your vocabulary notebook.*

## Learning Word Forms from Your Reading

In this unit, you have become familiar with a certain number of word families, but to make a real difference in your reading or writing, you need to continue this kind of vocabulary work in your reading.

### EXERCISE 13

A.   On a separate piece of paper, make a word family chart like the one in Exercise 12, but with 20 rows instead of 15. Look back at the first paragraph of the passage in Part 2, Unit 1, Exercise 1, on page 40 and underline the forms of these words.

| | | | | |
|---|---|---|---|---|
| combine | education | industry | serve | spread |
| customer | experience | nation | spend | various |

B.   Work with another student. Write the words from Part A in your word family chart and add as many other forms as possible. Then check your dictionary to see if the forms are correct. Correct your work and add missing forms.

C.   Look through the passage and find ten more words to add to your chart. Look for words that have two or more forms. Write them in your chart and add as many forms as possible.

D.   Check your dictionary to see if the forms are correct. Correct your work and add missing forms. Add any useful new words to your vocabulary workbook.

### EXERCISE 14

A.   On a separate piece of paper, make another word family chart with 20 rows. Look at the passage in Part 2, Unit 1, Exercise 2, on page 41 and underline the forms of these words in the text.

| | | | | |
|---|---|---|---|---|
| adjust | employ | feminine | inflation | period |
| decline | enter | growth | motivate | steadily |

B.   Work with another student. Write the words from Part A in your word family chart and add as many other forms as possible. Then check your dictionary to see if the forms are correct. Correct your work and add missing forms.

C.   Look through the passage and find ten more words to add to your chart. Look for words that have two or more forms. Write them in your chart and add as many forms as possible.

D.   Check your dictionary to see if the forms are correct. Correct your work and add missing forms. Add any useful new words to your vocabulary notebook.

Speakers and writers in English tend to use the same groups or combinations of words again and again. This is easier than trying to think of new ways to say things each time. It is also easier for listeners and readers if they recognize the group of words, since they do not have to think about each word separately.

If you can recognize many common phrases, your comprehension and fluency will improve in all language skill areas: listening, speaking, reading, and writing.

There are many types of phrases, including:

- Compound words
- Phrasal verbs
- Fixed phrases
- Idiomatic expressions
- Collocations

## Types of Phrases

### Compound Words

Compound words—two or more words that are used together with a single meaning—are very common in English in both informal and formal language, and more are constantly being created. They can usually be understood from the meanings of the single words. They may form one word, two separate words or two words with a hyphen (and this may differ in different sources).

***Examples:*** *fast food, fast(-)forward, answering machine, smartphone, organized crime, cost(-)effectiveness*

### Phrasal Verbs

Phrasal verbs—verbs followed by one or two prepositions—sometimes are understandable from the single words, but often they are not. A phrasal verb may have more than one meaning, so look for a dictionary definition that fits the context where you found it, as with a single word. As you are aware, many phrasal verbs are commonly used in general English.

Other phrasal verbs are used frequently in academic writing.

***Examples:*** *account for, rule out, seek to, deal with, put forward, come across as, give rise to, come up with*

### Fixed Phrases

Fixed phrases—phrases that generally do not vary in form—cannot be understood from knowing the single words. These include some very common phrases such as *of course* and *right away*. These and many other fixed phrases are truly "fixed"—that is, they are always used in exactly the same way. Others such as *make up your mind* can be altered to *made up your mind* or *make up my mind*, etc.

Certain fixed phrases are common in academic writing.

**Examples:** *by and large, by no means, with a view to, at any rate, give rise to, take into account*

## Idiomatic Expressions

These expressions may contain colorful metaphors or images. Though the meaning may not be obvious, it may be possible to guess it or at least to see the connection between the metaphor/image and the meaning. These are less common in formal academic writing, but may be used in spoken academic English or in emails.

**Examples:** *from A to Z, see eye to eye, get to the bottom of this, beat around the bush, bite the bullet*

## Collocations

A collocation is a pair or group of words that are frequently used together. They are not fixed phrases and the meaning is usually understandable from the single words. Collocations are an important part of general language as well as academic language.

**Examples:** General: *highly unlikely, immensely proud, pad of paper, catch sight of, get nowhere*
Academic: *the vast majority, entirely new, adversely affect, provide feedback, bear in mind*

Some words collocate (are used together) with many others.

**Examples:** *extremely + proud, happy, satisfied, angry* (and other adjectives for feelings)

Other words collocate only in limited ways.

**Examples:** *immensely proud* (but not immensely happy, satisfied, or angry)
*perfectly happy, satisfied* (but not perfectly proud, or angry)
*entirely satisfied* (but not entirely happy, proud, or angry)
*terribly angry* (but not terribly proud, happy, or satisfied)

---

### Reflecting on Your Learning

**1.** Look back at the examples for each of the different types of phrases.

- Are any of the examples expressed in a similar way in your language?
- How would you translate the ones that are different?

**2.** Work with another student.

- If you and your partner speak the same language, compare your answers to the questions in 1. Discuss any that were different.
- If you speak different languages, compare your answers to the first question in 1.

---

# Finding Phrases in the Dictionary

To find a phrase in the dictionary, look under the noun or verb if there is one, or under the word that seems most important. You may have to look in more than one place.

## *Examples:*

### keep an eye on someone

**eye**[1] /aɪ/ S1 W1 *n.*
**1** BODY PART [C] BIOLOGY one of the two parts of the body that you see with: *Erica has green eyes.* | *Her eyes were bright with happiness.* | ***Close your eyes** and go to sleep.* | *Tom **opened** his **eyes**.* | *There were **tears in** her **eyes**.* | **your eyes widen/narrow** (=you open your eyes wider, or close them slightly, in order to express an emotion) *Louise's eyes widened in surprise.*
**2** WAY OF SEEING/UNDERSTANDING [C usually singular] a particular way of seeing, judging, or understanding something: **critical/trained eye** *Always read your work again with a critical eye.* | *The story is told **through the eyes of** (=from the point of view of) a child.* | *More interesting, **to my eyes**, are his landscape paintings.* | *He became a hero **in the eyes of** (=in the opinion of) millions of Americans.*
**3 keep an eye on sb/sth** INFORMAL **a)** to carefully watch someone or something, especially because you expect something bad to happen: *Firefighters kept a wary eye on the dry hills.* **b)** to take care of someone or something and make sure that they are safe: *Could you keep an eye on my luggage?* | *I'll keep an eye on the kids for you.* **c)** to carefully watch something, especially in order to do something with it: *Keep your eye on the ball and swing the bat evenly.*

### at all

**all**[1] /ɔl/ S1 W1 *quantifier, pron.* **1** the complete amount or quantity of something; every one or every part of something: *He ate all the cake that was left.* | *Are you finished with all your chores?* | *They're all the same age.* | *I've heard it all before.* | **all of us/them/it etc.** *Put all of it in the garbage.* | **you/they/it all** *They all passed the test.* | *Bill talks about football **all the time** (=a lot).* → see Word Choice box at EACH[1] **2** used to emphasize the most basic or necessary facts or details about a situation: *All you need is a hammer and nails.* | *All I want is a few hours sleep.* **3 (not) at all** used in questions and negative statements to emphasize what you are saying: *Were they any help at all?* | *It's not at all uncommon.* | *I'm surprised the doctors said he could go at all.* | *"So you wouldn't mind if I came along?" "No, not at all!"* (=certainly not, please come) **4 all kinds/sorts of sth** very many different types of things, people, or places: *I met all kinds of people at the conference.*

### come to

**come to** *phr. v.* **1** to become conscious again after having been unconscious: *He came to a few minutes later.* **2 come to sth** to have a particular result, usually a bad result: *I never thought it would come to this.* **3 come to sb** if an idea, thought or memory comes to you, you suddenly realize or remember it: *The solution came to him in a dream.* | *I've forgotten her name, but maybe it'll come to me later.*

### day after day

**af•ter** /'æftɚ/ S1 W1 *prep.*
**1** WHEN STH IS FINISHED when a particular time or event has happened or is finished OPP **before**: *After the dance, a few of us went out for a drink.* | *I go swimming every day after work.* | *What's on after the 6 o'clock news?* | *Do you believe in life after death?* | **a month/3 weeks/4 years etc. after sth** *A year after the fire, they rebuilt the house.* | *We leave **the day after tomorrow**.* | **shortly/soon etc. after sth** *Not long after the wedding, his wife got pregnant.* | *Come home **right after** (=immediately after) school.*
**2** LIST following someone or something else on a list or in a series, piece of writing, line of people etc. OPP **before**: *Whose name is after yours on the list?* | *The date should be written after the address.*
**3 after 10 minutes/3 hours etc.** when a particular amount of time has passed: *After 25 minutes, remove the cake from the oven.* | *After a while, things started to improve.* | *After months of arguments, they decided to get a divorce.*
**4** TIME used when telling time to say how many minutes it is past the hour OPP **to**: *The movie starts at a quarter after seven.*
**5 day after day/year after year etc.** continuously, for a very long time: *I get bored doing the same exercises day after day.*

*Read the example phrases and sentences in the dictionary entry. Then complete each sentence with one or more words. (More than one answer may be possible.)*

1. In evolution, mutation can ___give___ *rise to* new species over time.

2. Interest in student politics seems to be ___on___ *the rise* at the university.

> **rise**² W2 *n.*   **1** [C] an increase in number, amount, or value: **+of** *Profits went up to $24 million, a rise of 16%.* | **rise in costs/prices/taxes etc.** *Official fear that sudden rises in food prices could cause riots.* | *Violent crime* **is on the rise** (=is increasing) *in some European nations.*
> **2** [singular] the achievement of importance, success, or power OPP **fall**: *the rise of Fascism* | **+of** *"Citizen Kane" details the rise of a ruthless tycoon.* | **rise to power/fame** *the band's sudden rise to fame in the 1960s* | **the rise and fall of** (=the achievement of importance, success, power etc. followed by a loss of it) *the Roman Empire*
> **3** [singular] a movement upward OPP **fall**: *the steady* **rise and fall of** *his chest as he slept*   **4 give rise to sth** a phrase meaning to be the reason why something happens or begins to exist, used especially in writing: *The success of "Pamela" gave rise to a number of imitations.* | *Daily shaving can give rise to a number of skin problems.*

**Notes:**

- When you write a phrase in your vocabulary notebook, it is very important to include the sentence where you found it, so you can also learn how it is used.

- You may remember an idiom or collocation better if you can find some connection between the meanings of the single words and the whole group. If you cannot find a connection, you can invent something that will make the phrase more memorable.

## EXERCISE 1

**A.**   *Read the example phrases and sentences in the dictionary entry. Then complete each sentence with one or more words. (More than one answer may be possible.)*

**1. a.** Messi _____ two goals for Argentina.

   **b.** To improve your reading rate, you should _____ goals for yourself.

   **c.** Their _____ goal was to achieve independence for the country.

   **d.** He needed to pass the exam in order to graduate, but to _____ this goal he would have to study very hard.

> **goal** /goʊl/ Ac S2 W1 *n.* [C]   **1** something that you hope to achieve in the future SYN **aim**: *We are all working toward a common goal.* | **+of** *We have set ourselves a goal of raising $100,000.* | **sb's/sth's goal is to do sth** *Our goal is to stop the spread of AIDS.* | **achieve/reach a goal** *Our division reached its sales goal for the month.* | *I try to* **set goals** *for myself every day.* | *My* **long-term goal** *is to make a million dollars by my 40th birthday.* ▶ see THESAURUS box at **purpose**¹   **2** the action of making the ball go into a particular area to win a point in games such as football or SOCCER, or the point won by doing this: *the game's winning goal* | *Ronaldo* **scored** *three* **goals** *for Brazil.*
> **3** the area between two posts where the ball must go for a point to be won [**Origin:** 1500–1600 *gol* limit, boundary (1300–1400)]

**2. a.** To prove her _____, the manager revealed the sales figures for the past year.

**b.** The files he sent her proved _____ for her research.

**c.** As the youngest runner, no one took her seriously. She felt she had to prove _____.

**d.** The new evidence proved his _____ beyond any doubt. After ten years in jail, he was free at last.

**B.** *Compare answers with another student. Write any useful new phrases in your vocabulary notebook.*

---

**prove** /pruv/ S2 W1 *v. past tense* **proved**, *past participle* **proved** *or* **proven** /ˈpruvən/ **1** [T] to show that something is definitely true, especially by providing facts, information etc. OPP **disprove**: *You're wrong and I can prove it.* | **prove (that)** *Can you prove that you had nothing to do with it?* | **prove sb right/wrong/innocent/guilty etc.** *They say I'm too old, but I'm going to prove them all wrong.* | **prove sb's guilt/innocence** *The trial proved her innocence.* ▶ see THESAURUS box at **demonstrate** **2** [linking verb] if someone or something proves to be difficult, helpful, a problem etc., you find out that they are difficult, helpful, a problem etc.: **prove (to be) useful/difficult etc.** *The recent revelations may prove to be embarrassing to the President.* | **prove (to be) a disaster/problem/benefit etc.** *The design proved to be a success.* **3 prove yourself** also **prove something** to show how good you are at doing something: *When I started the job, I felt I had to prove myself.* | *He's always acting like he's trying to prove something.* **4 What is sb trying to prove?** SPOKEN said when you are annoyed by someone's behavior, because you think they are trying too hard to show that they are right and that they know something **5 prove a/your point** if someone does something to prove a point, they do it to show that they are right or that they can do something without having any other good reason: *I'm not going to run the marathon just to prove a point.* **6** [T] LAW to show that a WILL has been made in the correct way —**provable** *adj.* —**provably** *adv.*

---

## EXERCISE 2

**A.** *Read the example phrases and sentences in the dictionary entry. Then complete each sentence with one or more words. (More than one answer may be possible.)*

**1. a.** The new students are _____ the lead of those who have done this before.

**b.** After the fifth mile, Hind _____ the lead and kept it until the finish.

**c.** A month before elections, Locke held a strong lead _____ the other candidates.

**d.** Security forces were _____ a number of leads in the investigation.

**B.** *Compare answers with another student. Write any useful new phrases in your vocabulary notebook.*

---

**lead²** S2 W2 *n.*
**1 RACES the lead** the position or situation of being in front of or better than everyone else in a race or competition: *Lewis is still **in the lead**.* | *Kent **took the lead** (=went ahead of others) in the fifth lap.*
**2 ACTION** [singular] an action that other people copy, often something that is intended to make other people copy you: *The French are **following** Germany's **lead** on this issue.* | *It was young people who **took the lead** (=were the first to start) in organizing a peace movement.*
**3 WINNING AMOUNT** [singular] the distance, number of points etc. by which one competitor is ahead of another: **+over** *Virginia holds a 12-game lead over Kentucky.* | **+of** *In March the Republican candidate had a lead of 35%.*
**4 INFORMATION** [C] a piece of information that may help you to make a discovery or help find the answer to a problem: *The police have no leads in the murder investigation.* | *Detectives are **following up** (=doing something as a result of) a number of **leads**.*
**5 ACTING ROLE** [C] ENG. LANG. ARTS the main acting part in a play, movie etc.: *Who's **playing the lead in** the school play?*
**6 ACTOR** [C] ENG. LANG. ARTS the main actor in a movie or play: **male/female lead** *They haven't chosen their male lead.*
**7 NEWS** [C] the first or most important story in a television news program, newspaper etc., or the first part of such a story
**8 be sb's lead** the right, in a game of cards, to play your card first
**9 FOR DOG** [C] a LEASH
**10 electric wire** [C] TECHNICAL a wire that is used to connect parts of a piece of electrical equipment

2. a. International students should bear _____ that employment is not always easy to find.

b. The proposal presented by Spears in 1791 bears _____ to Condorcet's writings on freedom of speech.

c. Joyce couldn't bear _____ of this young man as the new director, sitting at her desk and putting his pictures on the walls.

d. For the most part, the government has had to bear _____ of cleaning up industrial pollution.

e. Unlike human hands, chimpanzee hands are strong enough to bear _____ while walking on all fours.

**bear**[1] /bɛr/ [S3] [W2] *v. past tense* **bore** /bɔr/, *past participle* **borne** /bɔrn/ [T]
**1** BE RESPONSIBLE FOR FORMAL to be responsible for or accept something: **bear the cost/burden/expense etc.** *The company responsible for the oil spill should bear the expense of cleaning it up.* | **bear responsibility/the blame/the burden etc.** *U.N. agencies will bear the burden of resettling the refugees.* ▶see THESAURUS box at **carry**[1]
**2** DEAL WITH STH to bravely accept or deal with a painful, difficult, or upsetting situation [SYN] **stand**: *He bore the pain stoically.* | *They had borne untold suffering and hardship.* | *He wrote that he could hardly bear to be separated from her.* | *Make the water as hot as you can bear.* | *His job requires long hours, and their marriage was unable to bear the strain* (=continue despite having to deal with difficult problems).
**3 bear a resemblance/relation etc. to sb/sth** to be similar to or related to someone or something else: *Ed bore little resemblance to the man she had described.* | *The final script bore absolutely no relation to the one I'd originally written.* | *The blaze bears several parallels to a previous fire last month.*
**4 bear (sth) in mind** to remember a fact or piece of information that is important or could be useful in the future [SYN] **keep (sth) in mind**: *Thanks, I'll bear that in mind.* | **+(that)** *Tourists must bear in mind that they are visitors in another country.*
**5** SIGN/MARK FORMAL to have or show a sign, mark, or particular appearance [SYN] **have**: *The stone marker bears the names of those killed in the riot.* | *Staff members wear T-shirts bearing the company's logo.* | *He had the disease as a child and still bears its scars.*
**6 sb can't bear sb/sth a)** to be so upset about something that you feel unable to accept it or let it happen [SYN] **can't stand**: *I can't bear violence toward another human being.* | *I couldn't bear the thought of having to start all over.* | **can't bear to do sth** *She was the kind of person who just couldn't bear to throw anything away.* **b)** to dislike something or someone so much that they make you very annoyed or impatient: *I really can't bear him.* | **can't bear doing sth** *I can't bear swimming in cold water.*
**7** SUPPORT to be under something and support it [SYN] **hold**: *The ice wasn't thick enough to bear his weight.* | *An oak table bore several photographs of the family.*
**8 bear fruit a)** if a plan, decision etc. bears fruit, it is successful, especially after a long period of time: *The project may not begin to bear fruit for at least two years.* **b)** if a tree bears fruit, it produces fruit

**B.** *Compare answers with another student. Write any useful new phrases in your vocabulary notebook.*

# Using Concordances

A concordance is a computerized set of examples of the way a given word or phrase is used in a corpus (a collection of texts). Each example is shown with the word highlighted in the middle of the sentence or part of sentence where it was used. The concordance "sentences" are often incomplete because there is room for only a limited number of words on either side of the target word.

Looking at concordance sentences can help you understand how common a word or phrase is, and what other words it collocates with.

The concordance sentences in these exercises were taken from the Pearson International Corpus of Academic English. Other concordance programs are available on the Internet, including the free and very user-friendly program found on the Complete Lexical Tutor website: www.lextutor.ca.

### EXAMPLE

**A.** *Read the concordance sentences. Notice the way the target word* example *is used.*

1.           predict temperature changes. This **example** is typical in the sense that all of the
2.  program expects to achieve its effects. For **example** , a smoking prevention program offers activities
3.      solid minerals, is a similar method. For **example** , serpentine is a type of rock found in
4. developing countries. China and India, for **example** , with large populations but relatively
5.     strongest, the fastest. The most obvious **example** of this is competitive sport. Imperial
6.       an item, then what applies to cars, for **example** , can also apply to clothing; therefore,
7.    with simple exponential functions. One **example** is shown in figure 6(a). It shows a good
8.          across countries are very large. For **example** , there is one country that deflates almost
9.       through demonstration. Consider, for **example** , a 9-month-old infant who has never before
10.  equation? The banking industry is a good **example** of how the business model has changed and

**B.** *Write your answers to the questions.*

1. Look to the right of the target word. What words or phrases are used after it?

   is typical, a smoking prevention program, serpentine is, with large populations, of this, can

   also apply, is shown, there is, a 9-month-old infant, of how

2. Look to the left of the target word. What words or phrases are used before it?

   This, For (6), the most obvious, One, a good

3. Can you make any generalizations about the target word—what part of speech or what words or punctuation often come before or after it?

   The phrase "for example" is used often and is set apart from the sentence by commas.

   When not used in the phrase "for example," adjectives or numbers can be used before it

   (the most obvious, a good, One) and it can be followed by "is" or "can."

Even though concordance sentences may be incomplete, you can often understand what kind of text they come from. For example, the first sentence in the list above includes the phrase "a smoking prevention program," so it is probably from a medical or public health text. Can you tell where the other concordance sentences come from?

**Notes:**

- On most concordance programs you can access a larger sample of text by clicking on the target word in the concordance sentence.

- Entering a combination of words into a concordance program will tell you if it is commonly used in English. For example, putting in *immensely proud,* will give you a number of sentences. Putting in *perfectly proud,* won't give you any sentences.

## EXERCISE 3

**A.** *Read the concordance sentences. Notice the way the target word* assumption *is used.*

1. notes that this concept is based on the **assumption** that market competition, "as manifested
2. that while Webster is questioning the **assumptions** others are making, he is not necessarily
3. general. This claim is based on certain **assumptions** about the relationship between
4. the people involved and never make **assumptions** regarding what people need. As designers we
5. else about the table, it is a reasonable **assumption** that it has four legs. You will also know
6. and from the beginning the underlying **assumption** has been that the possessor, producer,
7. by her account which challenge common **assumptions** about art and society. Some are connected
8. when younger family members make the **assumption** that because their parents are growing
9. diagnostic related groups. "The basic **assumption** is that all illnesses can be grouped according
10. the question, moreover it makes the **assumption** that subjective risk is determined only
11. this approach rests on the fundamental **assumption** that good actions come from good people
12. distance-learning), lecturers may make **assumptions** about the ways you are using the material

**B.** *Write your answers to the questions.*

1. Look to the right of the target word. Write the words that follow it.

_____

2. Look to the left of the target word. Write the adjectives used before it.

_____

3. Write the verbs used before the target word (including phrasal verbs).

_____

4. What prepositional phrases are used after the target word?

_____

5. Can you make any generalizations about the target word—what part of speech or what words often come before or after it?

_____

C. _Compare answers with another student. Write the collocations in your vocabulary notebook. Underline or highlight the target word to help you find it more easily._

## EXERCISE 4

A. _Read the concordance sentences. Notice the way the target word_ evidence _is used._

1.   led to better health. However, there was little **evidence** that more aggressive care produced better
2.  to work three consecutive hours. There is strong **evidence** of on-campus employment improving
3.   cannot be expelled as long as they can provide **evidence** that they are seeking employment
4.   it was not just the police officer who showed **evidence** of stress but the partner as well. Even
5.   social workers will often be required to give **evidence** in court, it is essential to develop skills
6.   the relatively small amount of direct scientific **evidence** on the topic. There have been attempts
7.   health care system. However, there is no clear **evidence** that patients benefit, at least in terms
8.   apply if you can show by clear and convincing **evidence** that you took reasonable actions to
9.   be met. For applicants who need to provide **evidence** of English proficiency, please note that
10. literature. There does not seem to be any strong **evidence** for this. In fact, the most remarkable

B. _Write your answers to the questions._

1. Look to the right of the target word. Write the words that follow it.

_____

2. Look to the left of the target word. Write the adjectives used before it.

_____

3. Write the verbs used before the target word.

_____

4. In four of the sentences, a common phrase is used before the target word (with different tenses and additional words). What is it?

_____

5. Can you make any generalizations about what usually/often follows the target word?

_____

C. _Compare answers with another student. Write the collocations in your vocabulary notebook. Underline or highlight the target word to help you find it more easily._

**A.**  *Read the concordance sentences. Notice the way the target word* approach *is used.*

| | | | |
|---|---|---|---|
| 1. | markets in the North. Fair Trade is an alternative | **approach** | to conventional international trade. It |
| 2. | for some activities you can probably adopt an | **approach** | that is suited to the subject and methods |
| 3. | the course you are encouraged to adopt a critical | **approach** | to a wide range of problems, and you |
| 4. | Superman's story, coincides with a more general | **approach** | to popular culture, and comics in |
| 5. | aromatic rings. Recently, an advanced theoretical | **approach** | has been developed for the ET process |
| 6. | When reading it is important to adopt a critical | **approach** | , asking a range of questions as you |
| 7. | the event, the Times article took a more holistic | **approach** | to the issue, covering both the party |
| 8. | researchers at Bristol developed a theoretical | **approach** | that stressed the importance of group |
| 9. | strategic human resourcing. In this section a similar | **approach** | will be taken; however, the discussion |
| 10. | Galileo was the first to develop a quantitative | **approach** | to the study of motion. He addressed the |
| 11. | to predict future job behavior. The traditional | **approach** | assumes that past and present behavior |
| 12. | appears to be essentially arbitrary. An alternative | **approach** | was adopted by Heuer and Reisberg |

**B.**  *Write your answers to the questions.*

1. Look to the right of the target word. Write the words that follow it.

_____

2. Look to the left of the target word. Write the adjectives used before it.

_____

3. Write the verbs used before or after the target word.

_____

4. Can you make any generalizations about what follows the target word?

_____

**C.**  *Compare answers with another student. Write the collocations in your vocabulary notebook. Underline or highlight the target word to help you find it more easily.*

**A.** *Read the concordance sentences. Notice the way the target word* feature *is used.*

1. been that one of the striking and distinctive **features** of much of early Greek thought,
2. the show. And make sure to check out a special **feature** that we put on the blog this month.
3. that one of the principle distinguishing **features** of this organism which separates it from
4. and broad programs of study. A key **feature** of all of our degree programs is an
5. people in some cities have some characteristic **features** in their pronunciation, although they are
6. it is possible to identify a number of key **features** . First, they followed the approach of the
7. all world religions may share some common **features** , there are arguably some important
8. ought to be made. Despite these positive **features** , there are significant difficulties faced
9. companies also operate abroad. A significant **feature** is that for many of these companies their
10. about. There are three additional distinctive **features** of the book which make it a good choice
11. Despite this controversy, we may say a central **feature** of globalization is that it involves
12. it is possible to identify some common **features** that apply to most. Table 17.2 links these

**B.** *Write your answers to the questions.*

1. Look to the right of the target word. Write the words that follow it.

   _____

2. Look to the left of the target word. Write the adjectives used before it.

   _____

3. Write the verbs used before or after the target word.

   _____

4. Can you make any generalizations about what follows the target word?

   _____

**C.** *Compare answers with another student. Write the collocations in your vocabulary notebook. Underline or highlight the target word to help you find it more easily.*

A.   Work with another student. Write adjectives from the box in front of the nouns to form collocations.
     There may be more than five possibilities.

| alternative | characteristic | critical | key | strong |
|---|---|---|---|---|
| available | clear | distinctive | positive | theoretical |
| basic | common | distinguishing | quantitative | traditional |
| certain | convincing | fundamental | scientific | underlying |

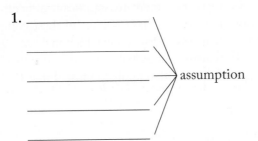

1. _____

_____

_____ > assumption

_____

_____

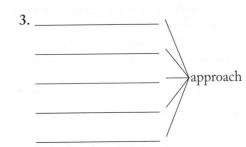

3. _____

_____

_____ > approach

_____

_____

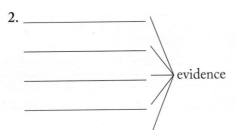

2. _____

_____

_____ > evidence

_____

_____

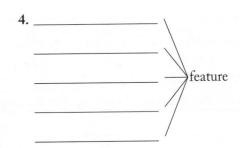

4. _____

_____

_____ > feature

_____

_____

B.   Compare answers with another student. Then check your answers using the concordance sentences
     in Exercises 3–6.

C.   Write the collocations in your vocabulary notebook. Underline or highlight the target word to help
     you find it more easily.

A.   Work with another student. Complete each sentence with an appropriate adjective.

1. This article takes a _____ approach in addressing this issue and attempts
   to provide a new perspective on the problem.

2. Although some of the _____ assumptions are questionable, the study
   raises some interesting points.

3. A _____ feature that set the economic and social elite apart was the way they educated their children.

4. There is _____ evidence from surveys and research that most individuals follow the proposed model of behavior.

5. There are two _____ approaches that are most commonly employed in management.

6. The _____ assumption of the scientists was that their theory could be applied to both men and women.

7. _____ evidence for this interpretation of his work includes the few color photographs that survive along with the much more numerous ones in black and white.

8. Many researchers have attempted to examine the _____ features of the economics of professional team sports.

**B.** *Compare answers with another student. Then check your answers using the concordance sentences on pages 90–93.*

## EXERCISE 9

**A.** *Work with another student. Write verbs from the box in front of the nouns to form collocations.*

| adopt | develop | make | share |
|---|---|---|---|
| based on | give | provide | show |
| check out | identify | question | take |

1. _____
   _____ $\rangle$ an/the assumption(s)
   _____

2. _____
   _____ $\rangle$ the evidence
   _____

3. _____
   _____ $\rangle$ an/the approach
   _____

4. _____
   _____ $\rangle$ (the) feature(s)
   _____

**B.** *Compare answers with another student. Then check your answers using the concordance sentences on pages 90–93.*

**C.** *Write the collocations in your vocabulary notebook. Underline or highlight the target word to help you find it more easily.*

**A.** *Work with another student. Complete each sentence with an appropriate verb.*

1. We also need to _____ assumptions about the people with whom we are interacting.

2. Keshet and Rosenthal (1980) _____ evidence which suggests that children of divorced parents can relate positively both to their biological parents and to a stepparent.

3. The random-walk model described in Section 6.2 is _____ the assumption that each possible state of the system is equally probable.

4. Hull (1986, 1987) has _____ this approach further and analyzed the stages in the reading process.

5. Here we can _____ one feature of that relationship which seems to me to be crucial to understand.

6. State and local governments favor projects which _____ evidence of user participation at the planning stage.

7. You could also find that some letters didn't _____ common features but sounded the same and tended to be confused as well.

8. This traditional approach has been _____ by many caregivers in community settings.

**B.** *Compare answers with another student. Then check your answers using the concordance sentences on pages 90–93.*

## Learning Phrases from Your Reading

Just as with single words, you can expand your vocabulary greatly if you notice phrases when you are reading and select useful ones to learn, focusing on those that are most frequent or that are related to your studies or work. In general, if you encounter a phrase in your academic reading and find it in a learner dictionary, it is probably worth learning.

When you write a phrase in your vocabulary notebook, be sure to include the sentence where you found it, since this will help you remember it and understand how to use it.

**Note:** You may remember an idiom or collocation better if you can find some connection between the meanings of the single words and the whole group. If the connection is not clear, you can create one— the more imaginative the better.

**A.** *Look back at the passage in Part 2, Unit 1, Exercise 1 on page 40. Read through it again and underline the phrases below. Did you underline or circle any of them when you did the exercise? Look up any phrases you are unfamiliar with or are uncertain how to use.*

a handful of                    values it embodies
a broad range of                a revolutionary force
get in line                     a complex interplay
place your order                on any given day
hand over                       a relatively brief period
take hold of                    popular culture
the whole experience            twice a day
taken for granted               a single bite
brushing your teeth

**B.** *Compare work with another student. Write any useful new phrases in your vocabulary notebook.*

## EXERCISE 12

**A.** *Some phrases have been underlined in the passage. Check that you understand the meaning of all of them. Look up the ones you are unsure about and write the definitions in the margin.*

The <u>extraordinary growth</u> of the <u>fast food industry</u> has been driven by <u>fundamental changes</u> in American society. <u>Adjusted for inflation</u>, the <u>hourly wage</u> of the average U.S. worker peaked in 1973 and then <u>steadily declined</u> for the next twenty-five years. During that period, women <u>entered the workforce</u> in <u>record numbers</u>, often motivated less by a feminist perspective than by a need to <u>pay the bills</u>. In 1975, about one-third of American mothers with young children worked outside the home; today almost two-thirds of such mothers are employed. As the sociologists Cameron Lynne Macdonald and Carmen Sirianni have noted, the entry of so many women into the workforce has <u>greatly increased demand</u> for the types of services that housewives traditionally perform: cooking, cleaning, and child care. <u>A generation ago</u>, three-quarters of the money used to buy food in the United States was spent to prepare meals at home. Today about half of the money used to buy food is spent at restaurants—mainly at fast food restaurants.

The McDonald's Corporation has become a <u>powerful symbol</u> of America's <u>service economy</u>, which is now <u>responsible for</u> 90 percent of the country's new jobs. In 1968, McDonald's operated about one thousand restaurants. Today it has about twenty-eight thousand restaurants worldwide and opens almost two thousand new ones each year. An estimated <u>one out of every eight</u> workers in the United States has <u>at some point</u> been employed by McDonald's. The company annually hires about one million people, more than any other American organization, public or private. McDonald's is the nation's largest purchaser of beef, pork, and potatoes—and the second largest purchaser of chicken. The McDonald's Corporation is the largest owner of <u>retail property</u> in the world. Indeed, the company <u>earns the majority of its profits</u> not from selling food but from <u>collecting rent</u>. McDonald's spends more money on advertising and marketing than any other brand. <u>As a result</u> it has replaced Coca-Cola as the world's most <u>famous</u> brand. McDonald's operates more playgrounds than any other private entity in the United States. It is one of the nation's largest distributors of toys. A survey of American schoolchildren found that 96 percent could identify Ronald McDonald. The only fictional character with a higher degree of recognition was Santa Claus. The impact of McDonald's on the way we live today is hard to overstate. The Golden Arches are now more <u>widely recognized</u> than the Christian cross.

**B.** *List phrases from the passage that are often used with economic topics. Note that some of the phrases may also be used with other topics.*

1. _____    7. _____

2. _____    8. _____

3. _____    9. _____

4. _____    10. _____

5. _____    11. _____

6. _____    12. _____

**C.** *List the other underlined phrases in the passage.*

1. _____    7. _____

2. _____    8. _____

3. _____    9. _____

4. _____    10. _____

5. _____    11. _____

6. _____    12. _____

**D.** *Compare work with another student. Write any useful new phrases in your vocabulary notebook.*

**A.** *Some phrases have been underlined in the passage. Check that you understand the meaning of all of them. Look up the ones you are unsure about and write the definition in the margin.*

One of the ironies of America's fast food industry is that a business so dedicated to conformity was founded by iconoclasts and <u>self-made men</u>, by entrepreneurs willing to <u>defy</u> <u>conventional opinion</u>. Few of the people who built fast food empires ever <u>attended college</u>, <u>let alone</u> business school. They worked hard, <u>took risks</u>, and followed their own paths. <u>In many respects</u>, the fast food industry embodies the best and the worst of American capitalism at the start of the twenty-first century—its <u>constant stream</u> of new products and innovations, its <u>widening gulf</u> between rich and poor.

The industrialization of the restaurant kitchen has enabled the fast food chains to rely upon a low-paid and <u>unskilled workforce</u>. While a handful of workers manage to rise up the <u>corporate ladder</u>, the <u>vast majority</u> lack <u>full-time employment</u>, <u>receive no benefits</u>, learn few skills, <u>exercise little control</u> over their workplace, quit after a few months, and float from job to job. The restaurant industry is now America's largest private employer, and it pays some of the lowest wages. During the <u>economic boom</u> of the 1990s, when many American workers enjoyed their first <u>pay raises</u> in a generation, the <u>real value</u> of wages in the restaurant industry continued to fall. The roughly 3.5 million fast food workers are <u>by far</u> the largest group of minimum <u>wage earners</u> in the United States. The only Americans who consistently earn a lower hourly wage are migrant <u>farm workers</u>.

A hamburger and french fries became the quintessential American meal in the 1950s, thanks to the <u>promotional efforts</u> of the fast food chains. The typical American now consumes approximately three hamburgers and four orders of french fries every week. But the <u>steady barrage</u> of fast food ads, full of thick juicy burgers and long golden fries, <u>rarely mentions</u> where these foods come from nowadays or what ingredients they contain. The birth of the fast food industry <u>coincided with</u> Eisenhower-era glorifications of technology, with <u>optimistic slogans</u> like Better Living through Chemistry and Our Friend the Atom. The sort of <u>technological wizardry</u> that Walt Disney promoted on television and at Disneyland eventually <u>reached its fulfillment</u> in the kitchens of fast food restaurants . . .The leading fast food chains still <u>embrace a boundless faith</u> in science—and as a result have changed not just what Americans eat, but also how their food is made.

**B.** *List phrases from the passage that are often used with economic topics. Note that some of the phrases may also be used with other topics.*

1. _____     7. _____

2. _____     8. _____

3. _____     9. _____

4. _____     10. _____

5. _____     11. _____

6. _____     12. _____

**C.** *List the other underlined phrases in the passage.*

1. _____     7. _____

2. _____     8. _____

3. _____     9. _____

4. _____     10. _____

5. _____     11. _____

6. _____     12. _____

**D.** *Compare work with another student. Write any useful new phrases in your vocabulary notebook.*

## Remember

To expand your knowledge of idioms and collocations in English:
- **Read extensively** (see Part 1).
  By reading a lot—not just a few passages or stories, but whole books—you have many opportunities to see how words are used and how they combine with each other. Research has shown that this is crucial for becoming a more effective and fluent reader (and writer).
- **Notice idioms and collocations as you read.**
  Look for them and mark them in your text.
- **Include them in your vocabulary study.**
  Look up the ones that are common or useful for you. Write them in your vocabulary notebook, as you would write single words, and review them regularly.

# Comprehension Skills

# Scanning and Previewing

In this unit, you will learn and practice ways to get information quickly from a text.

## Scanning

Scanning is a very fast type of reading. You use scanning when you need to get specific information from a text, such as a name, a date, or a number. When you scan, you move your eyes very quickly over the page until you find what you are looking for. You don't need to read many words, just enough to find the necessary information in the text. (Scanning is sometimes confused with skimming, another type of fast reading, which you will learn about in Part 3, Unit 7.)

You may already scan for information in English or in your first language, for example, when you are looking for information on a website, in a newspaper events listing, or on a bus schedule.

Practice in scanning helps you improve your reading ability in two important ways.

1. It leads to faster word recognition, a key aspect of the reading process and a significant factor in reading rate (speed).
2. It helps you develop more flexibility in your eye movements as you read. Many students move their eyes from left to right along the lines, and line by line down the page. This limits both reading rate and comprehension. Proficient readers often move their eyes along the lines, but they also skip words and look ahead or back, depending on their purpose for reading, the type of text, and their understanding of it.

There are two sets of exercises in this section: Scanning for Information and Scanning for Key Words.

For all these exercises, you should focus on finding the answers to the questions. You do not need to understand all the words in the texts. Use the words you do understand to help you look for the answers to the questions.

If you find unfamiliar words in the passages, skip them or try to guess them, but do not stop to look them up. You may go back to the passages later for vocabulary work.

## Scanning for Information

In these exercises, you will scan to find the answers to "Wh-" questions (*who, what, why, where, when,* and *how*). Use any bold headings to help you find the right place on the page. Focus your search on the kind of information indicated by the question. For example:

| | |
|---|---|
| *"When . . . ?"* | Look for a time, day, or date. |
| *"How many . . . ?"* | Look for a number. |
| *"Where . . . ?"* | Look for the name of a place. |

## EXERCISE 1

**A.** *Read the questions. Then scan the food festival events on the next page and underline the answers. You will have two minutes.*

1. Where can you go for a traditional New England-style clambake?
2. When can you try West African benne cake?
3. Which places include wine in the price of the meal?
4. How much does the Turkish feast cost?
5. Where can you learn about environmental sustainability?
6. Which is the most expensive event?
7. At which events can you listen to music?
8. Which events offer entertainment for children and families?

**B.** *Write three more questions about the list of events. Then ask another student to scan for the answers.*

_____

_____

_____

**C.** *Discuss these questions with your partner:*

1. If you could attend the Southport Food Festival, which event(s) would you attend?
2. Have you ever been to an outdoor festival? If so, where? What was it like? What kind of food was offered?
3. What is your favorite kind of street food or festival food?

Southport International Food Festival

**SEPTEMBER 1–30**

### BARBECUE ON THE PIER
### AT THE SEATON PIER
The Seaton Pier hosts a barbecue on the pier, prepared by chef Jane Shute and her team.
**WHERE:** 11 Hamilton Road
**COST:** $10 per person
**WHEN:** September 6; noon–3pm
**INQUIRIES:** 929-3999

### INTERNATIONAL BARBECUE
### AT QUEEN'S WHARF
The barbecue goes global: from Japanese teppanyaki to the Polynesian spit roast.
**WHERE:** Linden Street
**COST:** $10 per person
**WHEN:** September 6; noon–4pm
**INQUIRIES:** qwi.com

### THE PENDLETON PUB
### AT PENDLETON SQUARE
Treat yourself to classic pub fare—fish and chips, shepherd's pie, ploughman's lunch, and more—at one of five participating Pendleton pubs.
**WHERE:** 252 Pendleton Road
**COST:** $15 per dish
**WHEN:** September 13; noon–5pm
**INQUIRIES:** visitpendleton.com

### CLAMBAKE
### AT THE BRIGADE
A fresh, fun take on a traditional New England-style clambake: clams, mussels and lobster baked in the sand, and salads. Served with premium table wines.
**WHERE:** 200 Shoreline Drive
**COST:** $65 per person (includes wine)
**WHEN:** September 13; 2–4pm
**BOOKINGS:** 929-4144

### HARVEST LUNCH
### AT MADAM G'S
A bountiful spread of local seasonal offerings—from eggplant appetizers, to sweet pepper pasta, to pumpkin pie.
Something for everyone, mostly (but not entirely) vegetarian menu.
**WHERE:** 155 Victory Street
**COST:** $75 per person, includes wine
**WHEN:** September 20; 12.30–3pm
**BOOKINGS:** 937-1220

### ASHFORD'S TASTES OF ASIA
### AT ASHFORD ARCADE
Savor the exotic flavors of Ashford's Asian food outlets. Featuring Shanghai Chinese, Japanese, Korean, Thai, Vietnamese, Indian, Nepalese, and Sri Lankan cuisine. Street stalls serve tasting plates from local restaurants.
**WHERE:** Ashford Arcade, Center Street
**WHEN:** September 20; 6–9pm
**INQUIRIES:** 929-1920; ashfordarcade.com

### MEXICAN
### AT SOL AZTECA
There's a lot more to Mexican food than tacos and burritos. Discover chilaguiles, lengua, mole, and more—from the famous chef José Villazón.
**WHERE:** 27 Charter Street
**COST:** $15 per person
**WHEN:** September 27; noon–4pm
**INQUIRIES:** 928-1121; solaztecacharter.com

### TURKISH FEAST
### AT EFENDY
A Turkish feast of hot and cold mezze, and kebabs from the wood fire charcoal barbecue followed by the very best Turkish pastries and ice cream.
**WHERE:** 79 Endeavor Street
**COST:** $45 per person
**WHEN:** Saturdays; noon–3pm
**INQUIRIES:** 929-5466

### CULINARY CARNIVALE
### AT FALMOUTH SQUARE
A street party at Falmouth Square to celebrate South American food culture with an asado barbecue as the centerpiece. Dancers and drummers at this free family event.
**WHERE:** Falmouth Square
**WHEN:** September 20; 11am–4pm
**INQUIRIES:** 1927-3187

### SOUTH STREET ITALIAN FESTA
### AT SOUTH AND CANNING STREETS
South Street celebrates all things Italian with regional food stalls, street performers, concerts, carnival rides, and a children's masquerade.
**WHERE:** South Street and Canning Streets
**WHEN:** September 27; 10am–5pm
**INQUIRIES:** 926-9308; southstreetfesta.com

### FOOD 'N' FUN
### AT BAXTER PARK
A free, family-friendly festival of world music, food, and dance. Featuring multicultural entertainment, global cuisine, cooking demonstrations, children's rides, and information stalls with a focus on environmental sustainability.
**WHERE:** Baxter Park
**WHEN:** September 27; noon–5pm
**INQUIRIES:** 929-1666; baxterfoodnfun.com

### DUCK TO DUMPLINGS
### AT SONG
Newly opened Song takes you on a Cantonese journey. From roast duck to delicious dumplings, this is a chance to sample the highlights from Song's menu.
Minimum four people bookings.
**WHERE:** 3 Tower Lane
**COST:** $55 per person
**WHEN:** Saturdays; noon–3pm
**BOOKINGS:** 928-3000

### SWEET TOOTH FESTIVAL
### AT HOWELL HOUSE ARTS CENTER
Sample sweet treats from a range of cultures, including Turkey (lokum), Malaysia (ais kacang), West Africa (benne cake), India (gulab jamun), and China (nian gao). With locally produced tea and coffee, and live entertainment.
**WHERE:** 1 Charter Street
**COST:** $10 per person
**WHEN:** Saturdays; 10am-5pm
**INQUIRIES:** 928-1121; howellhousearts.com

**A.** *Read the questions. Then scan the results of the study about fast food on the next page and underline the answers. You will have two minutes.*

1. Which is the only fast-food restaurant in the study that routinely provides healthy choices?
2. How many of the 3,039 possible kids' meal combinations met nutrition criteria for preschoolers?
3. What percentage of parents reported that their child asks to go to McDonald's at least once a week?
4. How many calories did teens between the ages of 13 and 18 order in an average fast-food visit?
5. What is the name of the association that makes recommendations about calorie intake?
6. Which ethnic and minority groups are targeted by fast-food advertising?
7. What do restaurant employees serve with kids' meals 84 percent of the time?
8. Which websites are mentioned in the study?

**B.** *Write three more questions about the study results. Then ask another student to scan for the answers.*

_____

_____

_____

**C.** *Discuss these questions with your partner:*

1. How often do you eat at fast-food restaurants? Other kinds of restaurants?
2. When you choose fast food, what are your reasons?
3. Which fast-food restaurant(s) do you prefer? Why?
4. What do you usually order at your favorite fast-food restaurant?
5. Have you ever looked at the nutritional information for fast food?

# Evaluating Fast-Food Nutrition and Marketing to Youth
### Yale Rudd Center for Food Policy and Obesity

**Youth-targeted marketing has spread to company websites and other digital media.**
■ McDonald's web-based marketing starts with children as young as 2 at Ronald.com.

■ McDonald's and Burger King created sophisticated websites with 60 to 100 pages of advergames and virtual worlds to engage children (McWorld.com, HappyMeal.com, and ClubBK.com).

■ McDonald's thirteen websites attracted 365,000 unique child visitors and 294,000 unique teen visitors on average each month in 2009.

**Fast-food marketing also targets teens and ethnic and minority youth—often with less healthy items.**
■ Taco Bell TV and radio advertising reached more teens than adults and Burger King advertised teen-targeted promotions. Dairy Queen, Sonic, and Domino's also reached more teens with ads for their desserts and snacks.

■ Hispanic preschoolers saw 290 Spanish-language fast-food TV ads in 2009 and McDonald's was responsible for one quarter of young people's exposure to Spanish-language fast-food advertising.

■ African-American children and teens saw at least 50 percent more fast-food ads on TV than their white peers. That translated into twice as many calories viewed in fast-food ads daily compared to white children.

■ McDonald's and KFC specifically targeted African-American youth with TV advertising, websites, and banner ads. African-American teens viewed 75 percent more TV ads for McDonald's and KFC compared to white teens.

**Fast-food marketing works.**
■ Eighty-four percent of parents reported taking their child to a fast-food restaurant at least once in the past week; 66 percent reported going to McDonald's.

■ Forty-seven percent of parents who went to McDonald's reported that the main reason they went there was because their child likes it.

■ Forty percent of parents reported that their child asks to go to McDonald's at least once a week; 15 percent of preschoolers ask to go every day.

**Most restaurants do offer some healthful and lower-calorie choices on their regular and children's menus, but unhealthy options are the default inside the restaurants.**
■ Just 12 of 3,039 possible kids' meal combinations met nutrition criteria for preschoolers; 15 met nutrition criteria for older children.

■ Just 17 percent of regular menu items qualified as healthful choices. Most of these items were low or no-calorie beverages (e.g., coffee and diet soft drinks). Twelve percent of lunch/dinner sides met nutrition criteria, and 5 percent or less of lunch/dinner main dishes and breakfast items met the criteria.

■ Snacks and dessert items contained as many as 1,500 calories, which is five times more than the 200 to 300 calorie snack recommended by the American Dietetic Association for active teens.

■ The average restaurant had 15 signs promoting specific menu items, but just 4 percent promoted healthy menu items.

■ When ordering a kids' meal, restaurant employees at McDonald's, Burger King, Wendy's, and Taco Bell automatically served French fries or another unhealthy side dish more than 84 percent of the time.

■ Subway offered apple slices or yogurt and low-fat plain milk or 100 percent juice with their kids' meals 60 percent of the time, making it the only fast-food restaurant in our study to routinely provide healthy choices.

**As a result,**
■ At McDonald's, Burger King and Wendy's, approximately two-thirds of parents who ordered a kids' meal for their child ordered French fries and one-third to one-half ordered a soft drink. In contrast, two-thirds ordered fruit or yogurt and juice or plain milk with a kids' meal at Subway.

■ Parents of elementary school-age children were more likely to order a combo meal or dollar/value menu items for their child than a kids' meal.

■ Teens between the ages of 13 and 18 ordered 800 to 1,100 calories in an average fast-food visit. This age group ordered many of the highest-calorie, nutrient-poor items on fast-food menus, including large and extra-large french fries and soft drinks and large-sized burgers.

■ Teens were also more likely to visit a fast-food restaurant for an afternoon or evening snack compared to any other age group; and they purchased the most desserts, breads and sweet breads.

■ At least 30 percent of calories in menu items ordered by children and teens were from sugar and saturated fat. At most restaurants, young people ordered at least half of their maximum daily recommended sodium intake in just one fast food meal.

Jennifer L. Harris, Ph.D., M.B.A., Marlene B. Schwartz, Ph.D., Kelly D. Brownell, Ph.D.
http://fastfoodmarketing.org/media/FastFoodFACTS_Report.pdf

**Note:** You do not need to be concerned about understanding all of the ideas in the passages in Exercises 3 and 4. You will have an opportunity to think about them and discuss them in later exercises.

 **A.** *Read the questions. Then scan the article about the Amish community on the next page and underline the answers. You will have three minutes.*

1. What university was involved in the study?
2. What percentage of the general population of the United States is obese?
3. When did the Old Order Amish immigrate to the United States?
4. What do the Amish consume far less than the average American?
5. How many adults were involved in the study?
6. In the study, how many steps did Amish women accumulate per day?
7. What U.S. organization makes recommendations about activity?
8. What obesity-related diseases are mentioned?

**B.** *Write three more questions about the article. Then ask another student to scan for the answers.*

_____

_____

_____

**C.** *Discuss these questions with another pair of students:*

1. Do you know anything more about the Amish community in the United States?
2. Could you imagine living like the Amish, without a car or modern conveniences?
3. Do you do any activities for exercise (sports, dance, etc.)?
4. In the regular course of your day, how much physical activity do you do?
5. Without a major change in lifestyle, could you increase the amount of physical activity you do every day?

# Study Links Physical Activity in Amish Community with Low Rates of Obesity

A new study confirms previous reports that physical activity provides important health benefits, including weight management, and finds that lifestyle physical activity is one way to achieve a healthy level of activity. Lifestyle activity refers to physical activity performed in the regular course of daily work or routines.

Researchers at the Department of Exercise and Health Science at the University of Tennessee, Knoxville, studied an Old Order Amish community to examine the influence of modern technology on physical activity. The Old Order Amish population of Lancaster County, PA, immigrated to the United States from Western Europe in the late 1700s. There are now approximately 30,000 Amish individuals in the Lancaster area, nearly all of whom can trace their ancestry back 12–14 generations to a small number of founder families. The Amish have a high degree of consanguinity, well-documented genealogies, and a predominantly rural lifestyle. These features make this population attractive for genetic analysis and health studies.

Furthermore, the particular beliefs of the Amish make them an ideal population for the study of the health benefits of regular physical activity. Most Amish forgo the use of modern technology, including gasoline-powered vehicles, electricity, and most household conveniences. The men plow the fields of their farms with horses or oxen; the women do all the washing and housework by hand and produce most of the food consumed by their families.

The researchers hoped to discover how the lack of technology in the Amish lifestyle affects their levels of physical activity and rates of obesity. During the study, 98 adults wore a step counter for a period of seven days. They recorded their steps and listed three of the physical activities they performed each day. Each activity was categorized as a vigorous, moderate, walking, or sitting activity.

The results indicate that the levels of physical activity by the Amish far exceeded those reported in other parts of North America. Amish men averaged 18,425 steps per day, while Amish women accumulated approximately 14,196 steps per day. Furthermore, both Amish men and women performed a large amount of moderate to vigorous physical activity.

The researchers estimate that the amount of physical activity performed by Amish farmers is similar to that of distance runners, though their activity is performed at lower intensities over a longer duration. Of the Amish people studied, 100 percent surpassed the recommendation by the U.S. Centers for Disease Control and Prevention to perform at least 30 minutes of moderate physical activity per day on most days of the week. In comparison, only 60 percent of Americans achieve even the limited amount of moderate activity.

In addition, when the researchers looked at the health statistics in the Amish community, they found a low rate of obese and overweight adults. Only 4 percent of the adults were obese, and 26 percent were overweight, whereas the rate of obesity among adults in the general population of the United States is almost 31 percent, and a staggering 64.5 percent is overweight. The researchers concluded that the high levels of physical activity by the Amish adults contribute to their low rate of obesity. Not surprisingly, the Amish also have lower rates of obesity-related diseases such as type 2 diabetes and heart disease.

A decline in physical activity due to a more sedentary lifestyle has been identified as one factor in the recent significant increases in the rates of obesity, type 2 diabetes, and related health problems in the United States today.

Previous studies by the same researchers focusing on the diet of the Amish community found that it is comparable in many ways to the typical American diet. The Amish consumption of fat (including saturated animal fats) is average or above average, as is their consumption of carbohydrates. The main difference lies in the fact that the Amish consume far less industrially prepared food than the average American, relying instead on products from their farms and on traditional methods for conserving food.

**A.** *Read the questions. Then scan the article about fast food in Singapore on the next page and underline the answers. You will have three minutes.*

1. When was the study launched?
2. What kind of fat do Western-style fast-food restaurants use in Singapore?
3. How long was the follow-up to the study?
4. How much did the risk of heart disease increase among people who ate fast food often?
5. What was discovered about people who ate the most Western-style fast food?
6. What journal published a paper about "Big Food" in Brazil?
7. Who is the lead author of the study?
8. How many participants ate fast food more than four times a week?

**B.** *Write three more questions about the article. Then ask another student to scan for the answers.*

_____

_____

_____

**C.** *Discuss these questions with another pair of students:*

1. How prevalent is Western-style fast food in your country?
2. How often do you or your family eat Western-style fast food (in your country)?
3. Are there any traditional "fast foods"—prepared quickly and sold on the street or in restaurants?
4. What types of food do you prefer when you go out to eat? Why?
5. Are people in your country concerned about the effects of fast food on health?

# Western-style fast food linked to poorer health in Singapore, says U of M study

By Susan Perry | 07/05/12

Western-style fast food has had a dramatic health impact on people living in Singapore, according to a new study from researchers at the University of Minnesota's School of Public Health. And, as you might guess, it hasn't been a good impact.

Singapore residents who ate Western-style fast food at least twice a week were found to be 27 percent more likely to develop type 2 diabetes and 56 percent more likely to die from heart disease than those who avoided fast food and stuck with their traditional foods. For people who ate Western-style fast-food items four or more times each week, the heart disease risk increased by almost 80 percent. (There was no change in the diabetes risk.)

The study was published earlier this week in the American Heart Association's journal *Circulation*.

Past investigations into an association between fast food and type 2 diabetes and heart disease have been surprisingly few, and those that have been done focused almost exclusively on U.S. populations, said Andrew Odegaard, a U of M post-doctoral researcher and the study's lead author, in a phone interview Tuesday.

"Despite all the allusions to people having all these terrible health problems when you eat at McDonald's, there's really not a lot of research to substantiate that," he said. To help fill that research gap, Odegaard and his colleagues decided to turn to Singapore, which has recently witnessed a significant increase in diabetes and heart disease. For example, some 11.3 percent of Singapore's adults have diabetes, according to the Diabetic Society of Singapore—a number now as high as that in the United States.

Working with researchers at the National University of Singapore, the U of M researchers analyzed 16 years of dietary and other data from 52,584 participants in the Singapore Chinese Health Study, which was launched in 1993. All the participants were Chinese residents of Singapore who by the 1990s had found themselves suddenly able to buy Western-style fast food for the first time—things like burgers, French fries, hot dogs and pizza.

The data was collected from questionnaires filled out by the participants themselves. To confirm a diabetes diagnosis, the researchers used physician records and a separate questionnaire. A national death registry was used to determine deaths from heart disease. During the study's 16-year follow-up, 2,252 of the participants developed diabetes and 1,397 died of heart attacks or other heart-related illnesses. Of the 811 participants in the study who ate Western-style fast food four or more times a week, 17 died of heart disease. This group, therefore, had a nearly 80 percent greater relative risk of dying of heart disease than others in the study who avoided the Western food.

In addition to its major findings about the increased risk of diabetes and heart disease, the U of M study made two other interesting discoveries. One was the finding that the people in the study who were eating the most Western-style fast food tended to be younger, more educated, less likely to smoke and more physically active—just the kind of profile that is usually associated with a *lower* risk of type 2 diabetes and heart disease [in the United States]. The other interesting finding was that the study turned up no association between cardio-metabolic risk and *Eastern-style* snacks and fast food, such as *dim sum*.

"It's only speculation, but it may be because of the fat that those foods are cooked in," said Odegaard. Eastern-style fast foods tend to use vegetable-based oils, he explained, while the makers of Singapore's Western-style fast foods may be using trans fat, which has been linked to poor health outcomes … "Trans fat is not regulated in Singapore, and the Western [fast-food] companies don't share what they're using in their foods online."

The U of M study has several limitations. To begin with, it's an observational study, which means it can show only an association between fast food and health outcomes, not a cause-and-effect. In addition, as the authors themselves point out, self-reported dietary data can be unreliable. People don't always remember (or want to report) what they eat.

Still, the study is interesting, particularly in light of another paper published this week in the journal PLoS Medicine. As part of that journal's excellent series on "Big Food" and its impact on the world's health, two Brazilian epidemiologists, Carlos Monteiro and Geoffrey Cannon, describe how their country is trying to protect its traditional food system from the ultra-processed products made by transnational food corporations … Right now, the prevalence of diabetes in Brazil is 5.2 percent, half of what it is in the U.S. or Singapore. But that number is climbing, especially in Brazil's cities.

(http://www.minnpost.com/second-opinion/2012/07/western-style-fast-food-linked-poorer-health-singapore-says-u-m-study)

## Scanning for Key Words or Phrases

In these exercises you will continue to practice moving your eyes quickly as you look for key words and phrases. Key words or phrases can often be found in the title and are related to the important ideas in the passage.

## EXERCISE 5

A. *Look back at the article about the Amish on page 109. Scan it again for the key words or phrases below. Scan for one word or phrase at a time and circle that word every time you find it. Then write the number of times you found each key word.*

| Key words/phrases | Number of times |
|---|---|
| 1. Amish | _____ |
| 2. physical activity | _____ |
| 3. study/studies/studied | _____ |
| 4. researcher(s) | _____ |
| 5. health(y) | _____ |
| 6. (over)weight | _____ |
| 7. obese/obesity | _____ |
| 8. lifestyle | _____ |

B. *Now go back to the article and read it carefully. Look up any words or phrases that are necessary for comprehension and write the definitions in the margin. Then answer these questions:*

1. What was the main finding of the study?
2. Why did the study focus on the Amish?
3. How did the physical activity of the Amish compare with that of average Americans?
4. How did the health of the Amish compare with that of average Americans?
5. What was similar or different about the diet of the Amish compared with average Americans?

C. *Compare answers with another student.*

**A.** *Look back at the article on fast food in Singapore on page 111. Scan it again for the key words or phrases below. Scan for one word or phrase at a time and circle that word or phrase every time you find it. Then write the number of times you found each key word or phrase.*

| Key words/phrases | Number of times |
| --- | --- |
| 1. Singapore | _____ |
| 2. fast food | _____ |
| 3. Western-style | _____ |
| 4. study | _____ |
| 5. researchers | _____ |
| 6. health | _____ |
| 7. diabetes | _____ |
| 8. heart disease(s) | _____ |

**B.** *Now go back to the article and read it carefully. Look up any words or phrases that are necessary for comprehension and write their definitions in the margin. Then answer these questions:*

1. What is the "dramatic health impact" of fast food that the article mentions?
2. Why did Odegaard decide to do the study in Singapore?
3. What kind of people tend to eat fast food in Singapore?
4. What does Odegaard say might be the reason why Western-style fast foods have a negative effect on health, while Eastern-style fast foods do not?
5. What do you think is meant by "Big Food" in the last paragraph?

**C.** *Compare answers with another student.*

# Previewing

When you preview a passage, you take a quick look at it to get a sense of what kind of text it is and what it is about. This will help you read it more quickly and with better understanding.

Previewing can help you with all of your reading, including course assignments and tests. It takes a small amount of time before you read, but that will help you save time later.

How you preview depends on the kind of text you are going to read. In this unit, you will practice previewing articles and excerpts from books.

## Guidelines for Previewing

- Read the title (and subtitle if there is one) and formulate questions about them. What do you want to know about the topic?
- Look at any headings or illustrations, if there are any. How do they relate to the title?
- Read the first few lines of the text. Do they tell you more about the title?
- Look through the passage very quickly.
  —Does it contain many unfamiliar words?
  —Are there many numbers or proper names?
  —Are any words or phrases repeated often?

## EXERCISE 7

**A.** *Read the title of this article from a science magazine and discuss these questions with another student.*

1. What do you think the article will be about?
2. What more do you want to know about the topic?

### Bringing Back American Home Cooking
#### Could dinners at home resolve the obesity problem?

**B.** *Read these previewing questions for the article. Write one more with your partner.*

1. What has happened to home cooking in America?
2. Who says we should bring it back?
3. How does home cooking relate to the obesity problem?

4. _____

**C.** *Preview the passage, following the guidelines. <u>Do not</u> read it carefully. Just look quickly for the answers to the previewing questions.*

Americans used to cook and eat 98 percent of their meals at home. Not anymore. Now almost 50 percent of meals are eaten out, and the meals that are eaten at home are often bought ready-made. No one is spending much time in the kitchen anymore.

Researchers now believe that this may be related to the dramatic rise in levels of obesity. The prevalence of obesity in the United States has doubled since the 1970s for both adults and children, and tripled for adolescents.

Changes in demographics are part of the story, according to an article by Craig A. Lambert, in *Harvard Magazine.* "Compared to the 1950s, there are now relatively more divorced adults, more single-parent and single-person households, and more two-income households whose earners haven't time to cook dinner," he explains.

As families have become more fragmented, so have their mealtimes. Many families rarely eat all together sitting down at a table. Each family member may eat a different microwaved "food" at a different time and gobble it down while watching television, fiddling with the phone, or sitting in the car. More meals are probably eaten in the family car than in the kitchen. And the foods most conveniently eaten in front of a screen or on the run are not the most healthy ones.

But the fault doesn't lie entirely with families. The American food industry is also to blame—both fast food chains and industrial manufacturers of processed foods. They aim first and foremost for quantity, low cost, and immediate appeal to the taste buds, so foods are dosed heavily with fats, salt, sugar, corn syrup, and other unhealthy ingredients. These are cheap, first of all, which is why fast food and junk food can be sold at such low prices. Studies have also shown that a regular diet rich in these ingredients leads to a form of addiction, so that healthier foods with less fat, sugar, and salt don't seem as tasty or satisfying.

But the U.S. food industry wouldn't be selling such products if there weren't a market for them. Culturally, most Americans value quantity over quality. When it comes to food, as with everything else, they look first at the price and the size of the servings (which have expanded along with American waistlines). They often don't consider the quality of preparation, the nutritional content, or the social/cultural value (of traditional dishes, for instance). Not surprisingly, Americans spend less of their budget on food than Europeans, who place more value on quality and tradition (10 percent compared with 20 percent).

That might change, say the researchers, if Americans got back into their kitchens and prepared their own meals. Harvard researcher David Cutler and colleagues have studied cooking patterns across several cultures and found that the more time people spend preparing food, the lower the obesity rates in that culture. As Harry Balzer, author of *Eating Patterns in America 2012,* says, "Easy. You want Americans to eat less? I have the diet for you. It's short, it's simple. Here's my diet plan: *Cook it yourself.* That's it. **Eat anything you want—just as long as you're willing to cook it yourself.**"

**D.** *Discuss these questions with your partner. Do not look back at the article.*

1. Did you find the answers to your questions?
2. Are there lots of names or numbers? Difficult words?
3. Will it be difficult to read?
4. What is the general idea of the passage?

**E.** *Now read the passage carefully. Underline any unfamiliar vocabuary. Look up any useful words and add them to your vocabulary notebook.*

**F.** *Discuss these questions with your partner:*

1. Did reading carefully change your understanding of the article? If so, how?
2. When you were growing up, did your family usually eat at home? Who cooked the meals?
3. Do you eat at home now? Who cooks the meals?
4. When you go shopping, what kinds of foods do you buy?

**A.** *Read the heading of the passage from* In Defense of Food, *by Michael Pollan, and discuss these questions with another student:*

1. What do you know about the Aborigines of Australia?
2. What ideas or information might you find in the passage?
3. What more do you want to know about the topic?

**B.** *Work with your partner. Write three previewing questions on a separate piece of paper.*

**C.** *Preview the passage, following the guidelines.* <u>Do not</u> *read it carefully. Just look quickly for the answers to your questions.*

## The Aborigine in All of Us

In the summer of 1982, a group of ten middle-aged, overweight, and diabetic Aborigines living in settlements near the town of Derby, Western Australia, agreed to participate in an experiment to see if temporarily reversing the process of westernization they had undergone might also reverse their health problems. Since leaving the bush some years before, all ten had developed type 2 diabetes; they also showed signs of insulin resistance and elevated high levels of triglycerides in the blood—a risk factor for heart disease. "Metabolic syndrome," or "syndrome X," is the medical term for the complex of health problems these Aborigines had developed: Large amounts of refined carbohydrates in the diet combined with a sedentary lifestyle had disordered the intricate (and still imperfectly understood) system by which the insulin hormone regulates the metabolism of carbohydrates and fats in the body. Metabolic syndrome has been implicated not only in the development of type 2 diabetes, but also in obesity, hypertension, heart disease, and possibly certain cancers. Some researchers believe that metabolic syndrome may be at the root of many of the "diseases of civilization" that typically follow a native population's adoption of a Western lifestyle and the nutrition transition that typically entails follows.

The ten Aborigines returned to their traditional homeland, an isolated region of northwest Australia more than a day's drive by off-road vehicle from the nearest town. From the moment they left civilization, the men and women in the group had no access to store food or beverages; the idea was for them to rely exclusively on foods they hunted and gathered themselves. (Even while living in town, they still occasionally hunted traditional foods and so had preserved the knowledge of how to do so.) Kerin O'Dea, the nutrition researcher who designed the experiment, accompanied the group to monitor and record its dietary intake and keep tabs on the members' health.

The Aborigines divided their seven-week stay in the bush between a coastal and an inland location. While on the coast, their diet consisted mainly of seafood, supplemented by birds, kangaroo, and the fatty larvae of a local insect. Hoping to find more plant foods, the group moved inland after two weeks, settling at a riverside location. Here, in addition to freshwater fish and shellfish, the diet expanded to include turtle, crocodile, birds, kangaroo, yams, figs, and bush honey. The contrast between this hunter-gatherer fare and their previous diet was stark: O'Dea reports that prior to the experiment "the main dietary components in the urban setting were flour, sugar, rice, carbonated drinks, alcoholic beverages (beer and port), powdered milk, cheap fatty meat, potatoes, onions, and variable contributions of other fresh fruits and vegetables"—the local version of the Western diet.

After seven weeks in the bush, O'Dea drew blood from the Aborigines and found striking improvements in virtually every measure of their health. All had lost weight (an average of 17.9 pounds) and seen their blood pressure drop. Their triglyceride levels had fallen into the normal range. The proportion of omega-3 fatty acids in their tissues had increased dramatically. "In summary," O'Dea concluded, "all of the metabolic abnormalities of type 2 diabetes were either greatly improved (glucose tolerance, insulin response to glucose) or completely normalized (plasma lipids) in a group of diabetic Aborigines by a relatively short (seven week) reversion to traditional hunter-gatherer lifestyle."

O'Dea does not report what happened next, whether the Aborigines elected to remain in the bush or return to civilization, but it's safe to assume that if they did return to their Western lifestyles, their health problems returned too. We have known for a century now that there is a complex of so-called Western diseases—including obesity, diabetes, cardiovascular disease, hypertension, and a specific set of diet-related cancers—that begin almost invariably to appear soon after a people abandons its traditional diet and way of life. What we did not know before O'Dea took her Aborigines back to the bush . . . was that some of the most deleterious effects of the Western diet could be so quickly reversed. It appears that at least to an extent, we can rewind the tape of the nutrition transition and undo some of its damage. The implications for our own health are potentially significant.

[Source: Michael Pollan, *In Defense of Food,* The Penguin Press, 2008]

**D.** *Discuss these questions with your partner. Do not look back at the article.*

1. Did you find the answers to your questions?
2. Are there a lot of names or numbers? Difficult words?
3. Will it be difficult to read?
4. What is the general idea of the passage?

**E.** *Now read the passage carefully. Underline any unfamiliar vocabulary. Look up any useful words and add them to your vocabulary notebook.*

**F.** *Discuss these questions with your partner. Do not look back.*

1. Did reading closely change your understanding of the passage? If so, how?
2. Do you know of other populations suffering from a high rate of metabolic syndrome?
3. What do you think the Aborigines did after the study?
4. What do you think are the implications for our own health mentioned in the last line?

## EXERCISE 9

**A.** *Read the title of the passage on the next page from a sociology textbook and discuss these questions with another student:*

1. What is meant by the term "solid waste"? The expression "a disposable society"?
2. What ideas or information might you find in the passage?
3. What more do you want to know about the topic?

**B.** *Work with your partner. Write three previewing questions on a separate piece of paper.*

## Solid Waste: The Disposable Society

Across the United States, people generate a massive amount of solid waste—about 1.3 billion pounds *every day* . . . As a rich nation of people who value convenience, the United States has become a *disposable society*. We consume more products than virtually any other nation, and many of these products have throwaway packaging. For example, fast food is served with cardboard, plastic, and Styrofoam containers that we throw away within minutes. Countless other products, from film to fishhooks, are elaborately packaged to make the products more attractive to the customer and to discourage tampering and theft.

Manufacturers market soft drinks, beer, and fruit juices in aluminum cans, glass jars, and plastic containers, which not only consume finite resources but also generate mountains of solid waste. Then there are countless items intentionally designed to be disposable: pens, razors, flashlights, batteries, even cameras. Other products, from light bulbs to automobiles, are designed to have a limited useful life and then become unwanted junk. As Paul Connett (1991) points out, even the words we use to describe what we throw away—waste, litter, trash, refuse, garbage, rubbish—show how little we value what we cannot immediately use. But this was not always the case, as the Seeing Sociology in Everyday Life box . . . explains.

Living in a rich society, the average person in the United States consumes about 500 times more energy, plastics, lumber, water, and other resources than someone living in a low-income country such as Bangladesh or Tanzania and nearly twice as much as people in some other high-income countries such as Sweden and Japan. This high level of consumption means not only that we in the United States use a disproportionate share of the planet's natural resources but also that we generate most of the world's refuse.

We like to say that we throw things "away." But most of our solid waste never goes away. Rather, it ends up in landfills, which are, literally, filling up. Material in landfills can pollute underground water supplies. Although in most places laws now regulate what can be discarded in a landfill, the U.S. Environmental Protection Agency (2011) has identified 1,290 dump sites across the United States containing hazardous materials that are polluting water both above and below the ground. In addition, what goes into landfills all too often stays there, sometimes for centuries. Tens of millions of tires, diapers, and other items we bury in landfills each year do not decompose but will remain as an unwelcome legacy for future generations.

Environmentalists argue that we should address the problem of solid waste by doing what many of our grandparents did: Use less and turn "waste" into a resource. Part of the solution is *recycling*—reusing resources we would otherwise discard. Recycling is an accepted practice in Japan and many other nations, and it is becoming more common in the United States, where we now reuse about one-third of waste materials (U.S. Environmental Protection Agency, 2010). The share is increasing as laws require the recovery and reuse of certain materials such as glass bottles and aluminum cans and as the business of recycling becomes more profitable.

## Seeing Sociology in Everyday Life: Why Grandma Macionis Had No Trash

Grandma Macionis, we always used to say, never threw anything away. Not food, not bottles or cans, not paper. Not even coffee grounds. Nothing.

Grandma was born and raised in Lithuania—the "old country"—where life in a poor village shaped her in ways that never changed, even after she came to the United States as a young woman and settled in Philadelphia.

In her later years, when I knew her, I can remember the family traveling together to her house to celebrate her birthday. We never knew what to get Grandma, because she never seemed to need anything. She lived a simple life and had simple clothes and showed little interest in "fancy things." She had no electric appliances. She used her simple tools until they wore out. Her kitchen knives, for example, were worn narrow from decades of sharpening. The food that was left over from meals was saved. What could not be saved was recycled as compost for her vegetable garden.

After opening a birthday present, she would carefully save the box, refold the wrapping paper, and roll up the ribbon—all of these things meant as much to her as whatever gift they contained. We all knew her routines, and we smiled together as we watched her put everything away, knowing she would find a way to use each item again and again.

As strange as Grandma sometimes seemed to her grandchildren, she was a product of her culture. A century ago, in fact, there was little "trash." If socks wore thin, people mended them, probably more than once. When they were beyond repair, they were used as rags for cleaning or sewn with bits of other old clothing into a quilt. Everything had value—if not in one way, then in another.

During the twentieth century, as women joined men in working outside the home, income went up. Families began buying more appliances and other "timesaving" products. Before long, few people cared about the kind of recycling that Grandma practiced. Soon cities sent crews from block to block to pick up truckloads of discarded material. The era of "trash" had begun.

(Source: John J. Macionis, *Sociology* 14th edition, Pearson Education 2012)

**D.** *Discuss these questions with your partner. Do not look back.*

1. Did you find the answers to your questions?
2. Are there a lot of names or numbers? Difficult words?
3. Will it be difficult to read?
4. What is the general idea of the passage?

**E.** *Now read the passage carefully. Underline any unfamiliar vocabulary. Look up any useful words and add them to your vocabulary notebook.*

**F.** *Discuss these questions with your partner. Do not look back.*

1. Did reading carefully change your understanding of the passage? If so, how?
2. Compared with the United States, how much material is thrown away in your country?
3. Does recycling exist in your country? Is it informal, by individuals (like Grandma Macionis) or part of a recycling program?
4. Do you recycle things? If so, what things?
5. Besides recycling, what more do you think could be done about the problem of waste?

# Focus on Vocabulary

The words in all the Focus on Vocabulary exercises are included on the word list in the Appendix on page 310. The phrases are found in most learner dictionaries.

## EXERCISE 10

A.  *Read these sentences from the passage in Exercise 8. For each underlined word or phrase, choose the one that is closest in meaning.*

1. In the summer of 1982, a group of ten . . . Aborigines living in . . . Western Australia, agreed to participate in an experiment to see if temporarily <u>reversing</u> the process of westernization they had undergone might also reverse their health problems.

    a. reviewing           b. strengthening           c. undoing

2. . . . Aborigines living in . . . Western Australia, agreed to participate in an experiment to see if temporarily reversing the process of westernization they had <u>undergone</u> might also reverse their health problems.

    a. experienced           b. influenced           c. expected

3. Some researchers believe that metabolic syndrome may be <u>at the root</u> of many of the "diseases of civilization."

    a. related to           b. the main cause of           c. a small part of

4. From the moment they left civilization, the men and women in the group <u>had no access to</u> store food or beverages; the idea was for them to rely exclusively on foods they hunted and gathered themselves.

    a. had no money for           b. did not want any           c. could not get any

5. From the moment they left civilization, the men and women in the group had no access to store food or beverages; the idea was for them to rely <u>exclusively</u> on foods they hunted and gathered themselves.

    a. occasionally           b. only           c. mostly

6. Kerin O'Dea, the nutrition researcher who designed the experiment, <u>accompanied</u> the group to monitor and record its dietary intake and keep tabs on the members' health.

    a. went with           b. organized           c. sent away

7. While on the coast, their diet <u>consisted mainly of</u> seafood, supplemented by birds, kangaroo, and the fatty larvae of a local insect.

    a. included mostly        b. was entirely        c. contained some

8. O'Dea reports that . . . "the main dietary components in the urban setting were flour, sugar, rice, carbonated drinks, alcoholic beverages, powdered milk, cheap fatty meat, potatoes, onions, and <u>variable</u> contributions of other fresh fruits and vegetables."

    a. additional        b. important        c. changing

**B.** *Compare answers with another student. Check your answers in the dictionary. Then read through the passage on page 116 again. Can you remember the words you looked up the first time? If not, mark them for further review.*

## EXERCISE 11

**A.** *Read these sentences from the passage in Exercise 9. Write a word from the box in each blank. You may need to change the form of the word.*

| | | | | |
|---|---|---|---|---|
| convenience | disproportionate | finite | legacy | recovery |
| discard | elaborately | intentionally | massive | virtually |

1. Across the United States, people generate a _____ amount of solid waste—about 1.3 billion pounds *every day.*

2. As a rich nation of people who value _____, the United States has become a *disposable society.*

3. We consume more products than _____ any other nation, and many of these products have throwaway packaging.

4. Countless other products, from film to fishhooks, are _____ packaged to make the products more attractive to the customer and to discourage tampering and theft.

5. Manufacturers market soft drinks, beer, and fruit juices in aluminum cans, glass jars, and plastic containers, which not only consume _____ resources but also generate mountains of solid waste.

6. Then there are countless items _____ designed to be disposable: pens, razors, flashlights, batteries, even cameras.

7. This high level of consumption means not only that we in the United States use a _____ share of the planet's natural resources but also that we generate most of the world's refuse.

8. Although in most places laws now regulate what can be _____ in a landfill, the U.S. Environmental Protection Agency (2011) has identified 1,290 dump sites across the United States containing hazardous materials . . .

9. Tens of millions of tires, diapers, and other items we bury in landfills each year do not decompose but will remain as an unwelcome _____ for future generations.

10. The share is increasing as laws require the _____ and reuse of certain materials such as glass bottles and aluminum cans and as the business of recycling becomes more profitable.

B. *Compare answers with another student. Check your answers in the dictionary. Then read through the passage on page 118 again. Can you remember the words you looked up the first time? If not, mark them for further review.*

## EXERCISE 12

A. *Select six words or phrases from the passages in this unit which you think other students might not be familiar with (preferably words that are on the word list in the Appendix.)*

B. *On a separate piece of paper, make an exercise like Exercise 11:*
   * *Write the sentences where you found the words and phrases on your list, leaving a blank in place of the word or phrase.*
   * *Write the missing words/phrases in a box below the sentences—but not in order.*

C. *Exchange exercises with another student and complete your partner's exercise.*

D. *Look back at the passage and check your answers.*

E. *With your partner, give the definitions for the words or phrases you selected for your exercises. Look up any you are not sure about.*

### Reflecting on Your Learning

1. Discuss these questions with a group of students:
   * How do you think scanning could be useful to you in your course work? In other ways?
   * How does your reading change after you preview a text?
   * How can you help yourself remember to preview before you read?

2. Select useful vocabulary from this unit:
   * Look through the passages in this unit for more vocabulary that would be useful to learn. Write the words or phrases in your vocabulary notebook (with parts of speech, definitions and/ or synonyms, the sentences where you found them, and any helpful notes about usage).
   * Review the words in your notebook. Test yourself and then ask a classmate or friend to test you. Write the words you have trouble remembering on study cards. Review and test yourself until you know them well.

# UNIT 2  Making Inferences and Predictions

Good readers frequently make inferences as they read. They use information from the text, from other sources, and from their knowledge of the world to infer or guess more information or understand ideas.

As a language student, you will often need to make inferences about the meaning of unfamiliar words or phrases.

In both nonfiction and fiction texts, it may be necessary to infer information or ideas that are not directly stated by the writer. In this unit, you will learn how making inferences can help your comprehension of both types of text.

## Making Inferences in Fiction

Writers of fiction often choose not to tell "the whole story" to the reader. They may have stylistic reasons for this, or they may leave out some information in order to increase the mystery or the suspense. When you are reading fiction, you should look for clues in the dialogues or descriptions that will help you get a better sense of the characters, the situations, and the plot or story.

### EXERCISE 1

**A.**  *Read the title of a short story by Elizabeth Cullinan. Discuss these questions with another student:*

   **1.** What do you think the story might be about?
   **2.** What kind of prayer do you think it refers to?

---

**The Power of Prayer**

---

**B.**  *This passage is from the beginning of the story. Preview it quickly. Then read it carefully. Underline unfamiliar words and phrases. Look up those that are necessary for comprehension and write the definitions in the margin.*

---

   Nothing in their lives was natural any longer—that was what it amounted to. Nothing that touched them did not take on a certain kind of strangeness.
   That morning, the cold woke Aileen. She raised her head from the pillow and held it stiffly, straining her neck. Her eyes and her ears, her arms and legs and stomach—particularly her stomach—all were involved in the act of listening. There was no sound in the house, nothing but silence. A car passed. Three blocks away, on South Street, a bus went by. Aileen fell back onto her face, burrowing into the pillow and under the covers, tunneling down into softness and warmth.

"It's ten of seven," her mother said from the doorway. She stood there a moment, almost as though she were not quite sure what her next move should be, and then, when she saw Aileen push back the covers, she left.

The house was full of winter, the accumulated stuffiness of the long, cold months. Aileen stepped out of bed, picked up her underwear, and went out into the hall, looking neither to the left nor to the right, as though this were a strange house and she a timid guest. Safely inside the bathroom, she turned the big old-fashioned key in the lock; avoiding the face that looked out at her from the mirror, she ran the scalding hot and cloudy cold water, dipping her facecloth in one and then the other and rubbing it with a sliver of soap. She washed her face carelessly but gave great attention to the cleaning of her teeth, using a long ribbon of toothpaste and brushing hard, as though they would never be clean enough to suit her. Not taking any notice of her body (she was too thin, they told her—thin as a rail, skin and bones), she put on her underwear, threw her pajama coat about her shoulders, left the bathroom, and went over to her parents' bedroom. The bed was empty, and only one pillow had been slept on. The door of the spare room yawned upon a bed that hadn't been slept in at all.

So he hadn't come home; her father hadn't come home.

Feeling more at ease, she went back to her room and took a navy serge jumper and gray cotton blouse from their hanger . . .

(Source: Elizabeth Cullinan, "The Power of Prayer," *Growing Up Female: Stories by Women Writers from the American Mosaic*, ed. Susan Cahill, Mentor Books, Penguin Group, 1993)

**C.** *Discuss these inference questions with your partner. Look for evidence in the text and circle it.*

1. What can you infer about the setting (where it takes place)? About Aileen's house?
2. What can you infer about the time period, is it contemporary or in the past?
3. What can you infer about Aileen? How old is she? What does she look like?
4. What can you tell about her character?
5. What can you infer about her family? About her parents?
6. What do you think the writer means in the first sentence when she says: "Nothing in their lives was natural any longer"? What do you think is causing the "strangeness"?
7. What was she listening for?
8. Why is she "more at ease" in the last sentence?
9. What do you think might happen in the story?
10. Now what do you think might be the meaning of the title?

**D.** *Compare answers with another pair of students.*

## EXERCISE 2

**A.** *Read the title of a novel by Marjorie Kellogg. Discuss these questions with another student:*

1. What do you think the book might be about?
2. Who do you think Junie Moon might be?
3. Why is her name in the title?

**Tell Me That You Love Me, Junie Moon**

**B.** *This passage is from the beginning of the book. Preview it quickly. Then read it carefully. Underline unfamiliar words and phrases. Look up those that are necessary for comprehension and write the definitions in the margin.*

Once there were three patients who met in the hospital and decided to live together. They arrived at this decision because they had no place to go when they were discharged.

Despite the fact that these patients often quarreled and nagged each other, and had, so far as they knew, nothing in common, they formed an odd balance—like three pawnshop balls.

The first patient was called Warren. When he was seventeen, he and a friend were out hunting rabbits when the friend's gun went off and the bullet struck Warren in the middle of his spine. From then on he was a paraplegic and spent the rest of his days in a wheelchair.

The second patient was Arthur. He had a progressive neurological disease which no one had been able to diagnose. He estimated that he had been asked to touch his finger to his nose 6,012 times, and he could recite the laboratory findings on himself for the past five years, in case the doctors wanted them reviewed. Arthur walked with a careening gait and his hands fluttered about his face like butterflies.

The third patient was a woman named Junie Moon. That was her real name. An irate man had beaten her half to death in an alley one night and had topped off his violence by throwing acid over her. She had a number of pitiful and pesky deformities.

**C.** *Discuss these inference questions with your partner. Look for evidence in the text and circle it.*

1. What kind of hospital do you think this is?
2. What can you infer about each of these patients?
3. What can you infer about the families of these patients?
4. What do you think the next part will be about?

**D.** *Preview the next part of the story. Then read it carefully and work with the vocabulary as you did in Part B.*

The idea of their living together originated with Warren. He was fat and lazy and did not relish the thought of being alone or looking after himself. He was also a cheerful organizer of other people's time and affairs and could paint lovely pictures of how things would be later on.

"My dear friends," he said to Arthur and Junie Moon one night after the evening medications had been given out, "I have a solution to our collective dilemma." Junie Moon, who was playing checkers with Arthur in the far end of the corridor, scowled at Warren from her torn, disfigured face.

"With the various pittances we could collect from this and that source," Warren went on, as Arthur inadvertently knocked two checkers on the floor, "we could live fairly comfortably." Warren retrieved the checkers and patted Arthur on the shoulder. "What do you think?"

"Nobody wants to live with me," Junie Moon said, "so shut up about it."

"I think the idea stinks," Arthur said, as his hand flew into the air.

Then he and Junie Moon bent closer to the board as if to dismiss Warren's preposterous scheme.

"Don't pretend that either of you have a place to go," Warren said, leaning forward in his wheelchair so that his face was on a level with theirs, "because you haven't!" He gave Junie Moon a lascivious wink: "You'll end up at the old-ladies home and you know what goes on there!"

"At least it's better than nothing," she said. Her scarred mouth shifted painfully to permit a laugh. Warren was still not used to her face, but he loved her quick humor.

"But I'm better than a dozen old ladies," he said, "and more responsible."

"Baloney!" shouted Arthur, which set off a terrible spasm of his body and almost lifted him from his chair. Automatically, Warren and Junie Moon laid a hand on his shoulders to quiet him.

**E.** *Discuss these inference questions with your partner. Look for evidence in the text and circle it.*

1. What can you infer about the three patients' financial situation?
2. What can you infer about the relationship between Warren and the other two patients?
3. What can you infer from the fact that Junie Moon and Warren "automatically" laid a hand on Arthur's shoulder?

**F.** *Compare answers with another pair of students.*

## EXERCISE 3

**A.** *Preview the next passage from* **Tell Me That You Love Me, Junie Moon.** *Then read it carefully. Underline unfamiliar words and phrases. Look up those that are necessary for comprehension and write the definitions in the margin.*

"You are many things," Arthur said when he had regained control of himself, "but responsible is not one of them."

"But he may be better than the poorhouse at that," Junie Moon said. "What do you have in mind?"

"Well now!" Warren reared back in his wheelchair and stroked his bright blond beard. He said: "We will each have our own room. Junie Moon will do the cooking. Arthur will go to the store. I can see it all now."

"And I can see you have planned nothing for yourself in the way of expended effort," Arthur said.

"Who in their right mind would rent us an apartment?" Junie Moon said. "Three freaks, one a female."

"We'll do it by phone," Warren said. "We'll say we're much too busy to come in person."

"When the landlord takes one look at us, he will throw us out," Junie Moon said.

"He couldn't," Arthur said. "We represent at least three different minority groups." By making this last remark, Arthur had cast his vote in favor of the plan. Junie Moon held out a little longer.

**B.** *Discuss these inference questions with another student. Look for evidence in the text and circle it.*

1. What can you infer from what Arthur says about "three different minority groups"?
2. What can you infer about the relationship between Warren and Arthur?
3. What do you think the next part will be about?
4. What do you think Junie Moon will decide to do?

**C.** *The next passage continues from Part A. Preview it. Then read it carefully and work with the vocabulary as you did in Part A.*

"It's bad enough seeing the two of you in this hospital every day," she said, "let alone living with you."

At this, the two men banded together and attacked her.

"You're no prize yourself," Warren said.

"And you probably have a lot of disgusting personal habits of which we are not aware and to which you will expose us once we agree to a common arrangement," Arthur said.

"Let's not talk about prizes," Junie Moon said to Warren. "If we did, you might take the cake."

Arthur, who was the more sensitive of the men, realized by something in Junie Moon's voice that they had hurt her feelings. Because her face was so disfigured, it was difficult to read her emotions.

"I suppose none of us would take a prize," Arthur said. "On the other hand, we have a few things in our favor, I believe." He turned his head abruptly so the other two could not see him blush over this self-compliment.

"What are you three up to?" Miss Oxford, the chief nurse, asked, looking thin and suspicious.

"We are plotting your demise," Warren said, cheerfully. Miss Oxford scurried away, glancing over her shoulder.

Junie Moon then decided to join the two men in their plan. "I've thought of a number of ways to get that nurse," she said. "We must try a few of them before we leave here to set up housekeeping."

That was the way they decided.

(Marjorie Kellogg, *Tell Me That You Love Me, Junie Moon*, New York: Farrar, Strauss & Giroux. 1968.)

**D.** *Discuss these inference questions with your partner. Look for evidence in the text and circle it.*

1. What can you now infer about Junie Moon?
2. About Warren?
3. About the nurse, Miss Oxford, and her relations with patients?
4. Look back at the title of the novel. What do you think might happen later?
5. Does this novel appeal to you? Why or why not?

**E.** *Compare answers with another pair of students.*

## Inferring Information and Ideas in Nonfiction

How much you are able to infer from a text depends on

- your knowledge about the topic and the world.
- your understanding of the facts included in the text.

## EXERCISE 4

**A.** *Preview the title and the article quickly to get the gist. Then read it carefully. Underline unfamiliar words and phrases. Look up those that are necessary for comprehension and write the definitions in the margin.*

### Olive Oil Works as a Natural Painkiller

It is not just price or the flavor that distinguishes extra virgin olive oil from other oils. Now scientists have discovered that the olives it is made from contain a chemical compound that acts in many ways like the painkiller ibuprofen.

Paul Breslin from the Monell Chemical Sense Center in Philadelphia and colleagues describe in *Nature* how they isolated a compound called oleocanthal from extra virgin olive oil. Pouring 50 gm of the best olive oil on your food each day is equivalent to about 10 percent of the average ibuprofen dose.

The researchers further suggest that these anti-inflammatory properties may help explain why the Mediterranean diet appears to protect against some forms of cancer and other diseases.

*Work with another student. Read these statements, which match information in the passage. Find the matching information in the text and write the number of the statement beside it.*

1. Extra virgin olive oil is different from other kinds of oil.
2. It contains a chemical compound that is similar to ibuprofen.
3. Paul Breslin works at the Monell Chemical Senses Center in Philadelphia.
4. He and his colleagues discovered a compound called oleocanthal in olive oil.
5. Fifty grams of olive oil per day is the same as 10 percent of the average dose of ibuprofen.
6. People who eat a Mediterranean diet are at less risk of getting some forms of cancer.

C. *With your partner, use the information in the text and your general knowledge to answer these inference questions.*

1. How is the price and flavor of extra virgin olive oil different from that of other oils?
2. Do other oils contain natural painkillers?
3. What do you think *Nature* is?
4. How did Breslin and his colleagues "describe" their work in *Nature*?
5. How much oil do you need to consume to reach the equivalent of a full dose of ibuprofen?
6. What is an important ingredient of the Mediterranean diet?
7. What is one factor that promotes the growth of some cancers?

D. *Compare answers with another pair of students.*

**Notes:**

- Many of the questions for the exercises in this unit can be answered in more than one way. Any answer is acceptable if you can provide evidence from the text.
- Look up only the words or phrases that are necessary for comprehension. Skip unnecessary words, or try to guess a general meaning.

E. *Go back through the unit and look at the vocabulary you wrote in the margins. Choose words you want to learn and add them to your vocabulary notebook.*

## EXERCISE 5

A. *Read the title of the article and discuss these questions with another student:*

1. What do you think the article might be about?
2. What kind of "test scores" do you think it refers to?
3. Why do you think fast food affects test scores?

### Too much fast food harms children's test scores

By Graeme Paton

Pupils achieve lower scores in tests after eating takeaway meals such as burgers and chips more than three times a week, it is claimed.

The findings—in a study of more than 5,500 primary school children—even apply when parental income, race and pupils' weight is taken into account. Some children's scores in literacy and numeracy dropped by up to 16 per cent compared to the average, it was disclosed. The study provides some of the most conclusive evidence yet of a link between poor diet and academic ability . . .

One in three children [in the U.K.] are currently overweight and consumer groups have called for stricter controls on junk food advertising on television. The sale of fatty and sugary food has already been banned in school canteens and vending machines, following a high-profile campaign by Jamie Oliver, the TV chef. But the health drive has led to a sharp drop in the number of under-16s eating at school.

In the latest study, researchers from Vanderbilt University in Tennessee tracked the eating habits of children aged 10 and 11, then compared those habits to their performance in reading and math tests. They found that just over half of pupils had eaten at fast food restaurants such as McDonald's up to three times in the last week. One in 10 had eaten fast food between four and six times, and two per cent visited restaurants more than once a day.

In total, children scored between 58 and 181 points in the reading tests, with an average score of 141.5. But after taking other factors into account, pupils who ate fast food between four and six times a week scored almost seven points below average, those eating fast food once a day fell 16 points, and those indulging three times a day dropped by 19 points. Similar trends were noted in math. In total, children scored between 47 and 151 points in the test, with average results of 115. But those pupils eating fast food dropped by between 6.5 and 18.5 points.

Dr. Kerri Tobin, who carried out the study, said it found "statistically significant relationships between higher than average consumption of fast food and lowered test scores. It is possible that the types of food served at fast food restaurants cause cognitive difficulties that result in lower test scores."

The study said results may be influenced by other factors such as parental interest in children's work. "It is also possible that the tendency to eat fast food results from lower test scores, rather than resulting in lower test scores," added the report.

Last year, the [British] Government-funded School Food Trust recommended banning children from leaving school at lunchtime to stop them eating junk food.

(Source: Graeme Paton, "Too much fast food harms children's test scores," *The Telegraph* http://www.telegraph.co.uk/education/educationnews/5368637/Too-much-fast-food-harms-childrens-test-scores.html May 22, 2009)

C. *Discuss these comprehension questions with your partner and write the number of each question beside the answer in the passage.*

1. What was the reason for the lower scores of many primary school children?
2. Why has the sale of fatty and sugary foods been banned in schools?
3. What did the researchers compare in their study?
4. Which children scored the worst on the tests?
5. According to Dr. Tobin, what is one possible effect of fast food on children?
6. According to the report, what is another way that the results of the study might be interpreted?

**D.** *Discuss these inference questions with your partner. Look for evidence in the text and circle it.*

1. What can you infer about income, race, and weight?
2. About the food that used to be available in schools?
3. About Jamie Oliver?
4. About the food preferences of under-16s?
5. About parental interest in children's schoolwork?
6. About children's behavior at lunchtime?

**E.** *Compare answers with another pair of students.*

## EXERCISE 6

**A.** *Read the title of the passage from* **In Defense of Food,** *by Michael Pollan, and discuss these previewing questions with another student:*

1. Are you familiar with the expression "the elephant in the room"? If not, can you guess what it means?
2. What do you think the book might be about?
3. What do you think might be the "elephant in the room" in this passage?

### The Elephant in the Room

**B.** *Preview the passage quickly for the gist. Then read it carefully. Underline unfamiliar words and phrases. Look up those that are necessary for comprehension and write the definitions in the margin.*

In the end, even the biggest, most ambitious, and widely reported studies of diet and health [in the United States]—the Nurses Health Study, the Women's Health Initiative, and nearly all the others—leave undisturbed the main features of the Western diet: lots of processed foods and meat, lots of added fat and sugar, lots of everything except fruits, vegetables, and whole grains . . . Most nutrition researchers fiddle with single nutrients as best they can, but the populations they recruit and study are typical American eaters doing what typical American eaters do: trying to eat a little less of this nutrient, a little more of that one, depending on the latest thinking. The overall dietary pattern is treated as a more or less unalterable given. Which is why it probably should not surprise us that the findings of such research should be so modest, equivocal, and confusing.

But what about the elephant in the room—this pattern of eating that we call the Western diet? In the midst of our deepening confusion about nutrition, it might be useful to step back and gaze up on it—review what we do know about the Western diet and its effects on our health. What we know is that people who eat the way we do in the West today suffer substantially higher rates of cancer, cardiovascular diseases, diabetes, and obesity than people eating any number of different traditional diets. We also know that when people come to the West and adopt our way of eating, these diseases soon follow, and often, as in the case of the Aborigines and other native populations, in a particularly virulent form.

**C.** *Discuss these comprehension questions with your partner and write the number of each question beside the answer in the passage.*

1. What do you understand now about the title? *obvious*
2. What is the attitude of most nutrition researchers towards the typical American diet?
3. What do their studies usually test?
4. How does the Western diet affect health?
5. What happens to people who change from a traditional to a Western diet?

**D.** *Discuss these inference questions with your partner. Look for evidence in the text and circle it.*

1. What can you infer about the typical American attitude towards nutrition?
2. About nutrition science and research today?
3. About the health of people who eat traditional diets?
4. What do you think the next part of the passage will be about?

**E.** *This passage continues from Part B. Preview it quickly. Then read it carefully and work with the vocabulary as you did in Part B.*

The outlines of this story—the story of the so-called Western diseases and their link to the Western diet—we first learned in the early decades of the twentieth century. That was when a handful of European and American medical professionals working with a wide variety of native populations around the world began noticing the almost complete absence of the chronic diseases that had recently become common-place in the West. Albert Schweitzer and Denis P. Burkitt in Africa, Robert McCarrison in India, Samuel Hutton among the Eskimos in Labrador, the anthropologist Ales Hrdlicka among Native Americans, and the dentist Weston A. Price among a dozen different groups all over the world, sent back much the same news. They compiled lists, many of which appeared in medical journals, of the common diseases they'd been unable to find in the native populations they had treated or studied: little to no heart disease, diabetes, cancer, obesity, hypertension, or stroke; no appendicitis, diverticulitis, malformed dental arches, or tooth decay, no varicose veins, ulcers, or hemorrhoids. These disorders suddenly appeared to these researchers under a striking new light, as suggested by the name given to them by the British doctor Denis Burkitt, who worked in Africa during World War II: He proposed that we call them Western diseases. The implication was that these very different diseases were somehow linked and might even have a common cause.

**F.** *Discuss these comprehension questions with your partner and write the number of each question beside the answer in the passage.*

1. What is "the story" that is told in this passage?
2. What was the "news" sent back by Western medical professionals from around the world?
3. What were the "Western diseases" Burkitt was referring to and why did he call them that?

**G.** *Discuss these inference questions with your partner. Look for evidence in the text and circle it.*

1. What can you infer about the health of Western populations before the twentieth century?
2. About the diet of non-Western populations in the early twentieth century?
3. About the "common cause" of Western diseases?
4. What do you think the next part of the passage will be about?

**H.** *Compare answers with another pair of students.*

**A.** *Preview the next passage from* **In Defense of Food.** *Then read it carefully. Underline unfamiliar words and phrases. Look up those that are necessary for comprehension and write the definitions in the margin.*

Several of the researchers were on hand to witness the arrival of the Western diseases in isolated populations, typically, as Albert Schweitzer wrote, among "natives living more and more after the manner of the whites." Some noted that the Western diseases followed closely after the arrival of Western foods, particularly refined flour and sugar and other kinds of "store food." They observed too that when one Western disease arrived on the scene, so did most of the others, often in the same order: obesity followed by type 2 diabetes followed by hypertension and stroke followed by heart disease.

In the years before World War II the medical world entertained a lively conversation on the subject of the Western diseases and what their rise might say about our increasingly industrialized way of life. The concept's pioneers believed there were novelties in the modern diet to which native populations were poorly adapted, though they did not necessarily agree on exactly which novelty might be the culprit. Burkitt, for example, believed it was the lack of fiber in the modern diet while McCarrison, a British army doctor, focused on refined carbohydrates while still others blamed meat eating and saturated fat, or in Price's case, the advent of processed food and industrially grown crops deficient in vitamins and minerals.

**B.** *Discuss these comprehension questions with another student and write the number of each question beside the answer in the passage.*

1. What happened to people in distant places when they began to eat Western foods?
2. What did the researchers notice about the arrival of Western diseases in these places?
3. Who participated in the "lively conversation" and what was it about?
4. What aspects of the modern diet were cited as possible causes of Western diseases?

**C.** *Discuss these inference questions with your partner. Look for evidence in the text and circle it.*

1. What can you infer about the native populations' attitudes toward Western foods?
2. What can you infer about the medical views of industrialization before World War II?
3. What do you think the next part will be about?

**D.** *The next passage continues from Part A. Preview it quickly. Then read it carefully and work with the vocabulary as you did in Part A.*

Not everyone, though, accepted the idea that chronic disease was a by-product of Western lifestyles and in particular, that the industrialization of our food was damaging our health. One objection to the theory was genetic: Different races were apt to be susceptible to different diseases; white people were disposed to heart attacks, brown people to things like leprosy. Yet as Burkitt and others pointed out, blacks living in America suffered from the same chronic diseases as whites living there. Simply by moving to places like America, immigrants from nations with low rates of chronic disease seemed to quickly acquire them.

The other objection to the concept of Western diseases, one you sometimes still hear, was demographic. The reason we see so much chronic disease in the West is because these are illnesses that appear relatively late in life, and with the conquest of infectious disease early in the twentieth century, we're simply living long enough to get them. In this view, chronic disease is the inevitable price of a long life.

But while it is true that our life expectancy has improved dramatically since 1900 (rising in the United States from forty-nine to seventy-seven years), most of that gain is attributed to the fact that more of us are surviving infancy and childhood; the life expectancy of a sixty-five-year-old in 1900 was only about six years less than that of a sixty-five-year-old living today. When you adjust for age, rates of chronic diseases like cancer and type 2 diabetes are considerably higher today than they were in 1900. That is, the chances that a sixty- or seventy-year-old suffers from cancer or type 2 diabetes are far greater today than they were a century ago.

Cancer and heart disease and so many of the other Western diseases are by now such an accepted part of modern life that it's hard for us to believe this wasn't always or even necessarily the case. These days most of us think of chronic diseases as being a little like the weather—one of life's givens—and so count ourselves lucky that, compared to the weather, the diseases at least are more amenable to intervention by modern medicine. We think of them strictly in medical rather than historical, much less evolutionary, terms. But during the decades before World War II, when the industrialization of so many aspects of our lives was still fairly fresh, the price of "progress," especially to our health, seemed more obvious to many people and therefore more open to question.

(Source: Michael Pollan, *In Defense of Food,* Penguin Books, NY, 2008)

**E.** *Discuss these comprehension questions with your partner and write the number of each question beside the answer in the passage.*

1. What was the genetic argument about the cause of Western diseases?
2. What evidence does the writer give against that argument?
3. What is the demographic argument?
4. What logic does the writer use against that argument?
5. What is the attitude of most Westerners to diseases like cancer and heart disease?

**F.** *Discuss these inference questions with your partner. Look for evidence in the text and circle it.*

1. What can you infer about the people who argued for a genetic explanation?
2. What can you infer about the risk of chronic disease among young people today?
3. What can you infer about the risk of getting cancer in 1900?
4. Who does the phrase "most of us" (paragraph 4, line 3) refer to? Does it include the writer?
5. What can we infer about Western people's attitudes today towards the modern lifestyle?

**G.** *Compare answers with another pair of students.*

**H.** *Go back through the unit and look at the vocabulary you wrote in the margins. Choose words you want to learn and add them to your vocabulary notebook.*

# Making Predictions

Using their understanding of the facts and ideas in a text and their knowledge of the world, good readers make predictions about what will come next. This way they are thinking ahead and creating a mental framework that will help them process the text more quickly.

In these exercises, you will practice using your skills and knowledge to follow the ideas in the passages and predict the conclusion of each paragraph.

*Read the paragraph and choose the most logical ending.*

No one knows exactly how many children work in agriculture in the United States. In 2006, the Childhood Agricultural Survey carried out by the Department of Agriculture found 307,000 youth under the age of 20 employed on the nation's farmland. However, in an earlier study in 1998, another government agency estimated that there were 300,000 youths aged 15- to 17-years-old working in agriculture. In the same year, still another government report was released indicating that 431,730 youths aged 12- to 17-years-old had been hired for agricultural work. No studies have been done on the _____.

    **a.** health of farm workers in the United States
    **b.** average age of farm workers in U.S. agriculture
    **c.** number of child farm workers under the age of 12
    **d.** number of children who work on farms in Mexico

The best ending is *c. the number of child farm workers under the age of 12.* From the earlier sentences, you expect the last sentence to continue talking about children of different age groups working on farms in the United States. None of the other endings follow logically from the other sentences.

> **Note:** As in the earlier exercises, do not stop to look up unfamiliar vocabulary when you read these paragraphs the first time. Skip over new words or try to guess the general meaning. If you still don't understand when you reread it, and if the word or phrase is necessary for comprehension of the passage, look it up.

## EXERCISE 8

    **A.**  *Work with another student. Read the paragraphs from a news article and choose the best ending for each one.*

### Only Three in Ten Teens Have Summer Jobs

1. Not so many years ago, most American teenagers could count on getting a summer job. From June to August, some form of temporary employment was available, at a cash register, mowing lawns, washing dishes, pumping gas, or selling ice cream. However, this year only about 30 percent of 16-to-19-year olds found paid seasonal employment. This was the lowest level since World War II and _____.

    a.  a significant increase since 2000        c.  nearly twice that of 2000
    b.  about the same as in 2000           d.  a sharp decline since 2000

2. Unemployment for all ages is holding steady at about 8 percent, while the year-round teenage jobless rate has soared to about three times that, almost 25 percent. In the past decade, youth employment has suffered a much steeper drop than for other age groups. According to the U.S. Bureau of Labor Statistics, a number of long-term cultural and economic factors are depressing the teen labor market and it _____.

   a. will soon return to earlier levels
   b. may never return to previous levels
   c. is likely to recover quickly
   d. might affect the stock market

3. The situation is most critical for youths in lower-middle and lower-class families. Blacks, Hispanics, and teens in lower-income families were least likely to be employed in summer jobs. These young people are increasingly jobless, with few opportunities to earn wages and gain work experience. Economists say the teens who aren't getting summer jobs are often those who need them the most. According to the labor economist Bruce Powell, the gap between rich and poor is widened when lower-income youths are unable to _____.

   a. complete high school
   b. form social networks
   c. get skills and training
   d. help their families

4. As the economy has weakened, youths have also met with more competition for lower-skills employment from other categories of workers. Some older retirees who found themselves without adequate pensions have been forced back into the work force. Immigrants who may have aimed at more skilled positions in a stronger economy are now _____.

   a. working mostly in offices
   b. retiring at a younger age
   c. willing to take low-wage jobs
   d. pushing for higher wages

   B. *Compare answers with another pair of students. Then choose useful vocabulary from the article and add it to your vocabulary notebook.*

## EXERCISE 9

   A. *Read the paragraphs from a report and choose the best ending for each one.*

### Child Labor in the U.S.

1. Forms of child labor, including servitude and child slavery, have existed throughout American history. Children worked alongside their parents and relatives on farms and as apprentices or helpers to tradesmen of all kinds, including blacksmiths, weavers, candle makers, and printers. As industrialization moved workers from farms and small workshops into urban areas and factory work, children were often preferred as workers. Operating the power-driven machines did not require adult strength and with their small hands, children could perform better in certain jobs. They could be hired more cheaply than adults, and, furthermore, they were more manageable and _____.

   a. often absent from school
   b. expensive as workers
   c. less likely to protest
   d. difficult to discipline

2. It was a hard life for children working in factories in the late-eighteenth and early-nineteenth century. Many began working before the age of seven, tending machines in mills or factories, or carrying heavy loads. A child with a factory job might work twelve to eighteen hours a day, six days a week. These factory workers had no time to play or go to school, and little time to rest, with the result that their physical and mental development suffered and they _____.

   a. often became ill                c. learned to read
   b. became stronger                 d. had to eat often

3. By 1810, about 2,000,000 school-age children were working in factories, often for 50- to 60-hours per week. Most of them came from poor families who could not support their children and had no choice but to turn the children over to a mill or factory owner. One glass factory in Massachusetts was fenced in with barbed wire "to keep the young devils inside." The "young devils" were boys under twelve who carried loads of hot glass all day and were _____.

   a. treated well by the owner        c. given a generous wage
   b. told to go to school             d. paid less than a dollar

4. Protests by church and labor groups led to more public awareness of the cruelty of the factories, and to pressure on governments for reforms. The English writer Charles Dickens helped publicize the evils of child labor with his novel *Oliver Twist*. Britain was the first country to regulate child labor with a series of laws that gradually shortened working hours, improved conditions, and raised the age at which children could work. By the end of the 1800s, other European countries had _____.

   a. adopted similar laws             c. read *Oliver Twist*
   b. allowed child labor              d. started factories

5. In the United States, the number of child laborers continued to grow until the early decades of the twentieth century. In the nineteenth century, some states passed laws that limited child labor— Massachusetts, for example, passed a law in 1842 that limited children's working day to 10 hours. However, these laws were poorly enforced and did little to _____.

   a. worsen working conditions        c. increase the number of children
   b. improve working conditions       d. move the work to other states

6. It took many years and much effort by reformers to outlaw child labor on a national level. Two laws were passed by Congress in 1918 and 1922, but the Supreme Court declared both unconstitutional. In 1924, Congress proposed a constitutional amendment prohibiting child labor, but the states did not ratify it. Then, in 1938, Congress passed the Fair Labor Standards Act. It fixed a minimum age for certain kinds of work: 18 for dangerous jobs at any time, 16 for work during school hours, and _____.

   a. 65 for retirement from work      c. 18 for high school graduation
   b. 14 for most jobs after school    d. any age for jobs in factories

7. The Fair Labor Standards Act eliminated the worst evils of factory work for children, but it was not extended to all kinds of work and in particular not to farm work. Today, this has created a situation of cruel double standards, as the protections are applied to most young people in the United States, but not to those who work _____.

   a. in factories                     c. on farms
   b. in certain states                d. on weekends

**B.** *Compare answers with another pair of students. Then choose useful vocabulary from the report and add it to your vocabulary notebook.*

## EXERCISE 10

**A.** *Read the paragraphs from a report and choose the best ending for each one.*

### Childhood in the Fields

1. Without migrant workers in this country, fruits and vegetables would rot on the trees or in the fields. These workers and their families (many of them originally from Central America) travel from state to state, picking whatever is in season. At the farms where they work, visitors are told that kids don't work in the fields. They attend summer school or stay in the camps that house the workers and their families while their parents tend to the crops. That's the story many farm owners would like you to believe. However, _____.

   a. visitors usually believe this
   b. it's close to the truth
   c. the reality is quite different
   d. the children enjoy the camps

2. Classes are offered in a few model camps, but in the thousands of others, educational opportunities for the children of farm workers are limited during the summer. At the same time, these families cannot afford child care in the camps; nor can the mothers afford not to be working. If they don't want to leave their children alone in the camps, the only option left to them is to _____.

   a. send their children to school
   b. bring their children with them
   c. pay for a baby sitter
   d. let them stay in the camps

3. According to estimates provided by Farmworker Opportunity Programs in Washington D.C., up to 800,000 children work in agriculture. Farmers' organizations, dispute that number and argue that some of the child workers are members of farm families and should be allowed to help out on their parents' farms. But recent census reports tell a clear story: Over three quarters of those children are not from farm families. They are the children of hired farm workers. And they are not simply "helping out" with the farm chores after school; they are _____.

   a. doing housework at home
   b. studying for school
   c. making friends in the fields
   d. laboring long hours like adults

4. These children are working legally. Some states, such as Oregon, have set higher age limits, but according to federal law, the minimum legal age for paid farm workers is 12. Indeed, the Fair Labor Standards Act of 1938 removed children under the age of 16 from coal mines and factories, but it did not restrict the work of children on farms, except to forbid hiring children during school hours (a provision that is routinely ignored). Later laws strengthened protections for children in industry, defining many tasks as dangerous and off limits to those under 18, but not in agriculture, where sixteen-year-olds may _____.

   a. not operate farm equipment
   b. operate heavy machinery
   c. not work in the fields
   d. work during school hours

5. Many farmers do not even observe those very loose laws. In the fields, human rights investigators have often found children less than 12 years old treated just like adults. On an Oregon berry farm, 12-year-old Dora, together with her 9-year-old brother Elmo, picked blackberries for long hours all summer, both carrying buckets strapped to their shoulders with up to 15 pounds of fruit. Under the blazing Texas sun, 11-year-old Maria spent every day alongside her mother bent over the fields, pulling onions _____.

a. to cook for their supper
b. that they could sell

c. until her hands were bleeding
d. and laughing with her friends

**B.** *Compare answers with another pair of students. Then choose useful vocabulary from the report and add it to your vocabulary notebook.*

## EXERCISE 11

**A.** *These paragraphs continue from the ones in Exercise 10. Read them and choose the best ending for each one.*

1. Child labor is a pressing issue in the United States, but it remains hidden from public view. What little data are published, in any case, do not include underage workers like Dora and Elmo. But the reason for the lack of public scrutiny is simple: Those involved often prefer to leave things as they are. Farmers argue that their crops must be harvested cheaply to compete with imports from overseas. The farm workers themselves, who might prefer to keep their children in school and out of the fields,

_____.

a. need their children's income
b. already have a good income

c. don't care if their children work
d. don't need their children to work

2. When children work in the fields, they are at greater risk than adults in several ways. Their lack of experience, along with their small size makes them more vulnerable to accidents. They work long hours under the sun with sharp tools and heavy machinery; they climb tall ladders carrying heavy sacks and buckets. Approximately 100,000 children suffer agriculture-related injuries annually. And all too often, the injuries are fatal. More than half of all children who died of work-related injuries in 2010 worked _____.

a. in factories
b. at home

c. on weekends
d. on farms

3. During their long hours in the fields, children and adult workers are also exposed to the chemicals used on crops, which can cause acute poisoning, as well as chronic health problems, such as asthma and cancer. For children, with their smaller size and developing bodies and brains, the health consequences can also include neurological damage, leading to memory loss and poor coordination. Federal protections against pesticide do not take into consideration the presence of children among farm laborers. Federal guidelines for pesticide exposure are based on the typical adult male body weight of 154 pounds. The average 12-year-old weighs only about 100 pounds, but is allowed to re-enter fields sprayed with toxic pesticides _____.

a. at the same time as adults
b. at the same time as other children

c. only after a year has passed
d. only when adults are present

4. Then there are the challenges that child farm laborers face with regards to their education. It is in any case difficult for them emotionally and academically to change schools continually as their families follow the harvests. As a result of their long working hours in the fields, these children drop out of school at _____.

   a. a lower than average rate
   b. the same rate as other children
   c. less than the national rate
   d. four times the national rate

5. Farm worker advocates say the best way to prevent child labor in agriculture is first of all to raise wages for all farm workers. They are supposed to be paid the minimum wage, but investigations have revealed that they are often paid far less. For farm workers, federal law prohibits overtime pay and employers provide no benefits, such as health insurance or pensions. As a result, the average income of farm worker families is well below the poverty level and parents are desperate for any little extra income _____.

   a. the government might give
   b. their children might bring in
   c. employers might offer them
   d. they could earn in industry

6. The fact that the work is legal—for children over 12—further justifies their choice in the eyes of parents, children, and employers. Thus, the second key step in keeping children out of the fields, according to advocates, is to change the laws and eliminate the exceptions for agriculture contained in the Fair Labor Standards Act. Not only are these exceptions morally unacceptable in a democracy; they are an embarrassment internationally. The United States spends over $25 million a year to eliminate child labor around the world, while at the same time _____.

   a. banning it at home
   b. organizing it at home
   c. tolerating it at home
   d. eliminating it at home

   **B.**  *Compare answers with another pair of students. Then choose useful vocabulary from the report and add it to your vocabulary notebook.*

## EXERCISE 12

**A.**  *Read the paragraphs from a research report. For each one, write an ending that follows the logic of the other sentences.*

### Child Labor in the Global Economy

1. Popular opinion in high-income countries often seems to hold that child labor in developing countries is nearly always a form of child abuse, in which children work in hazardous conditions in run-down factories for callous businesses. There have been recent attempts to combat child labor by lowering employment opportunities for children through harmonized international child labor standards and by consumer boycotts of products produced by

   _____.

2. The U.S. Congress has repeatedly considered legislation that would prohibit imports into the United States of all products made with child labor. Under threat of such sanctions, export oriented garment factories in Bangladesh released more than 10,000 child workers under the age of 14 in the mid-1990s. More recently, the U.S. House of Representatives has deliberated the "Child Labor Elimination Act," which would impose general trade sanctions, deny all financial assistance, and mandate U.S. opposition to multilateral credits to 62 developing countries

_____.

3. But in fact, the broad term "child labor" covers a considerable diversity between and within countries in the types of activities in which children participate. Fortunately, horrifying images of children chained in factories or forced into prostitution stand out for their relative rarity. Most working children are at home, helping their family by assisting in the family business or farm and

_____.

4. Fundamentally, child labor is a symptom of poverty. Low income and poor institutions are driving forces behind the prevalence of child labor worldwide. As a result, some economic events or policies can have ambiguous effects on child labor; for example, a country that experiences an increase in labor demand, perhaps because of globalization, may experience greater demand for both adult and child labor. However, the greater demand for adult labor can raise family incomes in a way that tends to

_____.

5. The final section (of this report) assesses the policy options to reduce worldwide child labor. While some children do work in circumstances so hideous as to command immediate attention, development is the best overall cure for child labor. However, historical growth rates suggest that reducing child labor through improvements in living standards alone

_____.

6. If a more rapid reduction in the general incidence of child labor is a policy goal, improving educational systems and providing financial incentives to poor families to send children to school may be more useful solutions to the child labor problem than punitive measures designed to prevent children

_____.

B. **Compare endings with another student. Explain how your ending follows the logic of the paragraph. Then choose useful vocabulary from the report and add it to your vocabulary notebook.**

**A.** *Read the paragraphs from a research report. For each one, write an ending that follows the logic of the other sentences.*

1. Estimating the number of children working around the world is a difficult task. Most working children live in low-income countries. These countries often lack reliable data on many aspects of their labor market. Even more difficult, some policymakers have until recently defined "child labor" as economic activities that are deleterious

   _____.

2. There are some situations where it is hard to imagine how an activity could not be harmful to the child—forced prostitution, child soldiers—but . . . these activities are very rare. Most working children participate in activities that can be harmful or beneficial for the child, depending on the circumstances of the activity. Ultimately, the impact of child labor on the well-being of the child depends on . . . what the child would be doing

   _____.

3. The International Labor Organization (ILO) most recently estimated that 211 million children, or 18 percent of children 5–14, are economically active worldwide. A child is defined as economically active if he or she works for wages (cash or in-kind); works on the family farm in the production and processing of primary products; works in family enterprises that are making primary products for the market, barter or own consumption. The academic literature also uses the phrase "market work"

   _____.

4. Information on the domestic activities of children is unusual, and detailed data on time in school and time studying is generally not available. Moreover, a high fraction of children report neither attending school nor working in market or domestic work, and these so-called "idle" children are not well understood. Thus, in the available data, it is very hard to establish what children would do in the absence of participation in a particular type of work and therefore very difficult to evaluate the consequences

   _____.

5. Contrary to popular perception in high-income countries, most working children are employed by their parents, rather than in manufacturing establishments or other forms of wage employment. In 2000 and 2001, UNICEF coordinated detailed household surveys with virtually identical questionnaires in 36 low-income countries as a part of UNICEF's End of Decade Assessment. The surveys aimed to identify participation rates in market work

   _____.

6. Of the 25 percent of children ages 5–14 that participate in market work, few work outside of their own household. Less than 3 percent of children age 5–14 work outside of their household for pay, and this work for pay is actually more common in rural settings than

   _____.

7. In addition, 6 percent of children participate in unpaid work for someone outside of the child's household. We suspect that most of these children are involved in unpaid labor exchanges where neighboring families help one another in their business or farm, but these unpaid workers may also be children who are paid in-kind with meals or food (the questionnaire is unclear), or the work relationship may involve apprenticeships, children fostered out, that is, receiving food and board with another family in exchange for work, children held in bondage, that is, where the child's family has received a cash payment

_____

8. The minimal incidence of wage employment in these UNICEF surveys concords [agrees] with other datasets from countries as diverse as India, Nepal, South Africa, and Vietnam, where it is unusual to find more than 3 percent of children 5–14 working outside of the household for pay. Even in urban Bangladesh, where much attention has been paid to child labor in the garment industry, a 2002 child labor survey found only 1.2 percent of children 5–14 working as paid employees. In contrast, 20.8 percent of children 5–14 in countries surveyed by UNICEF work in their family business or farm. Participation rates in this category are highest in rural areas, but 14.8 percent of urban children 5–14

_____

(Source: Eric V. Edmonds and Nina Pavcnik, *Journal of Economic Perspectives*, Volume 19, Number 1, Winter 2005, Pages 199–220)

**B.** *Compare endings with another student. Explain how your ending follows the logic of the paragraph. Then choose useful vocabulary from the report and add it to your vocabulary notebook.*

### Reflecting on the Issues

*Discuss these questions with a small group of students:*

1. In your country, are there laws that regulate child labor? If so, how do they compare with the laws in the United States?

2. Have you seen children at work? If so, what kind of work and where?

3. Some people argue that laws against child labor only create more problems for the children and their families, who depend on the money the children bring home. What do you think?

# Focus on Vocabulary

## EXERCISE 14

**A.** *Read these sentences from the passage in Exercise 5. For each underlined word or phrase, choose the one that is closest in meaning.*

1. Pupils achieve lower scores in tests after eating takeaway meals such as burgers and chips more than three times a week, it is <u>claimed</u>.

   a. argued        b. believed        c. shown

2. Some children's scores in <u>literacy</u> and numeracy dropped by up to 16 percent compared to the average, it was disclosed.

   a. language learning        b. stories and books        c. reading and writing

3. Some children's scores in literacy and numeracy dropped by up to 16 per cent compared to the average, it was <u>disclosed</u>.

   a. discovered        b. decided        c. revealed

4. The study provides some of the most <u>conclusive</u> evidence yet of a link between poor diet and academic ability.

   a. selective        b. effective        c. decisive

5. The sale of fatty and sugary food has been <u>banned</u> in school canteens and vending machines, following a high-profile campaign by Jamie Oliver, the TV chef.

   a. allowed        b. restricted        c. promoted

6. In the latest study, researchers from Vanderbilt University in Tennessee <u>tracked</u> the eating habits of children aged 10 and 11, then compared those habits to their performance in reading and math tests.

   a. encouraged        b. changed        c. followed

7. . . . pupils who ate fast food between four and six times a week scored almost seven points below average, those eating fast food once a day fell 16 points, and those <u>indulging</u> three times a day dropped by 19 points.

   a. enjoying it        b. exceeding it        c. reducing it

8. It is possible that the types of food served at fast food restaurants cause <u>cognitive</u> difficulties that result in lower test scores.

   a. learning        b. emotional        c. physical

**B.** *Compare answers with another student. Check your answers in the dictionary. Then read through the passage on page 129 again. Can you remember the words you looked up the first time? If not, mark them for further review.*

## EXERCISE 15

**A.** *Read these sentences from the passage in Exercise 6. Write a word from the box in each blank. You may need to change the form of the word.*

| a handful of | compile | implication | recruit | substantially |
|---|---|---|---|---|
| chronic | gaze | nutrition | striking | unalterable |

1. Most _____ researchers fiddle with single nutrients as best they can, but the populations they . . . and study are typical American eaters doing what typical American eaters do.

2. . . . researchers fiddle with single nutrients as best they can, but the populations they _____ and study are typical American eaters doing what typical American eaters do.

3. The overall dietary pattern is treated as a more or less _____ given.

4. In the midst of our deepening confusion about nutrition, it might be useful to step back and _____ upon it—review what we do know about the Western diet and its effects on our health.

5. What we know is that people who eat the way we do in the West today suffer _____ higher rates of cancer, cardiovascular diseases, diabetes, and obesity than people eating any number of different traditional diets.

6. That was when _____ European and American medical professionals working with a wide variety of native populations around the world began noticing the almost complete absence of the . . . diseases . . .

7. . . . European and American medical professionals working with a wide variety of native populations around the world began noticing the almost complete absence of the _____ diseases that had recently become common-place in the West.

8. They _____ lists, many of which appeared in medical journals, of the common diseases they'd been unable to find in the native populations they had treated or studied.

9. These disorders suddenly appeared to these researchers under a _____ new light, as suggested by the name given to them by the British doctor Denis Burkitt. . . . He proposed that we call them Western diseases.

10. He proposed that we call them Western diseases. The _____ was that these very different diseases were somehow linked and might even have a common cause.

B. *Compare answers with another student. Check your answers in the dictionary. Then read through the passage on page 130 again. Can you remember the words you looked up the first time? If not, mark them for further review.*

## EXERCISE 16

A. *Select six words or phrases from the passages in this unit which you think other students might not be familiar with (preferably words that are on the word list in the Appendix.)*

B. *On a separate piece of paper, make an exercise like Exercise 15:*
   • *Write the sentences where you found the words and phrases on your list, leaving a blank in place of the word or phrase.*
   • *Write the missing words or phrases in a box below the sentences—but not in order.*

C. *Exchange exercises with another student and do your partner's exercise.*

D. *Look back at the text to check your answers.*

E. *With your partner, give the definitions for the words or phrases you selected for your exercises. Look up any you are not sure about.*

### Reflecting on Your Learning

1. Discuss these questions with a group of students.
   • Did you find it easier to make inferences in the fiction or nonfiction passages in this unit? Explain your answer.
   • Do you think you make more or fewer inferences when you are reading in your first language compared with English? Explain your answer.
   • How easy/difficult was it to predict the endings of the paragraphs? Do you think it would be easier in your first language?

2. Select useful vocabulary from this unit:
   • Look through the passages in this unit for more vocabulary that would be useful to learn. Write the words or phrases in your vocabulary notebook (with parts of speech, definitions and/ or synonyms, the sentences where you found them, and any helpful notes about usage).
   • Review the words in your notebook. Test yourself and then ask a classmate or friend to test you. Write the words you have trouble remembering on study cards. Review and test yourself until you know them well.

Paragraphs and longer passages in English usually focus on a single topic, which is generally stated near the beginning in a topic sentence. All the sentences relate directly or indirectly to that topic. They provide the supporting facts and ideas that help the reader understand the topic and the writer's idea about that topic.

In this unit, you will learn how to identify topics, as well as the supporting information in paragraphs and in longer passages. You will also learn how to recognize and restate the writer's ideas about the topic and how to follow the development of those ideas.

When reading the passages in these exercises for the first time, *do not stop to look up unfamiliar vocabulary.* Focus on what you do understand about the ideas and read through to the end. Skip over new words or try to guess the general meaning. Then go back and look up the words or phrases that you need for full comprehension. After you have completed the exercise, you may want to look up other words.

## Topics and Supporting Information in Paragraphs

The topic of a paragraph tells what it is about. The supporting facts and ideas give further information about the topic—describing, explaining, giving examples, or providing more details.

### EXAMPLE

A. *Read the topic and paragraph below. The supporting facts and ideas that describe or explain the topic have been underlined.*

Topic: _teenage workers in the U.S._

*SEF poverty*

With almost <u>six million workers</u>—a little over 4 percent of all the people employed—teenagers are a significant fraction of the work force in the United States. (Indeed), <u>most high school students work</u> for pay during their schooling, though their work is considered marginal since most 16-to-19-year olds still live with their parents and <u>do not have to support themselves.</u> They <u>work in order to put money in the bank for college, or, more often, to support lifestyle consumption</u>, that is, <u>to buy cell phones, cars, and so on</u>. Young people are found as <u>part-time workers in many occupations</u>, including secretarial jobs, retail sales, domestic services such as child care, and in industry or construction. However, they <u>are most heavily concentrated in the low-wage service sector</u>, above all in <u>fast-food restaurants.</u>

*SEF(3)*

**B.** *This diagram shows how the topic relates to the supporting facts and ideas in the paragraph in part A.*

| | | | |
|---|---|---|---|
| | **Topic:** <u>Teenage workers in the U.S.</u> | | |
| **Supporting facts and ideas** | **a.** How many teens work:<br>—6 million teenage workers<br>—most high school students work | **b.** Why they work:<br>—not to support themselves<br>—to put money in bank, to buy things | **c.** Where they work:<br>—part-time in many occupations<br>—most in low-wage service sector, above all fast food |

As you identify the topics in the following exercises, remember that the topic should not be too specific. It should be general enough to cover all the facts and ideas in the paragraph. At the same time, it should not be too general and should not refer to information or ideas that are not included in the paragraph. For example:

- *Teenage workers in the U.S.* is a good topic. It covers the ideas and information in the paragraph.
- *Teenage workers in fast-food restaurants* is too specific. Only one sentence in the paragraph mentions teenagers in fast-food restaurants.
- *Teenagers* is too general. It could include many different kinds of ideas about teenagers not mentioned in the paragraph.

**Notes:**

- Before underlining the supporting facts and ideas, read the whole passage to the end. Then use a pencil to underline so that you can change your underlining if your understanding of the passage changes as you read.

- Diagrams of other paragraphs may look different from the one above if they have a different number of supporting facts and ideas.

- Include only key words or phrases in your diagrams, not whole sentences.

## EXERCISE 1

**A.** *Read the paragraph. Then work with another student to write the topic and underline the supporting facts and ideas. Look up only the vocabulary you need for comprehension.*

Topic: <u>*Teenag job based on their race*</u>

The types of jobs held by teenage students are determined to some extent by their race and socioeconomic background. White students from advantaged socioeconomic origins are more likely to work in "good jobs" with fewer hours and higher status. They include clerical work or retail sales for females and industrial production or construction for males. These positions may not be prestigious in the general labor market, but for teenagers, they typically offer higher wages, more flexible work schedules, and possible opportunities for future employment as adults. Minority students (especially African-American) or those from disadvantaged backgrounds, whose parents have a low level of education, are more likely to work in the low-wage job sector, particularly fast-food restaurants, where they work longer hours, at a lower wage, and with limited career prospects.

**B.** *Work with your partner. Complete the diagram with the topic and supporting facts and ideas.*

Topic: _____

Supporting facts and ideas

a. *white students*
*good jobs*
*more opportunity*

b. *minority African American*
*low-wage*
*limited career prospects*

**C.** *Compare diagrams with another pair of students. Then choose useful vocabulary from the passage and add it to your vocabulary notebook.*

## EXERCISE 2

**A.** *Read each paragraph. Then work with another student to write the topic and underline the supporting facts and ideas.*

1. Topic: _____ *SOL lack of good schools*

*HEF*

One aspect of teenage employment that has been the focus of much debate is the impact of teenage work on education outcomes. This question is often framed in terms of a simple cause and effect—having a job is likely to lower grades and reduce the chances of finishing high school. However, research has shown that for students who work ten hours a week or less, working has no negative effect on school performance or completion. These students generally have higher grades to begin with and are more likely to come from families that are white and better off economically. On the other hand, students who work more than twenty hours per week are likely to see their academic performance decline. These also tend to be students who already have lower grades and who come from minority and less-advantaged backgrounds. Their schoolwork is likely to be further affected by the kind of job they do.

2. **Topic:** _____

Researchers have concluded the kind of job affects schooling as much as the number of hours students work. Teens who work traditional part-time jobs, such as lawn mowing or babysitting, can decide if and when they want to work, so they can adapt their jobs to the demands of school. However, teens who work in fast food are not usually allowed much flexibility in their work schedule, which may prevent them from becoming involved in extracurricular activities or sports. While traditional teen jobs are seen as temporary employment, jobs in retail and food service tend to be considered "real" jobs that could go on indefinitely. Students who work those jobs may lose sight of an alternative future—and a high school degree. Furthermore, the day-to-day routines of the workplace offer teenagers few opportunities to develop the self-esteem, skills, or autonomy necessary to leave the fast food sector and find other kinds of work.

3. **Topic:** _____

Certain characteristics are typical of the jobs available in the fast food employment sector. One is a high employee turnover rate—workers do not tend to stay in any job for long. This means that many establishments are continuously hiring, which may make these jobs more accessible to teenagers from disadvantaged backgrounds with no personal contacts. Another important aspect of jobs in this category is the fact that most positions are part-time so the companies will not have to pay benefits, such as pensions and health insurance. They are also low-wage, usually the minimum wage or only slightly higher. Furthermore, these jobs are not skilled in the technical sense, but like many of the positions that have traditionally been considered "women's jobs," they require high energy and good people skills, as well as a willingness to accept a part-time schedule and below-average pay.

**B.** *Write an overall topic for all three paragraphs:* _____

**C.** *Work with your partner. On a separate piece of paper, make a diagram for each paragraph to show the topic and the supporting facts and ideas.*

**D.** *Compare topics and diagrams with another pair of students. Then choose useful vocabulary from the passage and add it to your vocabulary notebook.*

## Ideas in Paragraphs

The main idea is the writer's idea about the topic. For any topic, writers may develop different ideas. As with the topic, the main idea should just fit the paragraph and should not be too general or specific. Unlike the topic, however, the main idea is best expressed in a complete sentence.

**Example:** Which of these main ideas best fits the example paragraph on page 146?

  a. Teenagers work so they can put money in the bank for college.
  b. Teenage workers are a significant part of the work force in the United States.
  c. There are many types of employment in the United States.

The best main idea is *b*. All the sentences in the paragraph discuss this idea.
Main idea *a* is too specific. Only one sentence mentions this idea.
Main idea *c* is too general. It refers to the employment of people of any age, but the paragraph discusses only teenagers.

| | | | |
|---|---|---|---|
| **Topic:** <u>Teenage workers in the U.S.</u> | | | |
| **Main idea:** <u>Teenage workers are a significant part of the work force in the U.S.</u> | | | |
| **Supporting facts and ideas** | **a.** How many teens work:<br>—6 million teenage workers<br>—most high school students work | **b.** Why they work:<br>—not to support themselves<br>—to put money in bank, to buy things | **c.** Where they work:<br>—part-time in many occupations<br>—most in low-wage service sector, above all fast food |

**Notes:**

- Paragraphs often, but not always, include a sentence that expresses the main idea. (This is sometimes called the topic sentence.) When there is one, it is likely to be near the beginning of the paragraph.

- When the main idea is not expressed in a topic sentence, you may need to use parts of several sentences to formulate it.

**A.** Re-read the paragraphs in Exercise 2 of this unit on pages 148–149. Then work with another student to write a main idea for each one.

**Main ideas:**

Paragraph 1 _____

Paragraph 2 _____

Paragraph 3 _____

**B.** Compare main ideas with another pair of students.

## EXERCISE 4

**A.** Read these paragraphs from the book Fast Food Nation by Eric Schlosser. Work with another student to write the main idea and underline the supporting facts and ideas for each paragraph. Then write the overall topic of the three paragraphs.

**Overall topic:** _Teengers are working in fast food resturant_

**1. Main idea:** _Teenagers ran fast food industry._

_____

Up and down Academy Boulevard, along South Nevada, Circle Drive, and Woodman Road, teenagers run the fast food restaurants of Colorado Springs. Fast food kitchens often seem like a scene from *Bugsy Malone,* a film in which all the actors are children pretending to be adults. No other industry in the United States has a workforce so dominated by adolescents. About two-thirds of the nation's fast food workers are under the age of twenty. Teenagers open the fast food outlets in the morning, close them at night, and keep them going at all hours in between. Even the managers and assistant managers are sometimes in their late teens. Unlike Olympic gymnastics—an activity in which teenagers consistently perform at a higher level than adults—there's nothing about the work in a fast food kitchen that requires young employees. Instead of relying on a small, stable, well-paid, and well-trained workforce, the fast food industry seeks out part-time, unskilled workers who are willing to accept low pay. Teenagers have been the perfect candidates for these jobs, not only because they are less expensive to hire than adults, but also because their youthful inexperience makes them easier to control.

**2. Main idea:** _____

_____

Although Richard and Mac McDonald introduced the division of labor to the restaurant business, it was a McDonald's executive named Fred Turner who created a production system of unusual thoroughness and attention to detail. In 1958, Turner put together an operations and training manual for the company that was seventy-five pages long, specifying how almost everything should be done. Hamburgers were always to be placed on the grill in six neat rows; French fries had to be exactly 0.28 inches thick. The McDonald's operations manual today has ten times the number of pages and weighs about four pounds. Known within the company as "the Bible," it contains precise instructions on how various appliances should be used, how each item on the menu should look, and how employees should greet customers. Operators who disobey these rules can lose their franchises. Cooking instructions are not only printed in the manual, they are often designed into the machines. A McDonald's kitchen is full of buzzers and flashing lights that tell employees what to do.

**3. Main idea:** _____

_____

The McDonald's Corporation insists that its franchise operators follow directives on food preparation, purchasing, store design, and countless other minute details. Company specifications cover everything from the size of the pickle slices to the circumference of the paper cups. When it comes to wage rates, however, the company is remarkably silent and laissez-faire. This policy allows operators to set their wages according to the local labor markets—and it absolves the McDonald's Corporation of any formal responsibility for roughly three-quarters of the company's workforce . . . In other mass production industries ruled by the assembly line, labor unions have gained workers higher wages, formal grievance procedures, and a voice in how the work is performed. The high turnover rates at fast food restaurants, the part-time nature of the jobs, and the marginal social status of the crew members have made it difficult to organize their workers. And the fast food chains have fought against unions with the same zeal they've displayed fighting hikes in the minimum wage.

**B.** *Work with your partner. Choose one of the paragraphs from Part A and make a diagram on a separate piece of paper to show the main idea and the supporting facts and ideas.*

**C.** *Compare diagrams with another pair of students. Then choose useful vocabulary to learn and add it to your vocabulary notebook.*

A. Read these paragraphs, also from **Fast Food Nation** by Eric Schlosser. **Work with another student to write the main idea and underline the supporting facts and ideas for each paragraph. Then write the overall topic of the three paragraphs.**

Overall topic: _____

1. Main idea: _____

_____

    Local fast food franchisees have little ability to reduce their fixed costs: their lease payments, franchise fees, and purchases from company-approved suppliers. Franchisees do, however, have some control over wage rates and try to keep them as low as possible. The labor structure of the fast food industry demands a steady supply of young and unskilled workers. But the immediate needs of the chains and the long-term needs of teenagers are fundamentally at odds.

2. Main idea: _____

_____

    At Cheyenne Mountain High School, set in the foothills, with a grand view of the city, few of the students work at fast food restaurants. Most of them are white and upper-middle class. During the summers, the boys often work as golf caddies or swimming pool lifeguards. The girls often work as babysitters at the Broadmoor. When Cheyenne Mountain kids work during the school year, they tend to find jobs at the mall, the girls employed at clothing stores like the Gap or the Limited, the boys at sporting goods stores like the Athlete's Foot. These jobs provide discounts on merchandise and a chance to visit with school friends who are out shopping. The pay of a job is often less important than its social status. Working as a hostess at an upscale chain restaurant like Carriba's, T.G.I. Friday's, or the Outback Steakhouse is considered a desirable job, even if it pays minimum wage. Working at a fast food restaurant is considered the bottom of the heap.

3. Main idea: _____

_____

    Jane Trogdon is head of the guidance department at Harrison High School in Colorado Springs. Harrison has the reputation of being a "rough" school, a "gang" school. The rap [reputation] is not entirely deserved; it may have stuck because Harrison is where many of the city's poorest teenagers go to school. Harrison is where you will find an abundance of fast food workers. About 60 percent of the students come from low-income families. In a town with a relatively low minority population, only 40 percent of the students at Harrison are white . . . Jane Trogdon has worked at the school since the day it opened in 1967. Over the past three decades, Trogdon has observed tremendous changes in the student body. Harrison was always the school on the wrong side of the tracks, but the kids today seem poorer than ever. It used to be, even in many low-income families, that the father worked and the mother stayed home to raise the children. Now it seems that no one is home and that both parents work just to make ends meet, often holding down two or three jobs. Many of the kids at Harrison are on their own from an early age. Parents increasingly turn to the school for help, asking teachers to supply discipline and direction. The teachers do their best, despite a lot of disrespect from students and the occasional threat of violence. Trogdon worries about the number of kids at Harrison who leave school in the afternoon and go straight to work, mainly at fast food restaurants. She also worries about the number of hours they're working.

4. **Main idea:** _____

_____

Although some students at Harrison work at fast food restaurants to help their families, most of the kids take jobs after school in order to have a car. In the suburban sprawl of Colorado Springs, having your own car seems like a necessity. Car payments and insurance easily come to $300 a month. As more and more kids work to get their own wheels, fewer participate in after-school sports and activities. They stay at their jobs late into the night, neglect their homework, and come to school exhausted. In Colorado, kids can drop out of school at the age of sixteen. Dropping out often seems tempting to sophomores who are working in the "real world," earning money, being eagerly recruited by local fast food chains and retail chains. Thirty years ago, businesses didn't pursue teenage workers so aggressively. Harrison usually has about 400 students in its freshman class. About half of them eventually graduate; perhaps fifty go to college.

5. **Main idea:** _____

_____

Trogdon's insights about teenagers and after-school jobs are supported by Protecting Youth at Work, a report on child labor published by the National Academy of Sciences in 1998. It concluded that the long hours many American teenagers now spend on the job pose a great risk to their future education and financial success. Numerous studies have found that kids who work up to twenty hours a week during the school year generally benefit from the experience, gaining an increased sense of personal responsibility and self-esteem. But kids who work more than that are far more likely to cut classes and drop out of high school. Teenage boys who work longer hours are much more likely to develop substance abuse problems and commit petty crimes. The negative effects of working too many hours are easy to explain: when kids go to work, they are neither at home nor at school. If the job is boring, overly regimented, or meaningless, it can create a lifelong aversion to work. All of these trends are most pronounced among poor and disadvantaged teenagers. While stressing the great benefits of work in moderation, the National Academy of Sciences report warned that short-term considerations are now limiting what millions of American kids can ever hope to achieve.

B. *Work with your partner. Choose two of the paragraphs from Part A. For each one, make a diagram on a separate piece of paper to show the main idea and the supporting facts and ideas.*

C. *Compare diagrams with another pair of students. Then choose useful vocabulary to learn and add it to your vocabulary notebook.*

## Main Ideas in Newspaper and Web Articles

The title of an article often includes the overall topic. The overall topic may also serve as the main idea for the first paragraph(s).

In newspapers and web articles, paragraphs are often quite short, sometimes no more than one sentence. A single paragraph may be too short to contain the writer's idea so you may need to read several paragraphs and think about them together in order to understand the ideas.

## EXERCISE 6

**A.** *Read the title and each group of paragraphs. Work with another student to write the main idea for each group.*

1. **Main idea:** _____

_____

### Western-style fast food linked to poorer health in Singapore, says U of M study

Western-style fast food has had a dramatic health impact on people living in Singapore, according to a new study from researchers at the University of Minnesota's School of Public Health. And, as you might guess, it hasn't been a good impact.

Singapore residents who ate Western-style fast food at least twice a week were found to be 27 percent more likely to develop type 2 diabetes and 56 percent more likely to die from heart disease than those who avoided fast food and stuck with their traditional foods. For people who ate Western-style fast food items four or more times each week, the heart disease risk increased by almost 80 percent. (There was no change in the diabetes risk.)

2. Main idea: _____

_____

### Too much fast food harms children's test scores

Pupils achieve lower scores in tests after eating takeaway meals such as burgers and chips more than three times a week, it is claimed.

The findings—in a study of more than 5,500 primary school children—even apply when parental income, race and pupils' weight is taken into account. Some children's scores in literacy and numeracy dropped by up to 16 per cent compared to the average, it was disclosed. The study provides some of the most conclusive evidence yet of a link between poor diet and academic ability.

**B.** *Compare main ideas with another pair of students.*

## EXERCISE 7

**A.** *Read the title of a news article and discuss it with another student. What do you think the article will be about?*

### Child labour: the tobacco industry's smoking gun by Kristin Palitza

**B.** *Work with another student. Read the article and group the paragraphs that have the same main idea. Show the groups with brackets, as in Exercise 6. (There are four groups.) Then compare work with another pair of students.*

At the height of the tobacco harvest season, Malawi's lush, flowing fields are filled with young children picking the big green-yellow leaves. Some can count their age on one hand.

One of them is five-year-old Olofala, who works every day with his parents in rural Kasungu, one of Malawi's key tobacco growing districts. When asked if he will go to school next year, he shrugs his shoulders.

One thing is clear to Olofala already: work comes first, education second. His sister, Ethel, 12, is only in year three. She attends school irregularly because she has to work, or because she is sick. "I cough," she says. "I have chest pains and headaches. Sometimes it feels like you don't have enough breath."

Such complaints are not uncommon. Many of Malawi's estimated 80,000 child tobacco workers suffer from a disease called green tobacco sickness, or nicotine poisoning. Symptoms include severe headaches, abdominal cramps, muscle weakness, breathing difficulties, diarrhoea and vomiting, high blood pressure and fluctuations in heart rate, according to the World Health Organisation.

Since the handling of the leaves is done largely without protective clothing, workers absorb up to 54 milligrams of dissolved nicotine daily through their skin, equal to the amount of 50 cigarettes, according to 2005 research by Prof Robert McKnight, of the College of Public Health at the University of Kentucky, Lexington. Farm owners routinely plead ignorance of the health implications. "I never heard about touching tobacco leaves being dangerous," says Fraston Mkwantha, who plants 15 hectares of tobacco in Kasungu district.

At the consumer end of the chain, smokers are constantly reminded of the associated health risks. Most are oblivious to the reality that, far from harming only themselves, their toxic habit is slowly killing the underage children involved in the production process.

Until the 1980s, much of the world's tobacco was grown in the US. Today, however, about 85% of worldwide production comes from the global south, where child labour is a major problem, according to a 2010 US Department of Labour report.

"In any developing country where tobacco is grown, you find child labour starting at the age of five," says Marty Otañez, a researcher at the University of California's tobacco control research and education centre.

Malawi, which has the highest number of child labourers in Africa, is a key offender. Health issues aside, children are also financially exploited. Olofala and Ethel often work 12-hour days, but neither earns a salary. They "help" their parents, who work on one of Kasungu's 22,000 registered tobacco farms and estates.

*Health HF*

At the heart of the problem is Malawi's poor economic situation. Parents involve their children in economic activities to provide food for the family.

Over the past decade, the country has become one of the five largest tobacco producers in the world, largely due to low tariffs on unmanufactured tobacco imports, cheap labour and lack of regulations. According to the UN's statistical division, more than 98% of Malawi's low-cost leaf is exported, with the EU and the US top destinations.

*Weak Laws LF*

*SEF(1)*

(Source: Kristin Palitza, "Child labour: the tobacco industry's smoking gun," guardian.co.uk, 09.56 BST Wednesday 14 September 2011)

**C.** *Work with your partner. For the paragraphs in each section, circle words and phrases connected to the main idea and underline the supporting facts and ideas. Write the main ideas on a separate piece of paper.*

**D.** *Compare work with another pair of students. Then add any useful vocabulary to your vocabulary notebook.*

# Following the Writer's Ideas

Understanding a passage often involves more than just identifying the topic and main idea. It also means following the writer's thinking from one idea to the next.

## Pronouns and Adjectives as Connectors

To avoid excessive repetition, writers often use pronouns or adjectives to replace words or ideas that have already been mentioned (and sometimes words or ideas that are mentioned later in the text).

Types of pronouns:

- Personal pronouns—*he, it, they, him, us,* etc.
- Possessive adjectives—*his, her, our, their,* etc.
- Demonstrative pronouns—*this, that, these, those*
- Demonstrative adjectives—*this book, that idea, these words,* etc.
- Relative pronouns—*which, who, that, whose,* etc.
- Other pronouns or adjectives—*one, another, each, most, none, the first, the last, such,* etc.

To follow the writer's thinking, you need to connect each pronoun to its referent—the word or idea it has replaced. Good readers do this automatically.

### Example:

Child labor is a pressing issue in the United States, but it remains hidden from public view. What little data are published, in any case, do not include underage workers like Dora and Elmo. But the reason for the lack of public scrutiny is simple: <u>those</u> involved often prefer to leave things as <u>they</u> are. Farmers argue that <u>their</u> crops must be harvested cheaply to compete with imports from overseas. The farm workers, who might prefer to keep <u>their</u> children in school and out of the fields, need <u>their</u> children's income.

| Pronouns | Referents |
|---|---|
| 1. it | child labor |
| 2. those | farmers and farm workers |
| 3. they | things (children working) |
| 4. their | farmers' crops |
| 5. their, their | farm workers' children |

**Note:** Some of the words in the list of pronouns on page 157 above can also function in different ways.

- *it*—often used as a subject of verbs such as *be, seem, look, happen, appear*. In this case, *it* does not replace a word or idea. ***Examples:*** *It's* snowing. *It* looks like he's won the elections.

- *that*—can also be a conjunction that introduces a clause. ***Examples:*** She was so happy *that* she cried. She promised *that* she'd be here.

## EXERCISE 8

**A.** *Work with another student. Reread this paragraph from Exercise 1. Write the underlined pronouns and their referents.*

The types of jobs held by teenage students are determined to some extent by race and socioeconomic background. White students from advantaged socioeconomic origins are more likely to work in "good jobs" with fewer hours and higher status. They include clerical work or retail sales for females and industrial production or construction for males. These positions may not be prestigious in the general labor market, but for teenagers, they typically offer higher wages, more flexible work schedules, and possible opportunities for future employment as adults. Minority students (especially African-Americans) or those from disadvantaged backgrounds, whose parents have a low level of education, are more likely to work in the low-wage job sector, particularly fast-food restaurants, where they work longer hours, at a lower wage and with limited career prospects.

| Pronouns | Referents |
|---|---|
| a. They | "good jobs" |
| b. These positions | work or retail for females / industrial production or construction for males |
| c. they | positions |
| d. those | another kind of minority students |
| e. whose | Minority students |
| f. they | Minority students |

**B.** *With your partner, underline the pronouns in the next paragraph and write the pronouns and their referents below.*

One aspect of teenage employment that has been the focus of much debate is the impact of teenage work on education outcomes. This question is often framed in terms of a simple cause and effect—having a job is likely to lower grades and reduce the chances of finishing high school. However, research has shown that for students who work ten hours a week or less, working has no negative effect on high school performance or completion. These students generally have higher grades to begin with and are more likely to come from families that are white and better off economically. On the other hand, students who work more than twenty hours per week are likely to see their academic performance decline. These also tend to be students who already have lower grades and who come from minority and less-advantaged backgrounds. Their schoolwork is likely to be further affected by the kind of job they do.

| Pronouns | Referents |
|---|---|
| 1. One aspect | the impact of teenage work |
| 2. This | the impact of teenage work on education outcomes |
| 3. who | students |
| 4. These | students |
| 5. who | students |
| 6. These | academic performance |
| 7. who | students |
| 8. who | students |
| 9. their | students schoolwork |

**C.** *Compare work with another pair of students.*

## Synonyms and Related Words as Connectors

Another way that writers avoid excessive repetition is by replacing words with:

- synonyms—words or phrases that have the same or similar meaning
- related words—words or phrases that have a similar but more specific or general meaning, or that have a related meaning in a particular context

**EXAMPLE**
..........

*In this paragraph, notice the underlined synonyms and related words the writer uses to replace the word* **teenagers***.*

With almost six million workers—a little over 4% of all the people employed—**teenagers** are a significant fraction of the work force in the United States. Indeed, most high school students work for pay during their schooling, though their work is considered marginal since most <u>16-to-19-year olds</u> still live with their parents and do not have to support themselves. They work in order to put money in the bank for college, or more often, to support lifestyle consumption, that is, to buy cell phones, cars and so on. <u>Young people</u> are found as <u>part-time workers</u> in many occupations, including secretarial jobs, retail sales, domestic services such as child care, and in industry or construction. However, they are most heavily concentrated in the low wage service sector, above all fast food restaurants.

**Synonyms:** high school students, 16-to-19-year olds, young people

**Related words:** six million workers, part-time workers

## EXERCISE 9

A.   *Work with another student. Read these passages from Eric Schlosser's* **Fast Food Nation**. *Underline the synonyms or related words for the bold word or phrase.*

1. **Local fast food franchisees** have a little ability to reduce their fixed costs: their lease payments, franchise fees, and purchases from company-approved suppliers. Franchisees do, however, have some control over wage rates and try to keep them as low as possible. The labor structure of the fast food industry demands a steady supply of young and unskilled workers. But the immediate needs of the chains and the long-term needs of teenagers are fundamentally at odds.

2. At Cheyenne Mountain High School, set in the foothills, with a grand view of the city, few of the **students** work at fast food restaurants. Most of them are white and upper-middle class. During the summers, the boys often work as golf caddies or swimming pool lifeguards. The girls often work as babysitters at the Broadmoor. When Cheyenne Mountain kids work during the school year, they tend to find jobs at the mall, the girls employed at clothing stores like the Gap or the Limited, the boys at sporting goods stores like the Athlete's Foot.

3. Up and down Academy Boulevard, along South Nevada, Circle Drive, and Woodman Road, **teenagers** run the fast food restaurants of Colorado Springs. Fast food kitchens often seem like a scene from *Bugsy Malone*, a film in which all the actors are children pretending to be adults. No other industry in the United States has a workforce so dominated by adolescents. About two-thirds of the nation's fast food workers are under the age of twenty.

B.   *Compare work with another pair of students.*

**A.** *Work with another student. Underline the synonyms or related words for the bold word or phrase.*

1. The types of **jobs** held by teenage students are determined to some extent by their race and socioeconomic background. White students from advantaged socioeconomic origins are more likely to work in "good jobs" with fewer hours and higher status. These include clerical work or retail sales for females and industrial production or construction for males. These positions may not be prestigious in the general labor market, but for teenagers, they typically offer higher wages, more flexible work schedules, and possible opportunities for future employment as adults. Minority students (especially African-Americans) or those from disadvantaged backgrounds, whose parents have a low level of education, are more likely to work in the low-wage job sector, including fast-food restaurants, where they work longer hours, at a lower wage, and with limited career prospects.

2. One aspect of teenage employment that has been the focus of much debate is the impact of teenage work on **education** outcomes. The question is often framed in terms of a simple cause and effect—working at a job is likely to lower grades and reduce the chances of finishing high school. However, research has shown that for students, who work ten hours a week or less, working has no negative effect on school performance or completion. These students generally have higher grades to begin with and are more likely to come from families that are white and better off economically. On the other hand, students who work more than twenty hours per week are likely to see their academic performance decline. These also tend to be students who already have lower grades and who come from minority and less-advantaged backgrounds. Their schoolwork is likely to be further affected by the kind of job they do.

3. Certain characteristics are typical of the jobs available in the **fast-food employment sector**. One is a high employee turnover rate—workers do not tend to stay in any job for long. This means that many establishments are continuously hiring, which may make these jobs more accessible to teenagers from disadvantaged backgrounds with no personal contacts. Another important aspect of jobs in this category is the fact that most positions are part-time so the companies will not have to pay benefits, such as pensions and health insurance. They are also low-wage, usually the minimum wage or only slightly higher. Furthermore, these jobs are not skilled in the technical sense, but like many of the positions that have traditionally been considered "women's jobs," they require high energy and good people skills, as well as a willingness to accept a part-time schedule and below-average pay.

**B.** *Compare work with another student.*

# Focus on Vocabulary

## EXERCISE 11

A. **Read these sentences from the passage in Exercise 4. For each underlined word or phrase, choose the one that is closest in meaning.**

1. Teenagers open the fast food <u>outlets</u> in the morning, close them at night, and keep them going at all hours in between.

   a. places          b. doors          c. kitchens

2. Unlike Olympic gymnastics—an activity in which teenagers <u>consistently</u> perform at a higher level than adults—there's nothing about the work in a fast food kitchen that requires young employees.

   a. always          b. occasionally          c. normally

3. Instead of <u>relying on</u> a small, stable, well-paid, and well-trained workforce, the fast food industry seeks out part-time, unskilled workers who are willing to accept low pay.

   a. focusing on          b. depending on          c. moving on

4. Instead of relying on a small, stable, well-paid, and well-trained workforce, the fast food industry <u>seeks out</u> part-time, unskilled workers who are willing to accept low pay.

   a. sorts out          b. sets up          c. looks for

5. Although Richard and Mac McDonald introduced the division of labor to the restaurant business, it was a McDonald's executive named Fred Turner who created a production system of unusual <u>thoroughness</u> and attention to detail.

   a. precision          b. efficiency          c. flexibility

6. In 1958, Turner put together an operations and training manual for the company that was seventy-five pages long, <u>specifying</u> how almost everything should be done.

   a. asking          b. changing          c. explaining

7. The McDonald's Corporation insists that its franchise operators follow directives on food preparation, purchasing, store design, and <u>countless</u> other minute details.

   a. a few          b. many          c. some

8. The high turnover rates at fast food restaurants, the part-time nature of the jobs, and the <u>marginal</u> social status of the crew members have made it difficult to organize their workers.

   a. powerful          b. low                    c. special

**B.** *Compare answers with another student. Check your answers in the dictionary. Then read through the passage on page 151 again. Can you remember the words you looked up the first time? If not, mark them for further review.*

## EXERCISE 12

**A.** *Read these sentences from the passage in Exercise 5. Write a word from the box in each blank. You may need to change the form of the word.*

> abundance    bottom of the heap    insights        merchandise    pose
> at odds       eagerly              make ends meet   overly         status

1. But the immediate needs of the chains and the long-term needs of teenagers are fundamentally _____.

2. These jobs provide discounts on _____ and a chance to visit with school friends who are out shopping.

3. The pay of a job is often less important than its social _____.

4. Working at a fast food restaurant is considered the _____.

5. Harrison is where you will find an _____ of fast food workers.

6. Now it seems that no one is home and that both parents work just to _____, often holding down two or three jobs.

7. Dropping out often seems tempting to sophomores who are working in the "real world," earning money, being _____ recruited by local fast food chains and retail chains.

8. Trogdon's _____ about teenagers and after-school jobs are supported by *Protecting Youth at Work*, a report on child labor published by the National Academy of Sciences in 1998.

9. It concluded that the long hours many American teenagers now spend on the job _____ a great risk to their future education and financial success.

10. If the job is boring, _____ regimented, or meaningless, it can create a lifelong aversion to work.

**B.** *Compare answers with another student. Check your answers in the dictionary. Then read through the passage on page xxx again. Can you remember the words you looked up the first time? If not, mark them for further review.*

## EXERCISE 13

**A.** *Select six words or phrases from the passages in this unit that you think other students might not be familiar with (preferably words that are on the word list in the Appendix).*

**B.** *On a separate piece of paper, make an exercise like Exercise 12:*
- *Write the sentences where you found the words and phrases on your list, leaving a blank in place of the word or phrase.*
- *Write the missing words or phrases in a box below the sentences—but not in order.*

**C.** *Exchange exercises with another student and do your partner's exercise.*

**D.** *Look back at the text to check your answers.*

**E.** *With your partner, give the definitions for the words or phrases you selected for your exercises. Look up any you are unsure about.*

### Reflecting on Your Learning

**1.** Discuss these questions with a group of students:
- Think about the way you write a paragraph or short passage in your first language. Do you organize it around a topic, as in English? Is the main idea stated in the passage?
- If a paragraph in your first language is different compared with a paragraph in English, how is it different?

**2.** Select useful vocabulary from this unit:
- Look through the passages in this unit for more vocabulary that would be useful to learn. Write the words or phrases in your vocabulary notebook (with parts of speech, definitions and/or synonyms, the sentences where you found them, and any helpful notes about usage).
- Review the words in your notebook. Test yourself and then ask a classmate or friend to test you. Write the words you have trouble remembering on study cards. Review and test yourself until you know them well.

# Identifying Patterns

To help us make sense of our lives, we create patterns and follow them: holidays and religious rites, calendars and schedules, programs and courses, rules of the road, and so on.

Writers also use patterns to organize and present ideas. As a reader, you can use these patterns to help you understand and follow the ideas. You probably do this automatically in your first language. However, the patterns used in different languages may be different. To improve you reading ability in English, you need to be familiar with the most common patterns used in English texts.

| Patterns Commonly Used in English Texts | | |
|---|---|---|
| Listing | Comparison-Contrast | Problem-Solution |
| Sequence | Cause-Effect | Definition |

With each pattern presented in this unit, there is also a list of the common *signal words and phrases* that writers use to help readers recognize the pattern and identify the important ideas. Writers do not always use those signals however. They may use other signals or none at all.

A paragraph usually has one main pattern, though it may include aspects of other patterns. In longer passages, different paragraphs or sections may have different patterns.

**Notes:**

- Do not stop to look up unfamiliar vocabulary when you first read a passage. Skip over it or try to guess the general meaning. When you re-read, look up only the words or phrases that are necessary for comprehension.

- In this unit, the main idea and supporting facts and ideas are shown in outline form, an alternative to the diagrams in Unit 3. After you have finished this unit, you can decide which method helps you better understand the ideas and information.

## The Listing Pattern

In this pattern, the main idea of the paragraph or passage includes a generalization and is followed by a list of facts or ideas. These are the supporting facts and ideas. The paragraph or passage usually gives some explanation or examples for each fact or idea listed.

**Main idea:**

*many, several, three, a lot of, lots of, some, a few, a number of, various, all kinds of*

**Supporting facts and ideas:**

*first, third, one, other, another, in addition, last, finally, and, also, too, yet another, for example*

***EXAMPLE:***

A.  *This paragraph follows the listing pattern. The main idea is underlined and marked with an asterisk (\*). The signal words and phrases are circled. Look at the student's outline below and find the supporting facts or ideas in the paragraph. Underline each one and mark the letter from the outline (a, b, c) beside it in the margin.*

## CAFOs

With the advent of industrial agriculture, a new method of raising livestock—in particular, cattle, pigs, and chickens—has come to dominate farming in the United States. <u>Known as</u>

&#42; <u>factory farms, or concentrated animal feeding operations (CAFOs), the new method has certain characteristics.</u> (One) is that the animals are bred and <u>selected to produce the maximum</u>    a
<u>quantity of meat</u>. Indeed, the chickens bred for these farms are so breast-heavy that some are unable to stand, and others suffer broken legs. On a CAFO, the animals <u>never leave the</u>    b
<u>buildings</u> where they are raised, never even see daylight, except when it is time for butchering.
(Furthermore), in the huge warehouses or pens where they live, the animals are <u>packed by the</u>    c
<u>thousands</u> with barely enough space for each one to lie down. They are <u>not fed their natural</u>    d
<u>diet</u>, but energy-rich food, such as grain and even some animal protein, which will contribute to rapid growth so they can be butchered sooner. (Finally), because they are confined in close quarters and severely stressed, these animals are highly susceptible to disease, so they are routinely <u>given antibiotics</u> as a preventive measure. Indeed, nearly three-quarters of all    e
antibiotics consumed in the United States are used in CAFOs.

---

**Main idea:** The new method of raising livestock on factory farms or CAFOs has certain
inhumane characteristics.

**Supporting facts/ideas**

    a. Animals bred to produce maximum quantity of meat

    b. Animals never leave the buildings

    c. Animals packed by thousands with little space

    d. Animals not fed their natural diet

    e. Animals given antibiotics

---

B.  *Compare work with another student. Add any useful vocabulary to your notebook.*

**A.** *Preview and read this web article. Then work with another student to find and underline the overall idea, the main ideas, and the supporting facts/ideas. Mark the main ideas with an asterisk. Look up only the vocabulary that is necessary for comprehension.*

### Smart Pasture Operations

One positive development in U.S. agriculture is the growing movement toward raising beef and dairy cattle, as well as pigs, chickens, and turkeys in what are called *smart pasture operations,* or SPOs. In a number of crucial ways, these farms take advantage of our understanding of natural systems to avoid the environmental damage and the health hazards of the industrial approach.

First of all, SPOs may be large operations, but they are usually not on the same scale as CAFOS, so the animals get better treatment. They are less crowded and spend extensive time outdoors, which keeps them healthier and greatly reduces the need for antibiotics or other medicines. The animals on SPOs are also not given conventional grain feeds, but live on the diet that is natural for the animals—grasses for cattle and insects for poultry. Because of this diet, animals on SPOs, particularly cattle, suffer little from digestive diseases and emit less methane [a global warming gas] than cattle that eat a rich grain diet.

Furthermore, the animals on SPOs are bred for a variety of traits, not just for the maximum quantity of meat in the shortest period of time. Valued traits include not only high quality meat and resistance to disease, but also better temperament, since the animals need to be moved periodically. Because of this (and the fact that they are less crowded), aggressive or violent behavior is much less common among these animals than on conventional factory farms.

Yet another distinctive aspect of SPOs is that there are no waste lagoons for the manure. These can cause all sorts of problems—from unpleasant and unhealthy odors to the contamination of drinking water and mass die-offs of fish in rivers and lakes. Instead, the manure produced by the animals at pasture is spread evenly around the fields, where it becomes a natural fertilizer and improves the quality of the grass.

**B.** *Work with your partner. Circle the listing signal words or phrases in the passage. On a separate piece of paper, write the overall idea and make an outline of the passage that shows the listing pattern. Follow the model below.*

| |
|---|
| *Smart Pasture Operations* |
|    *Overall idea: . . .* |
|       *1. Main idea: . . .* |
|          *a. Supporting fact/idea: . . .* |
|          *b. Supporting fact/idea: . . .* |
|          *c. Supporting fact/idea: . . .* |
|       *2. Main idea: . . .* |
|          *Supporting facts/ideas a, b, c, etc.: . . .* |

**C.** *Compare work with another pair of students. Add any useful vocabulary to your notebook.*

## The Sequence Pattern

In the sequence pattern, the main idea can describe **a series of events**, or it may list the **steps in a process**.

**Common Signal Words and Phrases for Sequence Pattern**

**Main idea / supporting facts and ideas for a series of events:**

- Words or phrases that refer to a date or period in time:
  *1955, during World War II, was born, history, began, yesterday, last week, a century ago, in later years, early in the morning, two o'clock, for an hour*

- Words or phrases that refer to a person's age or stage of life:
  *throughout his career, at the age of six*

**Main idea / supporting facts and ideas for a process:**

- Words or phrases that refer to a process—a description of, or instructions for, how something happens:
  *how to, make, prepare, process, development*

- Phrases that tell about the order of instructions or steps in a process:
  *first, second, before, soon, while, now, at last, finally, when, at first, then, last, after, during, until, no longer, prior to, following*

**PRACTICE 1:** A Series of Events

**A.** *This paragraph uses the sequence pattern to describe a series of events. The main idea is underlined and marked with an asterisk (\*). The signal words and phrases are circled. Look at the example outline below and find the supporting facts or ideas in the paragraph. Underline each one and mark the letter from the outline (a, b, c) beside it in the margin.*

### The Development of DDT-resistance in Mosquitoes

✱ In 1955, the World Health Organization (WHO) started a campaign to eliminate the mosquitoes that transmit malaria. This disease kills an estimated three million people each year in the world's tropical regions, particularly in southern Africa, southern Asia, and parts of South America. Scientists believed elimination was possible thanks to DDT, a chemical pesticide that had been discovered and used during World War II with spectacular effect; it apparently killed off all the insects when sprayed on the ground and plants of their habitat. In the early years of the WHO campaign, the results were promising. The mosquito had rapidly been eliminated from some of the areas of its usual geographic range. (Very soon), however, scientists also began to find evidence of resistance to the pesticide in the mosquitoes it was supposed to kill. DDT-resistant mosquitoes were discovered in Pakistan (in 1965), just five short years after DDT was introduced into the region. (By 1969), WHO had abandoned its DDT spraying programs, shifting its efforts to other methods for preventing and controlling the disease.

| Main idea: In the 50s and 60s, WHO used DDT to try to eliminate the mosquitoes that |
|---|
|       transmit malaria. |
| Supporting facts/ideas |
|     a. DDT discovered, used during World War II |
|     b. In early years, results promising, mosquitoes eliminated from some areas |
|     c. Very soon, scientists find evidence of resistance to DDT |
|     d. In 1965, five years after DDT introduced, DDT-resistant mosquitoes in Pakistan |
|     e. By 1969, WHO abandoned DDT spraying programs |

**B.** *Compare work with another student. Add any useful vocabulary to your notebook.*

**PRACTICE 2:** Steps in a Process

**A.** *This paragraph uses the sequence pattern to describe steps in a process. The main idea is underlined and marked with an asterisk (*). The signal words and phrases are circled. Read the paragraph and underline the supporting facts or ideas. Letter them (a, b, c) in the margin. Then write an outline to show the main idea and supporting ideas.*

**Evolution in Action**

✱ The (development) of insects' resistance to pesticide following its massive use in conventional agriculture demonstrates the process of evolution. (When) fields are sprayed with pesticide, most of the pests die. However, there are always a few that survive thanks to a slight difference in their genes. These survivors (then) reproduce and some of their offspring inherit the gene for pesticide resistance. (Over time), with continued spraying, the percentage of resistant insects increases, (until eventually) most of the population is resistant and the pesticide (no longer) protects the crop. Since insects breed quickly, (the time frame is quite short, a matter of a few years) rather than centuries. For example, the boll weevil, a pest found in cotton fields, produces a new generation every 21 days and as many as six generations in one growing season.

**B.** *Compare outlines with another student. Add any useful vocabulary from the passage to your notebook.*

**Note:** Writers do not always use a signal word or phrase for every step or event in a sequence. You may need to infer from the description that the writer has moved on to the next step.

## EXERCISE 2

A.  *Preview and read this web article. Then work with another student to find and underline the overall idea, the main ideas, and the supporting facts or ideas. Mark the main idea(s) with an asterisk. Look up only the vocabulary that is necessary for comprehension.*

### Integrated Pest Management

Integrated Pest Management (IPM) is an environmentally sensitive approach to pest management in farming. It uses a combination of pest control methods to manage pest damage by the most economical means, and with the least possible hazard to people, property, and the environment. IPM takes advantage of all appropriate pest control options, including the judicious use of pesticides. In practicing IPM, farmers follow a four-part approach.

Prior to undertaking any method of pest control, the farmer must have accurate knowledge of pests and a full understanding of their life cycles and their interaction with the environment. Not all insects, weeds, and other living organisms require control. Many organisms are innocuous, and some are even beneficial. With accurate monitoring and identification, pesticides will not be used unnecessarily or inappropriately.

As a first line of pest control, farmers in IPM programs work to manage the crop in a way that prevents pests from becoming a threat. Indeed, prevention is an essential aspect of the program. This means using methods that reduce the likelihood of infestation, such as rotating between different crops and selecting pest-resistant varieties. These methods can be very effective and cost-efficient, and they do not harm people or the environment.

An essential next step is to set a threshold for pest populations. Sighting a single pest does not always mean that pest control is needed. It is critical to establish the level at which pests will become an economic threat to the farmer and then follow up with constant monitoring and accurate identification of pests. Action should be taken only when populations reach the threshold.

Once it is clear that pest control is required, and preventive methods are no longer effective or available, the farmer must evaluate the situation and select the method of pest control that will be most effective and at the same time, least harmful for people and the environment. For example, IPM experts recommend the use of pheromones to disrupt pest mating, or mechanical control, such as trapping or weeding.

If further monitoring indicates that these controls are not working, then additional pest control methods may be employed, such as targeted spraying of specific pesticides. Widespread spraying of non-specific pesticides is only used as a last resort.

B.  *Work with your partner. Circle the sequence signal words and phrases in the passage. On a separate piece of paper, write the overall idea and make an outline of the passage that shows the sequence pattern.*

C.  *Compare work with another pair of students. Add any useful vocabulary to your notebook.*

# The Comparison-Contrast Pattern

In the comparison-contrast pattern, the main idea presents two or more things, people, or ideas, and tells how they are similar, different, or both. The paragraph or passage then gives various examples of the ways in which they are similar or different.

> **Common Signal Words and Phrases for the Comparison-Contrast Pattern**
>
> **The main idea:**
>
> - The main idea sentence usually introduces the two items that will be compared.
> - Any of the signal words below may be included with the main idea.
>
> **Supporting facts and ideas:**
>
> - Words that show similarity: *alike, like, similar, similarly, same, also, both, too, in the same way, in common*
> - Words that show difference or contrast: *different, unlike, but, however, although, while, whereas, on the other hand, in contrast, rather, instead*
> - Comparatives: *more (than), less (than), cheaper, more expensive, earlier than*

## PRACTICE

**A.** *This paragraph follows the comparison-contrast pattern. The main idea is underlined and marked with an asterisk (\*). The signal words and phrases are circled. Read the paragraph and underline the supporting facts or ideas. Letter each one (a, b, c) in the margin.*

### Conventional vs. Organic

\* In both conventional and organic agriculture, farmers are dependent on factors beyond their control, such as the weather and the global market. They also both aim to produce quality foods that will meet consumer demand. Beyond that, however, the differences are profound and go far beyond the basic fact that conventional farmers use large quantities of chemical pesticides and fertilizers, while organic farmers do not. In conventional agriculture, farms tend to be very large with vast fields planted in single crops. This makes planting and harvesting more efficient than on the smaller fields of organic farms. However, it increases the risk of damage or devastating crop failure due to viral disease, fungal pathogens, or insect pests that can spread quickly from plant to plant. Organic farmers, on the other hand, usually plant a number of different crops on smaller fields, sometimes with more than one crop in one field. This not only reduces the risk of crop failure but also provides a better habitat for wildlife, promoting greater biodiversity. Furthermore, whereas conventional farming tends to degrade soil quality, organic farming methods maintain and even improve soil quality over time.

**Main idea:** Though some factors and aims are similar, there are <u>fundamental differences</u> <u>between</u> conventional and organic agriculture.

| Conventional agriculture | Organic agriculture |
|---|---|

Similarities:

a. Depend on weather and markets

b. Aim to produce quality foods that meet demands

Differences:

| Conventional agriculture | Organic agriculture |
|---|---|
| a. Use of pesticides and fertilizers | a. No pesticides or fertilizers |
| b. Large farms, vast fields, single crops | b. Smaller fields with a number of different crops |
| c. Planting and harvesting more efficient | c. Less efficient |
| d. Increased risk of damage or failure | d. Reduces the risk of crop failure |
| e. Degrades soil quality | e. Promotes greater biodiversity |
| | f. Improves soil quality |

**B.**   *Compare work with another student. Add any useful vocabulary to your notebook.*

**Notes:**

- Along with comparison signal words and phrases, writers may also include listing or sequence signal words.

  **Examples :** . . . but <u>also</u> provides a better habitat for wildlife . . .
  <u>Furthermore</u>, whereas conventional farming tends to degrade soil quality . . .

- An outline for a comparison paragraph or passage should clearly show the items being compared. It is helpful to make two columns or boxes, as in the example outline. If there are also similarities, they can be listed in the middle.

**A.** *Preview and read this passage from an environmental science textbook. Work with another student to find and underline the overall idea, the main ideas, and the supporting facts or ideas. Mark the main idea(s) with an asterisk.*

### Genetic engineering is like, and unlike, traditional breeding

The genetic alteration of plants and animals by people is nothing new; through artificial selection, we have influenced the genetic makeup of our livestock and crop plants for thousands of years . . . Our ancestors altered the gene pools of our domesticated plants and animals through selective [traditional] breeding by preferentially mating individuals with favored traits so that offspring would inherit those traits. Early farmers selected plants and animals that grew faster, were more resistant to disease and drought, and produced large amounts of fruit, grain, or meat.

Proponents of genetically modified (GM) crops often stress this continuity with our past and say today's GM food will be just as safe as selectively bred food. Dan Glickman, head of the USDA from 1995 to 2001, remarked:

"Biotechnology's been around almost since the beginning of time. It's cavemen saving seeds of a high-yielding plant. It's Gregor Mendel, the father of genetics, cross-pollinating his garden peas. It's a diabetic's insulin, and the enzymes in your yogurt . . . Without exception, the biotech products on our shelves have proven safe."

However, as critics are quick to point out, the techniques geneticists use to create GM organisms differ from traditional selective breeding in several ways. For one, selective breeding mixes genes from individuals of the same or similar species, whereas scientists . . . routinely mix genes of organisms as different as viruses and crops, or spiders and goats. For another, selective breeding deals with whole organisms living in the field, whereas genetic engineering works with genetic material in the lab. Third, traditional breeding selects from combinations of genes that come together on their own, whereas genetic engineering creates the novel combinations directly. Thus, traditional breeding changes organisms through the process of selections, whereas genetic engineering is more akin to the process of mutation.

(Source: by Jay Withgott and Scott Brennan, Benjamin Cummings,
*Environment: The Science Behind the Stories*, 4th ed., 2001)

**B.** *Work with your partner. Circle the comparison signal words or phrases in the passage. On a separate piece of paper, write the overall idea and make an outline of the passage that shows the comparison/ contrast pattern.*

**C.** *Compare work with another pair of students. Add any useful vocabulary to your notebook.*

---

### Reflecting on the Issues

*Discuss these questions with a small group of students:*

**1.** Are organic foods available in your country?

**2.** If so, do you (or does your family) buy them? Why?

**3.** If you choose not to buy them, what are your reasons?

**4.** Do you think governments should invest in the development of organic farming?

# The Cause-Effect Pattern

In this pattern, the main idea states that something causes something else—or is caused by something else. The paragraph or passage explains and/or gives examples of the causes and/or the effects. Either the cause or the effect may come first in the sentence.

**Examples:**

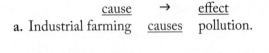

a. Industrial farming causes pollution.

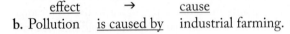

b. Pollution is caused by industrial farming.

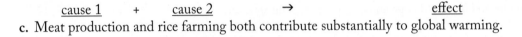

c. Meat production and rice farming both contribute substantially to global warming.

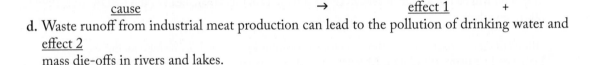

d. Waste runoff from industrial meat production can lead to the pollution of drinking water and
effect 2
mass die-offs in rivers and lakes.

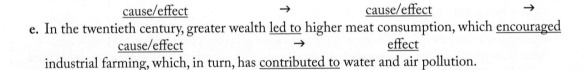

e. In the twentieth century, greater wealth led to higher meat consumption, which encouraged
cause/effect → effect
industrial farming, which, in turn, has contributed to water and air pollution.

---

### Common Signal Words and Phrases for Cause-Effect Pattern

**Main idea:**

Any of the signal words below may be included in the main idea sentence.

**Supporting facts and ideas:**

- When the cause comes first: *so, help, stop, start, become, create, make, produce, change, damage, affect, influence, increase, bring about, contribute to, result in, reason for, have an effect on, (be) a factor, cause, make, lead to, encourage, as a result, the cause of, give rise to*

- When the effect comes first: *because, because of, be due to, be caused by, be the reason for, be the effect of, be made by, be the consequence of, be damaged by, result from, follow*

**PRACTICE 1:** Several Causes with Effects

A. *This paragraph describes several causes with different effects. The main idea is underlined and marked with an asterisk (\*). The signal words and phrases are circled. Read the paragraph and underline the supporting facts or ideas. Letter each one (a, b, c) in the margin.*

## Biodiversity and Industrial Agriculture

\* Modern industrial agriculture tends to reduce biodiversity in aquatic and terrestrial ecosystems. The runoff of nutrients from fertilizer and manure can cause eutrophication (lack of oxygen) in bodies of water like rivers and streams, resulting in mass die-offs of fish and other organisms. Pesticides in rainwater runoff have been implicated in the reduction of both terrestrial and aquatic species in the wider landscape. A well-known example of this was the near elimination of a number of U.S. bird species during the second half of the twentieth century, due to the use of the insecticide DDT. Another major cause of declining farmland biodiversity was the simplification of the agricultural landscape following the adoption of modern single-crop farming. In previous centuries, farmland included diverse mixes of grazing land, crop land, orchards, wetlands, and managed forests, which could support a wide array of plant and animal species. Most industrial farms today, however, plant so as to maximize the harvestable land and minimize labor costs, which has led to uniform ecosystems and reduced biodiversity.

| Main idea: Industrial agriculture tends to <u>reduce</u> biodiversity in aquatic and terrestrial ecosystems. | | |
| --- | --- | --- |
| **Causes** | | **Effects** |
| a. Nutrient runoff from fertilizer and manure | → | Die-offs of fish |
| b. Pesticide runoff<br>    Example: Use of DDT | → | Species reduction<br>    near elimination of bird species |
| c. Single crop farming | → | Simplification of landscape<br>uniformity of ecosystems<br>declining biodiversity |

B. *Compare work with another student. Add any useful vocabulary to your notebook.*

**PRACTICE 2:** A Cause-Effect Chain

**A.** *This paragraph describes a chain of causes and effects. The main idea is underlined and marked with an asterisk (\*). The signal words and phrases are circled. Read the paragraph and underline the supporting facts or ideas. Letter each one (a, b, c) in the margin.*

## Agrobiodiversity

Agrobiodiversity refers to biodiversity among planned agricultural crops or livestock, such as the genetic diversity of wheat varieties or cattle breeds. Agrobiodiversity is (the result of) thousands of years of human intervention in selectively breeding traits in animals and crops for particular agricultural advantages. A famous example of the diversity that can exist within one crop species is found among the potatoes grown in the Andes of South America, where potatoes originated and some 4,000 known varieties exist. This abundance of diversity is (the result of) farmers artificially selecting traits over generations for specific purposes, like resistance to disease, tolerance to high altitudes, or poor soil, etc. This diversity is important for food security. In the event that a particular crop variety fails (due to drought), flooding or a disease, another variety might survive. In stark contrast to this model of agrobiodiversity, the Irish Potato Famine of the 1840s was (the result of) a fungus that completely destroyed the Irish potato crop (because) only a few varieties of potatoes had been imported from the Andes to Europe, none of which were resistant to the disease. (Because of) a lack of crop diversity and overreliance on one crop to feed many of its population, Ireland experienced widespread famine and death.

(Source: http://www.sustainabletable.org/home.php)

**Main idea:** Selective breeding <u>has created</u> agrobiodiversity, which <u>leads to</u> food security.

| | |
|---|---|
| **Cause** | |
| a. Farmers selected traits over generations | |
| Example of diversity: 4,000 varieties of potatoes in South America | |
| **Effect/Cause** | |
| b. Agricultural biodiversity | |
| **Effect** | |
| c. Food security | |
| Example of lack of security: Irish Potato Famine, when entire potato crop was destroyed by disease, causing famine and death | |

**B.** *Compare work with another student. Add any useful vocabulary to your notebook.*

**Notes:**

- Writers often use *may* or *can* with a verb when the cause or effect is possible but not certain.

  **Example:** Industrial agriculture *can reduce* biodiversity.

- In cause and effect sentences, writers often use the passive voice.

  **Example:** This diversity *is the result of* farmers artificially selecting traits.

- Listing or sequence signal words or phrases may also be included in a cause-effect paragraph.

  **Example:** *Another effect of* a poor diet may be weight gain or obesity.

## EXERCISE 4

**A.** *Preview and read this web article. Then work with another student to find and underline the overall idea, the main ideas, and the supporting facts or ideas.*

### Study Blames Pesticides for Bumblebee Decline

Remember bumblebees? We may soon be exchanging fond memories of those big fuzzy, buzzing bees that bumbled around from flower to flower in our gardens. Their decline has been dramatic in North America and Europe: two species are already extinct in the U.S., and another has nearly disappeared from the U.K.

Though various causes have been cited, including disease and habitat destruction, a new study published in *Nature* points to pesticide exposure as a major factor, particularly the commonly used pesticides neonicotinoid and pyrethroid.

Unlike previous studies which tested the reactions of bees to a single pesticide at high levels over 96 hours, this study recreated conditions more similar to those found in the field by subjecting the bees to low-level exposure to both pesticides for a period of four weeks. Bumblebees are known to travel considerable distances when foraging for food, and studies have proven that pesticides remain present at low levels in the environment long after initial application.

The findings showed that long term low-level exposure noticeably affected the bumblebees' ability to find food and return safely to their colonies, increasing the likelihood of a colony failing.

Neonicotinoid and pyrethroid are widely used for crops such as corn, soy, wheat, cotton, sorghum, and peanuts, during the growing cycle and also to treat seeds before planting. According to research by the Pesticide Action Network, at least 142 million acres of U.S. farmland were planted in neonicotinoid-treated seeds in 2012. As little as 2 percent of the pesticides applied to the seeds actually ends up in the plants; little is known about the environmental impact of the other 98 percent.

Scientists are concerned about the recent steep decline in both cultivated and wild bee populations because of the essential role these and other pollinators play in food production. An estimated one-third of all plant-based foods eaten by humans (including meat) rely on honey bees or wild bees and the disappearance of these pollinators could seriously affect global food production.

Governments in several European countries, including France, Italy, Germany and Slovenia, are debating measures to suspend the use of neonicotinoid until researchers can build a more solid case for or against their safety, but officials in the U.S. and U.K. seem reluctant to challenge agrochemical giants such as Bayer and Syngenta.

**B.** *Work with your partner. Circle the cause-effect signal words or phrases in the passage. On a separate piece of paper, write the overall idea and make an outline for the passage that shows the cause-effect pattern.*

**C.** *Compare work with another pair of students. Add any useful vocabulary to your notebook.*

---

### Reflecting on the Issues

*Discuss these questions with a small group of students:*

1. What do you know about the effects of pesticides in your country?

2. Have there been any declines in the populations of bees or other wildlife in your country (such as birds and bats)?

3. Do you or does anyone in your family use pesticides at home?

4. What do you know about the effects of pesticides on urban pests, such as cockroaches, bedbugs, or rats?

---

## The Problem-Solution Pattern

In this pattern, the main idea presents a problem of some kind. The paragraph or passage explains the problem, and then gives examples or details about one or more solutions to the problem.

> **Common Signal Words and Phrases for the Problem-Solution Pattern**
>
> **Main idea:**
> - Words that indicate a problem
>   - *Examples: problem, situation, trouble, crisis, issue, question, dilemma*
> - Words that indicate a solution
>   - *Examples: solution, solve, resolution, resolve, decide*
>
> **Supporting facts and ideas:**
>
> The explanation of the problem may include elements of any of the other patterns. For this reason, writers may use any of the signal words that are common in those patterns

### PRACTICE

**A.** *This paragraph follows the problem-solution pattern. The main idea is underlined and marked with an asterisk (\*). The signal words and phrases are circled. Read the paragraph and underline the supporting facts or ideas. Letter each one (a, b, c) in the margin.*

### World Hunger

Why do some 850 million people—many of them children—go to bed hungry? For those children, hunger means humiliation and suffering, and leaves a lifelong legacy of cognitive and physical impairment. Some scientists and corporations (as well as politicians) would have us believe that the more productive GM seeds they are developing will feed these children, but new seeds alone are unlikely to solve the problem. In fact, world agriculture already produces enough food to provide everyone on the planet with at least 2,720 kilocalories (kcal) per person per day, according to the FAO. Ending hunger will require (addressing the principle cause) of hunger, which is poverty, and (the main cause) of poverty, which is economic inequality, both within and between countries. Any long-term (solution to the problem) of world hunger must therefore be political. Countries such as Brazil and Ghana have shown how to reduce hunger dramatically through economic measures, such as cash transfers to poor people, raising the minimum wage, and investing in smallholder farmers (especially women). In both developed and developing countries, farmers and communities need to have a stake in the development of agricultural methods that will lead to a future of food security.

---

**Main idea:** Ending <u>world hunger</u> is possible only if we deal with the problems of poverty and economic inequality, <u>which will require political measures.</u>

**Problem:**

a. 850 million people suffer from hunger, including many children.

b. Hunger causes humiliation, suffering, cognitive and physical impairment

c. Some scientists, corporations, politicians say GMO seeds will solve the problem, but this seems unlikely

d. Agriculture already produces enough food to feed the world

e. Main cause of hunger = poverty; main cause of poverty = economic inequality

**Solution:**

a. Long-term solution requires political action

b. Brazil and Ghana are examples of how hunger can be reduced through economic measures

c. Farmers and communities need to be involved

---

B.   *Compare work with another student. Add any useful vocabulary to your notebook.*

**A.** *Preview and read this web article. Then work with another student to find and underline the overall idea, the main ideas, and the supporting facts or ideas. Mark the main idea(s) with an asterisk.*

### Wasted: How America Is Losing Up to 40 Percent of Its Food from Farm to Fork to Landfill
by Dana Gunders

Food is simply too good to waste. Even the most sustainably farmed food does us no good if the food is never eaten. Getting food to our tables eats up 10 percent of the total U.S. energy budget, uses 50 percent of U.S. land, and swallows 80 percent of freshwater consumed in the United States. Yet, 40 percent of food in the United States today goes uneaten. That is more than 20 pounds of food per person every month. Not only does this mean that Americans are throwing out the equivalent of $165 billion each year, but also 25 percent of all freshwater and huge amounts of unnecessary chemicals, energy, and land. Moreover, almost all of that uneaten food ends up rotting in landfills where it accounts for almost 25 percent of U.S. methane emissions . . .

The average American consumer wastes 10 times as much food as someone in Southeast Asia, up 50 percent from Americans in the 1970s. This means there was once a time when we wasted far less, and we can get back there again. Doing so will ultimately require a suite of coordinated solutions, including changes in supply-chain operation, enhanced market incentives, increased public awareness and adjustments in consumer behavior.

Much can be learned from work that is already under way in Europe. Both the United Kingdom and the European Union have conducted research to better understand the drivers of the problem and identify potential solutions. In January 2012, the European Parliament adopted a resolution to reduce food waste by 50 percent by 2020 and designated 2014 as the "European year against food waste." An extensive U.K. public awareness campaign called "Love Food Hate Waste" has been conducted over the past five years and 53 of the leading food retailers and brands there have adopted a resolution to reduce waste in their own operations, as well as upstream and downstream in the supply chain.

(Source: Dana Gunders, "Wasted: How America Is Losing Up to 40 Percent of Its Food from Farm to Fork to Landfill," National Resources Defense Council, http://www.nrdc.org/food/wasted-food.asp)

**B.** *Work with your partner. Circle the problem-solution signal words or phrases in the passage. (There may not be many.) On a separate piece of paper, make an outline for the passage that shows the problem-solution pattern.*

**C.** *Compare work with another pair of students. Add any useful vocabulary to your notebook.*

## Reflecting on the Issues

*Discuss these questions with a small group of students:*

**1.** What do you know about hunger and malnutrition in your country?

**2.** What do you know about food waste in your country?

**3.** What do you think governments should do to reduce hunger in your country? Around the world?

**4.** What could be done to reduce food waste?

# The Definition Pattern

In this pattern, the paragraph or passage presents something—a fact or concept. The overall idea may be a definition or description of the fact or concept. The supporting facts and ideas give further explanation or details.

---

**Common Signal Words and Phrases for the Definition Pattern**

**Main idea:**

- Verbs such as *be, seem, consist of, refers to*

    **Example:** Agrobiodiversity *refers to* biodiversity among planned agricultural crops or livestock . . .

- A dictionary definition
- Formatting signals such as bold or italic font
- Punctuation, such as parentheses, a colon (:) or comma (,) followed by the explanation

    **Examples:** Scientists believed elimination was possible thanks to *DDT, a chemical pesticide* that had been discovered and used during World War II.

    Because of this diet, cattle on SPOs emit less *methane (a global warming gas)* than cattle that eat a rich grain diet.

**Supporting facts and ideas:**

- The definition or explanation may include elements of any of the other patterns. For this reason, writers may use any of signal words that are common in any of those patterns.

There may not be any signal words for some facts or ideas.

**Note:** In textbooks, the important concepts which you may need to be able to define or explain are usually indicated in the text with bold or italics. In other kinds of texts, you need to decide which concepts are important and mark them yourself.

---

## PRACTICE

**A.** *This paragraph follows the definition pattern. The main idea is underlined and marked with an asterisk (\*). Read the paragraph and underline the supporting facts or ideas. Letter each one (a, b, c) in the margin.*

### Seed banks are living museums

Protecting areas and cultures that maintain a wealth of crop diversity is one way to preserve genetic assets for our agriculture. Another is to collect and store seeds from diverse crop ✱ varieties. This is the work of **seed banks**, <u>institutions that preserve seed types as a kind of living museum of genetic diversity</u>. These facilities keep seed samples in cold, dry conditions to encourage long-term viability, and they plant and harvest them periodically to renew the stocks. Major seed banks include the Royal Botanic Garden's Millennium Seed Bank in Britain, the U.S. National Seed Storage Laboratory at Colorado State University, and the Wheat and Maize Improvement Center in Mexico. In total, 1,400 such facilities house 1–2 million distinct types of seeds worldwide. The most renowned seed bank is the so-called "doomsday seed vault" established in 2008 on the island of Spitsbergen in Arctic Norway. The internationally funded Svalbard Global Seed Vault is storing millions of seeds from around the world (spare sets from other seed banks) as a safeguard against global agricultural calamity—"an insurance policy for the world's food supply." The doomsday seed vault is an admirable effort, but we would be well advised not to rely on it to save us. Far better to manage our agriculture wisely and sustainably so that we never need to break into the vault!

(Source: Jay Withgott and Scott Brennan, Benjamin Cummings, *Environment: The Science Behind the Stories,* 4th ed., Pearson Education, 2001)

| |
|---|
| **Seed banks:** institutions that preserve seed types as a kind of living museum of genetic diversity |
| a. Keep seeds in cold, dry conditions for long-term viability |
| b. Plant and harvest periodically to renew stocks |
| c. 1,400 seed banks house 1–2 million types of seeds worldwide |
| d. Svalbard Global Seed Vault storing millions of seeds from other seed banks |
| e. Svalbard is safeguard against global agricultural calamity |

B.   *Compare work with another student. Add any useful vocabulary to your notebook.*

## EXERCISE 6

A.   *Preview and read the passage from an environmental science textbook. Then work with another student to find supporting facts and ideas to define or explain the terms in bold and italics. Mark the main idea(s) with an asterisk.*

### Sustainable Agriculture

Industrial agriculture has allowed food production to keep pace with our growing population, but it involves many adverse environmental and social impacts. These range from the degradation of soils to reliance on fossil fuels to problems arising from pesticide use, genetic modification, and intensive feedlot and aquaculture operations. . . . Industrial agriculture in some form seems necessary to feed our planet's 7 billion people, but many experts feel we will be better off in the long run by raising animals and crops in ways that are less polluting and less resource-intensive.

**Sustainable agriculture** is agriculture that does not deplete soils faster than they form. It is farming and ranching that do not reduce the amount of healthy soil, clean water, and genetic diversity essential to long-term crop and livestock production. Simply put, sustainable agriculture is agriculture that can be practiced in the same way far into the future. Approaches such as no-till farming [when fields are not ploughed] and soil conservation methods helps move us toward sustainable agriculture. So do more traditional approaches, such as the Chinese practice of carp aquaculture in small ponds and the cultivation of diverse landraces of Mexican maize.

One key component of making agriculture sustainable is reducing the fossil-fuel-intensive inputs we invest in it and decreasing the pollution these inputs cause. *Low-input agriculture* describes agriculture that uses lesser amounts of pesticides, fertilizers, growth hormones, antibiotics, water, and fossil fuel energy than are used in industrial agriculture. Food-growing practices that aim to use no synthetic fertilizers, insecticides, fungicides, or herbicides—but instead rely on biological approaches such as composting and biocontrol—are termed **organic agriculture**.

(Source: Jay Withgott and Scott Brennan, Benjamin Cummings, *Environment: The Science Behind the Stories,* 4th ed., Pearson Education, 2001)

**B.** *Work with your partner. On a separate piece of paper, make an outline for this passage. Show the terms or concepts and their definitions or explanations.*

**C.** *Compare work with another pair of students. Then add any useful vocabulary to your notebook.*

## EXERCISE 7

**A.** *Preview and read this passage from* **Fast Food Nation.** *Work with another student to find two key terms in the passage and highlight them. Then underline the supporting facts and ideas that define or explain them.*

### Food Product Design

... The 1960s were the heyday of artificial flavors. The synthetic versions of flavor compounds were not subtle, but they did not need to be, given the nature of most processed food. For the past twenty years, food processors have tried hard to use only "natural flavors" in their products. According to the FDA, these must be derived entirely from natural sources—from herbs, spices, fruits, vegetables, beef, chicken, yeast, bark, roots, etc. Consumers prefer to see natural flavors on a label, out of a belief that they are healthier. The distinction between artificial and natural flavors can be somewhat arbitrary and absurd, based more on how the flavor has been made than on what it actually contains. "A natural flavor," says Terry Acree, a professor of food science technology at Cornell University, "is flavor that's been derived with an out-of-date technology." Natural flavors and artificial flavors sometimes contain exactly the same chemicals, produced through different methods. Amyl acetate, for example, provides the dominant note of banana flavor. When you produce it by mixing vinegar with amyl alcohol, adding sulfuric acid as a catalyst, amyl acetate is an artificial flavor. Either way it smells and tastes the same. The phrase "natural flavor" is now listed among the ingredients of everything from Stonyfield Farm Organic Strawberry Yogurt to Taco Bell Hot Taco Sauce.

A natural flavor is not necessarily healthier or purer than an artificial one. When almond flavor (benzaldehyde) is derived from natural sources, such as peach and apricot pits, it contains traces of hydrogen cyanide, a deadly poison. Benzaldehyde derived through a different process—by mixing oil of clove and the banana flavor, amyl acetate—does not contain any cyanide. Nevertheless, it is legally considered an artificial flavor and sells at a much lower price. Natural and artificial flavors are now manufactured at the same chemical plants, places that few people would associate with Mother Nature. Calling any of these flavors "natural" requires a flexible attitude toward the English language and a fair amount of irony.

(Source: Eric Schlosser, *Fast Food Nation,* Mariner Books, Houghton Mifflin, 2012)

**B.** *Work with your partner. On a separate piece of paper, make an outline to show the key terms and their definitions or explanations.*

**C.** *Compare work with another pair of students. Add any useful vocabulary to your notebook.*

# Recognizing Patterns

In these exercises, you will practice recognizing the patterns you have learned about. You will read longer pieces of writing, where the writer develops more than one idea and uses various patterns. As you read, think about the ideas and look for the signal words. Then decide which of the patterns the writer has used in each part of the text.

| | | |
|---|---|---|
| Listing | Comparison-Contrast | Problem-Solution |
| Sequence | Cause-Effect | Definition |

## EXERCISE 8

**A.** *Preview and read this passage from an environmental textbook. Then work with another student to find and underline the overall idea, the main idea(s), and the supporting facts or ideas. Mark the overall idea with an asterisk.*

### Sustainable Agriculture Mimics Natural Ecosystems

The best approach for making an agricultural system sustainable is to mimic the way a natural ecosystem functions. Ecosystems are sustainable because they operate in cycles and are internally stabilized with negative feedback loops. In this way they provide a useful model for agriculture.

One example comes from Japan, where some small-scale rice farmers are reviving ancient traditions and finding them superior to modern industrial methods. Takao Furuno is one such farmer. Starting 20 years ago, he and his wife added a crucial element to their rice paddies: the crossbred *aigamo* duck. Each spring after they plant rice seeds, the Furunos release hundreds of *aigamo* ducklings into their paddies. The ducklings eat weeds that compete with the rice, as well as insects and snails that attack the rice. The ducklings also fertilize the rice plants with their waste and oxygenate the water by paddling. Furuno and the scientists and extension agents [agricultural experts] who have worked with him have found that rice plants grow larger and yield far more rice in paddies that have ducks. Once the rice grains form, the ducks are taken out of the paddies (because they would eat the rice grains) and kept in sheds, where they are fed waste grain. They mature, lay eggs, and can be sold at market.

Besides the ducks, Furuno raises fish in the paddies, and these provide food and fertilizer as well. He also lets the aquatic fern *Azolla* cover the water surface. This plant fixes nitrogen, feeds the ducks, hides the fish, and provides habitat for insects, plankton, and aquatic invertebrates, which provide further food for the fish and ducks. Because fast-growing *Azolla* can double its biomass in 3 days, surplus plant matter is harvested and used as cattle feed. The end result is a productive, functioning ecosystem in which pests and weeds are transformed into resources and which yields organic rice, eggs, and meat from ducks and fish.

From 2 hectares of paddies and 1 hectare of organic vegetables, the Furunos annually produce 7 tons of rice, 300 ducks, 4,000 ducklings, and enough vegetables to feed 100 people. At this rate—twice the productivity of the region's conventional farmers—just 2% of Japan's people could supply the nation's food.

(Source: Jay Withgott and Scott Brennan, Benjamin Cummings, *Environment: The Science Behind the Stories*, 4th ed., Pearson Education, 2001)

**B.** *Write the overall pattern:* _____
*Circle the signal words or phrases for the pattern you wrote. Look for signal words for other patterns in the text. Underline them and write them in the margin.*

**C.** *On a separate piece of paper, make an outline to show the overall pattern in the passage.*

**D.** *Compare work with another pair of students. Add any useful vocabulary to your notebook.*

## EXERCISE 9

**A.** *Turn back to the following exercises from Part 3, Unit 1. Reread the passages and write the overall pattern for each one. Then look for other patterns in each text. Make a bracket in the margin beside each part with a pattern and write the pattern.*

1. Exercise 4: "Western-style fast food linked to poorer health in Singapore, says U of M study." (page 111)

2. Exercise 8: "The Aborigine in All of Us" (page 116)

**B.** *Compare work with another student.*

# Focus on Vocabulary

**A.** *Read these sentences from the passage in Exercise 2. For each underlined word or phrase, choose the one that is closest in meaning.*

1. It uses a combination of pest control methods to manage pest damage by the most economical means, and with the least possible <u>hazard</u> to people, property, and the environment.

   a. expense        b. danger        c. gain

2. IPM takes advantage of all appropriate pest control options, including the <u>judicious</u> use of pesticides.

   a. careful        b. generous        c. occasional

3. <u>Prior to</u> undertaking any method of pest control, the farmer must have an accurate knowledge of pests and a full understanding of their life cycles and their interaction with the environment.

   a. after        b. while        c. before

4. Not all insects, weeds, and other living organisms require control. Many organisms are innocuous, and some are even <u>beneficial</u>.

   a. alive        b. helpful        c. harmful

5. An essential next step is to set a <u>threshold</u> for pest populations.

   a. goal        b. model        c. limit

6. It is <u>critical</u> to establish the level at which pests will become an economic threat to the farmer . . .

   a. dangerous        b. unnecessary        c. essential

7. For example, IPM experts recommend the use of pheromones to <u>disrupt</u> pest mating, or mechanical control, such as trapping or weeding.

   a. stop        b. encourage        c. allow

8. Widespread spraying of non-specific pesticides is only used as <u>a last resort</u>.

   a. the end result        b. the only option left        c. a final step in a process

**B.** *Compare answers with another student. Check your answers in the dictionary. Then read through the passage on page 170 again. Can you remember the words you looked up the first time? If not, mark them for further review.*

## EXERCISE 11

**A.** *Read these sentences from the passage in Exercise 7. Write a word from the box in each blank. You may need to change the form of the word.*

| | | | | |
|---|---|---|---|---|
| arbitrary | catalyst | derive | dominant | nevertheless |
| associate with | compound | distinction | irony | trace |

1. The synthetic versions of flavor _____ were not subtle, but they did not need to be, given the nature of most processed food.

2. According to the FDA, these must be _____ entirely from natural sources— from herbs, spices, fruits, vegetables, beef, chicken, yeast, bark, roots, etc.

3. The _____ between artificial and natural flavors can be somewhat xxxxxxxxxx and absurd, based more on how the flavor has been made than on what it actually contains.

4. The xxxxxxxxxx between artificial and natural flavors can be somewhat _____ and absurd, based more on how the flavor has been made than on what it actually contains.

5. Amyl acetate, for example, provides the _____ note of banana flavor.

6. When you produce it by mixing vinegar with amyl alcohol, adding sulfuric acid as a _____, amyl acetate is an artificial flavor.

7. When almond flavor (benzaldehyde) is derived from natural sources, such as peach and apricot pits, it contains _____ of hydrogen cyanide, a deadly poison.

8. _____, it is legally considered an artificial flavor and sells at a much lower price.

9. Natural and artificial flavors are now manufactured at the same chemical plants, places that few people would _____ Mother Nature.

10. Calling any of these flavors "natural" requires a flexible attitude toward the English language and a fair amount of _____.

**B.** *Compare answers with another student. Check your answers in the dictionary. Then read through the passage on page 183 again. Can you remember the words you looked up the first time? If not, mark them for further review.*

## EXERCISE 12

A. *Select six words or phrases from the passages in this unit which you think other students might not be familiar with or might not remember well (preferably words that are on the word list in the Appendix).*

B. *On a separate piece of paper, make an exercise like Exercise 11:*
   - *Write the sentences where you found the words and phrases on your list, leaving a blank in place of the word or phrase.*
   - *Write the missing words/phrases in a box below the sentences—but not in order.*

C. *Exchange exercises with another student and do your partner's exercise.*

D. *Look back at the text to check your answers.*

E. *With your partner, give the definitions for the words or phrases you selected for your exercises. Look up any you are not sure about.*

---

### Reflecting on Your Learning

1. Discuss these questions with a group of students:
   - Think about how writers in your first language organize their ideas in writing. Do they use any of the same patterns of organization?
   - In written texts in your course of study or field of interest, which patterns are commonly used?
   - How can your understanding of patterns of organization help your writing in English?
2. Select useful vocabulary from this unit:
   - Look through the passages in this unit for more vocabulary that would be useful to learn. Write the words or phrases in your vocabulary notebook (with parts of speech, definitions and/ or synonyms, the sentences where you found them, and any helpful notes about usage).
   - Review the words in your notebook. Test yourself and then ask a classmate or friend to test you. Write the words you have trouble remembering on study cards. Review and test yourself until you know them well.

---

# UNIT 5

# Reading for Study

In this unit you will learn more about the strategies for improving comprehension that you have already used, such as marking texts and making diagrams or outlines. You will also learn some new strategies to help you retain important information.

Many students study by simply reading over parts of text that they have underlined or highlighted. However, this may not be a very effective method. You are much more likely to remember information and ideas if you work with them in some way, for example, by talking about them, by writing them down, or by creating a visual representation of them. The extra processing involved in these activities makes the material "stick" better in your brain.

Successful students use a combination of study strategies that they vary according to their needs. After you have tried out the strategies presented in this unit, you can decide which ones work best for you and create your own study method.

For maximum effectiveness, use a strategy from each of these categories:

1. Marking text (underlining, highlighting, etc.)
2. Making diagrams or outlines, or taking notes
3. Writing summaries or quiz questions

## Marking Text

In earlier units, you practiced marking the main idea and the supporting facts and ideas in a passage. Experienced readers make note of other aspects of text, including

1. connections among facts and ideas.
2. connections between the text and other materials (readings or lectures).
3. their reactions to parts of the text that are interesting, surprising, difficult, or unclear.

Each reader has his or her preferred techniques for marking, and these may change according to the purpose of the reading and the type of text. Here are some common techniques:

- Underlining (or highlighting)
- Circling or drawing a box around words or phrases
- Drawing asterisks or stars, or writing key words, dates, names in the margins
- Drawing brackets around sections of text of particular interest/importance
- Writing numbers in the margins to indicate points in a series
- Using symbols, such as ?, !, ★, ☺, to show your reactions

## Guidelines for Marking Text

1. *Always preview* before you start reading and marking a text. This will help you orient your thinking and find the ideas more quickly.

2. After previewing, read the passage more carefully and mark *in pencil*. You might need to change it later if your understanding of the passage changes.

3. Go back over the text and think about the ideas again. When you are sure you understand, add markings with highlighters or colored pens.

4. Don't underline a lot of text. Underline only the key words, phrases, or parts of sentences.

5. Vary your marking techniques to suit the type of text and your study needs. In a textbook, you may need to mark detailed definitions and explanations, but in other kinds of reading you may only need to mark more general concepts, theories, trends, etc.

### Example

*Notice the marking techniques used on this passage from the book in* Defense of Food, *by Michael Pollan. Which of these might you include in your own marking?*

### The Elephant in the Room

In the end, even the biggest, most ambitious, and widely reported studies of diet and health—the Nurses' Health Study, the Women's Health Initiative, and nearly all the others—leave undisturbed the main features of the Western diet: lots of processed foods and meat, lots of added fat and sugar, lots of everything except fruits, vegetables, and whole grains. In keeping with the limits of the nutritionism paradigm and reductionist science, most nutrition researchers fiddle with single nutrients as best they can, but the populations they recruit and study are typical American eaters doing what typical American eaters do: trying to eat a little less of this nutrient, a little more of that one, depending on the latest thinking. The overall dietary pattern is treated as a more or less unalterable given. Which is why it probably should not surprise us that the findings of such research should be so modest, equivocal, and confusing.

But what about the elephant in the room—this pattern of eating that we call the Western diet? In the midst of our deepening confusion about nutrition, it might be useful to step back and gaze upon it—review what we *do* know about the Western diet and its effects on our health. What we know is that people who eat the way we do in the West today suffer substantially higher rates of cancer, cardiovascular diseases, diabetes, and obesity than people eating any number of different traditional diets. We also know that when people come to the West and adopt our way of eating, these diseases soon follow, and often, as in the case of the Aborigines and other native populations, in a particularly virulent form.

*Margin annotations:* Western diet ↓ ↓ ↓ our health

**A.** *Read the next part of "The Elephant in the Room." Mark the main ideas and supporting facts and ideas. Use a pencil so you can change your marking later.*

The outlines of this story—the story of the so-called Western diseases and their link to the Western diet—we first learned in the early decades of the twentieth century. That was when a handful of European and American medical professionals working with a wide variety of native populations around the world began noticing the almost complete absence of the chronic diseases that had recently become common-place in the West. Albert Schweitzer and Denis P. Burkitt in Africa, Robert McCarrison in India, Samuel Hutton among the Eskimos in Labrador, the anthropologist Ales Hrdlicka among Native Americans, and the dentist Weston A. Price among a dozen different groups all over the world, sent back much the same news. They compiled lists, many of which appeared in medical journals, of the common diseases they'd been unable to find in the native populations they had treated or studied: little to no heart disease, diabetes, cancer, obesity, hypertension, or stroke; no appendicitis, diverticulitis, malformed dental arches, or tooth decay, no varicose veins, ulcers, or hemorrhoids. These disorders suddenly appeared to these researchers under a striking new light, as suggested by the name given to them by the British doctor Denis Burkitt, who worked in Africa during World War II: He proposed that we call them Western diseases. The implication was that these very different diseases were somehow linked and might even have a common cause.

Several of the researchers were on hand to witness the arrival of the Western diseases in isolated populations, typically, as Albert Schweitzer wrote, among "natives living more and more after the manner of the whites." Some noted that the Western diseases followed closely after the arrival of Western foods, particularly refined flour and sugar and other kinds of "store food." They observed too that when one Western disease arrived on the scene, so did most of the others, often in the same order: obesity followed by type 2 diabetes followed by hypertension and stroke followed by heart disease.

In the years before World War II the medical world entertained a lively conversation on the subject of the Western diseases and what their rise might say about our increasingly industrialized way of life. The concept's pioneers believed there were novelties in the modern diet to which native populations were poorly adapted, though they did not necessarily agree on exactly which novelty might be the culprit. Burkitt, for example, believed it was the lack of fiber in the modern diet while McCarrison, a British army doctor, focused on refined carbohydrates while still others blamed meat eating and saturated fat, or in Price's case, the advent of processed food and industrially grown crops deficient in vitamins and minerals.

Not everyone, though, accepted the idea that chronic disease was a by-product of Western lifestyles and in particular, that the industrialization of our food was damaging our health. One objection to the theory was genetic: Different races were apt to be susceptible to different diseases went the argument; white people were disposed to heart attacks, brown people to things like leprosy. Yet as Burkitt and others pointed out, blacks living in America suffered from the same chronic diseases as whites living there. Simply by moving to places like America, immigrants from nations with low rates of chronic disease seemed to quickly acquire them.

The other objection to the concept of Western diseases, one you sometimes still hear, was demographic. The reason we see so much chronic disease in the West is because these are illnesses that appear relatively late in life, and with the conquest of infectious disease early in the twentieth century, we're simply living long enough to get them. In this view, chronic disease is the inevitable price of a long life. But while it is true that our life expectancy has improved dramatically since 1900 (rising in the United States from forty-nine to seventy-seven years), most of that gain is attributed to the fact that more of us are surviving infancy and childhood; the life expectancy of a sixty-five-year-old in 1900 was only about six years less than that of a sixty-five-year-old living today. When you adjust for age, rates of chronic diseases like cancer and type 2 diabetes are considerably higher today than they were in 1900. That is, the chances that a sixty- or seventy-year-old suffers from cancer or type 2 diabetes are far greater today than they were a century ago.

Cancer and heart disease and so many of the other Western diseases are by now such an accepted part of modern life that it's hard for us to believe this wasn't always or even necessarily the case. These days most of us think of chronic diseases as being a little like the weather—one of life's givens—and so count ourselves lucky that, compared to the weather, the diseases at least are more amenable to intervention by modern medicine. We think of them strictly in medical rather than historical, much less evolutionary, terms. But during the decades before World War II, when the industrialization of so many aspects of our lives was still fairly fresh, the price of "progress," especially to our health, seemed more obvious to many people and therefore more open to question.

(Source: Michael V. Pollan, *In Defense of Food*. Penguin Press, 2008)

**B.**  *Compare texts with another student. How are your marking styles similar or different? Change yours if you see ways to improve it.*

## Making Diagrams and Outlines

When you make a diagram or an outline for a passage, you are forced to think about how the facts and ideas relate to each other. This requires more mental processing than when you simply underline in the text. Furthermore, a diagram or an outline gives you a visual image of the important ideas in the passage, which helps you remember them.

## Diagrams

The diagrams you learned how to make in earlier units can be improved by:

- Marking the text carefully first, and then referring to your marking to make the diagram. Your diagrams will be more accurate this way.
- Adding boxes around key words in your diagram (or highlighting them) to help you focus on the main ideas.

*Example*

*Here is an example of a student's diagram for the passage in the Example on page 190.*

---

The Elephant in the Room

(Main idea) ⟦Studies⟧ of diet and health do not question the ⟦typical American diet,⟧ which is why they are ⟦not very useful.⟧

⟦Western diet:⟧
processed foods,
meat, fat and sugar;
few fruits & vegetables

Americans in studies
⟦continue to eat⟧ this way!

Researchers never look
at ⟦whole picture⟧ so
studies are useless

(Main idea) The ⟦typical Western diet⟧ is like the elephant in the room, but we should look at it and think about its ⟦effects on health.⟧

American diet like the
⟦"elephant in the room:"⟧
something enormous that
everyone ignores

The effects of Western diet on health:
→ people who live on it get ⟦certain diseases⟧
→ people who start eating it, soon get the diseases

---

## EXERCISE 2

A.  *On a separate piece of paper, make diagrams for the passage in Exercise 1 on page 191. Show the main idea and the supporting facts and ideas for each of the paragraphs and mark the key words.*

B.  *Compare diagrams with another student. How are your diagrams similar or different? Change yours if you see ways to improve it.*

## Outlines

As you saw in Unit 4, an outline is similar to a diagram but more linear, so it does not always show the relationships among the ideas as well as a diagram. However, it does show the relative importance of the ideas. You can also use boxes to indicate key words or phrases in your outline.

*Example:*

Here is an example of an outline for the passage in the Example on page 190.

The Elephant in the Room
I.  Studies of diet and health do not question the typical American diet, which is why they are not very useful.
    A.  Western diet
        1.  Processed foods
        2.  Lots of meat, fats, and sugar
        3.  Few fruits and vegetables
    B.  American subjects in studies of diet continue to eat this way
    C.  Researchers never look at the whole picture (Western diet) so their results are useless
II.  The typical Western diet is like the elephant in the room, but we should look at it and think about its effects on health.
    A.  Western diet: like the "elephant in the room"
        1.  something important that everyone ignores
    B.  People on Western diet get diseases

## EXERCISE 3

**A.**  *On a separate piece of paper, make an outline for the passage in Exercise 1 on page 191. Label and indent clearly the main ideas and the supporting facts and ideas.*

**B.**  *Compare outlines with another student. How are your outlines similar or different? Change yours if you see ways to improve it.*

**C.**  *Discuss these questions with your partner:*
   1. Which do you find easier to make—diagrams or outlines?
   2. Which do you think will help you remember the material better?
   3. Think about your reading assignments. When might you use diagrams? When might you use outlines?

## Taking Notes

Another way of collecting important information and ideas from your reading is by taking notes, which may be more practical than diagramming when you have long passages or whole books to read, especially if you cannot mark the books.

The examples below show the two-column note-taking method used by many university students.

- The main ideas are written in a column on the left side of the page, and the supporting information and ideas are in a wider column on the right.
- Each main idea is across from its supporting facts and ideas.
- The supporting facts and ideas are written as phrases with the key facts and ideas (not whole sentences).
- The two-column format allows you to quiz yourself by covering up one column or the other and checking how well you remember the ideas and information on the side you have covered.

### Example:

*Here is an example of notes for the passage in the Example on page 190. Compare it to the example diagram and outline on pages 193 and 194. Which do you think presents the information most clearly?*

**The Elephant in the Room**

| Main ideas | Supporting information |
|---|---|
| 1. Health and diet studies don't question Western diet | Western diet: processed foods, meat, fat, and sugar; few fruits and vegetables |
| | Americans in diet studies still eat this way |
| | Researchers don't look at whole picture, so their studies are useless |
| 2. We need to look at and think about the Western diet and its effects | Western diet like elephant in the room: something important that everyone ignores |
| | What we know about the Western diet: |
| |    People who live on it get certain diseases |
| |    People who start eating it, soon get the diseases |

### PRACTICE

*Read the paragraph from a textbook and look at the notes that follow. Then use the notes to mark the main idea and supporting information in the paragraph.*

### Seed banks are living museums

Protecting areas and cultures that maintain a wealth of crop diversity is one way to preserve genetic assets for our agriculture. Another is to collect and store seeds from diverse crop varieties. This is the work of *seed banks*, institutions that preserve seed types as a kind of living museum of genetic diversity. These facilities keep seed samples in cold, dry conditions to encourage long-term viability, and they plant and harvest them periodically to renew the stocks. Major seed banks include the Royal Botanic Garden's Millennium Seed Bank in Britain, the U.S. National Seed Storage Laboratory at Colorado State University, and the Wheat and Maize Improvement Center in Mexico. In total, 1,400 such facilities house 1–2 million distinct types of seeds worldwide. The most renowned seed bank is the so-called "doomsday seed vault" established in 2008 on the island of Spitsbergen in Arctic Norway. The internationally funded Svalbard Global Seed Vault is storing millions of seeds from around the world (spare sets from other seed banks) as a safeguard against global agricultural calamity—"an insurance policy for the world's food supply." The doomsday seed vault is an admirable effort, but we would be well advised not to rely on it to save us. Far better to manage our agriculture wisely and sustainably so that we never need to break into the vault!

(Source: Jay Withgott and Scott Brennan, Benjamin Cummings, *Environment: The Science Behind the Stories*, 4th ed., 2001)

| Main ideas | Supporting information |
|---|---|
| Seed banks: | 1. Keep seeds in cold, dry conditions |
| places that hold seed | 2. Plant and harvest seeds regularly to renew them |
| samples for <u>genetic</u> | 3. 1,400 seed banks around the world with 1–2 million types |
| <u>diversity</u> and to protect | of seeds |
| the world's food | 4. Most famous is Svalbard Global Seed Vault in Arctic |
| | Norway—like an insurance police for world's food supply |

B.  **Look back at the way the paragraph is marked in the Practice exercise in Unit 4 on page 181. How is your marking similar or different?**

## EXERCISE 4

A.  *Turn to Unit 4, Exercise 5 on page 180. Re-read the passage* Wasted: How America is Losing 40 percent of its Food from Farm to Fork to Landfill. *Review the marking you did then and change it if you see ways to improve it.*

B.  *Take notes on the passage on a separate piece of paper:*
   *1. Draw two columns.*
   *2. Write each main idea on the left.*
   *3. On the right, across from each main idea, write the supporting facts and ideas*

C.  *Compare notes with another student. How are your notes similar or different? Change yours if you see ways to improve them.*

## EXERCISE 5

A.  *Turn to Unit 4, Exercise 8 on page 184. Re-read the passage* Sustainable Agriculture Mimics Natural Ecosystems. *Review the marking you did then and change it if you see ways to improve it now.*

B.  *Take notes on the passage on a separate piece of paper:*
   *1. Draw two columns.*
   *2. Write each main idea on the left.*
   *3. On the right, across from each main idea, write the supporting facts and ideas*

*Compare notes with another student. How are your notes similar or different? Make changes if you see ways to improve them.*

# Writing Summaries

A summary is a shorter version of a passage that includes only the most important facts and ideas. Writing a summary is an excellent way to check that you thoroughly understand the ideas in a text and to ensure that you remember them.

Summaries are also useful when you are writing reports or research papers and need to include information and ideas from original sources.

The key to writing a good summary is to include only the most important facts and ideas. You may want to include some details if you think you need to learn them, but do not include a lot of detail. In this unit and earlier units, you have practiced finding the important ideas in a text. You should use the same thinking process when you are deciding what to include in your summary.

## Guidelines for Writing Summaries

1. Before you write a summary, mark the text and make a diagram or outline or take notes.

2. Include key words and phrases from the original, but otherwise use your own words as much as possible. That forces you to think carefully about the ideas.

3. Follow the same pattern of organization as in the original and present the ideas in the same order.

4. Don't add any facts, ideas, or opinions that are not in the passage.

### EXAMPLE

*Look at the notes in the Practice on pages 196 and 197. Compare them with this summary. The supporting ideas from the notes are written in sentences. The sentences follow one another in a way that makes sense.*

**Seed banks** hold seed samples of crop varieties in order to preserve genetic diversity and protect the world's food supply. The seeds are kept alive and planted regularly to renew them. Of the thousands of seed banks around the world, the most famous is the Svalbard Global Seed Vault in Arctic Norway.

## EXERCISE 6

A. *Read this summary of the passage in Exercise 1 on page 191. Compare it to your diagram from Exercise 2. Does the summary include the same facts and ideas as your diagram?*

(1) The connection between Western diseases and the Western diet became evident in the early 20th century when American and European doctors working in other parts of the world noticed that people there were free of certain diseases common in the West. (2) The

doctors also noticed that when these people began to eat a Western diet, they began to suffer from Western diseases. (3) In those years, there was much debate about a possible link between Western diseases and the modern industrialized diet. (4) Some people rejected this connection because they believed the diseases had a genetic origin. (5) Others thought (and still think) that we see more of certain chronic diseases in Western countries simply because we are living longer, though the facts do not support this view. (6) These days, people often assume that the Western diseases are an inevitable part of modern life, but back then people were more willing to question this idea.

B.  *For each numbered sentence in the summary, find the corresponding part of the full passage on page 191 and write the number of the sentence beside it.*

C.  *Compare work with another student and discuss these questions:*

1. How do the sentences correspond to the paragraphs in the passage?
2. Based on this, what general rule can you make for writing summaries?


## EXERCISE 7

A.  *Use the notes you took in Exercises 4 and 5 to write summaries of these passages on a separate piece of paper:*

  *1.* Wasted: How America is Losing 40 percent of its Food from Farm to Fork to Landfill *in Unit 4, Exercise 5, page 180.*

  *2.* Sustainable Agriculture Mimics Natural Ecosystems *in Unit 4, Exercise 8, page 184.*

B.  *Compare summaries with another student. How are they similar or different? Change yours if you see ways to improve it.*


## EXERCISE 8

A.  *Turn back to Unit 4, Exercise 1 on page 191.*
  *1. Re-read the passage. Review your marking and revise it if necessary.*
  *2. Make a diagram or outline or take notes on another piece of paper.*
  *3. Write a summary.*

B.  *Exchange summaries with another student. Look at your own marking of the passage to check your partner's summary. Does your partner's summary include the main ideas? The important supporting facts and ideas?*

C.  *Make changes to your summary if you see ways to improve it.*

# Writing Quiz Questions

Another way to check your comprehension and review for exams is by writing quiz questions. These are questions about the information you have read, which you can use to quiz yourself (or another student).

As with summarizing, you can make your questions more or less detailed, depending on how much information you need to remember. Use the passage format—section titles, headings, subheadings, terms or concepts in bold print—to help you focus your questions. As with notes and summaries, the quiz questions should focus on the most important ideas.

## EXERCISE 9

A. *Read these quiz questions about the passage in Exercise 1, "The Elephant in the Room." Work with another student to answer the questions. Do not look back at the text.*

1. What is the writer referring to with the expression "the elephant in the room"?
2. What does the writer say about research on diet and health in the United States?
3. What are the main characteristics of a Western diet?
4. How does the Western diet affect health?
5. What does the writer say about a traditional diet compared with the Western diet?
6. What happens when people who have been eating a traditional diet change to the Western diet?

B. *Look back at the text to check your answers.*

## EXERCISE 10

A. *Turn back to Unit 4, Exercise 3 on page 173. Re-read the passage about genetic engineering and revise your marking if you see ways to improve it.*

B. *On a separate piece of paper, make a diagram or outline, or take notes for the passage. Use these to write quiz questions on a separate piece of paper. Write at least one question per paragraph.*

C. *Exchange questions with another student. Try to answer your partner's questions without looking back at the text. Then check your answers in the text.*

## Connecting Graphics to Text

Writers of textbooks and other materials often use graphics, such as tables, charts, or figures, to illustrate points made in the text and to provide additional information.

It is important to examine graphics carefully and look for connections between the information in the graphic and the text. You should indicate these connections in your marking of the text. It may also be useful to mark the graphic.

## EXERCISE 11

**A.** *Read the text and look at Figure 7-4. Then mark the important ideas in the text.*

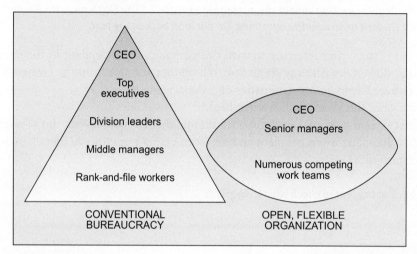

### FIGURE 7-4

The conventional model of bureaucratic organizations has a pyramid shape, with a clear chain of command. Orders flow from the top down, and reports of performance flow from the bottom up. Such organizations have extensive rules and regulations, and their workers have highly specialized jobs. More open and flexible organizations have a flatter shape, more like a football. With fewer levels in the hierarchy, responsibility for generating ideas and making decisions is shared throughout the organization. Many workers do their jobs in teams and have a broad knowledge of the entire organization's operation.

(Source: John J. Macionis, *Sociology*, Pearson Education, 2012)

**B.** *These sentences from the text contain information that is not included in the graphic in Figure 7-4. Add arrows, lines, words, or other marking to the graphic to show the information.*

1. Orders flow from the top down, and reports of performance flow from the bottom up.
2. Such organizations have extensive rules and regulations.
3. Workers have highly specialized jobs.
4. Responsibility for generating ideas and making decisions is shared throughout the organization.
5. Many workers do their jobs in teams.

**C.** *Use information from both the text and the graphic to discuss these questions with a partner.*

1. Which type of organization employs more people at the management level?
2. In which type of organization might workers get to know the top management better?
3. In which type of organization would you prefer to be a worker? A manager? Why?

**D.** *Compare answers with another pair of students.*

## EXERCISE 12

**A.** *Preview and read the text. Then mark the important ideas.*

### Unemployment

Every society has some unemployment. Few young people entering the labor force find a job right away; workers may leave their jobs to seek new work or stay at home raising children; others may be on strike or suffer from long-term illnesses; still others lack the skills to perform useful work.

But unemployment is not just an individual problem; it is also caused by the economy. Jobs disappear as occupations become obsolete and companies change the way they operate. Since 1980, the 500 largest U.S. businesses eliminated more than 5 million jobs while creating even more new ones.

Generally, companies downsize to become more competitive, or firms close in the face of foreign competition or economic recession. During the recession that began in 2008 in the United States, several million jobs were lost with unemployment rising in just about every part of the economy. Not only blue-collar workers but also white-collar workers who had typically weathered downturns in the past have lost jobs during this recession.

In 2008, just as the economy was falling into recession, 7 million people over the age of sixteen were unemployed, about 4.6 percent of the civilian labor force (U.S. Department of Labor, 2008b). But by the beginning of 2011, 14.5 million were unemployed with an unemployment rate of 8.9 percent, which was down from the high of 9.9 percent at the start of 2010. Even with this drop in the unemployment rate, however, the number of unemployed people had more than doubled since 2008, and the length of time people had been out of work had also increased—in 2011, more than 40 percent of unemployed people had been out of work for more than half a year (Tuttle, 2011). The unemployment rate is not the same everywhere in the country, of course. In some regions, especially rural areas, unemployment rates are usually far worse—about double the national average.

Figure 16-4 shows that in 2010, unemployment among African Americans (16.0 percent) was almost twice the rate among white people (8.7 percent). Regardless of sex or age, unemployment is lower among whites than among African Americans: the gap between white and black teenagers was especially large. For all categories of people, one of the best ways to avoid unemployment is to earn a college degree: As the figure shows, the unemployment rate for white college graduates was 4.3 percent—just half the national average.

(Source: John J. Macionis, *Sociology*, Pearson Education, 2012)

**B.** *Look at Figure 16-4 showing different groups of Americans and their levels of unemployment. Mark the text and the figure to show the connections between them.*

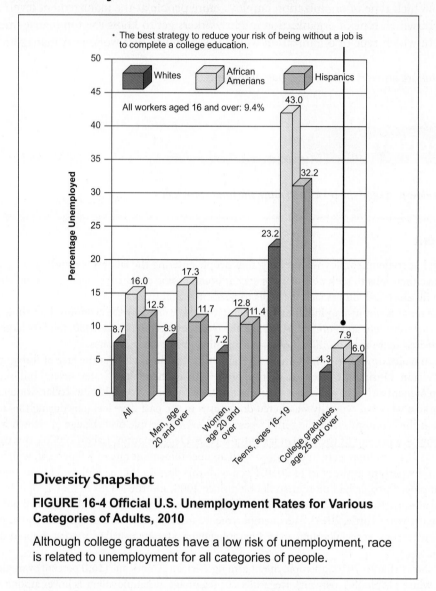

• The best strategy to reduce your risk of being without a job is to complete a college education.

Whites   African Amerians   Hispanics

All workers aged 16 and over: 9.4%

**Diversity Snapshot**

**FIGURE 16-4 Official U.S. Unemployment Rates for Various Categories of Adults, 2010**

Although college graduates have a low risk of unemployment, race is related to unemployment for all categories of people.

**C.** *Work with another student. Use information in the text or Figure 16-4 to answer these questions:*

1. Which group has the highest unemployment rate? The lowest?
2. Which racial minorities are discussed and how do their unemployment rates compare?
3. When was the unemployment rate highest in the U.S.? What was that rate?
4. In what areas of the country does unemployment tend to be higher?
5. How does the unemployment rate of women compare with that of men?

**D.** *Discuss these questions with your partner:*

1. Why do you think African Americans have the highest overall rate of unemployment?
2. Why do you think the rate is lower for women in each group than for men?
3. Based on this information, what advice would you give to a teenager worried about finding a job?

# Focus on Vocabulary

## EXERCISE 13

**A.** *Read these sentences from the passage in Exercise 1. For each underlined word or phrase, choose the one that is closest in meaning.*

1. . . . medical professionals working with a wide variety of native populations around the world began noticing the almost complete absence of the <u>chronic</u> diseases that had recently become common-place in the West.

   a. long-lasting      b. deadly      c. frequent

2. They <u>compiled</u> lists, many of which appeared in medical journals, of the common diseases they'd been unable to find in the native populations they had treated or studied.

   a. recorded      b. studied      c. created

3. The concept's pioneers believed there were <u>novelties</u> in the modern diet to which native populations were poorly adapted.

   a. dangerous chemicals      b. new things      c. strange foods

4. Burkitt . . . believed it was the lack of fiber in the modern diet while McCarrison, a British army doctor, focused on refined carbohydrates while still others blamed meat eating and saturated fat, or in Price's case, the <u>advent</u> of processed food . . .

   a. sale      b. idea      c. arrival

5. Different races were apt to be susceptible to different diseases went the argument; white people <u>were disposed to</u> heart attacks, brown people to things like leprosy.

   a. tended to have      b. rarely had      c. were treated for

6. But while it is true that our life expectancy has improved dramatically since 1900 . . . most of that gain is <u>attributed to</u> the fact that more of us are surviving infancy and childhood.

   a. probably due to      b. the probable reason for      c. likely to influence

7. When you adjust for age, rates of chronic diseases like cancer and type 2 diabetes are <u>considerably</u> higher today than they were in 1900.

   a. slightly      b. significantly      c. somewhat

8. We think of them <u>strictly</u> in medical rather than historical, much less evolutionary, terms.

    a. especially          b. partly                 c. only

**B.** *Compare answers with another student. Check your answers in the dictionary. Then read through the passage on page 191 again. Can you remember the words you looked up the first time? If not, mark them for further review.*

## EXERCISE 14

**A.** *Read these sentences from Exercises 11 and 12. Write a word from the box in each blank. You may need to change the form of the word.*

| | | | | |
|---|---|---|---|---|
| civilian | extensive | labor force | on strike | regardless of |
| downsize | generate | obsolete | recession | rural |

1. Such organizations have _____ rules and regulations, and their workers have highly specialized jobs.

2. With fewer levels in the hierarchy, responsibility for _____ ideas and making decisions is shared throughout the organization.

3. Jobs disappear as occupations become _____ and companies change the way they operate.

4. During the _____ that began in 2008 in the United States, several million jobs were lost with unemployment rising in just about every part of the economy.

5. Every society has some unemployment. Few young people entering the _____ find a job right away;

6. Workers may leave their jobs to seek new work or stay at home raising children; others may be _____ or suffer from long-term illnesses;

7. Generally, companies _____ to become more competitive, or firms close in the face of foreign competition or economic recession.

8. In 2008, just as the economy was falling into recession, 7 million people over the age of sixteen were unemployed, about 4.6 percent of the _____ labor force.

9. In some regions, especially _____ areas, unemployment rates are usually far worse—about double the national average.

10. _____ sex or age, unemployment is lower among whites than among African Americans: the gap between white and black teenagers was especially large.

**B.** *Compare answers with another student. Check your answers in the dictionary. Then read through the passage on page 201 again. Can you remember the words you looked up the first time? If not, mark them for further review.*

## EXERCISE 15

**A.** *Select six words or phrases from the passages in this unit that you think other students might not be familiar with or might not remember well (preferably words that are on the word list in the Appendix).*

**B.** *On a separate piece of paper, make an exercise like Exercise 14:*
- *Write the sentences where you found the words and phrases on your list, leaving a blank in place of the word or phrase.*
- *Write the missing words or phrases in a box below the sentences—but not in order.*

**C.** *Exchange exercises with another student and do your partner's exercise.*

**D.** *Look back at the text to check your answers.*

**E.** *With your partner, give the definitions for the words and phrases you selected for your exercises. Look up any you are not sure about.*

### Reflecting on Your Learning

**1.** Discuss these questions with another student.
- Which of the text marking techniques is easiest for you to use? Most effective? Explain.
- Do you find it easier to make diagrams or take notes? Which helps you retain information better? Explain.
- Is it easier to write summaries or quiz questions? Which helps you retain information better? Explain.
- Which do you think is more effective for reviews? Why?
- Consider the kinds of reading you need to do (or will need to do) for your courses. Which of the strategies in this unit do you think will work best for which kinds of reading or studying?

**2.** Select useful vocabulary from this unit:
- Look through the passages in this unit for more vocabulary that would be useful to learn. Write the words or phrases in your vocabulary notebook (with parts of speech, definitions and/ or synonyms, the sentences where you found them, and any helpful notes about usage).
- Review the words in your notebook. Test yourself and then ask a classmate or friend to test you. Write the words you have trouble remembering on study cards. Review and test yourself until you know them well.

# UNIT 6

# Genres of Writing

Writing in English varies a great deal, depending on the genre [type] and purpose of the text. For example, business emails, news articles, academic articles, and blogs are all structured very differently and all contain very different language.

Over the years, writers have developed typical structures, patterns, and styles for each genre so that the task of writing will be easier for them and they can concentrate on the content. It also makes reading easier—if the reader is familiar with the genre.

In this unit you will learn about the following five genres:

> news articles            opinion essays and blogs            textbooks
> background articles                                          academic articles

## News Articles (newspapers or websites)

These articles tell about recent events or about recent scientific, political, or economic developments. They may be short or long, depending on the publication and the importance of the event.

News articles typically

- present the most important information in the first few sentences (what happened, who was involved, when and where it happened, etc.).
- contain short paragraphs (sometimes just one sentence long).
- do not have a conclusion, since many readers do not read to the end.
- contain many facts, including names, places, dates, numbers, etc.
- are impersonal, written in the third person (*he/she/they*).
- do not include the writer's opinion, but may include opinions and quotation from others.

## EXERCISE 1

A. *Preview and read the article. What is the overall pattern from Unit 4 (listing, sequence, comparison, etc.)?*

_____

B. *Work with another student to identify and underline the overall idea, main ideas and supporting facts and ideas. Mark the overall idea and the main ideas. Look up only the vocabulary that is necessary for comprehension.*

# California Report: "Smart Growth" for a Sustainable Future

A new report released last week by Calthorpe Associates, a leading urban planning firm, highlights the stark contrasts between a "business as usual" approach to urban growth and a "smart growth" approach that aims for more sustainable land use, lower household costs, and significant reductions in energy and water consumption.

The report, entitled "Vision California: Charting Our Future" sets out the advantages of more compact and efficient development compared with the uncontrolled urban sprawl that has been the norm for the past 30 years. Communities that are more densely built would allow commuters in California to live closer to their jobs, saving them 3.7 trillion miles of driving and 140 billion gallons of gasoline by 2050.

The study, a $2.5 million undertaking, was promoted and funded by the California High Speed Train Authority and the Strategic Growth Council, formed under Governor Arnold Schwarzenegger.

According to the report, "smart growth" would save 240,000 acres of farm, forest and other open land and reduce the state's highway and infrastructure costs by $195 billion. Residential water use—a perennial issue in California—would drop by 60 percent, and overall energy use by 40 percent. Total vehicle miles traveled would be reduced by 34 percent and greenhouse gas emissions by two-thirds.

For individual households, the current annual average cost of $20,750 for auto travel and utilities would drop to $11,150.

Commenting on the report, the American Lung Association noted that smart growth would lead to fewer acute asthma and bronchitis attacks, heart attacks and premature deaths. Overall, it would reduce annual expenditures on pollution-related health issues by approximately $1.66 billion.

"If doctors and other health experts designed our cities, they would look quite different than the sprawling communities we see today," said Sonal R. Patel, M.D., Director of White Memorial Pediatric Medical Groups Division of Allergy and Immunology in Los Angeles.

The land use recommendations of the report include the development of infrastructure such as public transportation, parks and bike paths to encourage alternatives to vehicle use, as well as a healthier lifestyle.

In the words of Governor Schwarzenegger, "This analysis shows we are moving in the right direction in working to design communities that allow Californians to save money by spending less time in their cars and more time with their families. By working together at all levels of government, we can help create a brighter, more sustainable future for generations of Californians to enjoy."

C.   *Work with your partner. On a separate piece of paper, write the overall idea and make a diagram/outline or take notes to show the main ideas and the supporting facts and ideas. Then compare work with another pair of students.*

D.   *Add any useful vocabulary to your notebook.*

# Background Articles (newspapers, magazines, websites)

These articles are usually longer than news articles and give background information about people, places, issues in the news, or about economic, scientific, cultural, or other developments.

Background articles typically

- begin with something to catch the reader's attention: a description, an anecdote, a quotation, a question, a surprising statistic, etc.
- present the main idea in the first few paragraphs.
- contain longer, carefully structured paragraphs.
- end with a conclusion that summarizes or comments on the main idea.
- contain facts, as well as narratives, descriptions, explanations, or arguments.
- are more informal in tone, sometimes using the first *(I/we)* or second person *(you)*.
- may include the writer's personal experience or opinion.

## EXERCISE 2

**A.** *Preview and read the magazine article. What is the overall pattern from Unit 4 (listing, sequence, comparison, etc.)?* _____

**B.** *Work with another student to identify and underline the overall idea, main ideas, and supporting facts and ideas. Mark the overall idea and the main ideas. Look up only the vocabulary that is necessary for comprehension.*

### The Exurbs vs. Cities

By Sandra Shaw

Until recently, most Americans wanted to live in the suburbs. They wanted a big house and yard and everything else that went with it. However, as housing prices surged in the 80s and 90s, they could afford that lifestyle only by moving far out to the "exurbs"—the outermost distant suburbs.

But now the exurbs seem to have lost their appeal. The newest trend shows both younger and older households moving back towards the city. In fact, the demand for housing in the exurbs has remained low since the credit crisis of 2007–2008, despite the recovering economy. In city centers, on the other hand, housing prices have shown solid growth, even in central neighborhoods that had undergone decades of progressive decay.

One factor drawing people back into the city seems to be a general desire to participate more in social, political, or cultural life. When you live in the city, it's easier to attend courses or performances, visit museums and galleries, join movements or public events, or just meet up with friends. Whatever your particular interests, you're more likely to find others who share them than if you live in distant exurb where houses are far apart and neighbors hardly know each other.

But there's another factor that may loom larger for most people today: the cost of driving. Life in an exurb inevitably involves a long commute, and then more driving for everything else—shopping, school, sports or other activities. With fuel prices steadily increasing, lots of driving means major expenses.

Besides, how much can you enjoy a big exurban house and yard when you're trapped in your car for hours every day? And what about the quality of your life? Studies have shown that commuting long hours has a negative impact on health, partly because these commuters tend to get little exercise. Furthermore, it also places a good deal of stress on relationships and families, especially in the isolated context of the typical exurban home.

Indeed, sociologists are saying that Americans may be falling out of love with their cars. More and more people opt not to own a vehicle or they often leave it in their garage. But that's only possible if they live in a place where they can get around without a car. A study by Christopher B. Leinberger and Mariella Alfonzo for the Brookings Institution showed that the value of real estate today is closely related to its walkability index—how easy and pleasant it is to get around a neighborhood on foot (or bicycle). Good public transportation is also important, and, in fact, it usually coexists with high walkability.

To attract new residents, city planners and investors are working to improve their walkability indexes. Not surprisingly, the older cities are ahead of the game. New York, Boston, and San Francisco have always been great cities for walking, with streets full of people, day and night.

However, most American cities were built with cars in mind, and walking was discouraged. Now transportation policies and urban landscapes are being re-evaluated and redesigned to include wider sidewalks, more green areas, trees and benches. The aim is to create "complete streets" that are usable and attractive for everyone, not just drivers.

**C.** *Work with your partner. On a separate piece of paper, write the overall idea and make a diagram/outline, or take notes to show the main ideas and supporting facts and ideas. Then compare work with another pair of students.*

**D.** *Add any useful vocabulary to your notebook.*

# Opinion Essays and Blogs

Journalists, academics, and others write essays in newspapers and magazines and on news websites to express their opinions about current issues.

Opinion essays typically

- begin with something to catch the reader's attention (like background articles).
- present the overall idea—the writer's opinion about the issue—in the first paragraph or two.
- end with a conclusion that summarizes or comments on the main idea.
- may include the writer's own experiences, as well as opinions.
- are informal in tone and use first, second, or third person.
- often include persuasive language with the aim of influencing the reader's thinking.

**A.** *Preview and read this blog post. What is the overall pattern?* _____

**B.** *Work with another student to identify and underline the overall idea, main ideas, and supporting facts and ideas. Mark the overall idea and main ideas. Look up only the vocabulary that is necessary for comprehension.*

### Commuting My Life Away

I did it for eight years. Every morning I drove from my home in New Hampshire to my job in Boston and every evening I drove home again. My husband also commuted, but to Portland, Maine, so we couldn't share driving or expenses. We bought a lovely old house in a village and enjoyed fixing it up over the weekends. The commute was a burden that weighed on me, but I listened to a lot of radio and told myself that having our dream home made it all worthwhile.

But then my first child was born. When my maternity ended, I hated spending three hours or more every day in a car. It was time away from my little girl and my husband, who had a shorter commute. It was time out of my life, when I couldn't relax or do any of the things I like doing. Instead, I was trapped in my little metal box, trying to focus on the radio, but worrying all the time about the baby.

Indeed, commuting is not just unpleasant; it is highly stressful. Studies have found that a long commute is associated with migraines and back pain, as well as obesity and all the health problems that go with it, including diabetes and heart disease. Researchers at Brown University found an inverse relationship between length of commute and health: the longer the commute, the poorer the commuter's physical condition. An important factor—as I knew all too well—was that long commutes left little time for engaging in physical activity. The researchers also found that people with long commutes were far more likely to buy unhealthy, ready-made meals, rather than preparing their own.

Other research has shown that people with long commutes express greater dissatisfaction with their lives in general. Long commutes correlate closely with loneliness and social isolation. As the political scientist Robert Putnam has written, every 10 minutes of commuting results in 10 percent fewer social connections. A study in Sweden found that couples in which one partner had a long commute were 40 percent more likely to divorce. The fatigue, the stress, the lack of time together, problems relating to child care—I know something about these issues and can imagine all too well how they could undo a marriage.

In the United States, commuting time has been steadily increasing over recent decades. For one in six American workers, travel time each way to work is at least 45 minutes, and for about 3.5 million people—the "extreme commuters" like me—it is more than 90 minutes. Why do they do it? I suspect many of them have motives that are similar to mine at that time: We loved our house and the village; we were very attached to the idea that our daughter would grow up in the country; I had a good job in Boston that I didn't want to leave.

The turning point for me was my second pregnancy. Continuing to commute with a second child at home was simply not feasible. At that point, we were faced with a decision: I could give up my career and we could keep our lovely house in New Hampshire, or I could keep my job and we

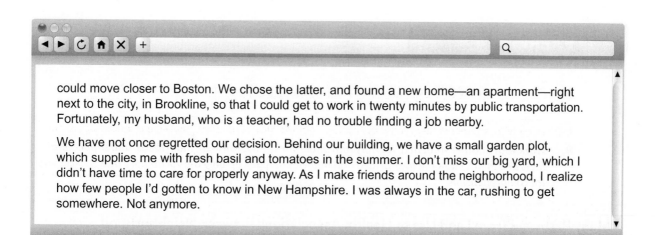

could move closer to Boston. We chose the latter, and found a new home—an apartment—right next to the city, in Brookline, so that I could get to work in twenty minutes by public transportation. Fortunately, my husband, who is a teacher, had no trouble finding a job nearby.

We have not once regretted our decision. Behind our building, we have a small garden plot, which supplies me with fresh basil and tomatoes in the summer. I don't miss our big yard, which I didn't have time to care for properly anyway. As I make friends around the neighborhood, I realize how few people I'd gotten to know in New Hampshire. I was always in the car, rushing to get somewhere. Not anymore.

**C.** *Work with your partner. On a separate piece of paper, write the overall idea and make a diagram/outline or take notes to show the main ideas and supporting facts and ideas. Then compare your work with another pair of students.*

**D.** *Add any useful vocabulary to your notebook.*

## Academic Articles

Academic papers and articles are written by researchers to share the results of their research.

Academic papers typically

- begin with an abstract [summary] that describes findings of the research—the overall idea.
- are divided into sections with headings that relate to stages in the research (current evidence, methods, conclusions, implications, etc.).
- include an author biography, acknowledgments, notes, and a list of references.
- include many references to other researchers, and citations from other studies or publications.
- include graphic illustrations.
- are formal in tone, using mostly third person and occasionally "we" to refer to the researcher(s).
- contain technical language relating to the topic and the field.
- are very dense with information and ideas.
- are written with sentences that contain complex noun phrases (***Examples:** low-density land development, a single index of walkability that incorporated land use mix, street connectivity, net residential density and retail floor area ratios*).

**A.** *Preview and read this excerpt from an academic article. What is the overall pattern?*

**B.** *Work with another student to identify and underline the overall idea, main ideas, and supporting facts and ideas. Mark the overall idea and main ideas. Look up only the vocabulary that is necessary for comprehension.*

## Many Pathways from Land Use to Health: Associations between Neighborhood Walkability and Active Transportation, Body Mass Index, and Air Quality

Lawrence D. Frank, James F. Sallis, Terry L. Conway, James E. Chapman, Brian E. Saelens & William Bachman

### Abstract

The literature shows single-use, low-density land development and disconnected street networks to be positively associated with auto dependence and negatively associated with walking and transit [public transportation] use. These factors in turn appear to affect health by influencing physical activity, obesity, and emissions of air pollutants. We evaluated the association between a single index of walkability that incorporated land use mix, street connectivity, net residential density, and retail floor area ratios, with health-related outcomes in King County, Washington. We found a 5% increase in walkability to be associated with a per capita 32.1% increase in time spent in physically active travel, a 0.23-point reduction in body mass index, 6.5% fewer vehicle miles traveled, 5.6% fewer grams of oxides of nitrogen (NOx) emitted, and 5.5% fewer grams of volatile organic compounds (VOC) emitted. These results connect development patterns with factors that affect several prevalent chronic diseases.

### Full Text
### Associations between Neighborhood Walkability and Active Transportation, Body Mass Index, and Air Quality

Growing evidence documents the adverse health impacts of common land use patterns in the U.S. (Frank & Engelke, 2005; Frumkin, Frank, & Jackson, 2004; Handy, Boarnet, Ewing, & Killingsworth, 2002). Thus, according to some researchers, many zoning and subdivision regulations are doing a poor job of protecting public health, safety, and welfare (Jackson, 2003; Lavizzo-Mourey & McGinnis, 2003; Schilling & Linton, 2005).

Zoning ordinances [regulations] often require separation between residential and other land uses and restrict mixed-use development capable of supporting local retail and regional transit service (Knaap & Nelson, 1992). Subdivision regulations often favor disconnected cul-de-sac street designs over more connected grid networks. As a result, the distances between places where people live, work, and play are often too great to walk. In the Seattle region, where this study was based, 85.5% of all work trips and 86.0% of all non-work trips are made in private vehicles (Puget Sound Regional Council, 1999).

Traveling in vehicles rather than on foot can produce adverse health effects through a variety of mechanisms. For example, a survey of 10,898 people in Atlanta, Georgia (Frank, Andresen, & Schmid, 2004), showed that each additional hour spent in a car per day was associated with a 6% increase in the odds of being obese, while each additional kilometer walked per day was associated with a 4.8% reduction in the odds of being obese. Obesity and inactivity are both widespread, and increase the risk of several common chronic diseases (Andersen, 2003; U. S. Department of Health and Human Services, 1996). Increased numbers of vehicle trips and vehicle miles of travel are also associated with higher levels of several air pollutants resulting from vehicle emissions that have adverse respiratory health impacts.

This article examines the following three pathways by which single-use, low-density land use patterns can adversely affect health:

1. If the built environment reduces opportunity for active transportation [walking or cycling], this may reduce total physical activity, and potentially increase risk for chronic disease.

2. If the built environment stimulates increased time spent in vehicles, it may reduce physical activity, and both of these may contribute to obesity, potentially increasing risk for chronic disease.

3. If the built environment stimulates increased vehicular travel, this may increase per capita vehicle emissions, and these may increase exposure to pollutants and risk of respiratory and cardiovascular ailments.

**Current Evidence Linking the Built Environment to Physical Activity and Obesity**

Recent reviews show consistent associations between neighborhood design and walking and cycling for transportation (Frank, Engelke, & Schmid, 2003; Saelens, Sallis, Black, & Chen, 2003; Sallis, Frank, Saelens, & Kraft, 2004; Transportation Research Board & Institute of Medicine, 2005). People who live in neighborhoods with "traditional" or "walkable" designs report about 30 minutes more walking for transportation each week (Saelens, Sallis, & Frank, 2003) and more total physical activity (Frank, Schmid, Sallis, Chapman, & Saelens, 2005; King et al., 2003; Saelens, Sallis, Black, et al., 2003), compared to those who live in neighborhoods with less walkable "suburban" designs. (For a different approach and result, see also Rodriguez, Khattak, & Evenson in this issue.)

If the built environment affects physical activity, it is reasonable to expect it to affect weight as well. At least five studies demonstrated people were more likely to be heavier, overweight, or obese if they lived in less walkable areas (Ewing, Schmid, Killingsworth, Zlot, & Raudenbush, 2003; Frank, Andresen, & Schmid, 2004; Giles-Corti, MacIntyre, Clarkson, Pikora, & Donovan, 2003; Saelens, Sallis, Black, et al., 2003; Lopez, 2004). Moreover, one study related sprawl in metropolitan areas directly to the prevalence of chronic diseases (Sturm & Cohen, 2004). (See also Doyle, Kelly-Schwartz, Schlossberg, & Stockard in this issue.) This body of work links the built environment with physical activity, obesity, and chronic diseases.

(Source: Journal of the American Planning Association January 1, 2006, Taylor and Francis for permissions http://www.tandfonline.com/doi/abs/10.1080/01944360608976725#preview)

C.   *Work with your partner. On a separate piece of paper, write the overall idea, and make a diagram/outline, or take notes to show the main ideas and the supporting facts and ideas. Then compare work with another pair of students.*

D.   *Add any useful vocabulary to your notebook.*

# Textbooks

Textbooks are written by professors or experts to teach concepts and terminology related to academic subjects.

Textbooks typically

- begin each chapter or section with an introduction to the key concepts.
- conclude each chapter or section with a summary of those concepts.
- include references to research and citations from academic publications.
- include definitions for important new terms.
- use bold or italic print to emphasize important terms and concepts.
- include color illustrations, photographs, and graphics.
- are formal in tone, using the third person.
- contain technical language relating to the subject.

## EXERCISE 5

**A.** *Preview and read this passage from an environmental science textbook. What is the overall pattern?*

_____

**B.** *Work with another student to identify and underline the overall idea, main ideas, and supporting facts and ideas. Mark the overall idea and main ideas. Look up only the vocabulary that is necessary for comprehension.*

### SPRAWL

The term *sprawl* has become laden with meanings and suggests different things to different people. To some, sprawl is aesthetically ugly, environmentally harmful, and economically inefficient. To others, it is the collective outgrowth of reasonable individual desires and decisions in a world of growing human population. We can begin our discussion by giving **sprawl** a simple, nonjudgemental definition: the spread of low-density urban or suburban development outward from an urban center.

**Urban areas spread outward**

As urban and suburban areas grow in population, they also grow spatially. This is clear from maps and satellite images of rapidly spreading cities such as Las Vegas. Another example is Chicago, whose metropolitan area now consists of more than 9.5 million people spread across 23,000 km2 (9,000 mi2)—an area 40 times the size of the city. All in all, houses and roads supplant over 1 million ha (2.5 million acres) of U.S. land each year—over 2,700 ha (6,700 acres) every day.

Several types of development approaches can lead to sprawl. These approaches allot [give] each person more space than do cities. For example, the average resident of Chicago's suburbs takes up 11 times more space than a resident of the city. As a result, the outward spatial growth of suburbs across the landscape generally outpaces growth in numbers of people. In fact, many researchers define *sprawl* as the physical spread of development at a rate that exceeds the rate of population growth. For instance, the population of Phoenix grew 12 times larger between 1950 and 2000, yet its land area grew 27 times larger. Between 1950 and 1990, the population of 58 major U.S. metropolitan areas rose by 80%, but the land they covered rose by 305%. Even in 11 metro areas where population declined between 1970 and 1990 (for instance, Rust Belt cities such as Detroit, Cleveland, and Pittsburgh), the amount of land covered increased.

## Sprawl has several causes

There are two main components of sprawl. One is human population growth—there are simply more people alive each year. The other is per capita land consumption—each person takes up more land. The amount of sprawl is a function of the number of people added to a region times the amount of land the average person occupies.

A study of U.S. metropolitan areas between 1970 and 1990 found that each of these two factors contributes about equally to sprawl but that cities varied in which was more important. The Los Angeles metro area increased in population density by 9% between 1970 and 1990, becoming the nation's most densely populated metro area. Increasing density should be a good recipe for preventing sprawl. Yet L.A. grew in size by a whopping 1,021 km2 (394 mi2). This spatial growth, despite the increase in density, resulted from an overwhelming influx of new people. In contrast, the Detroit metro area lost 7% of its population between 1970 and 1990, yet it expanded in area by 28%. In this case, sprawl clearly was caused solely by increased per capita land consumption.

We discussed reasons for human population growth in Chapter 8. As for the rise in per capita land consumption, factors just mentioned—better highways, inexpensive gasoline, and technologies such as telecommunications and the Internet—fostered movement away from city centers by freeing businesses from dependence on the centralized infrastructure a major city provides and by giving workers greater flexibility to live where they desire. The primary reason for greater per capita land consumption, however, is that most people simply like having space and privacy and dislike congestion. Furthermore, the consumption-oriented American lifestyle promotes bigger houses, bigger cars, and bigger TVs, and having more space to house one's possessions becomes important. Unless there are overriding economic or social disadvantages, most people prefer living in less congested [crowded], more spacious, more affluent communities.

Economists, politicians, and city boosters have encouraged the unbridled [uncontrolled] spatial expansion of cities and suburbs. The conventional assumption has been that growth is always good and that attracting business, industry, and residents will enhance a community's economic well-being, political power, and cultural influence. Today, however, this assumption is being challenged. As growing numbers of people feel the negative effects of sprawl on their lifestyles, they have begun to question the mantra [belief] that all growth is good.

## What is wrong with sprawl?

*Sprawl* means different things to different people. To some, the word evokes strip malls, homogenous commercial development, and tracts of cookie-cutter houses encroaching on farmland or ranchland. It may suggest traffic jams, destruction of wildlife habitat, and loss of natural land around cities.

For other people, sprawl represents the collective result of choices made by millions of well-meaning individuals trying to make a better life for themselves and their families. In this view, those who decry sprawl are being elitist and fail to appreciate the good things about suburban life. Let us try, then to leave the emotional debate aside and assess what research can tell us about the impacts of sprawl.

**Transportation** Most studies show that sprawl constrains transportation options, essentially forcing people to drive cars. These constraints include the need to own a vehicle and to drive it most places, the need to drive greater distances or to spend more time in vehicles, lack of mass transit options, and more traffic accidents. Across the United States, during the 1980s and 1990s the average length of work trips rose by 36%, and total vehicle miles driven rose three times faster than population growth. An automobile-oriented culture also increases dependence on nonrenewable petroleum, with its economic and environmental consequences.

**Pollution** By promoting automobile transportation, sprawl increases pollution. Carbon dioxide emissions from vehicles contribute to global climate change while nitrogen- and sulfur-containing air pollutants lead to tropospheric ozone, urban smog, and acid precipitation. Motor oil and road salt from roads and parking lots pollute waterways, posing risks to ecosystems and human health. Runoff of polluted water from paved areas is estimated to be about 16 times greater than from naturally vegetated areas.

**Health** Aside from the health impacts of pollution, some research suggests that sprawl promotes physical inactivity because driving cars largely takes the place of walking during daily errands. Physical inactivity increases obesity and high blood pressure, which can in turn lead to other ailments. A 2003 study found that people from the most-sprawling U.S. counties weigh 2.7 kg (6 lb) more for their height than people from the least-sprawling U.S. counties and that slightly more people from the most-sprawling counties show high blood pressure.

**Land use** The spread of low-density development means that more land is developed while less is left as forests, fields, farmland, or ranchland. Of the estimated 1 million ha (2.5 million acres) of U.S. land converted each year, roughly 60% is agricultural land and 40% is forest. These lands provide vital resources, recreation, aesthetic beauty, wildlife habitat, air and water purification, and other ecosystem services. Sprawl generally diminishes all these amenities.

**Economics** Sprawl drains tax dollars from existing communities and funnels them into infrastructure for new development on the fringes of those communities. Money that could be spent maintaining and improving downtown centers is instead spent on extending the road system, water and sewer system, electricity grid, telephone lines, police and fire service, schools, and libraries. These costs of extending infrastructure are generally paid by taxpayers of the community and are not charged to developers. For instance, one study calculated that sprawling development at Virginia Beach, Virginia, would require 81% more in infrastructure costs and would drain 3.7 times more from the community's general fund each year than compact urban development. Advocates for sprawling development argue that as owners of newly developed homes and businesses pay property taxes, this revenue eventually reimburses the community's investment in extending infrastructure. However, studies have found that in most cases taxpayers continue to subsidize new development unless municipalities specifically require that developers pay new infrastructure costs.

(Source: Jay Withgott and Scott Brennan, Benjamin Cummings, *Environment: The Science Behind the Stories,* 4th ed., Pearson Education, 2001)

C. *Work with your partner. On a separate piece of paper, write the overall idea and make a diagram/outline, or take notes to show the main idea and the supporting facts and ideas. Then compare work with another pair of students.*

D. *Add any useful vocabulary to your notebook.*

## Reflecting on the Issues

*Discuss these questions with a small group of students:*

1. Do you live in a city neighborhood, a suburb, an exurb, or in the country? Are you happy with the location, or would you rather live in a different area?
2. Do you commute to work or school? If so, how long does it take you?
3. Do you know any "extreme commuters"?
4. Would you accept a job if it involved a long commute?
5. Have commuting habits changed in your country in recent years? If so, how?

# Focus on Vocabulary

**A.**  *Read these sentences from the passage in Exercise 4. For each underlined word or phrase, choose the one that is closest in meaning.*

1. The literature shows single-use, low-density land development and disconnected street <u>networks</u> to be positively associated with auto dependence and negatively associated with walking and transit use.

   a. lighting            b. systems            c. maps

2. We evaluated the association between a single index of walkability that <u>incorporated</u> land use mix, street connectivity, net residential density, and retail floor area ratios, with health-related outcomes in King County, Washington.

   a. organized           b. showed             c. included

3. We evaluated the association between a single index of walkability that incorporated land use mix, street connectivity, net residential density, and retail floor area ratios, with health-related <u>outcomes</u> in King County, Washington.

   a. results             b. problems           c. causes

4. These results connect development patterns with factors that affect several <u>prevalent</u> chronic diseases.

   a. rare                b. frequent           c. serious

5. Growing evidence documents the <u>adverse</u> health impacts of common land use patterns in the U.S.

   a. positive            b. typical            c. negative

6. Obesity and inactivity are both <u>widespread</u>, and increase the risk of several common chronic diseases.

   a. serious             b. unhealthy          c. common

7. If the built environment reduces opportunity for active transportation, this may reduce total physical activity, and <u>potentially</u> increase risk for chronic disease.

   a. possibly            b. powerfully         c. probably

8. If the built environment <u>stimulates</u> increased time spent in vehicles, it may reduce physical activity, and both of these may contribute to obesity, potentially increasing risk for chronic disease.

   a. prevents             b. encourages             c. discourages

B.   *Compare answers with another student. Check your answers in the dictionary. Then read through the passage on page 212 again. Can you remember the words you looked up the first time? If not, mark them for further review.*

## EXERCISE 7

A.   *Read these sentences from the passage in Exercise 5. Write a word from the box in each blank. You may need to change the form of the word.*

| a function of | challenge | diminish | foster | outpace |
|---|---|---|---|---|
| affluent | constrain | evoke | outgrowth | spatially |

1. To others, it is the collective _____ of reasonable individual desires and decisions in a world of growing human population.

2. As urban and suburban areas grow in population, they also grow _____.

3. As a result, the outward spatial growth of suburbs across the landscape generally _____ growth in numbers of people.

4. The amount of sprawl is _____ the number of people added to a region times the amount of land the average person occupies.

5. As for the rise in per capita land consumption, factors just mentioned . . . _____ movement away from city centers by freeing businesses from dependence on the centralized infrastructure a major city provides . . .

6. Unless there are overriding economic or social disadvantages, most people prefer living in less congested, more spacious, more _____ communities.

7. Today, however, this assumption is being _____.

8. To some, the word [sprawl] _____ strip malls, homogenous commercial development, and tracts of cookie-cutter houses encroaching on farmland or ranchland.

9. Most studies show that sprawl _____ transportation options, essentially forcing people to drive cars.

10. These lands provide vital resources, recreation, aesthetic beauty, wildlife habitat, air and water purification, and other ecosystem services. Sprawl generally _____ all these amenities.

B.   *Compare answers with another student. Check your answers in the passage on page 214. With your partner, give definitions for the words in the box (as they are used in the sentences) Look up any you are not sure about and write them in your notebook.*

## EXERCISE 8

A.   *Select six words or phrases from the passages in this unit which you think other students might not be familiar with or might not remember well (preferably words that are on the word list in the Appendix).*

B.   *On a separate piece of paper, make an exercise like Exercise 7:*
  - *Write the sentences where you found the words and phrases on your list, leaving a blank in place of the word or phrase.*
  - *Write the missing words or phrases in a box below the sentences—but not in order.*

C.   *Exchange exercises with another student and do your partner's exercise.*

D.   *Look back at the text to check your answers.*

E.   *With your partner, give the definitions for the words and phrases you selected for your exercises. Look up any you are not sure about.*

---

### Reflecting on Your Learning

**1.** Discuss these questions with another student:
  - Which of the genres of writing presented in this unit have you read before?
  - Which is the easiest to read? Why?
  - Which is the most difficult to read? Why?
  - Which genre do you think you will have to read the most in your university courses?

**2.** Select useful vocabulary from this unit:
  - Look through the passages in this unit for more vocabulary that would be useful to learn. Write the words or phrases in your vocabulary notebook (with parts of speech, definitions and/ or synonyms, the sentences where you found them, and any helpful notes about usage).
  - Review the words in your notebook. Test yourself and then ask a classmate or friend to test you. Write the words you have trouble remembering on study cards. Review and test yourself until you know them well.

# Skimming

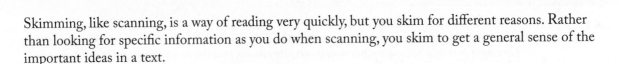

Skimming, like scanning, is a way of reading very quickly, but you skim for different reasons. Rather than looking for specific information as you do when scanning, you skim to get a general sense of the important ideas in a text.

You may skim a text

- to get a sense of what it's about before you read it (previewing).
- to find out what a reviewer thinks about a book, movie, product, etc.
- to understand a writer or a blogger's opinion about an issue.
- to decide if an article will be useful for a research assignment.

Which of these uses of skimming have you tried? Which could be useful for you?

The key to skimming is *skipping* text. You skim by reading some parts of the text and skipping the rest. The more text you skip, the faster you can skim. It is also true, however, that the more you skip, the less you will understand and remember.

For this reason, good readers do not skim when they need a detailed or complete understanding of a text. In those cases, they read carefully. And they change the way they skim—skipping more or less text—according to what they are skimming and why.

How do you know which parts to read and which to skip? In fact, there is no precise formula. That is why skimming requires concentration and active thinking. You need to adapt the way you skim to the kind of text, to your knowledge and understanding of the topic, and to your reason for skimming.

When you skim, you also make use of many other reading skills:

- You scan the text for key words and phrases.
- You look for the most important ideas.
- You make inferences to fill in the gaps for the parts of the text you skip.
- You follow the logic of the writer's ideas.
- You recognize patterns of organization and the different ways texts are structured.

## Guidelines for Skimming

1. Read the title and ask yourself questions about it (as you do when you are previewing).

2. Looking at the passage as a whole, think about the type of text it is and the way it is structured.

3. Continue to ask yourself questions as you look quickly through the parts of the passage that often contain important information or ideas, including
   - the first paragraph(s).
   - the first sentence of other paragraphs (when the paragraphs are long).
   - sentences that include key words or seem important.
   - the last paragraph (except in news articles).

Many students find that skimming is quite difficult. It requires great concentration to move your eyes quickly through a text and decide rapidly what parts to focus on.

The exercises in this unit are timed to help you work on this skill. Your skimming time will naturally vary according to the passage and your understanding of the ideas. In general, as you go through the unit, you should try to skim more quickly with each passage.

Keep in mind that good readers can skim much faster than they normally read—twice as fast or faster. Compare your skimming time in these exercises with your reading time in Part 4. For example, if you read a Part 4 passage (1,000 words) in four minutes (4:00), you should be able to skim a passage in this unit (650 words) in about one minute thirty seconds (1:30).

## Remember

You only want the important ideas from a passage when you skim. You can skip most of the details.

## Skimming Book Reviews

In these exercises, you will read two reviews of the same book. As you skim, ask yourself questions about the book and the reviewer's opinion of the book. Use the title of the book and subtitles of the reviews to help you think of questions (as you do when you are previewing).

# EXERCISE 1

**A.** *Read the title of the book and the subtitle of this review. What do you think the book is about? What is the reviewer's opinion of it?*

**Moonwalking with Einstein: The Art and Science of Remembering Everything by Joshua Foer**
One man's memory odyssey reveals the astonishing potential of the human brain—and its limitations

by Tim Radford

 **B.** *Write your exact starting time. Then skim the review very quickly for the gist [general idea] of the book and the reviewer's opinion.*

Starting time: _____

This is the book of a journey: a young American reporter identifies a puzzle, and sets out to solve it, mostly by talking to the people who set him the puzzle—and therefore must have the answers—and then by trying for himself, and discovering he can do it . . .

At its best, *Moonwalking with Einstein* is a delightful book. It begins with a young journalist who goes out on an interview, gets to thinking about superlatives of strength and intellect, goes home again, searches Google for the cleverest human, and discovers "if not the smartest person in the world, at least some kind of freakish genius" who can memorise 1,528 random digits in one hour and any poem handed to him. It ends with Foer—who cannot remember where he put his car keys—in the finals of the USA Memory Championship, the product not so much of intellectual firepower as determination, technique and luck.

Early in the story he observes astonishing feats of mental athletics at a memory championship—someone recites back 252 random digits as effortlessly as if it had been his own telephone number—and is told that "anybody can do it." He encounters Ed, a shambling 24-year-old from Oxford who becomes his mentor; he meets Tony Buzan, the trim 67-year-old English self-help guru who founded the World Memory Championships in 1991 and who insists the brain is "like a muscle": exercise it and it gets stronger.

These starting points take Foer back in time to the classical world, and the first essay on memory, in a little Latin textbook from 82 BC; and to the legend of Simonides of Ceos, the poet from the 5th century BC who is credited with inventing the notional "memory palaces" in which contestants "place" the objects or abstractions they wish to remember, first having given them physical characteristics with which to recall them. The memory palace technique exploits the fact that we have a better memory for spaces, places and faces than for names and numbers: it's much easier to recall that someone is a baker, than that his surname is Baker.

It also takes Foer to the laboratories of cognitive science, and to the literature of memory: to the famous Russian journalist identified in 1928 who could remember everything; and to those tragic victims of illness and injury who can recall nothing for more than a few seconds.

He gets to know the psychologist who first identified the "phenomenon of seven"—the number of things you can keep in your head at any time, give or take one or two—and explores the still uncertain mechanics and neuroscience of short-term, working and enduring memory.

He recalls Jorge Luis Borges's famous story Funes the Memorious. He explores the historic past: the traditions of memory that existed before the invention of writing. He contemplates the bardic tradition of recited poems; he reflects on Homer and the repetitive insistence on a sea that is wine-dark and a dawn that is rosy-fingered.

He discovers, to his surprise, that learning a poem is harder than memorising a string of nonsense numbers or the order of a shuffled deck of cards. He crosses the Atlantic and puts himself under the tutelage of Ed, and gets to know the eccentric collection of souls who compete in the memory championships: "a bunch of guys (and a few ladies) widely varying in both age and hygienic upkeep."

*Moonwalking with Einstein* is huge fun to read, intellectually rewarding and chronicles a lot of drunk and nerdy behaviour. But what in the end does Foer gain from his newfound capacity for total recall under testing conditions? A good book, certainly, and a better memory—but not vastly better. He goes to dinner with friends and afterwards doesn't just forget where he parked his car: he goes home by subway having forgotten that he drove to dinner in the first place.

(Source: Joshua Foer, "Moonwalking with Einstein: The Art and Science of Remembering Everything," *Guardian*)

**Finishing time:** _____

 **C.** *Write your finishing time. Then calculate and write your skimming time:*

*Finishing time – Starting time = Skimming time:* _____

**D.** *Talk with another student about the book review. Do not look back. What is the book about? Does the reviewer recommend it?*

**E.** *Read the review carefully and check your understanding. Look up the words or phrases that are necessary for comprehension. Then answer these questions (you may look back):*

1. What is the "puzzle" that the writer refers to in the first sentence?
2. How does Foer end up in the finals of the National Memory Championship?
3. What is the "memory palace" technique?
4. What is the author's overall opinion of the book?

**F.** *Compare answers with another pair of students.*

## EXERCISE 2

**A.**   *Read the subtitle of this review of the same book as in Exercise 1. How do you think this review will differ from the one in Exercise 1?*

**Moonwalking with Einstein: The Art and Science of Remembering Everything by Joshua Foer**
Foer's account of his quest to become U.S. memory champion is a dreary and pointless celebration of trivia.

by Peter Conrad

 **B.**   *Write your exact starting time. Then skim quickly to find out more about the book and about this reviewer's opinion.*

Starting time: _____

Memory was once a cerebral lodestar, training us to be rational and ensuring that we were moral. For classical sages it regulated judgment, citizenship and piety, and for medieval scholars, who used books as mnemonic aids, it compressed and codified the history of the world. In modern times memory was redefined as an emotional and spiritual treasury: the taste of a cake brings back Proust's lost childhood.

This noble faculty has not yet been made redundant by electronic search engines such as Google or gadgets such as satnav, since our smart cards and online accounts require us to memorise an ever-longer list of pin numbers, passwords and security codes. But the contests chronicled by Joshua Foer, who in 2006 acquired the title of USA Memory Champion, reward competitors for the retention of trivia: the sequence of cards in a rapidly shuffled deck, the birthdates of total strangers, random glossaries of unfamiliar words. Such is the sadly diminished, demeaning role that the information age allots to our proudest and most precious mental skill.

Foer presents this account of his year spent training for the championship as an induction into the "art and science" of remembering. In fact the useless [tricks] he learns to perform are neither artistic nor scientific; they are sporting feats, which is why he hypes up his associative tricks as exhibitions of strength. Thus the sedentary act of reading becomes a leap from a board poised high above an Olympic-sized pool: "I decided it would be a good idea to dive (bellyflop, really) into the scientific literature." Foer works this mock-heroic metaphor to death, honouring his colleagues—ill-groomed and unsocialised wonks, who wear blinkers and blacked-out goggles when competing—as "mental athletes" or "warriors of the mind."

The grotesque array of professional rememberers lined up by Foer includes a fellow from Utah called Kim Peek, the inspiration for the character played by Dustin Hoffman in *Rain Man*, who died in 2009. The "Kimputer," as this idiot savant called himself, could instantly memorise whatever his eyes scanned, whether it was the text of a Shakespeare play or the telephone directory of some unknown city. Despite the library of factoids crammed into his buzzing skull, Kim had an IQ of only 87. He was at best a neurological oddity, rendered unfit for ordinary existence by his inability to select, edit or erase the information he indiscriminately absorbed.

"Participatory journalism," which is how Foer classifies his book, requires the reporter to step into the frame as a performer, and he tries to keep us interested in his arid quizzes and numerical quirks by going on journeys to conduct interviews. He visits one expert in "a bright bungalow in suburban San Diego" and calls on another in "a plush office complex on the outskirts of Tallahassee"; he even manages a picturesque detour to Oxford, "one of the world's most storied centers of learning" where there are many "storied old buildings, with tall Gothic windows." A pity that his capacity for total recall didn't alert him to his slack or dozy stylistic repetitions.

Foer's self-improvement manual reads like the script for a reality TV series, so we are meant to experience a climactic thrill when a cable network "for the first time ever airs the Memory Championship on national television," devising "television-friendly 'elimination' events" to dramatise the dreary proceedings. Foer's win earns him invitations to fill a few minutes of otherwise empty air on early morning talk shows, though he understands how temporary his "newfound stardom" (or loserdom, depending on your perspective) actually is. After performing the tricks required of him, he is ushered off into oblivion; by telling the story all over again five years later, he is hoping to prolong his meagre allocation of fame and persuade the world to remember his name. But I have too much on my mind, and now intend to exercise my prerogative as a thinker by forgetting him.

(Source: Joshua Foer, "Moonwalking with Einstein: The Art and Science of Remembering Everything," *Guardian*)

**Finishing time:** _____

**C.** *Write your finishing time. Then calculate and write your skimming time:*

*Finishing time – Starting time = Skimming time:* _____

*How does this compare with your skimming time in Exercise 1?*

**D.** *Talk with another student about the book review. Do not look back. Did you learn anything new about the book form this review? Did the reviewer recommend it?*

**E.** *Read the review carefully and check your understanding. Look up the words or phrases that are necessary for comprehension. Then answer these questions (you may look back):*

1. What is this writer's opinion of memory contests?
2. What is his point about Kim Peek?
3. What does the writer think about Foer's style of writing?
4. What is his overall opinion of the book?

**F.** *Compare answers with another pair of students and discuss these questions:*

1. Would you be interested in reading a book about memory?
2. How would you rate your own memory? Have you ever tried to improve it?
3. Have you ever met anyone, read about, or seen a movie about someone with an extraordinary memory (*Rain Man*, for example)?
4. Do you think that modern technology (computers, smart phones, GPS, etc.) affects our ability to remember things?

# Skimming Blogs

The passages in these exercises are both from one writer's blog. As you skim, ask yourself questions about the topic of the article, the issues involved, and the blogger's views.

## EXERCISE 3

**A.** *Read the title of the blog and of this post. Discuss these questions with another student:*

1. What kinds of ideas and information can you expect from this blog? This post?
2. Can you guess what the phrase "Minimize Me" refers to?
3. What current issues do you think the post will address?
4. Can you infer anything about the blogger's point of view?

### Harvard Business Review Blog Network

**A Swedish Burger Chain Says "Minimize Me"**

by Andrew Winston

 **B.** *Write your exact starting time. Then skim the blog post quickly to find out about the topic and the writer's point of view.*

**Starting time:** _____

Last week I wrote about how eating less meat was the best way to reduce your food's carbon footprint. But what do you do if you want to be a responsible corporate citizen and you sell fast food? Well, I think your company would look a lot like Max Burgers, based in Sweden.

I recently spoke to Richard Bergfors, the CEO (and son of the founders) of this unusual 44-year-old "fast" food chain. With 3,000 employees and about $200 million in revenue, Max Burgers is a great example of how a midsize company can carve out a profitable niche through a focus on sustainability—even in an unexpected sector.

In 2000, the company set a new strategy focused on the word "fresh." The leaders looked closely at every ingredient and reduced fat, salt, and sugar, and eliminated genetically modified organisms (GMOs) and trans fats. The menu got healthier, with multiple side options besides fries, 10 drinks with no added sugar, and a selection of darker, healthier breads. The company now sources 100% of its beef and chicken—and 90% of all its product—locally.

To explore its broader climate impact, the firm started working with Swedish thought leaders Natural Step, which, not surprisingly, identified beef as the biggest problem for the company (80 to 85 percent of the footprint). Bergfors acknowledges that industry-wide climate-friendly beef is still a long way off, so Max Burgers plants trees in Africa to offset its carbon footprint. New stores also use solar panels for 15 to 20 percent of electric needs.

But perhaps the most surprising thing this company does is try to influence its customers to buy less meat. Quick reminder: the chain is called Max Burgers. This counterintuitive strategy is the kind of heresy I love—asking customers to use less of your core product. Max Burgers accomplishes this by adding more non-meat items to the menu, prominently displaying climate footprint data in stores (there's transparency for you), and suggesting customers buy chicken, fish, or veggie sandwiches periodically (a là Meatless Mondays).

In 2004, a golden marketing opportunity came along with the launch of the documentary *Supersize Me,* which followed director Morgan Spurlock as he ate only McDonald's food for 30 days. Max Burgers decided to launch a tongue-in-cheek "Minimize Me" campaign. A customer, much like Subway's famous Jared, ate only Max Burgers for 90 days and lost 77 pounds. Two years later, the company re-ran the promotion with multiple people competing on the Max-only diet.

The result of all these efforts is a more sustainable burger chain that's telling everyone to eat less meat, and doing so profitably. The mix of non-beef products is 30% higher than it used to be. But the profit margins are very high.

Bergfors reports that his stores are averaging 11 to 15 percent profit margins versus 2 to 5 percent at the big name competitors. He says Max Burgers is the most profitable, fastest growing chain in Sweden, expanding at 20% per year (and 5% same store sales growth) in a flat market. Granted, higher-end niche brands generally do have higher margins, but this is not an overly small company, and it doesn't seem to be sacrificing anything with its "minimize me" strategy—quite the contrary.

Of course a family run company always has more leeway to act on values (see Patagonia, the prime example). As Bergfors told me, "we've always done things a bit differently—the goal is greater than to just maximize profit." But it's still a business, and in the next breath he said, "we're profit driven and like to make a profit like everyone else . . . but we don't put profit first . . . we don't have to maximize profit and we can care for people and the planet we're living on."

But given Max Burgers' profit levels, it seems that maximizing all value, not just profits, can be darn good business.

(Source: Andrew Watson, "A Swedish Burger Chain Says 'Minimize Me,'" June 30, 2011
http://blogs.hbr.org/winston/2011/06/a-swedish-burger-chain-says-mi.html)

**Finishing time:** _____

C.   *Write your finishing time and calculate your skimming time:* _____
     *How does it compare with your skimming time in the previous exercises?*

D.   *Talk with your partner about the blog post. Do not look back. What is it about? What is the blogger's opinion? Why do you think he chose to write about this topic?*

E.   *Read the blog post carefully and check your understanding. Look up the words or phrases that are necessary for comprehension. Then answer these questions (you may look back):*

1. What does Max Burgers want to "minimize"?
2. What was the company's strategy in 2000?
3. What was the company's campaign in 2004?
4. How is the Max Burger chain different from other fast food chains?
5. What point does this blog post make about sustainability and profitability?

F.   *Compare answers with another pair of students and discuss these questions:*

1. Have you ever eaten at a Max Burger restaurant? If so, how was your experience?
2. Have you ever eaten at other "fast food" restaurants that advertise higher quality, sustainability, or local ingredients (for example, Chipotle Mexican Grill or Chop't)? If so, how was your experience?
3. Are you willing to spend more money for better quality "fast food"? For fast food that is produced locally or more sustainably?

G.   *Write any useful vocabulary in your notebook.*

**A.** *Read the title of the blog and of this post. Discuss these questions with another student:*

1. What current issues do you think this post will address?
2. How might it be similar or different from the blog post in Exercise 3?
3. Can you infer anything about the blogger's point of view?

## Harvard Business Review Blog Network

### Greening Pepsi, from Fertilizer to Bottles

by Andrew Winston

 **B.** *Write your exact starting time. Then skim the blog post quickly to find out about the topic and the writer's point of view.*

**Starting time:** _____

Pepsi recently demonstrated its commitment to reducing its environmental impacts up and down the value chain with two rapid-fire announcements about new initiatives. The old-school approach to greening is to focus on operations within the proverbial "four walls." But Pepsi, like other leaders, is approaching sustainability more holistically, with much greater impact . . .

First, on the downstream side, Pepsi looked for ways to raise the recycling rate of beverage containers from a relatively paltry 34% to 50% or higher. Working with GreenOps, a division of Waste Management, Pepsi launched a new program called "Dream Machine." These "reverse" vending machines, now being placed in high-traffic areas such as gas stations and stadiums, take back those often-abandoned and often-unrecycled empty bottles and give users points toward rewards from sponsors or local merchants.

But Pepsi has gone beyond those relatively minor incentives to add on a social mission. The program will also help fund Pepsi's donation to a group called Entrepreneurship Bootcamp for Veterans with Disabilities (EBV), which trains vets at business schools around the country. Pepsi expects that the combined immediate points and larger mission will drive new, greener customer behaviors—and help solve one of the beverage industry's most intractable value chain problems.

Second, Pepsi has embarked on a very unusual supply chain effort to reduce the carbon emissions associated with its Tropicana orange juice. After conducting a full life-cycle analysis of the product line, the company was relatively surprised to find that the biggest portion of the carbon footprint was found not in manufacturing, or distribution, but actually back in the agriculture stage—primarily the result of the heavily natural-gas dependent process of making fertilizer . . .

The analysis showed Pepsi executives where the largest impacts were, and thus where they'd get the biggest bang for their buck on carbon reductions. The company started working with suppliers and farmers to find new ways to make and apply fertilizer. For example, instead of using natural gas from as far away as Russia (which then requires shipping heavy fertilizer across the world), Pepsi is using biomass from closer to home. Wood waste and agricultural by-products are two sources, but execs are hopeful they can also use the large number of their own orange rinds left over in manufacturing, which would fully close the loop.

The company is also working with scientists on the root chemistry of orange trees, applying fungi and bacteria to increase the uptake of nutrients. All that techno-speak means that the trees will need less fertilizer in total, which means less manufacturing and shipping of that fertilizer and, voila, a smaller footprint.

A 100-acre test run of these new methods of working with new, low-carbon fertilizer is underway. A few years from now, Pepsi and its suppliers will know what's working and what isn't.

But here's the best part: the cost of these changes to consumers and growers will be about zero. And it had to be. Let's face it, this kind of carbon reduction isn't easy to convey to consumers. . . So the sustainability team needed to find ways to lower the fertilizer footprint without causing any additional cost to suppliers or farmers. How did they do it?

By focusing its efforts on the real footprint—identified through a solid lifecycle analysis and good data—Pepsi found the approach with the highest payback. As sustainability executive Tim Carey put it, "It's not unusual to spend tens of millions of dollars removing some carbon from a manufacturing process at returns that can be 10% or less . . . or we can take 15% of total carbon out in the fertilizer step without costing anything."

The impacts of these tests—and future rollout—will not be small; Pepsi buys a fairly shocking one-third of the Florida orange harvest. And the recycling work could shift millions of bottles out of landfills. Pepsi's full value chain view on sustainability is deep green stuff—this is how you implement green thinking.

(Source: Andrew Winston, "Greening Pepsi, from Fertilizer to Bottles," May 19, 2010
http://blogs.hbr.org/winston/2010/05/greening-pepsi-from-fertilizer.html)

**Finishing time:** _____

**C.** *Write your finishing time and calculate your skimming time:* _____
*How does it compare with your skimming time in Exercise 3? In the first exercises?*

**D.** *Talk with your partner about the blog post. Do not look back. What is it about? What is the blogger's opinion? Why do you think he chose to write about this topic?*

**E.** *Read the blog post carefully and check your understanding. Look up the words or phrases that are necessary for comprehension. Then answer these questions (you may look back):*

1. What is different about Pepsi's new initiatives compared with green initiatives in other companies?
2. How does Pepsi plan to increase recycling?
3. What aspect of orange juice production emits the most carbon?
4. How does Pepsi intend to reduce those emissions?
5. How will Pepsi's new initiatives affect customers? The environment?
6. What point does this blog post make about sustainability and profitability?

**F.** *Compare answers with another pair of students and discuss these questions:*

1. What differences or similarities are there between the policies of Max Burgers and Pepsi?
2. Do you know about "green" initiatives at any other company? If so, explain.
3. How effective do you think these policies are environmentally—do they make a difference?
4. How effective do you think they are in terms of public relations for the company?
5. If you were the CEO of a big company like Pepsi, what would you do to make the company "greener"?

**G.** *Write any useful vocabulary in your notebook.*

# Skimming for Research

When you need to write a research report or paper, you can use skimming to find out quickly if articles or books will be useful or not. Ask yourself questions about the ideas and information they contain, and whether they are relevant to your research.

## EXERCISE 5

**A.** *Read the title of the website and article. Discuss these questions with another student:*

**1.** What kind of information or ideas might you expect from this website?

**2.** Do you think this article would be useful for a report on climate change and agriculture?

### CLIMATE NEWS

**The Future Lies in "Climate-smart Agriculture"**

 **B.** *Write your exact starting time. Then skim the article to find out about the issue and the writer's point of view.*

Starting time: _____

In agriculture, "business as usual" has become untenable. This is the conclusion of a year-long study by the Commission on Sustainable Agriculture and Climate Change, chaired by Sir John Beddington, chief scientific adviser to the UK government. According to the commission's report, current agricultural practices will not bring food security for the growing global population, estimated to reach 9 billion by 2050.

The solution lies in "climate-smart" policies, which would generate more output without generating more greenhouse gas (GHG) emissions. As Beddington says, "You've got to massively increase agricultural production, but you can't do it using the same agricultural techniques we've used before because that would seriously increase greenhouse gas emissions for the whole world, with further climate change consequences."

At present, agriculture accounts for about one third of all greenhouse gas (GHG) emissions from human activity—only slightly less than industry and more than transportation. Some of these emissions are a direct consequence of farming: plowing fields releases carbon dioxide in the soil; rice cultivation and livestock breeding both emit large quantities of methane; chemical fertilizers release nitrous oxide. GHG emissions also result indirectly from land-use changes, including deforestation and desertification of fragile grasslands. These changes alter the earth's ability to absorb or reflect heat and light.

Not all farming contributes equally to GHG emissions. The report points to large-scale industrial agricultural practices, and particularly livestock production, as the principle culprits. Major changes are recommended to avoid further global warming, particularly as demand intensifies in developing countries for poultry, beef, and dairy products.

Apart from the issue of emissions, the current agricultural system is also inherently inefficient. The amount of food produced globally "could feed a population of 8 billion, possibly even 9 billion," says U.N., Population Fund advisor Michael Herrmann, but "a large share of the food does not actually end up as food on our plates." About 80% of the worldwide soybean harvest and 35% of cereals are used to manufacture feed for animals.

The solutions needed in different regions will vary widely depending on the climate, soil conditions, economic resources, as well as cultural and other factors. Dr. Christine Negra, coordinator of the commission, says, "In places where organic methods, for example, are appropriate or economically advantageous and produce good socio-economic and ecological outcomes, that's a great approach. In places where, using GMOs, you can address food security challenges and socio-economic issues, those are the right approaches to use, where they've been proven safe."

The report highlights a number of regional projects, including the return to indigenous cattle breeds in India (they emit less methane gas) and the practice of no-till rice farming in Vietnam (also to reduce methane).

As a model for development, it cites the Productive Safety Net Program in Ethiopia. Started in 2003, this program aims to build household and community assets so that people will be better able to withstand times of food shortage. According to Prof. Tekalign Mamo, advisor to the Ethiopian Ministry of Agriculture, the program helps communities share knowledge and resources, and develop small-scale infrastructure such as irrigation, storage, and local seed banks. He says the program has lifted about 1.3 million of the population from poverty and into food security, and at the same time, conserved and rehabilitated the environment.

However, the report also recommends extensive changes in policies governing food production and consumption in developed countries. With better information about the long-term environmental and health consequences, governments can help consumers make more sustainable choices in their shopping for food. They can be encouraged to reduce their consumption of meat through the promotion of campaigns such as "Meatless Mondays," which have gained considerable following in the UK and in several U.S. cities.

Measures can also be taken to reduce food waste, especially in households and at the retail level. As Dr. Negra notes, "The less we waste food, the less food we have to produce, and the fewer greenhouse gases are emitted."

**Finishing time:** _____

C. *Write your finishing time and calculate your skimming time:* _____
*How does it compare with your skimming times in previous exercises?*

D. *Talk with your partner about the article. Do not look back. What is the article about? In what ways might this article be useful for a report on agriculture and climate change?*

E. *Read the article carefully and check your understanding. Look up the words or phrases that are necessary for comprehension. Then answer these questions (you may look back):*

1. What is the topic of the "report" and who produced it?
2. What does Sir John say is the problem with the agricultural techniques used until now?
3. What does he mean by "climate smart" agriculture?
4. What two different approaches to farming does Dr. Christine Negra mention?
5. What programs in what countries are mentioned as examples?

F. *Compare answers with another pair of students and discuss these questions:*

1. What do you think about the examples that are mentioned in the article? Could any of these be applied in your country?
2. Do you know about any "climate smart" initiatives regarding agriculture in your country? If so, explain.
3. If you were in the government in your country, what would you do to increase food production and/or make agriculture more sustainable?

G. *Write any useful vocabulary in your notebook.*

**A.** *Read the title and subtitle of the article and discuss it with another student. What do you think it is about? Will it be useful for a research report on the causes or effects of climate change?*

## CLIMATE NEWS

### Report: U.S. Agriculture threatened by climate change
Current trends point to a bleak future for American farmers

 **B.** *Write your exact starting time. Then skim the article to find out about the issue and the writer's point of view.*

**Starting time:** _____

Climate change could devastate agriculture in the United States said a major government report released by the Agriculture Department Tuesday. Farmers could be forced to shift crops and change practices, and could face millions of dollars in additional costs battling the weeds, pests, and diseases that thrive in the warming temperatures.

The report cites the rise in average global temperatures caused by greenhouse gases in the atmosphere, which, in turn, can affect weather patterns and lead to bouts of extreme conditions, such as prolonged drought or severe downpours and flooding. Evidence of this trend, says the report, has been seen in recent years in some areas of the United States, where drought and flooding decimated crops and livestock and cost farmers millions in recovery costs.

According to the U.S. Department of Agriculture (USDA), U.S. agriculture has been able to adapt to climate challenges in the past, but those represented temporary variations over the past 150 years of "relative climatic stability." However, scientists predict that global warming will accelerate in pace and intensity over the next few decades, and may soon present a more critical challenge for the sector.

The lead author of the study, Jerry Hatfield, a laboratory director and plant physiologist with the USDA, says, "We're going to end up in a situation where we have a multitude of things happening that are going to negatively impact crop production. In fact, we saw this in 2012 with the drought."

The records of the National Oceanic and Atmospheric Administration show that 2012 was the hottest year ever in the United States since meterological record-keeping began in 1895. The temperatures in 2012 broke the previous record by a full degree Fahrenheit. The drought that hit large areas of the Midwestern states was the most devastating in more than 50 years, destroying up to 80% of crops, most notably corn.

The report states that the next twenty years will present manageable challenges for farmers, which they should be able to minimize by, among other practices, modifying the timing of planting and harvesting, using crop varieties that are more resistant to drought and heat, and increasing irrigation. Farmers may also be able to shift production of crops to regions where the temperature will permit better output. Some northern areas may benefit from the warmer temperatures (as long as rainfall is sufficient), while areas further south or west will be faced with difficult dilemmas.

By mid-century, however, adaptive measures may not be enough to mitigate the consequences of climate change, and serious action must be taken to reduce the greenhouse gas emissions that are driving it, says the USDA.

"Continued increases in greenhouse gas emissions will increase the amount of climate change the United States will experience in the next 100 years," the report said. "Limiting the increase in greenhouse gas emissions will reduce the rate and amount of climate change during this period."

Climate models show the entire United States warming significantly over the next 40 years, with an increase of 2–4° F (1–2° C) over most of the country. The report says that the warming will probably be more noticeable in the interior, where temperatures are likely to increase 3–5°F (2–3° C).

If no action is taken by mid-century, adaptation to climate change may become overwhelming and costly for farmers, and the productivity of crops and livestock will become increasingly unpredictable. Temperature increases and more extreme swings in precipitation could lead to a drop in yield for major U.S. crops and reduce the profitability of many agriculture operations. Higher temperatures cause crops to mature and ripen too quickly, reducing the production of grain, forage, fiber, and fruit if the plants do not receive enough nutrients or water.

Another threat to crops is the increased growth of weeds, due to rising temperatures and higher levels of carbon dioxide, and of insects and diseases, which also thrive in the warmer weather. The higher temperatures will also directly affect livestock productivity because changes in the core body temperature of animals can inhibit growth and production of milk or eggs.

The 146-page report, written by a team of 56 experts from the federal government, universities, and the private sector, was based on a review of more than 1,400 publications, but it made no recommendation on how to stop or curb global warming.

**Finishing time:** _____

C.   *Write your finishing time and calculate your skimming time:* _____
     *How does it compare with your skimming time in Exercise 5? In previous exercises?*

D.   *Talk with your partner about the article. Do not look back. What is the gist? In what ways might it be useful for research on the causes or effects of climate change?*

E.   *Read the article carefully and check your understanding. Look up the words or phrases that are necessary for comprehension. Then answer these questions (you may look back):*

   1. What is the topic of the "report" and who produced it?
   2. What does it say about the immediate impact of global warming on U.S. farms?
   3. What does it say about long-term adaptation to global warming?
   4. What are some of the consequences of global warming mentioned in the article?

F.   *Compare answers with another pair of students and discuss these questions:*

   1. Have you noticed any signs of global warming where you live?
   2. What evidence of global warming have you read or heard about?
   3. Do you think it will have any noticeable effect on your life?
   4. Do you think governments should be concerned about global warming? If so, what do you think should be done?

G.   *Write any useful vocabulary in your notebook.*

# Focus on Vocabulary

EXERCISE 7

**A.** *Read these sentences from the passage in Exercise 3. For each underlined word or phrase, choose the one that is closest in meaning.*

1. I recently spoke to Richard Bergfors, the CEO (and son of the <u>founders</u>) of this unusual 44-year-old "fast" food chain.

   a. people who built      b. people who directed      c. people who started

2. With 3,000 employees and about $200 million in revenue, Max Burgers is a great example of how a midsize company can carve out a profitable niche through a focus on sustainability—even in an unexpected <u>sector</u>.

   a. area of business or trade      b. geographical area      c. part of a company

3. To explore its broader climate <u>impact</u>, the firm started working with Swedish thought leaders Natural Step, which, not surprisingly, identified beef as the biggest problem for the company.

   a. change      b. policy      c. effect

4. This counterintuitive strategy is the kind of heresy I love—asking customers to use less of your <u>core</u> product.

   a. best      b. main      c. favorite

5. Max Burgers <u>accomplishes</u> this by adding more non-meat items to the menu, prominently displaying climate footprint data in stores . . . and suggesting customers buy chicken, fish, or veggie sandwiches periodically (a là Meatless Mondays).

   a. prevents      b. promises      c. achieves

6. Max Burgers accomplishes this by adding more non-meat items to the menu, prominently displaying climate footprint data in stores . . . and suggesting customers buy chicken, fish, or veggie sandwiches <u>periodically</u> (a là Meatless Mondays).

   a. regularly      b. frequently      c. occasionally

7. In 2004, a golden marketing opportunity came along with the <u>launch</u> of the documentary *Supersize Me*, which followed director Morgan Spurlock as he ate only McDonald's food for 30 days.

   a. review      b. success      c. opening

8. Granted, higher-end <u>niche</u> brands generally do have higher margins, but this is not an overly small company, and it doesn't seem to be sacrificing anything with its "minimize me" strategy . . .

   a. specialized          b. healthy          c. popular

**B.** *Compare answers with another student. Check your answers in the dictionary. Then read through the passage on page 226 again. Can you remember the words you looked up the first time? If not, mark them for further review.*

## EXERCISE 8

**A.** *Read these sentences from the passage in Exercise 4. Write a word from the box in each blank. You may need to change the form of the word.*

| close the loop | convey | embark on | incentive | shift |
|---|---|---|---|---|
| commitment | donation | implement | portion | stage |

1. Pepsi recently demonstrated its _____ to reducing its environmental impacts up and down the value chain with two rapid-fire announcements about new initiatives.

2. But Pepsi has gone beyond those relatively minor _____ to add on a social mission.

3. The program will also help fund Pepsi's _____ to a group called Entrepreneurship Bootcamp for Veterans with Disabilities (EBV), which trains vets at business schools around the country.

4. Second, Pepsi has _____ a very unusual supply chain effort to reduce the carbon emissions associated with its Tropicana orange juice.

5. . . . the company was relatively surprised to find that the biggest _____ of the carbon footprint was found not in manufacturing, or distribution, but actually back in the agriculture . . .

6. . . . the company was relatively surprised to find that the biggest . . . of the carbon footprint was found not in manufacturing, or distribution, but actually back in the agriculture _____.

7. . . . execs are hopeful they can also use the large number of their own orange rinds left over in manufacturing, which would fully _____.

8. Let's face it, this kind of carbon reduction isn't easy to _____ to consumers.

9. And the recycling work could _____ millions of bottles out of landfills.

10. Pepsi's full value chain view on sustainability is deep green stuff—this is how you _____ green thinking.

B. *Compare answers with another student. Check your answers in the dictionary. Then read through the passage on page 228 again. Can you remember the words you looked up the first time? If not, mark them for further review.*

## EXERCISE 9

A. *Select six words or phrases from the passages in this unit which you think other students might not be familiar with or might not remember well (preferably words that are on the word list in the Appendix).*

B. *On a separate piece of paper, make an exercise like Exercise 8:*
   - *Write the sentences where you found the words and phrases on your list, leaving a blank in place of the word or phrase.*
   - *Write the missing words or phrases in a box below the sentences—but not in order.*

C. *Exchange exercises with another student and do your partner's exercise.*

D. *Look back at the text to check your answers.*

E. *With your partner, give the definitions for the words and phrases you selected for your exercises. Look up any you are not sure about.*

### Reflecting on Your Learning

**1.** Discuss these questions with another student.
   - Which text(s) seemed more difficult to skim? Why?
   - Which text(s) seemed easier to skim? Why?
   - How could skimming help you in your studies? In other contexts?

**2.** Select useful vocabulary from this unit:
   - Look through the passages in this unit for more vocabulary that would be useful to learn. Write the words or phrases in your vocabulary notebook (with parts of speech, definitions and/or synonyms, the sentences where you found them, and any helpful notes about usage).
   - Review the words in your notebook. Test yourself and then ask a classmate or friend to test you. Write the words you have trouble remembering on study cards. Review and test yourself until you know them well.

# Critical Reading

In order to come to a full understanding of a text, it is often important to look beyond the ideas that have been included and consider who the writer is, why he or she has written the piece, what point of view (or bias) it expresses, and how the ideas compare with others you have read or heard. This will allow you to form your own opinion about the text and ideas.

The ability to analyze and evaluate a piece of writing in this way is known as critical reading. It is essential to academic success in any field of study. In this unit, you will consider these aspects of a text and form an opinion about the writer's ideas.

## Evaluating Web Sources

Since the web is open to everyone and anyone can create web pages or create blogs, you need to look critically at any piece of writing or information that you find online.

The essential first step with an online text is to determine who wrote it and who published or posted it (if it was not the writer him or herself). The guidelines below can help you focus your thinking:

### Guidelines to Evaluating Websites

1. Does the writer identify himself or herself?

2. Is he or she qualified to write about this topic? (For example, if the topic is medical, is the writer a doctor?)

3. Does the website belong to an organization or company that you have heard of? If not, you should do a web search to find out more about it.

4. If the text is a blog post, is the blog hosted by a known organization, such as a news site? If it is on a personal website, is the person well known? If you have not heard of the person, do a web search to find out about him or her.

Sometimes, however, information about the writer and/or source is not available or not helpful. Then you need to figure out what you can about the writer and the source from the text.

**A.** *Read these excerpts from emails. Then work with another student to decide who or what kind of organization sent each one (a company, a news organization, a non-profit organization, etc.). Look up only the vocabulary that is necessary for comprehension.*

1. The weather forecast calls for sustained strong winds for several more hours. Because of this, we expect that our system will continue to take on more damage, resulting in additional outages. We would like to warn our customers that service may not return for an extended period of time. If you experience an outage, please call the emergency number or go to our website (via PC or mobile device) to report it. Consult the attached list of Important Safety Reminders and be safe!

   Sender: _____

2. What Kevin Jones says in his TV ads is one thing, how he votes is another:

   • Last fall, with almost a quarter of a million people out of work here in Massachusetts, Kevin Jones voted against three jobs bills.

   • When some of us were working to stop the excess on Wall Street, Kevin Jones tried to weaken the rules and give the big banks a 19 billion dollar break.

   • Kevin Jones voted against funding for summer jobs and voted twice to double the interest rate on student loans.

   • And Kevin Jones voted to limit the authority of the Environmental Protection Agency and repeatedly voted to give billions in subsidies to big oil companies.

   It's clear where Kevin Jones stands—and it's not with the people of Massachusetts. Do you want him to be your senator?

   Sender: _____

3. After significant declines in the second quarter, equity markets staged a strong rally to establish new highs for the year. International emerging markets generated total returns of 7.7 percent, followed by the developed international markets at 6.9 percent and domestic markets at 6.4 percent. The gains were due in part to the simultaneous announcements of central bank bond purchases by the Chairman of the U.S. Federal Reserve and the Chairman of the European Central Bank.

   Sender: _____

4. Two years ago, cholera struck Haiti for the first time in 100 years, quickly spreading around the country until it became the worst cholera epidemic in the world. Since then, our work has contributed to a substantial decline in the number of cases. Every month we have been treating hundreds of patients with cholera—more than 900 last month.

Now our emergency funding is nearly exhausted, but the disease is not going away. Thousands of patients who could be saved will become sick, and many of them will die unnecessarily—if we can't come up with more funding soon.

That's why we're turning to you . . .

Sender: _____

B.   *Compare answers with another pair of students. Explain your answers with evidence from the texts.*

C.   *Write any useful vocabulary in your notebook.*

## Determining the Purpose

Writers may have many reasons for writing a particular text, but the purpose of a piece of writing generally belongs to one of these categories:

- To **inform**—the writer presents facts and explains ideas to the reader.
- To **persuade**—the writer uses facts and opinions to argue for or against something.
- To **entertain**—the writer tries to catch and hold the reader's attention, using narrative, humor, surprise, suspense, a particular writing style, etc.

## EXERCISE 2

A.   *Re-read the emails in Exercise 1. Then work with another student to decide what the main purpose was for each one: to inform, persuade, or entertain. Write the purpose below.*

1. Purpose: _to inform_____

2. Purpose: _to persuade_____

3. Purpose: _to inform_____

4. Purpose: _to persuade_____

B.   *Compare answers with another pair of students. Explain your answers with evidence from the texts. Then discuss these questions with your partner:*

1. Which emails are asking you to do something?
2. What pronoun(s) is/are used in each text?
3. What examples of persuasive language can you find?
4. Which email uses the most informal language? The most formal language?

A. *Read these passages from various websites. Then work with another student to decide who or what kind of organization wrote each one and what the main purpose was: to inform, persuade, or entertain. Look up only the vocabulary that is necessary for comprehension.*

1. Global Exchange has been a nationally recognized leader of the Fair Trade movement in the United States for years. We support Fair Trade because it revolutionizes the global economy by setting minimum standards for economic, social, and environmental performance of companies. Global Exchange's Fair Trade campaign particularly focuses on coffee, cocoa, and crafts. At present, the campaign is promoting Fair Trade cocoa, for several reasons. After our corporate campaign victories with Fair Trade coffee, we believe that Fair Trade cocoa is the logical next step. Second, we are passionately committed to ending child and forced labor in the cocoa industry, which is a serious problem. Also, Fair Trade cocoa is a great way to introduce the concept of Fair Trade to chocolate lovers (in other words, nearly everyone), and to start a dialogue about poverty in the global economy.

Writer: *Global Exchange Employee — News*

Purpose: *to inform — persuade*

2. Africa Gold is a specialty coffee of exceptional quality from a small farmer group in Cameroon. With our assistance, this local coffee cooperative in the western region of Moungo has begun producing a premium quality coffee bean, bringing enhanced taste and smoothness to your cup and helping Cameroonian farmers earn a better return on their labor. If you like our Boyo Blend coffee, you'll love Africa Gold. If you're interested in single origin coffees, you should try this product of Cameroon, a country with a diverse culture and history, unique geographical features, and numerous endangered species. Your purchase of Africa Gold will help improve sustainability in the area and improve the lives of our partner farmers throughout the Moungo region. Supplies are limited for this special offering, so place your order now.

Writer: *Africa Gold Employee Advertisment*

Purpose: *to persuade*

3. During the past two decades, extensive research has been conducted on the health aspects of caffeine consumption. The U.S. Food and Drug Administration (FDA) classified caffeine as Generally Recognized as Safe (GRAS) in 1958. A more recent review "found no evidence to show that the use of caffeine in carbonated beverages would render these products injurious to health." The American Medical Association (AMA) has a similar position on caffeine's safety, stating that "moderate tea or coffee drinkers probably need have no concern for their health relative to their caffeine consumption. . . ." Most experts agree that moderation and common sense are the keys for consuming caffeine-containing foods and beverages. Moderate caffeine consumption is considered to be about 300 mg, which is equal to 3 cups of coffee, but this depends on the individual and can vary from one to several beverages.

Writer: *Reporter News / Health Resources*

Purpose: *to inform*

**4.** This coffee falls into your stomach, and straightway there is a general commotion. Ideas begin to move like the battalions of the Grand Army on the battlefield, and the battle takes place. Things remembered arrive at full gallop, flags flying. The light cavalry [horsemen] of comparisons deliver a magnificent charge to gain their positions, the artillery of logic hurry up with their train and ammunition, the spears of wit start up like sharpshooters. Similes arise, the paper is covered with ink; for the struggle commences and is concluded with torrents of black water, just as a battle with gun powder.

Writer: _____Writer – advertisement_____

Purpose: ____to entertain_____

**B.** *Compare answers with another pair of students. Explain your answers with evidence from the texts. Then discuss these questions with your partner:*

**1.** Which passages are asking you to do something?
**2.** What pronoun(s) is/are used in each text?
**3.** What examples of persuasive language can you find?
**4.** Which passage contains the most informal language? Most formal? Explain your answers.

**C.** *Write any useful vocabulary in your notebook.*

# Assessing Reliability

When you have a general idea about who wrote a text and why it was written, you can assess the reliability: Is the information in the text likely to be accurate? Can you take the writer's views seriously?

One important clue to reliability is the source of the text. Another clue is the presence or lack of citations from outside sources. Yet another clue is the tone or style of writing—is it factual and objective or emotional and personal?

## Guidelines for Assessing Reliability

**Very reliable:**
- A trusted, well-known news source, an academic journal, a government agency website
- A highly qualified author with academic qualifications, known experience, previous publications
- Containing facts that can be verified and references to well-known outside sources
- Written in a factual, objective style, using formal language

**Somewhat reliable:**
- From a lesser-known, small or local news source, the website of an organization
- Author with modest qualifications, experience, previous publications
- Containing some facts that can be verified
- Written in a generally (though not entirely) objective style, using some informal language

**Not reliable:**
- From a personal blog, an unknown website, or an organization with religious or political aims
- Author with no qualifications, experience, previous publications
- Containing mostly opinions and few facts that can be verified
- Written in an emotional, personal style, using informal language and punctuation (e.g., !)

A. *Read each of these passages from websites. Work with another student to decide who or what kind of organization wrote each one and what the main purpose was. Then assess the reliability (very reliable, somewhat reliable, not reliable). Look up only the vocabulary that is necessary for comprehension.*

1. **Signing for your lunch**
   By Sandra Shaw

   It opened in 2003 as a gamble—the first café/restaurant in France, or anywhere in the world, to be staffed mainly by the deaf. Ten years later, the Café Signes is a solid success, popular in the neighborhood, sought out by Parisians from around the city, and written up in tourist guidebooks.

   The café was the brainchild of Martine Lejeau Perry, who runs a workshop for deaf people across the street. When the bar that used to be on the premises closed, she got the idea of moving the cooking workshop to a restaurant and opening it to the public. Before the café could open, however, she spent several years struggling to find funds for renovation and staff training. Eventually she got backing from a mixture of government agencies and private sponsors.

   Daniel Seguret is spokesman for Entraide Universitaire, an association that manages work projects for the handicapped in Paris, which contributed to the start-up and assists in the management of the café. He says that the café functions amazingly well. "We have ordinary regulars who come in, say 'hello' in sign language, sit down next to a deaf person and quite happily have a go at communicating. It's changing people's perception of the handicap and making a huge difference to the deaf staff."

   Many of the waiters are working with the public for the first time and have had to overcome their shyness and fear that they wouldn't be understood. As waitress Valerie Plume says (through an interpreter), "It's difficult communicating sometimes, but we have charts on the tables with the signs for different things. People try to use the signs and it works most of the time—we do understand. If not, they can write it down."

   At lunch time, with waiters moving quickly around the tables inside and on the sidewalk, the Café Signes seems like any other busy Parisian café—except that it's quieter. There are no calls from the kitchen to announce dishes that are ready (the cook uses a pager that vibrates in the pockets of the waiters). No calls from customers for more coffee. As Lejeau Perry says, "Perhaps the loudest sound in this café is laughter."

   Writer: _Reporter Shaw_

   Purpose: _to inform_

   Reliability: _s high_

### 2. AT&T: Discriminating against the deaf
By Randy Kaufman

My sister has been deaf ever since she was ill with spinal meningitis as a small child. My parents and I can all sign, so communication in the family is not a problem when we're together, only when we're apart.

But modern technology has solved that problem too, with the invention of FaceTime. We used to use Android platforms, but we all switched to iOS to use the iPhone FaceTime app because it just plain works. It's a completely straightforward video calling solution that anyone can use. You look up a contact on your iPhone and there's the option to make a FaceTime call listed right beside the voice and texting options.

The only hitch up until now was that you could only access FaceTime through WiFi, not through the mobile network. Now Apple has announced that the FaceTime app will be available to all iPhone users on the mobile network, and not just on WiFi. The benefits of mobile FaceTime cannot be overstated. It allows for the use of video chat anywhere and anytime, without the uncertainties of WiFi connections. In emergencies where texting may not be an option, mobile FaceTime could be a lifesaver.

But—and this is a huge *but*—the iPhone FaceTime app is only available if the customer signs up for an expensive unlimited voice plan with AT&T. This is outrageous. A deaf person has no use for a voice plan. Basically, AT&T is charging these customers for being disabled. Other companies, such as Verizon and Sprint, allow their customers full accessibility to FaceTime. So why not AT&T?

Writer: _Randy Kaufman        blogger_

Purpose: _to persuade_

Reliability: _how reliable_

**B.**   *Compare work with another student. Explain your answers with evidence from the text.*

**C.**   *Write any useful vocabulary in your notebook.*

# Recognizing Point of View and Bias

Like everyone else, writers have a way of thinking—a point of view—that has been influenced by their own experiences and background. It is important to recognize the point of view so you can better evaluate the ideas and information and form your own opinion.

When a point of view is part of a general attitude in favor of (or against) one belief or group of people, it is called bias. In some situations, bias can interfere with balanced judgment or fair treatment. For example, a television channel is biased in its reporting if it regularly presents candidates from one political party more often than candidates from another political party.

In some genres, such as serious news articles, journalists generally try to report the facts, without expressing their personal point of view or allowing any personal bias to influence the reporting. In a personal blog post, on the other hand, the writer's point of view and bias may be very evident.

*Read the email excerpt. Then read the notes about the purpose, point of view, and bias.*

What Kevin Jones says in his TV ads is one thing, how he votes is another:

- Last fall, with almost a quarter of a million people out of work here in Massachusetts, Kevin Jones voted against three jobs bills.
- When some of us were working to stop the excess on Wall Street, Kevin Jones tried to weaken the rules and give the big banks a 19 billion dollar break.
- Kevin Jones voted against funding for summer jobs and voted twice to double the interest rate on student loans.
- And Kevin Jones voted to limit the authority of the Environmental Protection Agency and repeatedly voted to give billions in subsidies to big oil companies.

It's clear where Kevin Jones stands—and it's not with the people of Massachusetts. Do you want him to be your senator?

Point of view: *The writer doesn't want Kevin Jones to win the election, so she tells about the things he's done that readers probably won't agree with.*

Possible bias: *The writer probably belongs to a different and opposing political party.*

## EXERCISE 5

A. **Work with another student. Decide on the point of view and possible bias for the passages in Exercise 4.**

1. **Signing for your lunch**
   Point of view: _Positive about the cafe_
   Possible bias: _None_

2. **AT&T: Discriminating against the deaf**
   Point of view: _negative_
   Possible bias: _negative bias about companies who discriminate against deaf people._

B. **Compare answers with another pair of students. Explain your answers with evidence from the text.**

**A.** *Read each of these passages from websites. Work with another student to decide who or what kind of organization wrote each one and what the main purpose was. Then assess the reliability and the point of view and possible bias. Look up only the vocabulary that is necessary for comprehension.*

1. Doctors around the country are all saying the same thing: Americans are overweight, and part of the cause is their poor diet, fast food in particular. This is certainly a serious problem in this country. Many people think the way to solve it is with laws or regulations to force the fast food companies to change the way they make, serve, and advertise their food. But let's face it: Can we really blame the fast food chains? They're just serving what people want to eat. We should blame ourselves. No one is forcing us to buy those hamburgers! What's needed is more self-discipline and responsible behavior. We could perfectly well go to a supermarket and cook ourselves a healthy meal at home instead of going to McDonald's. If we did that more often, we'd be thinner and healthier. So stop complaining and get yourself a better lifestyle! Then maybe McDonald's will have to change, too.

Writer: _Normal person, blogger, commentor, personal trainer_

Purpose: _to persuade_

Reliability: _low_

Point of view: _negative_

Possible bias: _negative toward ppl who doesn't have good nutrition habits._

2. A new study by economists at the University of California, Berkeley, has a clear message for school administrators and town planners: Keep the fast food away from the schools.

   According to the findings, California's nearly 3 million 9th graders are at least 5.2 percent more likely to be obese if there is a fast food restaurant close to their school (within a tenth of a mile). No correlation was found between obesity and the presence of fast food restaurants if they were farther away (at least a quarter of a mile). Nor was the rate of obesity affected by the presence of other kinds of restaurants near a school.

   Obesity among children ages 6–16 in the United States has increased from about 5 percent in the early 1970s to nearly 20 percent today. During that same period, the number of fast food restaurants has almost tripled, and many schools now offer fast food in machines or at snack bars inside school buildings.

   The report concluded that policies restricting access to fast food at school could result in significantly less obesity among school children.

   School administrators and town planners can no longer ignore the facts. As many health professionals and parents have been demanding for years, it is time for schools and towns to revise their policies. The sale of fast food in schools must come to an end, and towns must not issue licenses for fast food outlets in the immediate vicinity of schools.

Writer: _____

Purpose: _____

Reliability: _____

Point of view: _____

Possible bias: _____

3. The McDonald's fast-food chain recently began listing calorie information for all food items on its menus in stores across the country. According to the company, this new policy will inform customers about healthy menu options and help them make nutritional choices.

In addition to listing calorie-content on menus, McDonald's released its first nutrition report and introduced several upcoming menu options that will include recommended food groups from the Department of Agriculture's *Guidelines for Healthy Dietary Choices*. With these efforts, the company intends to meet the promises set out in its 2011 "Commitments to Offer Improved Nutrition Choices." The aim is to educate and help customers and employees make smart nutritional choices.

In order to make healthy menu options more convenient and accessible, McDonald's also announced today that it will experiment with a number of additional new food items, including

- seasonal fruits and vegetables, such as strawberries and green beans.
- more vegetarian options, like those already featured in European McDonald's restaurants, and a grilled chicken option for children's meals.
- new choices for breakfast, including an egg-white sandwich on a whole-grain English muffin.

Writer: _____

Purpose: _____

Reliability: _____

Point of view: _____

Possible bias: _____

B.  **Compare answers with another student. Explain your answers with evidence from the text. Then discuss these questions:**

1. Do you agree with the views of any of these writers? Explain.
2. Who or what do you think is to blame for the problem of obesity among American children?
3. What can be done about this problem and who should do it, in your opinion?

C.  **Write any useful vocabulary in your notebook.**

**A.** *Preview and read these two passages. Work with another student to decide who or what kind of organization wrote each one and what the main purpose was. Then assess the reliability and the point of view and possible bias. Look up only the vocabulary that is necessary for comprehension.*

1. Fast-food chain Top Chef recently sent a group of discerning moms to Hansfield, Ohio, for an all-access tour of one of the chicken farms that produces the meat for those delicious chicken nuggets your children love so much. Here's what one mom, Jane Emerson, wrote after the visit:

   From what I saw, I'm convinced that these farmers really care about the welfare of the animals! The farm is family owned, so that's a guarantee of quality and integrity. Besides, the farmer has to meet the very strict standards specified by Top Chef, which buys a lot of its chicken from the Parker Farms processing plant nearby.

   The barns are kept nice and warm (28–32 degrees Celsius), and we saw chickens roaming around freely. They have all the space they need. (The farmer says he follows government recommendations—no more than 31 kilos per meter square.) The chickens always have access to food and water. They don't roam outside, so they're not completely free-range, but that doesn't matter for these birds. They're not egg layers, just meat birds (broiler chickens). If they were allowed to go outside, they'd be more susceptible to disease.

   The feed given to the chickens is 88 percent grain, 10 percent protein, and 1–2 percent vitamin supplements. Thanks to this diet, they grow fast—in five to six weeks, they're nice and plump, ready for processing.

   We talked with Travis Smith, one of the employees who's involved in catching and transporting the animals. He said he'd had special training and received a license in animal welfare practices.

   When it's time for processing, the live birds are put into crates and loaded on trucks. The processing plant is not far from the farm, but it's a busy place—it processes approximately 80,000–90,000 chickens daily—so sometimes the trucks have to wait, but never more than 8 hours. In the summer, when the weather is warmer, the chickens get sprayed with water so they won't overheat. Parker Farms really cares about its chickens!

   Our next post—a visit to the processing plant. Stay tuned!

   Writer: _____

   Purpose: _____

   Reliability: _____

   Point of view: _____

   Possible bias: _____

2. Formerly signifying Kentucky Fried Chicken, now signifying nothing, KFC is arguably the company that has increased the sum total of suffering in the world more than any other in history. KFC buys nearly a billion chickens a year—if you packed those chickens body to body, they would blanket Manhattan from river to river and spill from the windows of the higher floors of office buildings—so its practices have profound ripple effects throughout all the sectors of the poultry industry.

KFC insists that it is "committed to the well-being and humane treatment of chickens." How trustworthy are these words? At a slaughterhouse in West Virginia that supplies KFC, workers were documented tearing the heads off live birds, spitting tobacco into their eyes, spray-painting their faces, and violently stomping on them. These acts were witnessed dozens of times. This slaughterhouse was not a "bad apple," but a "Supplier of the Year." Imagine what happens at the bad apples when no one is looking.

On KFC's website, the company claims, "We are monitoring our suppliers on an ongoing basis to determine whether they are using humane procedures for caring for and handling animals they supply to us. As a consequence, it is our goal to only deal with suppliers who promise to maintain our high standards and share our commitment to animal welfare." That is half true. KFC does deal with suppliers that *promise* to ensure welfare. What KFC doesn't tell you is that anything the suppliers practice is necessarily considered welfare.

A similar half-truth is the claim that KFC conducts welfare audits of its suppliers' slaughter facilities (the "monitoring" alluded to above). What we are not told is that these are typically *announced* audits. KFC announces an inspection meant (at least in theory) to document illicit behavior in a manner that allows plenty of time for the soon-to-be-inspected to throw a tarp over whatever they don't want seen.

(Source: Jonathan Safran Foer, *Eating Animals,* Back Bay Books, Little Brown and Company, 2010)

Writer: _____

Purpose: _____

Reliability: _____

Point of view: _____

Possible bias: _____

**B.** *Compare answers with another pair of students. Explain your answers with evidence from the text. Then discuss these questions:*

1. Which of the passages do you think is the most reliable? The least reliable?
2. What is your opinion of the views expressed in each passage?
3. Have you ever watched a farm animal being slaughtered?
4. Do you eat meat? If so, do you think about where the meat comes from?

**C.** *Write any useful vocabulary in your notebook.*

A. *Read each of these passages from websites. Work with another student to decide who or what kind of organization wrote each one and what the main purpose was. Then assess the reliability and the point of view and possible bias. Look up only the vocabulary that is necessary for comprehension.*

### 1. Smoking laws limit heart attacks

There is no longer room for doubt: people's health improves in a community when smoking is banned. In a report published last month in *Archives of Internal Medicine*, researchers analyzed medical data in Olmsted County, Minnesota, before and after a ban on smoking in public places, and they found that the heart attack rate dropped by one-third in the five-year period after the ban, compared with the period before.

A co-author of the report, Richard Hurt from the Mayo Clinic in Rochester, Minnesota, said the study was the longest analysis to date of the effects of a smoking ban on cardiovascular health and that it provides definitive proof of an association between secondhand smoke and heart attacks.

Olmsted County's first anti-smoking ordinance prohibited smoking in restaurants on January 1, 2002. The ban was extended to all workplaces, including bars, on October 1, 2007. The researchers examined the county's medical records for the population of about 145,000, focusing on the 18 months before the first ordinance in 2002 and the 18 months after the full ban became effective in 2007. Their analysis was facilitated by the extensive medical database available in this county.

The records showed 187 heart attacks in the earlier period, but only 139 in the later period after the full ban. When adjusted for demographic changes in the county's population, this revealed an annual heart attack rate of 151 per 100,000 people before and 101 per 100,000 afterward. Other studies have shown that cigarette smoke inhalation increases heart attack risk, but this is the first to show that a ban on smoking can have such a direct positive effect on cardiovascular health.

Even the promoters of the smoking ban were surprised at the strength of the evidence that smoke-free policies could affect medical outcomes. According to Pamela Ling, an internist at the University of California, San Francisco, "One of the arguments against the ban was that smoke-free policies would restrict [smoking] in the workplace, but that people would smoke more at home, but, actually, studies suggest . . . that people don't compensate." She believes that the data reflect not only less exposure to secondhand smoke but probably also people smoking less overall.

The next battle for antismoking activists: a ban on smoking in cars. According to some studies, smoking in an automobile creates a very high concentration of secondhand smoke.

Writer: _____

Purpose: _____

Reliability: _____

Point of view: _____

Possible bias: _____

## 2. You Smoke? You're Fired!

Stephanie Armour

More companies are taking action against employees who smoke off-duty, and, in an extreme trend that some call troubling, some are now firing or banning the hiring of workers who light up even on their own time.

The outright bans raise new questions about how far companies can go in regulating workers' behavior when they are off the clock. The crackdown is coming in part as a way to curb soaring health care costs, but critics say companies are violating workers' privacy rights. The zero-tolerance policies are coming as more companies adopt smoke-free workplaces.

Weyco, a medical benefits provider based in Okemos, Michigan, this year banned employees from smoking on their own time. Employees must submit to random tests that detect if someone has smoked. They must also agree to searches of briefcases, purses, or other belongings if company officials suspect tobacco or other banned substances have been brought on-site. Those who smoke may be suspended or fired.

About 20 employees have quit smoking under the policy, and a handful were fired after they opted out of the testing. "The main goal is to elevate the health status of our employees," says Gary Climes, chief financial officer.

At Investors Property Management in Seattle, smokers are not hired. Employees who smoked before the ban was passed about two years ago are not fired; however, they can't get medical insurance through the company.

Alaska Airlines has a no-smoking policy for employees, and new hires must submit to a urine test to prove they're tobacco-free. "The debate has gone from where they can smoke to whether they can smoke," says Marshal Tanick, a Minneapolis-based employment lawyer.

Such bans are not legal everywhere: More than 20 states have passed laws that bar companies from discriminating against workers for lifestyle decisions.

There are other ways that companies are taking action against off-duty smoking, such as raising health care premiums for smokers.

Employers say it's about creating a healthy workforce. But it's also a bottom-line issue: Tobacco causes more than 440,000 deaths annually and results in more than $75 billion in direct medical costs a year, according to the Centers for Disease Control and Prevention.

Some smokers' rights groups are vowing legal action. "These matters will be decided in the courts," says Redmond, Washington-based Normon Kjono with Forces, a smokers' rights group. "You're creating a class of unemployable citizens. It won't stand."

And legal experts fear companies will try to control other aspects of employees' off-duty lifestyle, a trend that is already happening. Some companies are firing, suspending or charging higher insurance premiums to workers who are overweight, have high cholesterol or participate in risky activities.

(Source: *USA TODAY*, May 11, 2005)

Writer: _____

Purpose: _____

Reliability: _____

Point of view: _____

Possible bias: _____

### 3. Smoke Screen

We are in favor of policies that encourage people to reduce or quit smoking, but we feel that the measures taken by the World Health Organization go against the rights of individuals.

The organization has adopted a policy that puts smoking at the center of their hiring decisions. As of December 1, it will no longer hire people who are smokers unless they pledge to stop.

The WHO spokesperson said that since they are the leaders of an international drive to reduce the use of tobacco they could not allow smoking among their employees and remain credible in the eyes of the world.

However, there is a difference between smoking and smokers. Their battle against smoking is an admirable one, but smokers are not criminals—they are people with a failing that harms only themselves. It's all too easy to target them and lose sight of the fact that they are only human.

In the same way that the rights of free speech must be extended to people expressing views we may not like, so too should people with unhealthy habits—which harm only themselves—be free from discrimination at the workplace.

(Source: *The Boston Star*, December 3, 2009)

Writer: _____

Purpose: _____

Reliability: _____

Point of view: _____

Possible bias: _____

**B.** *Compare answers with another pair of students. Explain your answers with evidence from the text. Then discuss these questions:*

1. Which of the passages do you think is the most reliable? The least reliable?
2. What is your opinion of the views expressed in each passage?
3. In your country, is smoking allowed in the workplace? In public places like restaurants?
4. What are your views about smoking in the workplace or in public places?

**C.** *Write any useful vocabulary in your notebook.*

# Focus on Vocabulary

## EXERCISE 9

**A.** *Read these sentences from the passage in Exercise 7. For each underlined word or phrase, choose the one below that is closest in meaning.*

1. Fast-food chain Top Chef recently sent a group of <u>discerning</u> moms to Hansfield, Ohio, for an all-access tour of one of the chicken farms that produces the meat for those delicious chicken nuggets your children love so much.

   a. having good judgment    b. having poor skills    c. having great interest

2. From what I saw, I'm convinced that these farmers really care about the <u>welfare</u> of the animals!

   a. size and strength    b. economic value    c. health and happiness

3. Formerly signifying Kentucky Fried Chicken, now signifying nothing, KFC is <u>arguably</u> the company that has increased the sum total of suffering in the world more than any other in history.

   a. certainly    b. probably    c. possibly

4. KFC buys nearly a billion chickens a year . . . so its practices have <u>profound</u> ripple effects throughout all the sectors of the poultry industry.

   a. minor    b. slight    c. strong

5. These acts were <u>witnessed</u> dozens of times.

   a. seen    b. done    c. filmed

6. "We are <u>monitoring</u> our suppliers on an ongoing basis to determine whether they are using humane procedures for caring for and handling animals they supply to us . . ."

   a. changing constantly    b. watching carefully    c. visiting regularly

7. A similar half-truth is the claim that KFC conducts welfare audits of its suppliers' slaughter <u>facilities</u> (the "monitoring" alluded to above).

   a. methods    b. workers    c. places

8. A similar half-truth is the claim that KFC conducts welfare audits of its suppliers' slaughter facilities (the "monitoring" <u>alluded to</u> above).

   a. reviewed    b. mentioned    c. arranged

**B.** *Compare answers with another student. Check your answers in the dictionary. Then read through the passage on page 247 again. Can you remember the words you looked up the first time? If not, mark them for further review.*

## EXERCISE 10

**A.** *Read these sentences from the passage in Exercise 8. Write a word from the box in each blank. You may need to change the form of the word.*

| compensate | facilitate | outcome | prohibit | submit |
|---|---|---|---|---|
| exposure | opt out | premium | reveal | substance |

1. Olmsted County's first anti-smoking ordinance _____ smoking in restaurants on January 1, 2002. The ban was extended to all workplaces, including bars, on October 1, 2007.

2. Their analysis was _____ by the extensive medical database available in this county.

3. When adjusted for demographic changes in the county's population, this _____ an annual heart attack rate of 151 per 100,000 people before and 101 per 100,000 afterward.

4. Even the promoters of the smoking ban were surprised at the strength of the evidence that smoke-free policies could affect medical _____.

5. "One of the arguments against the ban was that smoke-free policies would restrict [smoking] in the workplace, but that people would smoke more at home, but, actually, studies suggest . . . that people don't _____."

6. She believes that the data reflect not only less _____ to secondhand smoke but probably also people smoking less overall.

7. Employees must _____ to random tests that detect if someone has smoked.

8. They must also agree to searches of briefcases, purses, or other belongings if company officials suspect tobacco or other banned _____ have been brought on-site.

9. About 20 employees have quit smoking under the policy, and a handful were fired after they _____ of the testing.

10. There are other ways that companies are taking action against off-duty smoking, such as raising health care _____ for smokers.

**B.** *Compare answers with another student. Check your answers in the passage on page 249. With your partner, give definitions for the words in the box (as they are used in the sentences). Look up any you are not sure about and write them in your notebook.*

A.   *Select six words or phrases from the passages in this unit which you think other students might not be familiar with or might not remember well (preferably words that are on the word list in the Appendix).*

B.   *On a separate piece of paper, make an exercise like Exercise 10:*
   • *Write the sentences where you found the words and phrases on your list, leaving a blank in place of the word or phrase.*
   • *Write the missing words or phrases in a box below the sentences—but not in order.*

C.   *Exchange exercises with another student and do your partner's exercise.*

D.   *Look back at the text to check your answers.*

E.   *With your partner, give the definitions for the words and phrases you selected for your exercises. Look up any you are not sure about.*

---

## Reflecting on Your Learning

**1.** Discuss these questions with another student.

   • Which do you think is more difficult to evaluate—purpose, reliability, point of view, or bias?

   • Outside of class, do you read critically? If so, what kinds of material? (e.g., newspapers, websites, blogs, etc.)

   • Do you think it is easier to read critically in English or in your first language? Explain.

   • Were you expected to read critically at school (or university) in your home country?

**2.** Select useful vocabulary from this unit:

   • Look through the passages in this unit for more vocabulary that would be useful to learn. Write the words or phrases in your vocabulary notebook (with parts of speech, definitions and/ or synonyms, the sentences where you found them, and any helpful notes about usage).

   • Review the words in your notebook. Test yourself and then ask a classmate or friend to test you. Write the words you have trouble remembering on study cards. Review and test yourself until you know them well.

# Reading Fluency

# An Introduction to Reading Fluency

The ability to read fluently—quickly and with adequate comprehension—can make an enormous difference in an academic context. Your reading fluency may improve somewhat with work on vocabulary and comprehension skills. But the only way to make a real difference is through a lot of reading (as you learned in Part 1) and through practice with timed readings. This is what you will learn about and practice in this part of the book.

## Why Read Faster?

There are three important reasons for learning to read faster:

### 1. You can be a more efficient reader.

This will help you with homework, class work, and tests. It will also make reading books, magazines, and newspapers more enjoyable—so you'll probably read more.

### 2. You can improve your knowledge of English.

If you read faster and you read more, you'll encounter more words and phrases and get more language input from your reading. You will have more practice getting meaning from sentences and longer passages. This will help you:

- learn more vocabulary.
- understand how sentences work.
- learn what words are used together.
- become a better writer.

### 3. You can improve your comprehension.

How is this possible? The answer is very simple: when you read slowly, you read one word at a time. Your eyes and your brain take in each word separately. This is like reading a text with extra spaces between the words.

### Example:

*Try reading these sentences with separated words. Is it easier or harder to read this way?*

> What      really    happens    when    we
> read?   Many    people     think    we      read
> one      word      at      a     time.    They
> think       we       read     a
> word,     understand     it,      and
> then    move     on   to    the    next     word.

You probably found it harder to read this way. The separate words are separate pieces of information that your short-term memory must try to hold on to. With short sentences, this may not matter much. But when you read longer sentences, you may not be able to keep the words in your memory long enough to make sense of the sentences.

When you read faster, on the other hand, your eyes and your brain group words together to form ideas. Your brain works more efficiently with these than with single words, so it is easier to make sense of the sentences and of the passage.

In fact, your brain tends to groups words together in a way that makes sense. This is true for both reading and listening. You can hear the "thought groups" [groups of words that form an idea] when you listen to fluent speakers, especially when they are reading aloud or giving a lecture or speech. They naturally make pauses between thought groups to allow listeners to understand better.

### Example:

*Read the sentences silently while your teacher reads them aloud. What groups of words do you hear?*

> What really happens when we read? Many people think we read one word at a time. They think we read a word, understand it, and then move on to the next word.

Different readers group words differently, depending on how they interpret the text. Readers who are more fluent tend to group more words together than slow readers. Here is the way a reader might group the sentences above:

> What really happens / when we read? / Many people think / we read one word / at a time. / They think / we read a word, / understand it, / and then move on / to the next word.

When you read faster, you naturally group words together. This is why you understand better.

**Note:** You should not try to read faster all the time. Certain types of text need to be read slowly and carefully—such as, instructions, cookbook recipes, poetry, or technical explanations. You should aim for flexibility, speeding up or slowing down as necessary.

# Strategies for Reading Faster

You can learn to improve your reading rate—read faster—by following these strategies.

## 1. Check your reading habits.

Some habits can slow you down when you are reading. Think about your own reading habits:

### Do you try to pronounce each word as you read?

You will probably understand less this way. If you are trying to say and understand the words, your brain has to do two things at the same time. (You can practice saying the sentences after you read them silently.)

### Do you move your lips when you read silently?

If you do, you are probably thinking each word to yourself. You will have the same problems as someone who pronounces the words.

### Do you point at the words with your finger or a pencil?

If you do, your eyes will follow your finger or pencil word by word across the lines. However, your eyes need to be free to follow your thinking. You may need to go back and check a word, or you may want to skip ahead.

### Do you try to translate into your native language while you are reading in English?

If you do, you will have to stop often to think about the translation, and it will be harder to follow the story or the ideas. When you translate, you will also be thinking in your language, not in English.

## 2. Skip or guess unknown words.

### Skip words that are not necessary for understanding the passage.

It is not necessary to know the meaning of every word. You may be able to follow the story or understand the ideas even when there are words you don't know. (See Part 1, Unit 1, Exercise 1, page 5.).

### Guess the general meaning of the words you need to understand the passage.

You can learn a lot about a word from the words or sentences around it (the context). It is often possible to understand the general meaning. This will allow you to continue reading and follow the story or ideas. (See Part 2, Unit 3, for more about guessing meaning.)

### 3. Time yourself.

**Time yourself with passages for fluency practice.**
By timing how long it takes you to read a series of passages of the same length, you can find out how fast you read now and then work on improving your reading rate. Questions following the readings allow you to check your comprehension. The units in Part 4 include three sets of six timed reading passages.

**Time yourself in your extensive reading book.**
In Part 1, Unit 3, on page 27, you learn how to time yourself and do reading sprints in your extensive reading book.

## Guidelines for Timed Reading

1. Before you start, write down the *exact* time shown on your watch or clock (minutes and seconds).

2. Preview each passage quickly before reading it.

3. Read the passage and write down the exact time you finish.

4. Answer the questions without looking back at the passage. Then check your answers with your teacher.

5. Read the passage again. Look for the answers to the questions that were incorrect.

6. Find your reading time: your finishing time minus your starting time.

   *Example:* *Finishing time:*  *10:14:30 (14 minutes and 30 seconds after 10 o'clock)*
   *Starting time:*   *10:10:45*
   *Reading time:*   *3:45 (3 minutes and 45 seconds)*

7. Find your reading rate on the Reading Rate Table on page 263. Write your reading rate and your comprehension score [the number of correct answers] on the progress chart on page 264.

8. After reading four passages, check your progress.

9. If your reading rate has stayed the same, you should push yourself to read faster.

10. If you have more than three incorrect answers on any passage, you might be trying to read too quickly. Slow down a little and read more carefully.

## Using Cell Phones: Cultural Differences

What do you do if your cell phone rings while you are with a group of people? If you are French, you will probably ignore the call. If you are English, you may walk away from the group to answer it. If you are Spanish, you are likely to answer it there in the middle of the group and invite everyone around you to join the conversation.

As many travelers have noticed, there are significant differences from one country to another in the way people use their cell phones. This has been confirmed by a recent study of cell phone use in three European cities—Madrid, London, and Paris. In spite of the fact that these cities are all in the European Union and share a great deal of history and culture, local customs still vary considerably. These customs influence the way people in these cities make use of their phones in public.

According to Amparo Lasén, the Spanish sociologist who conducted the study, there were no real surprises for anyone who is familiar with the customs in these countries. Lasén interviewed people and observed their behavior in three different settings in each city: a major train station, a commercial area, and a business district.

She found that Londoners use their cell phones the least in public. If they are with others, they prefer to let calls be answered by voice mail [a recorded message], and then they check for voice messages later. If the English do answer a call on the street, they seem to dislike talking with others around. They tend to move away from a crowded sidewalk and seek out a place where they cannot be heard, such as the far side of a subway entrance or even the edge of a street. They seem to feel that the danger of stepping into speeding traffic is preferable to the risk of having their conversation be overheard. Even when it is raining—as it often is in London—people still prefer not to hold their conversations where others could hear. It seems they'd rather stay out in the rain than move into a protected doorway where there are other people.

This has led to a behavior that Lasén has called "clustering." At a busy time of day on the streets of London, you may find small crowds of cell phone users grouped together, each one talking into a cell phone. They seem to assume that others on phones are too occupied with their own calls to listen in.

In Madrid, on the other hand, few people use voice mail because the Spanish dislike talking to a machine rather than a real person. If no one answers a call, they prefer not to leave a message, but try again later or wait for a return call. And since the Spanish are not shy about answering their calls in public, the return call may come sooner than it would in London or Paris. In fact, in Madrid it is common to hear loud and lively phone conversations on the street, accompanied by shouts, laughter, and the waving of hands. In fact, sometimes it happens that a group of friends may be walking down the street together, each talking on their own phone, but smiling and nodding as though it were one large conversation that everyone could hear.

Even when they are not using their phones, the Spanish often hold them in their hands as they walk down the street or put them on the table at a restaurant, so they will not miss any incoming calls. In a movie theater, not only do cell phones occasionally ring, but people sometimes answer them and have brief conversations.

This would not be acceptable in Paris, however. The French have much stricter rules about how and when to use cell phones in public. It is not considered polite to use a phone in a restaurant, for instance, though it might be acceptable in the more informal setting of a café. In general, the French are very disapproving of phone use in public and are quick to express that disapproval, even to strangers. One special custom that has developed in cafés seems unique to Paris. Young women often place their cell phones on the table beside them to signal that they are expecting someone. When the friend arrives, the phone is put away.

In one area, the study found that the French and Spanish behaved in a similar way. Both were quite willing to continue a phone conversation in a romantic situation, even kissing someone present while continuing a conversation on the phone. These people were clearly not using videophones. In London, on the other hand, no one was ever observed to be kissing while on the telephone. The English apparently prefer to have more privacy for their phone calls and their romantic moments.

The study thus confirms certain cultural stereotypes about the people in each of the three cities. Lasén reported that the reactions to her as she was conducting her research were also interesting—and in line with the stereotypes. When people noticed her in Paris, they frowned at her; in London, they pretended not to notice; in Madrid, however, they did not seem to mind.

Understanding the habits of these European cell phone users has become a lively topic of study for sociologists and psychologists at European universities. But with one billion cell phone users around the world, the subject is of interest not only to academic researchers. Habits of cell phone use are also a matter of serious study by telecommunications companies. If they can understand the local customs and customers better, they might be able to change people's behavior and increase cell phone use. For example, if phone companies want to increase their profits in France, they need to convince people that it is acceptable to use their phones in restaurants. The Spanish need to be persuaded that voice mail is not so bad, and the English must learn to leave their phones on all the time.

**B.** *Write your finishing time: _____ Then turn the page and answer the questions. Do not look back at the passage.*

1. Which statement best expresses the overall idea of this passage?
   a. People in different European cities have different social customs.
   b. People use their cell phones differently in London, Paris, and Madrid.
   c. People in Madrid tend to speak more loudly than those in Paris or London.

2. A Spanish sociologist has said that the way people use their cell phones
   a. fits in with their local habits and customs.
   b. is the same in all European countries today.
   c. is related to the person's sex and age.

3. Londoners use voice mail a lot because they
   a. enjoy leaving recorded messages.
   b. like having conversations with others.
   c. prefer not to answer calls in public.

4. Which of the following was NOT mentioned in the passage?
   a. Cell phone users in London tend to cluster together on the street.
   b. Londoners tend not to make phone calls when it is raining.
   c. The English don't like to be overheard on the phone.

5. When they are in groups, the people in Madrid
   a. continue to answer calls and have phone conversations.
   b. stop talking and wait when a cell phone rings.
   c. prefer to leave messages with voice mail.

6. In a café in Paris, a young woman might leave her phone on the table
   a. to show that she is waiting for someone.
   b. to remind herself to make a call.
   c. to make sure she hears it ringing.

7. Parisians
   a. do not like other people to use cell phones in public.
   b. use cell phones more than the English or the Spanish.
   d. never continue a phone conversation at a romantic moment.

8. You can infer from this passage that
   a. cell phone companies will make less money in European countries.
   c. weather can be an important factor in the way people use cell phones.
   d. technology may be global, but the way people use it is not.

C.  *Check your answers with your teacher. Write your comprehension score (number of correct answers) in the progress chart.*

D.  *Calculate your reading time: Finishing time – Starting time = Reading time: _____ Find your reading rate on page 263. Write it in the progress chart on page 264.*

E.  *Re-read the passage and look for the answers to any questions that you missed.*

F.  *Go back through the passage again and underline the new vocabulary. Select the useful words or phrases you would like to learn and write them in your vocabulary notebook.*

# Reading Rate Table

*All of the passages are about 1000 words long. To find your reading rate, find the reading time that is closest to yours. Then look across at the reading rate column.*

| Reading time (minutes) | Reading rate (words per minute) |
|---|---|
| 1:00 | 1000 |
| 1:10 | 857 |
| 1:20 | 750 |
| 1:30 | 667 |
| 1:40 | 600 |
| 1:50 | 545 |
| 2:00 | 500 |
| 2:10 | 462 |
| 2:20 | 429 |
| 2:30 | 400 |
| 2:40 | 375 |
| 2:50 | 352 |
| 3:00 | 333 |
| 3:10 | 315 |
| 3:20 | 300 |
| 3:30 | 285 |
| 3:40 | 273 |
| 3:50 | 261 |
| 4:00 | 250 |
| 4:10 | 240 |
| 4:20 | 231 |
| 4:30 | 222 |
| 4:40 | 214 |
| 4:50 | 207 |
| 5:00 | 200 |
| 5:10 | 194 |
| 5:20 | 188 |
| 5:30 | 182 |
| 5:40 | 176 |
| 5:50 | 171 |
| 6:00 | 167 |

# Faster Reading Progress Chart

Next to the exercise number, write the date. Then write the reading rate that is closest to yours and your comprehension score (number of correct answers).

| Passage and Date | Reading Rate (WPM) | Comprehension Score | Comments |
|---|---|---|---|
| Practice | | | |
| **Unit 2** | | | |
| 1 | | | |
| 2 | | | |
| 3 | | | |
| 4 | | | |
| 5 | | | |
| 6 | | | |
| **Unit 3** | | | |
| 1 | | | |
| 2 | | | |
| 3 | | | |
| 4 | | | |
| 5 | | | |
| 6 | | | |
| **Unit 4** | | | |
| 1 | | | |
| 2 | | | |
| 3 | | | |
| 4 | | | |
| 5 | | | |
| 6 | | | |

# UNIT 2

## People Who Have Made a Difference

**A.** *Write your starting time:* _____ *Then preview and read the passage.*

### Dr. Paul Farmer

In Dr. Paul Farmer's view, health is a fundamental human right. He believes it should not be dependent on income or education, and he has devoted his life to bringing medical care to the poorest people in developing countries. Many doctors assumed that people in these countries were too poor and uneducated to manage complex medical treatments, but Dr. Farmer has demonstrated that this is not true.

Farmer was born in Massachusetts in 1960, and he grew up in Florida with his parents and five brothers and sisters. They lived for a while in a converted school bus and then in a broken-down boat, much of the time without running water. One summer, when the family needed cash, Farmer, his father, and his two brothers got jobs picking oranges. That is where he first heard Haitians speaking Creole, the language that would become so important to him later in his life. In spite of their financial difficulties, the Farmer home was filled with books, and the children were encouraged to pursue their interests and talents.

After graduating from high school at the top of his class, Farmer received a full scholarship to Duke University in North Carolina. As a college student, he heard about the terrible conditions for migrant workers on nearby farms. Among these workers were some Haitians whom he got to know and who invited him to visit their homes in Haiti. This was the beginning of his interest in this small Caribbean island country, one of the poorest in the world. He eventually took a trip there and spent time in the central highland region where vast areas had been stripped of their forests and the soil was poor and unproductive. Families lived in mud huts, had little food, and almost no medical care. But Farmer came to admire the spirit of these people and their ability to adapt.

Farmer continued his studies at Harvard Medical School, where he earned degrees in both Medicine and Medical Anthropology. He returned to Haiti many times, learning the language and working with local doctors. In 1987, with a few friends, he founded a charity organization, Partners in Health (PIH), based in Boston, Massachusetts. Their first project was to build a small clinic in the village of Cange in central Haiti. Over two decades, the Cange center—named Zanmi Lasante—expanded into a large facility. It now cares for more than 220,000 patients a year, with a 104-bed hospital and clinics for women's and children's health, eye care, and surgery.

The Cange center has become a world-wide model for community-based health care. Three principles guide care at the clinic. First and foremost, no patient is ever turned away. Second, to ensure long-term success, Haitians are involved in all levels of care. Thus, most of the doctors and nurses at Cange are Haitian, with some starting their medical experience at the clinic itself. And third, the health workers go out to the people so that the patients do not have to travel long distances, as did the woman Farmer met the first year who walked three hours with her child in her arms. It is important for health workers to get out of the clinic and see where and how the patients live. In a poor country like Haiti, improvements in health are only possible if living conditions also improve. When Farmer visits a village, he looks not only at people with health problems, but also at the houses and the general situation.

Thanks to PIH, the villages around Cange have acquired clean drinking water, and the houses have been rebuilt with rain-proof roofs and concrete floors.

Over the years, PIH has expanded and now works in many countries around the world, including Peru, Mexico, Rwanda, Russia, and Kazakhstan, as well as in poor neighborhoods in the United States and Canada. However, Haiti continues to be the main focus of Farmer's work, especially since the devastating earthquake in 2010. In 2012, PIH opened a new hospital outside the capital, Port-au-Prince, which now provides care for up to 500 people a day.

As a leading expert in HIV/AIDS and tuberculosis, Farmer attends conferences and consults with doctors around the world. His goal is to convince the world's medical experts that even in the most difficult social and economic conditions, it is possible to treat people successfully. In developing countries, for example, most international health organizations refused until recently to treat patients with drug-resistant tuberculosis. They claimed that the treatment was too expensive and that the patients would not be capable of following doctors' instructions. Partners in Health has shown, however, that the same treatment that works in the United States can work with patients anywhere. Furthermore, they have shown that it is possible to get the medicines at a lower cost.

For his work among the world's most vulnerable populations, Dr. Farmer has won many important awards. He continues to consult and teach part of the year at some of the world's most famous hospitals and universities. He is also the subject of a best-selling book by Tracy Kidder, *Mountains Beyond Mountains: The Quest of Dr. Paul Farmer, a Man Who Would Cure the World.*

But most of the money Farmer earns from his work or his awards is immediately given to Partners in Health. And despite his fame, Dr. Farmer still thinks of himself first and foremost as a doctor. He has not given up a doctor's simplest pleasures and responsibilities, such as walking for hours along dirt tracks to treat sick people in Haitian hill villages. Farmer says it helps remind him why he became a doctor in the first place: to treat the patient at hand. The title of Kidder's book comes from a Haitian saying that Farmer likes to quote: "After mountains there are mountains." In other words, beyond every problem there is another; the best we can do is to solve each problem, one at a time.

**B.** *Write your finishing time: _____ Then turn to page 274 and answer the questions. Do not look back at the passage.*

## EXERCISE 2

**A.** *Write your starting time: _____ Then preview and read the passage.*

### Christo and Jeanne-Claude

For more than forty years, artists Christo and Jeanne-Claude have been challenged the public's idea of what art can be. Working together, they create pieces known as "installation art" on a giant scale. In these pieces, entire bridges or buildings were wrapped in colorful fabric, or a nylon fence was stretched for miles along country fields. These "gentle disturbances," as the artists named them, temporarily changed places that we often take for granted and inspired people to see their world anew.

The two artists were born on the same day: June 13, 1935. Christo Javacheff was born in Bulgaria and studied art in Sofia, Bulgaria, and Vienna, Austria, before moving to Paris in 1957. Jeanne-Claude de Guillebon was born to French parents in Morocco and grew up in Morocco, Tunisia, Switzerland, and Paris. When he arrived in Paris, Christo was supporting himself by painting portraits. He took an assignment to paint a portrait of Jeanne-Claude's mother, and met and fell in love with her daughter. Christo and Jeanne-Claude were married and began collaborating on art work, though in the first years only Christo took credit for their work. Throughout their careers, both artists were known professionally by their first names only.

In 1964, they moved to New York City where Christo has continued to live after Jeanne-Claude passed away in 2009. When the two artists met, Christo had already begun creating the art work that they became famous for—wrapped objects. At first, the objects were relatively small, such as a motorcycle or a tree, and they were covered with cloth or sheets of plastic. They believed that the shape and beauty of the object was more visible when the details of the surface were hidden. As interest in their work grew, they went on to wrap larger objects, such as buildings and bridges. In 1968, they wrapped an entire art museum in Switzerland and another in the United States. Christo and Jeanne-Claude also began wrapping landscapes and over the next 30 years, they completed nearly 20 major projects. Among the most dramatic were the wrapped cliffs of the seacoast at Little Bay, Australia, the 11 islands in Florida wrapped with pink skirts, a 24-mile (38-kilometer) cloth fence in California, and 3,100 20-foot-tall (6 meter) blue and yellow umbrellas in Japan and California.

Probably their most famous project, however, was in New York City in February, 2005. They designed and organized the installation of 7,500 tall black metal "gates" hung with orange-colored fabric along 23 miles (37 kilometers) of walkways in Central Park. For the two weeks that the gates were up, the park was filled with thousands of people. Both New Yorkers and visitors from out of town wanted to see this transformation of the park. Just to keep going through the gates, people walked to corners of the park where they had never been before. Under the gates, the walkers felt as though they were strolling under saffron-colored sails. The bright fabric fluttering in the wind created a whole new dimension to the normally black and white winter scenery. Observed from one of New York City's skyscrapers, the gates looked like a river of bright color flowing through the park. They created a feeling of joyful celebration and brought New Yorkers together.

The inspiration for The Gates, as the installation was officially called, came from the initial 1854 design for Central Park. The original designers had planned for gates along the park's surrounding walls, but those gates were never built. Christo and Jeanne-Claude focused on the fact that New Yorkers love walking, and that Central Park is one of their favorite places for walking and meeting. The gate structures were designed to mirror the grid of the city streets near the park, so they were tall and narrow and people could pass through them. The fabric was chosen carefully and cut in a way so that it could swing freely in the wind and seem to follow the curving paths on which they were built.

Christo and Jeanne-Claude first proposed the idea for The Gates many years earlier, but New York officials at that time did not welcome the project. In the course of the long process of trying to get permission from the city offices in charge of the park, the artists collected a huge pile of documents. Christo and Jeanne-Claude kept all these documents, along with all the drawings and papers regarding the design, which they considered to be part of the art work itself. No matter how long and frustrating it was, getting permission was part of the process of creating The Gates. Christo and Jeanne-Claude recognized that their artwork, in this case, was not made *about* Central Park; it was made *out of* Central Park.

In spite of all the delays and objections, the artists persisted. They received building permits for The Gates in 2003, by order of Mayor Bloomberg. Several more years were required for the design and the construction of the 7,500 structures with their pieces of orange fabric. And finally, on February 13, 2005, The Gates were open. For the actual installation and removal of the gates, 900 workers were required. However, it is important to note that no public money was used for The Gates. As for all of their installations, Christo and Jeanne-Claude accepted no sponsors. They raised all the money themselves by selling drawings, artwork, and models of their projects to collectors. When The Gates came down, Christo and Jeanne-Claude gave away or recycled all the materials used in the project. This is another important part of their artistic philosophy. Nothing they made was permanent, and what they made should not harm the environment in any way.

When asked about the meaning of The Gates, Jeanne-Claude said: "We do not build meanings; we do not build messages; we do not build symbols; we only build art." Some art experts have criticized their work, saying it was not serious, not attractive, or simply not art. However, the crowds in Central Park seemed to feel otherwise.

**B.** *Write your finishing time:* _____ *Then turn to page 275 and answer the questions. Do not look back at the passage.*

## EXERCISE 3

**A.** *Write your starting time:* _____ *Then preview and read the passage.*

### Wangari Maathai

Until her death in 2011, Wangari Maathai was one of the world's most honored environmentalists. She fought to protect the fragile landscape of her native Kenya and helped to raise awareness about the need to address environmental concerns through development and anti-poverty programs in Africa and other parts of the world. The Green Belt Movement, which she founded in 1977, has established over 6,000 tree nurseries and planted more than 20 million trees across Kenya. For her remarkable successes, Wangari Maathai was awarded the Nobel Peace Prize in 2004.

Born in 1940, Wangari Maathai grew up on a farm in Nyeri, Kenya. She traveled to the United States to earn a master's degree in science, and then to Germany and back to Kenya for a Ph.D. The first woman in eastern and central Africa to earn a Ph.D. degree, she then became the first woman to be the head of a university department in Kenya. She was director of the Kenya Red Cross in the 1980s and was elected to Parliament in 2002. A woman of many firsts, she became the first African woman to win a Nobel Prize and only the twelfth woman to receive the award since it was established in 1901.

Maathai's commitment to the environment began when she returned to Kenya from her studies abroad and saw how the environment was being destroyed by uncontrolled deforestation. The trees were being cut down by poor families who needed firewood for cooking. However, cutting down the trees made the situation worse for these families in the long run. With the trees gone, the fertile topsoil blew away with the wind or was washed away by rainstorms. As a result, the land became dusty, stony, and unproductive. People were no longer able to grow enough food for their families, and since the cattle and goats could no longer find enough grass, there was also less milk and meat. In general, families who lived in areas where trees had been cut down became poorer. They also suffered from increased health problems because the soil that washed away contained human and animal waste that ended up in rivers, polluting the water supplies and leading to more disease.

Because the Kenyan government was weak and corrupt at the time, Maathai knew that it was not going to address this environmental problem. The solution had to come from elsewhere. Maathai decided to turn to the women of Kenya. African women are often responsible not only for cooking and taking care of their families, but also for farming and food production. She felt that since the women usually suffered the most from environmental destruction, they would be the most willing to work for change. Others told her that poor and uneducated women would not be capable of understanding environmental problems, but she did not believe this was true.

The idea of a widespread tree-planting program came to Maathai in 1976, but she knew that education about the environment had to be part of the program, or any new trees would also be cut down. She began with a small group of women and the planting of seven trees in a park in Nairobi. Then she went out into the countryside to teach ordinary women in villages about trees—not only how to plant them on their small farms, near schools and churches, but above all, why trees are necessary for their farms and families. At first, she had no tree nurseries, no staff, and no money, but other women joined her and the movement started to grow. Small grants of money arrived from international environmental organizations and the program soon developed into the "Green Belt Movement." Along with the environmental benefits it brings, the organization provides paid work and financial stability to thousands of Kenyan women.

After establishing the tree-planting program, Maathai turned to other aspects of Kenyan society. She challenged the government to improve education, food distribution, and other areas of concern to women. As a well-known voice against the corrupt governments of those years, she was often a target for threats and violence. She was put in prison several times, and after one arrest in 1991, she was freed only through pressure from international human rights organizations. In 1992, she was badly beaten by the police for participating in a hunger strike to protest government torture. In spite of continuing persecution, however, she went on with her work. In the years after founding the Green Belt Movement, Wangari Maathai expanded her interests beyond Kenya. Under her guidance, at least six other African countries developed tree-planting programs like the Green Belt Movement and launched them with similar success. In 1995, Maathai joined forces with other women leaders at the Fourth World Conference on Women in Beijing, China. Dressed in bright yellow, she marched with a thousand others to protest violence against women worldwide. In the late 1990s, Maathai led the Jubilee 2000 Coalition in Africa. This organization works to convince world leaders and banks to cancel the debts of the world's poorest countries.

When the political situation finally changed in Kenya, in 2002, Maathai was elected to parliament, and soon after, the new government appointed her Assistant Minister for the Environment, Natural Resources and Wildlife.

Dozens of international organizations have honored Maathai for her efforts to protect the environment and improve the lives of the poor in Africa. In deciding to give her the Peace Prize in 2004, the Nobel Committee changed its definition of peace for the first time since the Prize was founded in 1901. In fact, the award to Maathai was the first to be given to someone in the environmental field. Maathai said she understood why the Nobel Committee chose to offer an environmentalist an award normally given to politicians or human rights leaders.

"People are fighting over water, over food, and over other natural resources. When our resources become scarce, we fight over them. In managing our resources and in sustainable development, we plant the seeds of peace."

**B.**   *Write your finishing time:* _____ *Then turn to page 276 and answer the questions. Do not look back at the passage.*

## EXERCISE 4

**A.**   *Write your starting time:* _____ *Then preview and read the passage.*

### Rosa Parks

On December 1, 1955, Rosa Parks, a 42-year-old African-American woman, became the inspiring public face of the civil rights struggle in the United States. On that day, in Montgomery, Alabama, she sat at the front of a bus and refused to give up her seat to a white man. In Alabama, as in many other states, there were laws stating that black people could only sit in the back seats of buses. Parks was arrested for not giving up her seat. This set off a protest among blacks in Montgomery and all over the country and marked a turning point in the fight for equality for all American citizens.

Rosa was born in 1913 in Tuskegee, Alabama. Her parents separated when she was still young, so she and her younger brother were raised by her maternal grandparents on a farm outside of Montgomery, Alabama.

The world she grew up in was defined by race. In Alabama, as in all the former slave-holding states in the South, the black slaves had been freed at the end of the Civil War in 1865. But freedom had not brought equality. Many of these states passed laws to segregate blacks—that is, to keep them separate from whites and to deny them an equal position in society. These were called the "Jim Crow" laws. Blacks could not eat at the same restaurants, attend the same schools, or worship at the same churches as whites. They could not even walk on the same sidewalk, but had to step down when a white person passed. Aside from their second-class social and legal standing, blacks in the southern states were often the victims of violence by whites. White racists burned down black people's homes and churches and kidnapped, tortured, and murdered black men they accused of wrongdoing or disrespect. As a child, Parks would lie awake at night, listening for the sound of men coming to burn down the house. Parks once said: "Back then we didn't have any civil rights. It was just a matter of survival, of existing from one day to the next."

After studying at a private school for black girls and at the Alabama State Teachers College, Rosa married Raymond Parks, a barber. At that time, he was already active in the civil rights movement. Rosa had not yet become involved herself. Indeed, because of the dangers of violence or arrest, women usually were not active in the struggle. But Rosa wanted to participate. Despite her husband's fears for her, she attended meetings, joined protests, and became a member of several major civil rights groups.

In 1955, the nation's civil rights leaders decided it was time to challenge the Jim Crow laws, and they needed a case that would test those laws under the U.S. Constitution. They needed a person of great moral strength and courage, a woman rather than a man who might simply be beaten or murdered. That person was Rosa Parks, and the case would depend on her refusal to give up her seat. As they had expected, she was arrested immediately. In response, the black leaders in Montgomery formed the Montgomery Improvement Association (MIA), and elected a young minister as president. The minister was the Reverend Martin Luther King, Jr., only 26 years old at the time.

The next year was difficult for blacks in Montgomery. To call attention to their fight for civil rights, MIA organized a boycott of the city buses. Since few blacks owned cars, they had to walk everywhere, some traveling many miles on foot to get to work every day. Black men were arrested for no reason, and violence against black families increased. At the same time, news about the protests spread around the country and Reverend King's inspired leadership captured the nation's attention. The court case brought by MIA went to the Supreme Court, which ruled, on November 13, 1956, that the separation of blacks and whites on buses was illegal. From then on, access to public services had to be open to all, with no discrimination on the basis of race.

The day after the ruling became final, Rosa Parks took a front seat on a Montgomery bus, a white man sitting behind her. She and other blacks of Montgomery could now ride the bus freely. But the struggle for equality for blacks was not over. The Reverend Martin Luther King, Jr., who had made a name for himself in Montgomery, continued to fight for civil rights in schools and in the workplace, becoming the greatest civil rights leader America has known.

Both Rosa and Raymond Parks lost their jobs in Montgomery because of their activism. Following the court ruling, they received threats to their lives and safety, so they decided to move out of the South, settling in Detroit, Michigan in 1957, where they lived out the rest of their days. From the 1960s until she retired in the late 1980s, Rosa Parks worked as a staff member for U.S. Representative John Conyers. Colleagues and friends remember her as a quiet and modest woman, who never wished to be the center of attention, even when Nelson Mandela, president of South Africa, called her on stage during a visit to Detroit in the 1990s.

After her husband's death in 1987, Rosa Parks co-founded the Rosa and Raymond Parks Institute for Self-Development, an organization that sponsors programs to help teenagers learn about the country's civil rights history. President Bill Clinton awarded Rosa the Presidential Medal of Freedom in 1996, and, in 1999, the U.S. Congress gave her a Congressional Gold Medal.

When she died at age 92, the U.S. Congress passed a resolution that allowed her body to lie in state in the rotunda of the U.S. Capitol Building. Rosa Parks was the first woman in history to be given this honor. Speaking after her death, the civil rights leader Reverend Jesse Jackson summed up why Rosa Parks was so important to America's struggle for civil rights: "She sat down in order that we might stand up."

**B.** *Write your finishing time:* _____ *Then turn to page 277 and answer the questions. Do not look back at the passage.*

## EXERCISE 5

**A.** *Write your starting time:* _____ *Then preview and read the passage.*

### Tim Berners-Lee

What would the world be like today if Tim Berners-Lee hadn't invented the Web? It's impossible to know if someone else could have come up with something similar. Before his invention, computer users could transfer information only within local networks of computers, such as those used by large companies or universities. But now, thanks to Berners-Lee, we can access a vast universe of information, commerce, and communication on the Internet.

A future in computers seemed almost inevitable for young Tim. He was born in Great Britain to parents who were both computer experts. They met on a project to build an early computer at the University of Manchester. As a child in the 1960s, his interest in math and computers was encouraged from an early age. He played math games with his parents at the dining table and built make-believe computers out of boxes and whatever he could find. Later, when he was a student at Oxford University, he was caught hacking into computer files and was banned from using the university computer. His reaction to that ban was to build his own computer out of extra electronic parts and an old TV set. After graduation, he worked for a few years as a computer programmer and then, in 1980, was hired for six months to work at CERN, the European nuclear research center in Switzerland.

During these six months, he began the project that made him famous. Like many great inventors, Berners-Lee started out wanting to solve a simple problem for himself. Many files on his computer contained data that was related to other data in his system, but he could not always remember how all the data was connected. He decided to create a computer program that would help him keep track of these connections.

To do this, Berners-Lee made use of a technique already known to computer programmers called "hypertext." These are specially chosen words in a document that can serve as links to text in other files. He gave a number to each piece of hypertext so that he could refer to it easily. This was in the days before the invention of the computer mouse and touch screens, so he had to type in the long link numbers when he came upon hypertext in one of his documents. Then his computer would connect him to the related document. This system, which he developed with the help of a colleague, was named Enquire, after a British encyclopedia that he had loved as a boy.

At first, Enquire was designed to work on Berners-Lee's computer alone. However, other scientists at CERN were also eager to have access to information on other computers at the lab, so he expanded it to work with any computer at CERN. But Enquire could not be used outside of the lab. This was a serious limitation, and his next ambition was expand Enquire into a system that could work with computers anywhere, not just in a lab.

After working several years in Britain, Berners-Lee returned to CERN in 1984. As the largest Internet center in Europe, it was a good place for him to work towards his vision of a common set of Internet rules and regulations. He began by inventing HTML, the simple computer language that programmers still use to write pages with links. Next, he devised URLs, a way of giving web pages an address, and HTTP, a set of common rules that control the way web pages are set up and accessed. He then invented the first web browser program to move from web page to web page. Finally, after thinking long and hard, Berners-Lee decided to give a name to this new, expanded Internet system. He called it The World Wide Web (WWW).

The first website, which belonged to CERN, went online on August 6, 1991. It provided an explanation of the World Wide Web, how to obtain a browser, and how to set up a web server. Basically, Berners-Lee—with CERN's approval—announced his invention to the world and shared it with anyone interested. Enthusiasm for the new system was immediate. Computer experts around the globe began working on further inventions for the Web. Many programmers have earned millions of dollars from programs that they have developed to expand the functions of the Web. Berners-Lee, however, never patented his inventions and did not make any money from them.

He has always seen the Internet as a means for people around the world to share knowledge, and he believes it is important to keep the Internet open to everyone. Some critics have wondered whether we are paying too high a price for this universal access, since it also allows people to build and access websites that are dangerous for society, such as those that promote terrorism or other crimes. For Berners-Lee, though, the problems with the Internet are no different from the general problems in our society and they will not be solved by limiting access. In his view, we need to encourage the good aspects and try to keep out the bad, but we must keep the Web open and neutral. "A neutral communications medium is essential to our society," he says. "It is the basis of democracy."

The world has hardly ignored Tim Berners-Lee's contribution to technology and communications. He has won dozens of prizes, honorary degrees, and other honors, including the European Millennium Technology Prize in 2004, worth $1.2 million. Also in that year, Britain's Queen Elizabeth made Berners-Lee a Knight Commander of the British Empire. In his typically modest fashion, he insisted on sharing the credit with others, saying "This is an honor which applies to the whole Web development community and to the inventors and developers of the Internet, whose work made the Web possible."

Berners-Lee still drives every day to his modest office at the Massachusetts Institute of Technology, in Cambridge, Massachusetts. There he oversees an international organization called WC3, which fights to keep the World Wide Web available to everyone regardless of age, nationality, or income level.

**B.** *Write your finishing time:* _____ *Then turn to page 278 and answer the questions. Do not look back at the passage.*

## EXERCISE 6

**A.** *Write your starting time:* _____ *Then preview and read the passage.*

### José Antonio Abreu

Almost forty years ago, José Antonio Abreu dreamed that music could serve as a route out of poverty for the poorest children in Venezuela. He began working with eleven children in a garage in Caracas and from there, created a program of classical music study and performance known today as "El Sistema" (The System). More than two million children have gone through the program. Most of them have come from neighborhoods where drug abuse, violence, and hunger are daily facts of life. But in the music schools and orchestras, these children become part of a community and learn that there is more to life. They also make music that is praised around the world.

Born in 1939, Abreu grew up with a love of music, but focused his early studies on economics, first in Venezuela and then in the United States. He became a professor of Economics at Simón Bolívar University, got involved in politics, and was elected deputy to the Congress of Venezuela. However, he did not give up on music and his musical studies, which eventually led him to receive a second degree in music composition and organ from Venezuela's national music academy.

The idea for a music program came to Abreu in 1975. His first step was to found the National Youth Symphony Orchestra in order to give young musicians the opportunity to play regularly and train under good conductors. The two symphonic orchestras in Venezuela at the time were both filled mainly with European and North American musicians. Abreu wanted to see more Venezuelans playing in the orchestras, but there were relatively few Venezuelans studying classical music and young musicians in Venezuela also had few opportunities to gain musical experience.

Beyond simple music training, however, Abreu had a larger social vision. Music, he believed, could rescue some of his country's most at-risk children from the desperate conditions of their lives. As he has said, "Poverty generates anonymity, loneliness. Music creates happiness and hope in a community, and the triumph of a child as a musician helps him aspire to even higher things."

Over the years this hope has been fulfilled. Abreu has seen his students cut ties with the criminal gangs they used to belong to. Many have become music teachers themselves, becoming a source of pride for their families and inspiring others to give up their destructive behavior. One student came to music at the age of fifteen after nine arrests for robbery and drugs. He said that the first person who really understood him and had confidence in him was his music teacher. He credits his orchestra experience with literally saving his life.

Crime and violence are still a problem in Venezuela, but studies evaluating the program have been unanimous: Most of the participating children attain above-average results in school and become more involved in their communities. If they do not become professional musicians, they go on to productive lives in other fields.

The success of the first youth orchestra attracted attention and funds from the government, and other youth orchestras were started around the country. Before long, the program was adopted by the government as part of its official social and educational policy. Every government since then has supported the program financially, covering 90 percent of the costs. This has been an essential aspect of the success of Abreu's vision. Before the program, music lessons had been too expensive for the great majority of Venezuelans; in the program, both lessons and instruments are free for the children and their families. Children attend the neighborhood music centers for several hours on weekday afternoons and practice on the weekends.

From the very first lesson, each student also becomes a member of an orchestra, starting with one of the country's 60 children's orchestras and moving on to one of the 120 youth orchestras. Being part of a group inspires all the students to work hard and quickly gain technical ability. Because they are playing in an orchestra, they also learn about making music together and many other aspects of musical performance. The quality of playing has been widely praised when the Simón Bolívar Youth Orchestra has toured abroad and joined with youth orchestras from other countries in international music festivals. People who hear the Venezuelans for the first time are amazed at the quality of their playing, often far beyond that of other youth orchestras. They find it hard to believe that many of the teenagers come from very poor families.

As word about the program has spread, musicians and educators from other countries have traveled to Venezuela to see how it all works. From Sir Simon Rattle to Claudio Abbado, famous musicians have praised Abreu and "El Sistema" for its innovative approach to music education and community involvement. As the young musicians have matured, some have left Venezuela to make their careers abroad. One of the biggest stars is Gustavo Dudamel, conductor of the Los Angeles Symphony. Other young Venezuelan musicians who are making their name in Europe include the conductors Diego Matheuz and Christian Vasquez, and the bass player Ericson Ruiz.

As well as serving as Venezuela's Minister of Culture in the 1980s, Abreu has received many honors. In 1998, he was named as a United Nations Cultural Ambassador for Peace. In 2000, he received Sweden's Right Livelihood Award, known as the Alternative Nobel Prize, given to people who have made important contributions to the betterment of humanity.

In his own country, Abreu and his youth symphonies have established a minor cultural revolution. While many countries honor young athletes or pop stars, Venezuelan society embraces its young classical musicians. The country now hosts 28 professional orchestras, and Venezuelan musicians who, in the past, had trouble finding jobs even in their own country, are now also playing in American and European orchestras.

How has all this come about? "El Maestro," as Abreu is called by the thousands and thousands of students who love him, has always kept to his simple view: "Music makes our children better human beings."

**B.** *Write your finishing time: _____ Then turn to page 279 and answer the questions. Do not look back at the passage.*

## QUESTIONS For Unit 2

*After you answer the questions for each exercise, follow these steps:*

1. *Check your answers with your teacher. Write your comprehension score (number of correct answers) in the progress chart.*

2. *Calculate your reading time: Finishing time – Starting time = Reading time: _____ Find your reading rate on page 263. Write it in the progress chart on page 264.*

3. *Re-read the passage and look for the answers to any questions you missed.*

4. *Go back through the passage again and underline the new vocabulary. Add any useful vocabulary to your notebook.*

### 1. Dr. Paul Farmer

1. Which statement best expresses the overall idea of the passage?
   a. Dr. Paul Farmer treats patients with HIV/AIDS and tuberculosis.
   b. Dr. Paul Farmer is a famous doctor who went to Harvard University.
   c. Dr. Paul Farmer works to bring better health care to poor people.

2. You can infer from this passage that Farmer's parents
   a. cared more about learning than money.
   b. pushed their children to become rich.
   c. wanted to have a middle-class lifestyle.

3. Who were the first Haitians that Farmer met?
   a. college students
   b. health workers
   c. farm workers

4. The Cange center—Zanmi Lasante—is a

   a. large community health facility in central Haiti.
   b. charity organization in Boston, Massachusetts.
   d. project for the treatment of HIV/AIDS and tuberculosis.

5. Which of the following is NOT mentioned in the passage?

   a. Health workers at Cange travel to see patients at their homes.
   b. Patients are never sent away from Cange without treatment.
   c. Farmer spends little time with the patients in Cange.

6. PIH believes that the health of people in poor countries

   a. depends on the political situation.
   b. is related to their living conditions.
   c. is mostly a matter of better medicine.

7. Farmer has shown that poor people in developing countries

   a. should pay the same amount as people in wealthy countries.
   b. must be treated differently from people in wealthy countries.
   c. can manage the same treatments as people in wealthy countries.

8. You can infer from this passage that Farmer

   a. cares a lot about the patients he treats.
   b. would like to dedicate more time to research.
   c. enjoys earning lots of money and getting awards.

## 2. Christo and Jeanne-Claude

1. Which statement best expresses the overall idea of the passage?

   a. Christo and Jeanne-Claude believed all art work should have a deep meaning.
   b. Christo and Jeanne-Claude made art that allows people to see places in a new way.
   c. Christo and Jeanne-Claude are famous for wrapping buildings and bridges.

2. Which of the following is NOT mentioned in the passage?

   a. Christo and Jeanne-Claude were not born in France.
   b. Christo was born the same day as Jeanne-Claude.
   c. Christo does most of the work on their installations.

3. Christo and Jeanne-Claude began to wrap objects so that

   a. they could be unwrapped later.
   b. that the real shape could be seen.
   c. they could get the attention of the public.

4. Where were The Gates installed?

   a. in New York's Central Park
   b. in an art museum in New York
   c. along the streets of New York

5. How did people in New York react to The Gates?

   a. It made many people in New York upset and angry.
   b. It made no difference to most people in New York.
   c. It had a positive effect on people walking among them.

6. When Christo and Jeanne-Claude first proposed The Gates 26 years earlier

    a. the city of New York refused permission.
    b. the artists did not have enough money.
    c. the drawings and plans were not yet ready.

7. How were the artists' projects funded?

    a. by the local government
    b. by the artists themselves
    c. by corporate sponsors

8. We can infer from this passage that Christo and Jeanne-Claude

    a. preferred to work mostly in the United States.
    b. were not able to sell much of their artwork.
    d. wanted to keep their artistic independence.

## 3. Wangari Maathai

1. Which statement best expresses the overall idea of the passage?

    a. Maathai worked to improve the environment and the lives of poor people in Africa.
    b. Maathai started the Green Belt Movement by planting trees in Kenya in 1976.
    c. Maathai was the first African woman to win a Nobel Peace Prize.

2. Which of the following was NOT mentioned in the passage?

    a. Maathai studied in both Kenya and the United States.
    b. Maathai ran for Parliament and was elected.
    c. Maathai preferred to stay out of politics.

3. What did Maathai realize when she returned to Kenya after her studies abroad?

    a. Deforestation had changed the environment.
    b. Families were leaving the poor villages.
    c. Politicians in Kenya were stealing money.

4. When poor people cut down the trees in their villages,

    a. they became even poorer.
    c. they moved to other villages.
    d. they were able to grow more food.

5. We can infer from this passage that

    a. women in Kenyan villages were only interested in health problems.
    b. men in Kenyan villages were very interested in the environment.
    c. most women in Kenyan villages were not educated.

6. The Green Belt Movement

    a. helps villagers plant and grow food for their families.
    c. teaches children in schools about the environment.
    d. teaches women to plant and keep trees in their villages.

7. Why was Maathai beaten and put in prison?

    a. because she was not recognized by the police
    b. because she spoke out against the government
    c. because she was a member of Parliament

8. Maathai believes that environmental destruction
    a. can lead to fighting over water, food, and resources.
    b. cannot be avoided in poor African countries.
    c. is an inevitable result of economic development.

## 4. Rosa Parks

1. Which statement best expresses the main idea of the passage?
    a. Rosa Parks became involved in civil rights in Montgomery.
    c. Rosa Parks is an important figure in modern American history.
    d. Rosa Parks played a key role in the fight for civil rights in America.

2. What were the "Jim Crow" laws?
    a. Law that allowed whites to keep slaves.
    b. Laws that kept blacks and whites separate.
    c. Laws that gave blacks the same rights as whites.

3. Which of the following is NOT mentioned in the passage?
    a. Whites sometimes set fire to the homes of black people.
    b. Whites sometimes tortured and killed black men.
    c. Whites were often the victims of violence by blacks.

4. You can infer from this passage that in mid-twentieth century America,
    a. blacks did not commit violent crimes against whites.
    b. whites who were violent against blacks were not severely punished.
    c. violent actions were always severely punished by the courts.

5. The Montgomery Improvement Association
    a. worked for civil rights for blacks.
    b. was a religious association.
    c. organized activities for black women.

6. Reverend Martin Luther King, Jr.,
    a. was arrested for his work on Park's case.
    b. worked as a lawyer on Park's case.
    c. brought Park's case to national attention.

7. Why did Rosa and Raymond Parks move out of Montgomery?
    a. They wanted to be closer to their family.
    b. They had no jobs and did not feel safe.
    c. They hoped to improve their financial situation.

8. Rosa Parks was the first woman in American history to
    a. lose her job because of her political activism.
    b. meet Nelson Mandela, the president of South Africa.
    c. lie in state in the U.S. Capitol Building after her death.

## 5. Tim Berners-Lee

1. Which statement best expresses the main idea of the passage?
   a. Berners-Lee is a famous computer programmer from Great Britain.
   b. Berners-Lee invented the World Wide Web so people could share information.
   c. Berners-Lee developed an interest in computers during his childhood.

2. Berners-Lee made his first computer
   a. at the Massachusetts Institute of Technology.
   b. when he was working at CERN.
   c. when he was a student at Oxford.

3. Why did Berners-Lee begin working on his invention?
   a. He wanted to solve a problem he was having on his computer.
   b. He and his colleagues wanted a better way to share information.
   c. He wanted to remember information from a British encyclopedia.

4. Which of the following is NOT mentioned in the passage?
   a. Enquire could work only with computers at CERN.
   b. Enquire was named after an encyclopaedia.
   c. Enquire made Berners-Lee famous in Britain.

5. To create the World Wide Web, Berners-Lee had to
   a. get help from colleagues.
   b. build a new kind of computer.
   c. invent a series of new things.

6. What information did the first website provide?
   a. about the CERN research center
   b. about the World Wide Web
   c. about Tim Berners-Lee

7. How is Berners-Lee different from many other computer programmers?
   a. He made no money from his inventions.
   b. He patented only a few of his inventions.
   c. He lost interest in the Internet after his inventions.

8. You can infer from this passage that
   a. Berners-Lee values other things more than money.
   b. Berners-Lee would like to limit access to the Web.
   c. Berners-Lee wishes he had made money from the Web.

## 6. José Antonio Abreu

1. Which statement best expresses the overall idea of the passage?

   a. Abreu started a music program that has helped many young Venezuelans.
   b. Abreu's music program includes many youth symphony orchestras.
   c. Abreu believes it is important to teach music to young children.

2. Abreu hoped that the National Youth Symphony Orchestra would

   a. attract more foreign musicians to Venezuela.
   b. allow him to conduct a large symphony orchestra.
   c. give young Venezuelans more orchestral experience.

3. Abreu believes that music can

   a. improve the economy of a poor country.
   b. help young people learn positive values.
   c. encourage young people to leave home.

4. Which of the following is NOT mentioned in the passage?

   a. Some students in the program used to belong to criminal gangs.
   b. Most of the students could not afford private music lessons.
   c. Few of the students continue with music after the program.

5. How does the program survive financially?

   a. with funds from the Venezuelan government
   b. with donations from international organizations
   c. with money from the families of the students

6. Which of the following is NOT mentioned in the passage?

   a. All the students in the program play in orchestras.
   b. Students pay a small fee to rent their instruments.
   c. Music keeps students busy after school and on weekends.

7. What is the reaction of people who hear the Venezuelan youth orchestras?

   a. They are surprised by the kind of music they play.
   b. They are surprised by the high level of their playing.
   c. They are surprised by the youth of the musicians.

8. You can infer from this passage that in the past

   a. many young Venezuelans were interested in classical music.
   b. young Venezuelans went to the United States to study music.
   c. there were few opportunities for Venezuelans to learn music.

# The Impact of Modern Technology

**A.** *Write your starting time:* _____ *Then preview and read the passage.*

## New Uses for Cell Phones

Only a short time ago, few people could have imagined that cell phone use would expand so rapidly. Cell phones have now spread to every corner of the world, even in the poorest countries. And they have been adapted to many different purposes beyond their original use as a way to talk to someone.

The spread of cell phones has been most surprising and dramatic in developing areas of the world, especially in Africa. Much of the African population still lives in rural areas where travel is difficult because of the terrible road conditions. People lack basic services such as electricity or running water. Huge areas also lack landline phone service because of the high cost of laying out wires across jungles or deserts.

At the same time, the need for communication has been growing. As in many other parts of the world, millions of Africans have moved far away from friends and family in their small villages in order to look for work in the big cities, in other African countries, or abroad. The changing economy is also a factor in the increased need for communication. Farmers, fishermen, traders, businessmen— all those involved in buying or selling—need to be in touch with markets and customers all over Africa and beyond. They need to know about the prices and availability of products in the big cities or internationally.

In the developed countries, the need for more information and better communication has largely been met through the use of computers, smart phones and tablets connected to the Internet. As people and businesses have become dependent on the Internet, devices to access it have become more portable, and software applications have multiplied. But in Africa and other developing countries, the use of computers and the Internet is not widespread. Computers—not to mention smart phones or tablets— are too expensive for most people and require too much electric power. Furthermore, Internet service is unavailable in most rural areas and may be unreliable even in the cities.

Thus, Africans have turned to their cell phones for many of their needs. Cell phones are cheaper, simpler to use, and more easily recharged than computers. There are many devices now that recharge cell phones through solar power, human power (with a bicycle), or by other relatively cheap means. Cell phone networks can also be established relatively easily, since they send their signals from towers, not through lines, and the towers can be constructed inexpensively by hand out of scraps of metal.

One result has been the rapid development of mobile banking. A company called M-Pesa, in Kenya, was one of the first to provide mobile banking services. MTN soon followed with a mobile banking service in South Africa. These companies' success inspired others, so that today, almost every country on the African continent offers mobile banking. It allows users to store money with their cell phones and use the phone to send money or make payments. For example, if a worker in Nairobi wishes to send money to a relative in a distant village, he sends her a text message. She then goes to her local M-Pesa office to pick up the cash. Since M-Pesa offices or kiosks are found everywhere in Kenya, this process is simple and easy for everyone. For the millions of Africans without access to traditional banks or without the money to pay the banks' high fees, mobile banking has been revolutionary.

Other kinds of phone services have followed mobile banking. Some companies, like SlimTrader in Nigeria, have made it possible for cell phone users to access commercial websites more easily and efficiently. Other companies make the exchange of information easier. In Namibia and nine other countries, the company Umuntu has created "mimiboards," allowing people in a specific area to post and read messages. People can post notices to their local mimiboard—for example, a fisherman can post information about his catch of the day, or a shop owner can announce the arrival of new stock.

Special programs for cell phones have also helped governments and aid workers deal with medical issues. In South Africa, for instance, cell phones help doctors treat the enormous number of patients with HIV/AIDS. It is impossible for doctors to visit all the patients themselves and patients often cannot travel, but trained health workers can check on the patients and communicate with the doctors by text message. In the fight against malaria, researchers have made use of cell phone technology in a different way. Using cell phone records, they can keep track of human travel in a given area, which allows them to predict where malaria cases are likely to be most numerous. Malaria control programs can then concentrate on those areas to make the best use of their limited resources.

Yet another way that cell phones can be of use to the community is through the Ushahidi software. This was developed during a period of violence in Nairobi, Kenya, to help people find out what was happening and allow them to get help. An open source program, it allows users to gather information via text message from people at the scene of a crisis and then plot that information on a computer map so that aid workers and international monitors can organize their efforts and keep track of developments. It has been used after natural disasters in Haiti and Pakistan and during political conflict in Sudan and the Congo.

Though Africa has been leading the way, cell phone use has expanded in similar ways in other parts of the developing world, particularly in India, Pakistan, Bangladesh, and South American countries. In the developed world as well, people have recognized the huge market for cell phone services, particularly mobile banking. Some big U.S. companies, like Visa, have decided to invest in African mobile banking services. Other companies are looking for ways that cell phone services could be expanded in the United States, for example, for the nine million Americans without banking services.

**B.** *Write your finishing time:* _____ *Then turn to page 289 and answer the questions.*

## EXERCISE 2

**A.** *Write your starting time:* _____ *Then preview and read the passage.*

### A New World of DNA Testing

Genetics is one of the most exciting areas of science today. Not only have discoveries about genetics greatly expanded our knowledge of the human body, they have also led researchers to discover dramatic new applications for knowledge about our genes, in particular, DNA testing.

Since the early 20th century, scientists have known that most physical characteristics, from eye color to body height, nose size, or blood type, are contained in an individual's genes and passed on from parents to children. Genes work like a chemical instruction manual for each part and function of the body. Their basic chemical element is called DNA, a copy of which can be found in every cell. The existence of genes and the chemical structure of DNA were understood by the mid-1900s and at that time, scientists thought that genetics would open the door quickly to treatments for many diseases, such as cancer. More recent discoveries have revealed that genes work in far more complex ways than were thought, and definitive cures have not yet been found for cancer or other diseases.

Still, knowledge about genetics is changing health care in important ways. Scientists now know which diseases are genetic in origin and, often, which genes are responsible. Though scientists were hoping that this knowledge might lead to effective cures for diseases with genetic origins, such as cystic fibrosis and

Huntington's disease, that has not been the case. But it has allowed some women for example, to take preventive measures when they learn that they are very likely to get certain forms of breast cancer.

For many other diseases that are only partly genetic, like Type 2 diabetes, knowledge of genetic risk factors allows doctors and their patients to focus on other ways to reduce risks, for example, by not smoking, and by exercising regularly and eating a healthy diet. If a patient contracts diabetes, genetic information can help doctors customize treatment to make it more effective. Thus, given that prevention usually costs far less than treatment of these diseases at later stages, genetic information can also help reduce the cost of health care.

The fact that DNA is unique to each individual also means that it can be used for purposes of identification. DNA testing is often called for in problematic family situations, such as a divorce where there is disagreement about the paternity (who is the father) of a child. Definite knowledge of paternity may be important in decisions about who will care for the child and who is financially responsible. DNA testing is also useful for people who were adopted and who decide as adults to search for their biological parents. Yet another use for DNA testing is for people applying for family-based immigration to the United States, Canada, or the U.K. These days, they can present DNA evidence in support of their application.

Another very important social benefit of DNA testing is in criminal justice. With just a drop of blood or saliva or a single hair, it is possible to prove definitively whether someone who is suspected of a crime is guilty or innocent. This technique was first used in 1985 in the U.K. when a man confessed to killing a young woman. Because police had found samples of the killer's DNA at the scene of the crime, a biologist suggested that it might be possible to compare that DNA to some from the confessor's blood. To everyone's surprise, the tests showed he was not the killer. At that point, he explained that he had confessed to the crime out of fear and police pressure. Soon after, the police found a positive match for the DNA, and the first man was set free.

The successful conclusion of this case in England made a big impression on lawyers and law enforcement officers around the world, especially in the United States. Studies at that time showed that perhaps five percent of U.S. prison inmates were, in fact, innocent of the crimes they had been accused of. That added up to almost 10,000 people. Some, like the man in the U.K., had been pushed to confess to crimes they had not committed. Others had never had a chance to defend themselves in court because of incompetent lawyers. Still others had been convicted on false evidence given by dishonest police officers who wanted to put someone in jail.

In 1992, two law professors, Peter Neufeld and Barry Scheck, decided to use DNA evidence to help set free such mistakenly convicted inmates. With the help of their students, they created an organization called the Innocence Project, which is still operating. Most of their clients are poor men, many from racial and ethnic minorities. Studies have shown that U.S. judges and juries are often influenced by racial and ethnic background and that people from minority groups are more likely to be convicted. Some of these men had even been sentenced to death. Since it was founded, the Innocence Project has helped free 299 men and 1 woman. Some of them had been in jail for ten, twenty years or longer for crimes they did not commit.

In some cases, DNA testing has brought about larger changes to the criminal justice system. In Illinois, a group of journalism students were able to use DNA testing to prove the innocence of state jail inmates with problematic cases. Thirteen men were set free and the governor of the state stopped all executions of death sentences until after further study of the cases. Four more men were then freed and sentences were changed for 167 more. More important, the state worked to address the problems that had led to such injustice.

Some people fear that DNA testing could be used in evil or undemocratic ways by governments. Others mistrust the science and the lawyers who use it. But for those whose innocence has been proven and who are now free men, DNA testing has meant nothing less than a return to life.

**B.**   *Write your finishing time:* _____   *Then turn to page 290 and answer the questions. Do not look back at the passage.*

**A.**  *Write your starting time:* _____ *Then preview and read the passage.*

## The Growing Success of Organ Transplants

The successful transplanting of human body parts is one of modern medicine's most remarkable achievements. A transplant is when surgeons remove an organ or other part from one person's body and put it into another person's body in order to replace a diseased or damaged body part. At present, the body parts that have been transplanted with success include organs such as the heart, kidneys, liver, lungs, pancreas, and intestines, as well as bones, tendons, trachea, corneas, veins, skin, and recently even a few hands and faces.

Attempts at transplants were recorded far back in human history, but they always ended in failure. In the late 1500s, Italian doctor, Gasparo Tagliacozzi, wrote about his experiments with skin transplants. He was able to replace skin successfully, but only when it was taken from another part of the patient's body. When he tried the same operation with skin from a different person, the skin died. Even at that date Tagliacozzi knew enough about medicine to succeed in the operation itself; what he didn't know was how to prevent the recipient's body from reacting negatively to the foreign skin and rejecting it.

The problem of rejection continued to limit the success of transplants. As early as 1905, a Czech doctor named Eduard Zirm transplanted a cornea. A few years later, a French doctor, Alexis Carrel, transplanted veins. Then, in 1954, Dr. Joseph Murray and his team in Boston were the first to perform a kidney transplant operation after which the patient survived. Transplants of other organs soon followed, with the dramatic first heart transplant in 1968 by Dr. Christian Barnard in South Africa. However, despite successful operations, most early recipients of organs did not survive long.

That changed only after 1980, when scientists discovered new drugs to prevent the recipient from rejecting a transplanted body part. The most important of these was called cyclosporine. Before the arrival of this drug, the chances of surviving transplant surgery were almost zero, but with cyclosporine, transplants became a life-saving treatment. Since then, organ transplants have allowed thousands of people with damaged organs to live for many more years. At the same time, however, cyclosporine and similar drugs have created other problems. Though they reduce the risk of rejection, they also reduce the body's ability to defend itself against infection. After every operation, doctors must keep adjusting drug doses—enough to prevent reaction, but not so much as to leave the patient open to infection and disease.

The problem of rejection is pushing scientists to look for different ways of replacing damaged body parts. For a while it seemed that artificial organs might be the answer, and there was much publicity about the first artificial hearts in the 1990s. Those devices are still used temporarily by some patients awaiting transplants, but they are not living organs. They are really just sophisticated machines, and like machines, they can break down, wear out, or need new parts.

Research is now heading in another direction—regenerative medicine, also known as tissue engineering. Scientists working in this field aim to create new body parts from the patient's own cells, or a combination of the patient's cells and other material. They want to make organs with cells, blood vessels, and nerves that can become a living, functioning part of the body. Some scientists, such as Paolo Macchiarini at the Karolinska Institute in Sweden, hope to go even further. He would like to make use of the body's ability to repair itself, so that it can remake a damaged organ on its own.

Macchiarini has focused on the trachea [windpipe inside the neck], which is a relatively simple organ. In his first operations, he used windpipes from dead people, which had been cleaned and seeded with cells from the patient. Those cells re-formed the lining that is naturally inside the windpipe. Since it is difficult to find suitable human windpipes, Macchiarini has developed an artificial windpipe that can be lined with the patient's cells. One of these was implanted into a man from Eritrea who was studying engineering in Iceland and who had cancer of the windpipe. He regained his health and afterwards was able to make full use of his new windpipe.

So far, scientists have made and transplanted only simple organs like windpipes and bladders, but they are working towards building more complex organs, such as blood vessels, livers, and kidneys. There are several very important advantages to these "bioartificial" organs. One is that, since they are built from the patient's own cells, there is no risk of rejection. The other is that there is no need to find a donor of the same age, size, and blood type. For delicate organs, such as the heart, kidney, and liver, there is a serious shortage in the United States and many people die while waiting for a transplant.

More recently, doctors have begun to transplant complex body parts, such as hands. Dr. Jean-Michel Dubernard in France was the first to transplant a hand onto the arm of an Australian prison inmate in 1998. However, the patient was not satisfied with the hand, and, after several years, he had it removed. The next hand transplant patients—in the United States and Austria—received better follow-up care and kept their hands. The Austrian, who received two new hands, took a round-the-world motorcycle trip afterwards to publicize them.

The last frontier in transplant medicine is the face. Though some question the idea of replacing a person's face, the alternatives may be far worse. Someone whose face has been severely damaged may have trouble breathing and eating. Transplants of the patient's own skin may require up to 50 operations with limited results. The first partial face transplant was performed in France in 2005 for a woman who had been badly bitten by her dog. The first full face transplant took place in Spain and since then there have been many others with ever better results. A patient in the United States whose whole face was replaced in 2011 even recovered his sense of smell.

**B.** *Write your finishing time:* _____ *Then turn to page 291 and answer the questions. Do not look back at the passage.*

## EXERCISE 4

**A.** *Write your starting time:* _____ *Then preview and read the passage.*

### The Past and Future of Robots

The idea of inventing machines to do things for humans is not a new one. Mechanical figures with moving parts were invented long ago in ancient China. A third century Chinese text describes how an engineer presented the emperor with a life-size human figure that could move. In Renaissance Italy, Leonardo da Vinci was very interested in machines, and drew plans for a mechanical human figure, though it is not known if he tried to build it.

The art of building mechanized figures became highly developed in Japan after 1700. Japanese craftsmen built mechanized puppets that were used in theater to act out traditional myths and legends. They also created extremely complex mechanical toys, some of which served tea or fired arrows. Programmable mechanical figures, or automata as they were called, became popular in Europe in the eighteenth century. But these were really just toys.

The word robot comes from the Czech word robotnik, meaning "worker." It came into use in 1921 when a play by Czech writer Karel Capek became very popular. In the play, a man makes a machine that can think, which he calls a robot and which ends up killing him. In the 1940s, the American science fiction writer Isaac Asimov wrote a series of stories about robots and invented the term robotics, the science of robots.

Meanwhile, in the real world, the first robots were developed by an engineer, Joseph F. Engelberger, and an inventor, George C. Devol. Together they started Unimation, a manufacturing company that produced the first true robot, called the Unimate. Robots of this type were installed at a General Motors automobile plant and proved to be a success. They worked reliably and saved money for General Motors, so other companies soon began acquiring robots as well.

Industrial robots are nothing like the terrifying creatures that can be seen in science fiction films. In fact, these robots do not look or behave like humans. They are simply pieces of computer-controlled machinery with metal "arms" or "hands." Since they are made of metal, they can perform jobs that might be difficult or dangerous for humans, particularly those that require high heat. And since robots never get tired, hungry, or distracted, they are useful for repetitive tasks that would be tedious for humans. Though the use of robots in factories has meant the loss of some jobs, at the same time other jobs have been created for robot technicians, engineers, and programmers, as well as for other workers in the factories that produce them.

Robots have also been developed by governments and scientists for use in situations where humans might be in danger. For example, robots can be sent in to investigate a possible bomb threat or an accident at a nuclear power plant. Researchers use robots to collect samples of hot rocks or gases in active volcanoes. In space exploration, robots have performed many key tasks where humans could not be present, such as on the surface of Mars. In 2004, two robotic Rovers—small six-wheeled computerized cars—were sent to Mars. The Rovers had lasers that functioned as eyes and software that was designed to help them travel around holes or rocks. In their first two years on Mars, they performed many scientific experiments and took over 16,500 photographs, sending all the results back to Earth. Among other things, the Rovers discovered that Mars probably once had water on its surface just like Earth.

As robots were developed for industry and science, some inventors also found uses for smaller and less expensive robots. The first of these appeared in the 1980s as an educational tool for learning about computers. Then in the 1990s, further technological improvements led to the invention of robot toys, especially in Asian countries, where robots are viewed more favorably than in western countries. The most famous of these was AIBO, a robotic dog produced by Sony. It could run around a room and chase a ball like a real dog. However, in spite of great enthusiasm for AIBO when it first appeared, it was too expensive ($2,000) for popular appeal. The more recent Topio, a humanoid robot that is designed to play table tennis has also had limited success.

Inventors have been more successful with robots that can help with housework. The Roomba, for example, is a robotic vacuum cleaner. Made of lightweight plastic, it is low and round, with wheels. Before it begins cleaning, Roomba first moves all around to "learn" about the shape of the room and the furniture in it. Then it starts vacuuming, avoiding the walls and furniture. When it begins to run out of power, it returns to a base to recharge. It does all of this without any human direction. With a reasonable price tag ($400-600), the Roomba has sold millions in the ten years since it appeared. The same company that makes Roomba, has developed a series of other robots to wash floors, clean swimming pools, and do other household jobs.

What is the future for robots in society? Other uses will undoubtedly be developed for industry and for research. In Asia, robots are being developed for use in schools and in homes for the elderly, but they are less accepted in western countries. A more likely application could be in cars. Robot specialists at Stanford University have shown with a robot-controlled car called Stanley that robots are capable of dealing with many of the tasks required of a driver—reading a map, finding a location, judging what is ahead, and making decisions based on this information.

Robots have come a long way. Once, story writers and movie makers imagined them as dangerous human-like machines that could take over the Earth. Now robots help people at home, in factories, and in scientific research. In the next decade, many new uses will be found for robots, especially in cars. As one designer said, "A person's role in the car is changing. People will become more planners than drivers." Robots will do the rest.

**B.** Write your finishing time: _____ Then turn to page 291 and answer the questions. Do not look back at the passage.

**A.** *Write your starting time:* _____ *Then preview and read the passage.*

## How AC Shaped the Nation

Heating systems go back to the very first human settlements in cold climates, when people started bringing fires indoors. Cooling systems were much slower to develop, not arriving on the scene until the twentieth century.

Before air conditioning (AC), people in hot climates found other ways to deal with the heat. In the Middle East, for example, houses had no windows to the south and were positioned to encourage air circulation. In the United States, houses in the southern states had high ceilings and several stories so that the hot air could rise away from the main living areas. They also had porches, where people often slept during the summer months. In general, people in hot climates avoided activity during the hottest part of the day.

With industrialization, however, productive activity in factories had to continue throughout the day. Thus the first air conditioners were not inspired by a desire to make workers more comfortable, but by the need to keep machines and products in better condition. The first machine that could cool a room and remove humidity was invented in 1902 by a 25-year-old engineer, Willis Carrier. His "Apparatus for Treating Air," which sent air through water-cooled coils, was built for a printing company in Brooklyn, New York, so that humidity would not make the paper stick in the machines.

Carrier's machine was such a success that he started a company to produce more. In the early years, these were installed mostly in factories, as owners began to realize that cooler temperatures benefitted workers as well as machinery, resulting in higher production levels. Air conditioning undoubtedly was an important factor in the growth of industry, since it allowed manufacturing to continue at the same pace year round even in the warmest states.

These early machines—like the early computers—were enormous and costly. Carrier designed a new model in 1925 with a central compressor to reduce the size. It was first used on Memorial Day weekend at the Rivoli Theater in Times Square, New York. After that, the use of AC units gradually spread to department stores, movie theaters, railroad cars, and offices, but not yet in most homes. Few except the very wealthy could afford them. For most people, air conditioning was a luxury to be experienced and enjoyed only while shopping or watching a movie.

It was not until after the Second World War that smaller, less expensive air-conditioning units became available. This resulted in a boom in the sales of home air conditioning units. As British scholar S.F. Markham wrote in 1947, "The greatest contribution to civilization in this century may well be air-conditioning—and America leads the way." Many of the returning soldiers and their new families moved to the suburbs outside America's major cities with a desire to put the war behind them and live the good life. Air-conditioned homes were part of that life.

The consequences of this trend were far reaching, starting with the architecture of homes. With AC, inexpensive single-story homes could be made comfortable all year round. Porches were no longer necessary, and since people tended to stay indoors in any case, new houses were built without them. The fact that people were no longer spending time on their front steps or porches also meant that neighborhood residents met and talked less. Along with other factors, such as the advent of television, this led to a weakening of America's sense of community.

The rise of AC also allowed the creation of large malls with shops, walkways, movie theaters, and restaurants that are comfortable in all seasons. In suburban America in the second half of the twentieth century, the air-conditioned mall became the preferred place to go for shopping or for an afternoon's entertainment. Shoppers stopped going to the town and city centers, which led to the closing of many small family-owned businesses, and to the general decline of downtown areas.

The architecture of the cities also changed thanks to AC. Since windows were no longer necessary for fresh air in every room, builders could now take full advantage of the new engineering and materials to create structures that were much larger and taller than ever before. Buildings were designed to take up entire city blocks or to rise more than 100 stories. Furthermore, since the windows did not need to open, glass could be used for entire outside walls. Air conditioning is one of the reasons cities from Shanghai to New York have so many shiny glass-fronted skyscrapers.

In the United States, air conditioning has also influenced the movement of the population from the cooler northern states to the southern states. The hot climate of the south had always made it unattractive to northerners. But once homes could be cooled in summer, states like Florida and Arizona began to draw people who wanted to escape from northern winters. This population shift has affected regional economies, as well as the balance of political power between northern and southern states.

The massive use of AC has not been without side effects, some of them very serious. One is the risk of spreading disease through large AC systems. This was recognized in the 1970s after an epidemic of Legionnaire's disease in a hotel, which killed 26 people. However, this risk can be avoided with regular cleaning. Another problem is less easily solved. Air conditioning is a major factor in levels of energy consumption. More recent AC models are more efficient than the early ones, but they still consume a great deal of energy and thus contribute to pollution and global warming.

In spite of the cost and the environmental consequences, the use of AC continues to expand. In the United States, people are so used to living with AC, they can't imagine life without it. People in other parts of the world are also discovering the comfort and increased productivity that comes with AC. Furthermore, the worldwide growth of information technology has greatly increased the need for cooling systems that will prevent large computers and servers from overheating.

**B.** *Write your finishing time:* _____ *Then turn to page 292 and answer the questions. Do not look back at the passage.*

## EXERCISE 6

**A.** *Write your starting time:* _____ *Then preview and read the passage.*

### The Uses and Misuses of GPS

As a technology for finding location, GPS (Global Positioning System) is the latest in a long series of developments. Travelers once checked on the sun or the stars to find their way through unknown lands or seas. As early as 6200 BCE, people in the Middle East began to make and use maps. But until quite recently, maps did not give a very accurate picture of the geography. They became more realistic as European explorers traveled to all corners of the globe, bringing with them equipment for calculating time, locations, and distances.

But no map can compete with GPS. All you need now is a receiver—which costs as little as $100 and can fit in your pocket—and a clear view of the sky. You'll never be lost again. The receiver connects to a satellite navigation system that provides location and time information in all weather conditions anywhere on Earth. The satellites, which send continuous signals from 12,000 miles (19,000 kilometers) above Earth, are owned and operated by the United States government. Anyone with a GPS receiver can access the system.

The system had its beginnings in the 1940s, when the U.S. military developed a navigation system using radio signals from different ground locations. However, this system was not very reliable. The signals could easily be interrupted in wartime or get lost in bad weather. The idea of using satellites for sending signals came to some American scientists soon after the first man-made satellite, the Sputnik, was launched by the Soviet Union in 1957. The scientists could easily follow the satellite's path across the sky and track its radio beams. Knowing their exact location on Earth, they could calculate the position of the satellite and its traveling speed. They realized that if there were several satellites with signals, they could figure out their own position on Earth. A system using signals sent from satellites was clearly the solution for global navigation.

The first such system was developed by the U.S. Navy in the 1960s. It sent signals from five satellites and was used mainly by military ships and airplanes. However, with only five satellites, it was not always possible to get a signal everywhere on the globe. This meant ships or planes could not depend on the system when they needed it most, in emergency situations such as extreme weather or war. More satellites and better signals were needed. After years of research, the first GPS satellite was launched in 1978, ten more by 1989, and a complete set of 24 satellites were in orbit by 1994. Since then some satellites have been replaced, and the system has been updated. Other countries and regions have also developed, or are developing, similar satellite systems, including the Russians, the Chinese, the Europeans, and the Indians.

Though it was originally created for military uses, GPS has by now become an essential global navigation tool. Around the world, large commercial ships depend on GPS, as do smaller boats and airplanes. With the development of smaller and more inexpensive receivers, GPS has become a common feature on most newer vehicles and is included on many rental cars. The system shows your route on a map as you are driving and also gives directions by computerized voice. Trucking companies have put receivers in their trucks, so drivers will not get lost, and so the companies can better keep track of them. The same is true of companies that run taxi or other services.

Another use of GPS is for emergency services. In 2002, a new rule of the Federal Communications Commission required that telephone companies had to allow for GPS capability so that the people who call emergency numbers could be located. This has been an enormous help for the police and ambulance drivers and shortened the time needed for them to arrive at the scene of the emergency. It has also allowed disaster relief organizations to find people who are injured or in danger after natural disasters such as earthquakes or floods. Families who are worried about their children getting lost or kidnapped can have their children wear GPS receivers. Receivers can also be worn by elderly people who are likely to get lost. Owners of dogs and cats can prevent their pets from getting lost or stolen with a receiver on a collar.

However, the GPS technology can also be misused. In the United States, several cases have been brought to court to question the right of the government or private companies to track people without their knowledge. One case came before the Supreme Court in the state of Washington in 2003. The police there wanted to learn more about the habits of a man they suspected of a crime, so they hid a GPS receiver in his car. However, under American law, the police are not allowed to investigate a person's private life if there is no evidence that he or she has committed a crime. The Washington Supreme Court agreed that the police in Washington had broken this law. In their view, hiding a GPS receiver in a car was like putting an invisible police officer in the back seat.

In 2005, a different issue came up in a case involving GPS in Connecticut. This time it was a rental car company that had hidden GPS receivers in all their rental cars so they could find out how fast people were driving. If one of their cars was driven faster than 80 miles per hour (120 km/hour), the renter was charged an extra $150. However, renters were not told about this policy. One angry customer decided to sue the company and his case went to the Connecticut Supreme Court, which agreed that the charge was unfair and told the rental company to refund him. The use of GPS in this way was not illegal, according to the decision, but the rental company had to inform customers beforehand about the existence of a GPS receiver in the car and about the speeding charges.

**B.** *Write your finishing time: _____ Then turn to page 293 and answer the questions. Do not look back at the passage.*

# QUESTIONS For Unit 3

*Follow these steps for each exercise:*

1. *Check your answers with your teacher. Write your comprehension score (number of correct answers) in the progress chart.*

2. *Calculate your reading time: Finishing time – Starting time = Reading time: _____ Find your reading rate on page 263. Write it in the progress chart on page 264.*

3. *Re-read the passage for any questions you answered incorrectly.*

4. *Go back through the passage again and underline the new vocabulary. Add any useful vocabulary to your notebook.*

## 1. New Uses for Cell Phones

1. Which statement best expresses the overall idea of the passage?
   a. Cell phone use in Africa is mainly for banking.
   b. Cell phone use has expanded dramatically in Africa.
   c. Cell phones have helped many African businesses.

2. Which of the following is NOT mentioned in the passage?
   a. Many rural areas have no running water or electricity.
   b. The terrible condition of the roads makes travel difficult.
   c. Landline networks are inexpensive to build.

3. What is one reason why the need for communication has increased?
   a. People enjoy using their phones.
   b. People do not have access to the Internet.
   c. People move around more than before.

4. Which of the following is NOT mentioned in the passage?
   a. Cell phone towers are cheap and easy to build.
   b. Cell phones are smaller and lighter than landline phones.
   c. Cell phones are easier to charge than computers.

5. Mobile banking allows someone to send money
   a. by sending a text message.
   b. through their local bank.
   c. with a phone conversation.

6. A "mimiboard" allows people
   a. to get in touch with friends.
   b. to post notices about things for sale.
   c. to get better medical treatment.

7. How can mobile phone technology help fight malaria?
   a. by helping governments find patients
   b. by helping doctors contact health workers
   c. by helping scientists predict where it will hit

8. You can infer from this passage that cell phones

    a. are helping economic development in Africa.

    b. are changing the political situation in Africa.

    c. are not relevant to social status in Africa.

## 2. A New World of DNA Testing

1. Which statement best expresses the overall idea of the passage?

    a. DNA testing is useful in many different fields today.

    b. DNA testing has freed many men from American jails.

    c. DNA testing was developed in the twentieth century

2. The use of genetics to cure diseases like cancer

    a. has been less successful than scientists expected.

    b. has led to some successful new treatments.

    c. has been simplified by recent discoveries.

3. How can genetic information help reduce healthcare costs?

    a. If doctors know which diseases are genetic, they can cure those diseases.

    b. If doctors know that a patient is at risk, they can provide better preventive care.

    c. If doctors know that a patient is a smoker, they can test for type 2 diabetes.

4. Which of the following is NOT mentioned in the passage?

    a. Divorcing couples sometimes use DNA paternity testing.

    b. Applicants for immigration use DNA testing as evidence.

    c. Doctors use DNA testing to identify their patients.

5. In 1985 in England, DNA testing

    a. proved that the killer was a man.

    b. confirmed the killer's confession.

    c. freed a man accused of murder.

6. The Innocence Project uses DNA testing to

    a. help the police put killers in prison.

    c. prove that lawyers are incompetent.

    d. free people who shouldn't be in jail.

7. Why are the students in Illinois mentioned in the passage?

    a. They used DNA testing to prove that some sentences were unjust.

    b. They proved that men from minorities are convicted less often.

    c. They showed that the governor of Illinois was influencing justice.

8. You can infer from this passage that DNA testing

    a. is used in the same ways around the world.

    b. may not be reliable in some cases

    c. will continue to be used in the United States.

## 3. The Growing Success of Organ Transplants

1. Which statement best expresses the overall idea of the passage?
    a. Modern medicine and technology can save the lives of many patients.
    b. The first successful transplants were done in the early twentieth century.
    c. Over the past century, transplant medicine has made constant progress.

2. Why were early transplant operations unsuccessful?
    a. Because the patient's body rejected the transplant.
    b. Because doctors did not know how to operate.
    c. Because the body parts came from the same person.

3. Transplant recipients began to live longer
    a. after it was possible to transplant veins.
    b. after the discovery of a new drug.
    c. after they rejected the new body part.

4. Which of the following is NOT mentioned in the passage?
    a. Regenerative medicine aims to create sophisticated machines.
    b. Regenerative medicine uses the patient's cells to create body parts.
    c. Regenerative medicine sometimes uses artificial materials.

5. What has Paolo Macchiarini developed?
    a. an artificial heart
    b. a new kind of cell
    c. a bioartifical windpipe

6. Which of the following is NOT mentioned in the passage?
    a. Bioartifical organs are extremely expensive.
    b. Bioartifical organs are not rejected by patients.
    c. Bioartifical organs do not require suitable donors.

7. The first recipient of a hand transplant
    a. lost his new hand in an accident
    b. decided not to keep the new hand.
    c. received a double hand transplant.

8. You can infer from this passage that
    a. until recently many people refused to have transplant operations.
    b. early transplant operations were more for research than for treatment.
    c. the shortage of organs has led doctors to use organs that are not suitable.

## 4. The Past and Future of Robots

1. Which statement best expresses the overall idea of the passage?
    a. The word *robot* was invented by a Czech writer in 1921.
    b. Some kinds of robots are used in industry and scientific research.
    c. Robots can be used to perform many complex tasks these days.

2. Figures that could move mechanically

   a. did not exist until the age of electronics.
   b. were created by people in ancient China.
   c. were first imagined in science fiction.

3. The first real robot was

   a. installed in an automobile plant.
   b. a machine that could think like a person.
   c. was similar to a human in appearance.

4. Which of the following is NOT mentioned in the passage?

   a. Industrial robots often look and behave just like humans.
   b. Industrial robots can perform jobs that are dangerous for people.
   c. Industrial robots are useful for jobs that involve repeated movements.

5. Robots are useful in space exploration because they

   a. travel much faster and farther than humans.
   b. can go places where people cannot go.
   c. take better photographs than humans.

6. Which of the following is NOT mentioned in the passage?

   a. Robots are sold as toys.
   b. Robots are used for housework.
   c. Robots are most popular in the United States.

7. Why did researchers at Stanford invent Stanley, the robot-controlled car?

   a. to show that robots could replace drivers
   b. to show that robots drive better than humans
   c. to show that robots aren't as good as humans

8. You can infer from this passage that

   a. robots will not be as useful in the future.
   b. future robots probably will not look like humans.
   c. robots could be dangerous to humans in the future.

## 5. How AC Shaped the Nation

1. Which statement best expresses the overall idea of the passage?

   a. Air conditioning has affected the way houses are constructed in the United States.
   b. Air conditioning has contributed to economic development in the United States.
   c. Air conditioning has had an impact on various aspects of life in the United States.

2. Which of the following is NOT mentioned in the passage?

   a. The first air conditioners reduced humidity in a room.
   b. The first air conditioners were used mostly in southern states.
   c. The first air conditioners helped improve the quality of products.

3. Air conditioners were not used in homes in the 20s and 30s

   a. because most people couldn't afford them.
   b. because few people knew about them.
   c. because people didn't want them.

4. How did people's behavior change as a result of air conditioning?

    a. They moved indoors and saw fewer people.
    b. They spent more time visiting their neighbors.
    c. They went more often to the movies.

5. Which of the following is NOT mentioned in the passage?

    a. Air conditioning led to the rise of large shopping malls.
    b. Air conditioning allowed for the creation of lively town centers.
    c. Air conditioning made possible the construction of tall office buildings.

6. The invention of air conditioning led to population growth in

    a. the northern states.
    b. the southern states.
    c. the middle states.

7. One problem with air conditioning today is that it

    b. consumes a lot of energy.
    c. takes up a lot of space.
    d. is difficult to install.

8. We can infer from this passage that most Americans today

    a. miss socializing with friends and neighbors.
    b. would prefer to live in the cooler northern states.
    c. can afford to have air conditioning in their homes.

## 6. The Uses and Misuses of GPS

1. Which statement best expresses the overall idea of the passage?

    a. GPS is easier to use than a map.
    b. GPS receivers depend on satellites above Earth.
    c. GPS has a wide range of different uses today.

2. The first radio navigation system

    a. was developed by the Soviet Union.
    b. followed the path of a man-made satellite.
    c. depended on signals sent from the ground.

3. What did American scientists learn from Sputnik?

    a. They realized that signals from satellites could be used to find location.
    b. They realized they had to send up more satellites than the Soviet Union.
    c. They realized that satellite signals could be interrupted in wartime.

4. Having twenty-four satellites in the system means that

    a. it may not be possible to get a signal in some places.
    b. it is possible to get a signal from any place on Earth.
    c. signals are easily interrupted or lost in some places.

5. Which of the following is NOT mentioned in the passage?

    a. GPS helps relief workers after natural disasters.
    b. The police use GPS to locate people who call 911.
    c. The army has used GPS to find enemy ships or planes.

6. What did the Washington Supreme Court decide?

   a. The police can investigate people if they have done something suspicious.
   b. The police cannot use GPS to follow someone except in certain conditions.
   c. The police should never sit in the back seat behind a criminal.

7. Which of the following is NOT mentioned in the passage?

   a. A rental car company charged customers extra for driving too fast.
   b. A customer got angry with the company and decided to sue.
   c. The court said the charges were legal, and the customer had to pay.

8. You can infer from this passage that in the United States

   a  private companies are allowed to use GPS to locate customers.
   b. the use of GPS has reduced the number of airplane accidents.
   c. people's privacy is protected by the law and the courts.

# Issues and Ideas

## EXERCISE 1

**A.** *Write your starting time:* _____ *Then preview and read the passage.*

### The Perks of Reading Fiction

Think back over the last week—have you read any fiction?

Many young people probably haven't. They may have spent their free time online, posting Facebook or Twitter updates, or streaming episodes of The Big Bang Theory. Or they may have dedicated it to keeping up to date with the news, reading course materials, or professional journals. Reading stories and novels, after all, is old-fashioned and irrelevant, a waste of time.

Or is it? Recent research has shown, on the contrary, that reading fiction is good for your brain. Some benefits have been known for a while. Language teachers are well aware that reading extensively in the target language helps students acquire vocabulary, syntax, and, more generally, a feel for the way the language is used. Students can also learn about the culture, people, and places associated with their language of study. And all this is more likely to happen when you are reading fiction because a good novel draws you in: You want to know the people better and find out what happens, so you keep reading.

School teachers also know all about the positive effects of reading, starting with parents reading stories aloud to their children. Numerous studies have found that children who are read to regularly become better readers themselves and generally perform better in school—not surprising, given the importance of reading for most school subjects. Children who become habitual readers get better grades and test scores throughout their academic careers.

But that's only the beginning of what reading can do for you. In recent years, thanks to fMRI scanning (functional magnetic resonance imaging), scientists have learned a great deal about what happens in the brain during reading. The traditional view was that reading involved mainly the language centers of the brain, particularly Broca's and Wermicke's areas, which are responsible for interpreting written symbols and transforming them into meaning. Scientists now believe that much more of the brain is involved.

In a study in Spain, for example, researchers scanned participants' brains while they read words with strong associations of smell, such as "perfume" and "coffee." The scans showed activity in the primary olfactory cortex—the part of the brain that deals with smell. When participants read words with no smell associations, such as "chair" or "key," there was no activity there.

A similar study in France examined brain activity while participants read about body movements. Their brains were scanned while they read sentences such as "John grabbed the stick." and "Paul kicked the ball." Reading these sentences stimulated activity in the motor cortex, the part of the brain that coordinates body movements. Furthermore, within the motor cortex, the activity changed location according to whether the sentences mentioned a leg or an arm—as if the participants had actually moved their own leg or arm.

In fact, it seems that reading about something is a lot like the real experience, as far as the brain is concerned. And where are you most likely to find a wealth of evocative details and colorful descriptions of people, places, situations, and actions? In fiction, of course. Reading a good novel stimulates all kinds of neurological activity in your brain.

But, as any avid reader is well aware, the experience of reading a novel is far more than gymnastics for the brain. In fiction, you can enter into the heads of characters and try to imagine what they are thinking and feeling. You can explore unknown emotional territory and experience novel social situations. According to Keith Oatley and his colleagues in neuropsychology at the University of Toronto, fiction provides us with a "simulation of reality" and gives the brain an opportunity to practice understanding and relating to other people. In fact, studies have found that people who read fiction are better able to guess the emotions of others than people who don't. As he has written: "We have discovered that fiction at its best isn't just enjoyable; it measurably enhances our ability to empathize with other people."

Aside from a better understanding of an individual's motives and actions, fiction also gives the brain practice in understanding human relations, what happens when people get together. Oatley says: "Just as computer simulations of atmospheric pressure, winds, and humidity are used to generate weather forecasts, novels can be thought of as simulations of how people react to combinations of social forces." Research seems to confirm this: The more practice you get in navigating the complexities of fictional social worlds—whether with *Anna Karenina* or *Harry Potter*—the better your social skills will be in real life.

Oatley's theory about fiction has sparked interest in various fields, most notably in business. In a blog post by Jane Kreamer for the Harvard Business Review, "The Business Case for Reading Novels," she discusses the importance of emotional intelligence (the ability to understand people's emotions) in the business world. "Emotions have an impact on the bottom line," she writes. She mentions studies showing that people with higher emotional intelligence receive the biggest pay raises and are promoted more. If emotional intelligence is so important, how can you improve it? Her answer is, by reading fiction. "It's when we read fiction that we have the time and opportunity to think deeply about the feelings of others, really imagining the shape and flavor of alternate worlds of experience."

Though business people might find the idea of learning from fiction surprising, Oatley's studies serve only to confirm what many others know from their experiences as teachers or readers. Oatley himself notes that there is nothing really new about his theory. Two thousand years ago, Oatley writes: "Aristotle claimed that poetry—he meant the epics of Homer and the tragedies of Aeschylus, Sophocles, and Euripides, which we would now call fiction—is a more serious business than history. History, he argued, tells us only what has happened, whereas fiction tells us what can happen, which can stretch our moral imaginations and give us insights into ourselves and other people."

**B.** *Write your finishing time:* _____ *Then turn to page 304 and answer the questions. Do not look back at the passage.*

## EXERCISE 2

**A.** *Write your starting time:* _____ *Then preview and read the passage.*

### Connection or Addiction?

If you are a student in the United States, you are naturally going to spend some time on the Internet. Everything relating to college courses is online these days, including registration, scheduling, announcements, assignments, and grades. But outside of coursework, how much time do you spend online? If you're like most college students, the answer is probably: a lot.

Many students start checking their text messages and social media accounts first thing in the morning, and keep checking frequently until they go to bed. Having grown up with the Internet, they take for granted a world with WiFi and instant communication. Neuroscientists believe this has changed the way they think. It seems also to have changed the way young people relate to each other. Time to move on from a relationship that is beginning to go sour? No need for an awkward phone call or an even more awkward meeting. You can send an SMS, or even better, "unfriend" the person, denying them access to your Facebook page.

In a University of Maryland study, 200 students were disconnected from all electronic media for twenty-four hours, and many of them said the experience was traumatic. They reported feeling anxious, unhappy, nervous, and physically restless. The researchers noted similarities between the students' reactions and withdrawal symptoms suffered by people with addictions to alcohol or drugs. The students said they missed "the feeling of comfort" that they got from social media. With their devices turned off, they felt out of touch. As the study concluded, "Going without media meant, in their world, going without their friends and family."

The Maryland researchers described the students' relation to media in terms of addiction, but not all experts would agree. Dr. Larry Rosen, a California psychologist, has looked closely at the way people relate to Facebook and found that for younger users, it is indeed a crucial part of their social world. He says they see it "as a part of everyday life, whether listening to music or communicating. For them, it's the same as talking on the phone. It's a part of everything they do."

But he would not call this addiction. He believes it is more accurate to speak about compulsion—a strong, unreasonable desire to do something. "Addictions," he says, "are about finding pleasure. Compulsions are born from anxiety, and Facebook is psychologically important. It allows us to project on the world, in a way that we've never been able to before, who we are and what we want to say about ourselves."

In some people, he warns, it may make certain tendencies worse. A narcissist [someone who admires himself] is likely to become more narcissistic. Someone who suffers from depression may end up more depressed. In an anxious person, the compulsion to check their Facebook page may become an unhealthy obsession that can interfere with normal life.

A certain level of anxiety does seem to be common among Facebook users. Many have mentioned the "fear of missing out"—or "FOMO"—which drives them to keep looking at their device. Patrick Mott, a teenage blogger from Canada, wrote that "sheer panic set in" when technical problems kept him disconnected for two days. He couldn't stop thinking that he might be missing something important.

If social media is so central to the lives of students, how does it affect the college experience? Parents, as well as college administrators, wonder if social media has made it easier or harder for young people to make the big move from high school and hometown to college and campus. On the one hand, the fact that it's easy for students to stay in touch with family and friends is reassuring for everyone. But it may also mean there is less incentive to make new friends.

For students who are studying abroad the effect may be even more critical. If they are checking back with friends and families all the time, they may not be open to new social or cultural opportunities where they are. As Robert Huesca has written: "These new communication tools come at a cost not only to cross-cultural immersion but also, and more important, to personal growth. . . . When I studied in Mexico City in 1980, telephone access was neither easy nor inexpensive nor of good quality. Attempts to call home were infrequent, costly, and often unsuccessful, which led to feelings of isolation and vulnerability. Although painful at the time, the periods of intense loneliness and homesickness I experienced taught me a great deal about empathy, tolerance, perseverance, perspective, and gratitude."

In terms of academic performance, Dr. Rosen has noticed a negative effect on students who are unable to turn off social media for part of the day. If they keep checking Facebook, they can't concentrate fully on their reading, their papers, or the lectures they attend. According to Rosen, "students who checked Facebook while studying tended to have lower grade point averages than their peers who resisted looking at the social network while doing their homework."

This could be compared with a similar phenomenon—the way email has become a major drain on productivity among office workers. In a blog post, Elizabeth Lupfer writes: "All too often, employees disrupt their activity to check email and then switch back to the activity, eroding overall productivity. This behavior tends to feed on itself, leading to further distraction."

No one expects students to close down their Facebook pages and become media hermits. For better or worse, as Dr. Rosen observes, Facebook and other social media are part of the way people interact and get information today. He recommends instead that young people try to find a balance in the way they use the media. When it's time to study, the best thing is to turn everything off. It's also important to prioritize. Do you really care about all the names and groups on your lists? Sort through them and cut them down. You may find that you will enjoy fewer contacts more and can focus better on those who truly matter in your life.

**B.**   *Write your finishing time:* _____   *Then turn to page 305 and answer the questions. Do not look back at the passage.*

## EXERCISE 3

**A.**   *Write your starting time:* _____   *Then preview and read the passage.*

### Not Enough Nature

A new term has been invented to fit a new condition in our society: nature deficit disorder. A generation ago, there was little need for the term. On a sunny day, parents would open the front door and send children out to play—in the yard, in the neighbor's yard, or in a park down the street. Not anymore. Children don't go outside much. They have other things to do (lessons in French, clarinet, yoga); they have other kinds of play (electronic), and their parents fear the evils that might be lurking behind the bushes.

Is it really so dangerous? Roads definitely have become more dangerous for small pedestrians, but parents usually aren't thinking of the traffic. They're worried about molesters and kidnappers. It doesn't seem to matter that the chances of a stranger attacking their child are actually very slim. Compared with a generation ago, violent crime has gone down dramatically in the United States and the U.K. All the statistics indicate that children in urban and suburban areas are just as safe, if not safer than their parents were as children.

But today's parents don't seem aware of this. It's no wonder, when day after day the television and newspapers are full of gruesome details about kidnappings and school shootings, and constantly show the faces of missing or dead children. That these are the same cases and the same cute faces again and again hardly seems to matter. They get our attention, as the media intended. Then if worried mothers or fathers go online to parenting websites, they'll find those same cases discussed by other worried parents, all their fears are reinforced and of course they'll decide never to let their children out of their sight.

Not surprisingly, children themselves have become fearful, too. Christine Odone writes in *The Telegraph* about her nine-year-old daughter, who used to walk down their London street alone on Sunday mornings to the bakery. She considered this a special treat and was proud of herself. Then a little girl named April went missing in England. The news was full of the story. As Odone says: "It doesn't matter that child abduction [kidnapping] is an extremely rare occurrence; the 'man in a van' has become a terrifying spectre that haunts the playground. My daughter and her friends swap scare stories about bad men who prey on children just like them." Now Christine's daughter doesn't want to go to the bakery alone. "What if someone takes me?" she says.

Fear is one factor that keeps children inside. Another is the attraction of electronic activities indoors. Thirty years ago, educators and doctors worried about the influence of television on children's development, but those children had only televisions. Today they not only watch television, but also, and above all, spend time in front of computers, video games, tablets, and smartphones. According to George Monbiot, "Eleven- to fifteen-year-olds in Britain now spend, on average, half their waking day in front of a screen."

Richard Louv, author of *Last Child in the Woods* puts it this way: "The point isn't that technology is bad, but that daily, monthly, yearly, lifelong electronic immersion, without a force to balance it, can drain our ability to pay attention, to think clearly, to be productive and creative. What to do? Match screen time with stream time. Research suggests that the best antidote to the downside of electronic immersion will be an increase in the amount of natural information we receive."

However, children today aren't getting much "stream time"—that is, time spent playing in natural environments with woods, fields, and streams. As Monbiot notes, the technological boom has coincided with "the remarkable collapse of children's engagement with nature." Children spend far less time outdoors and have many fewer opportunities for experiencing the natural world. "In one generation the proportion of children regularly playing in wild places in the U.K. has fallen from more than half to fewer than one in 10. In the United States, in just six years (1997-2003) children with particular outdoor hobbies fell by half."

For centuries, nature lovers have been saying that contact with nature is beneficial, and now scientific research has examined and confirmed their claims. Studies of animal behavior, for example, have demonstrated that animals in empty and unnatural environments suffer from social, psychological, and physical breakdown. Studies of humans come to basically the same conclusion. People with access to green environments are fitter and healthier than those without access. They are also happier, with lower levels of anxiety and depression. Furthermore, they have more opportunities for positive social interaction and enjoy a greater sense of community. People without access to nature, on the other hand, are more likely to have physical and psychological problems, and neighborhoods without green space have higher rates of violence and crime, even taking into account differences of income.

Research has proven the particular benefits of a natural environment for children. As might be expected, time spent playing outside in green spaces lowers the risk of obesity, hypertension, and diabetes. It also helps prevent asthma, vitamin D deficiency, nearsightedness, and attention deficit/hyperactivity disorder (ADHD). Studies have found, furthermore, that spending time in a natural environment reduces negative emotions in children, including anger, fatigue, anxiety, and sadness.

In fact, time spent in green spaces can positively influence children's development in a number of critical ways, as Dr. Stephen R. Kellert of Yale University has concluded: "Play in nature, particularly during the critical period of middle childhood, appears to be an especially important time for developing the capacities for creativity, problem-solving, and emotional and intellectual development."

The message is clear for parents: Your children need to see (and climb) trees, to smell flowers, grass, and wet earth, to hear birds and bees. But there is a message also for community leaders and policy makers. Trees and parks are not just ways to make communities prettier or to raise property values; they play a central role in the development of healthy and happy individuals.

**B.** *Write your finishing time:* _____ ***Then turn to page 306 and answer the questions. Do not look back at the passage.***

## EXERCISE 4

**A.** *Write your starting time:* _____ ***Then preview and read the passage.***

### Americans—at Home and in Rome

When you're heading off for a new job, for travel or study abroad, you may receive the advice: "When in Rome, do as the Romans do." In other words, do your best to fit in. But is that always possible or desirable? Let's say you are an American who actually does go to live in Rome. There are many aspects of the Italian lifestyle you may be happy to experience. You have a mid-morning coffee standing at the bar counter like everyone else. You eat lots of pasta and pizza and risotto and tiramisu. On Sundays you have a big lunch with a big group of friends, you take a siesta, and then you go out for a stroll in the main square.

But sooner or later, in Italy or anywhere else, you run up against something you don't want to do, something that just seems too alien. It's often a strange food. Americans think they know all about Italian food, for example, but the Italian restaurants in Cleveland or Houston probably don't serve rabbit or horsemeat or veal brains, which are considered delicious and healthful dinner options in Italy.

As an American, however, you may have grown up reading books about cute little rabbits, and you may not like the idea of rabbit on your plate. Likewise with horsemeat, if you dreamed all your childhood of a pony in your backyard. As for the veal brains, Americans have gotten out of the habit of those odd animal parts, such as brains, kidneys, liver, and tripe [stomach], that have a strong flavor and strange consistency.

Once you're clear on the Italian names for those items, you can avoid them on menus. Another kind of problem arises if you're a guest in an Italian home. Many Italians shower, dress, and leave the house in the morning without eating anything. They get their breakfast at the bar later on—a pastry to go with their caffè latte [warm milk with a shot of coffee].

Or, when Italians do have something to eat at home in the morning, it's usually cookies or cornflakes with caffè latte or warm milk. That doesn't mean a cup of coffee or milk alongside the cookies or cereal, but both together in a bowl—the cookies or cereal are served sodden and warm. Cold milk is out of the question—for adults, and even more so for children. The fact that millions of American children drink cold milk daily doesn't seem to matter. For Italians, it's bad for the digestion.

Digestion for Italians is evidently a delicate process that is easily disrupted. Not only cold milk, but any kind of cold drink, they believe, is sure to create problems. Far worse than drinking something cold, however, is actual bodily contact with water after a meal, which could cause cramps and other unnamed disorders. An Italian mother never allows her children near the water for at least two hours after eating, not even the warm water of the Mediterranean. An American mother who does so is eyed with concern. If she lets her children dive right in the deep end of the pool, she's considered totally irresponsible. True, there might be some risk of sinking like a stone after a full Italian Sunday lunch, but the size of the lunch seems to matter little to Italians. They're just as worried when it's a sandwich.

This concern about water extends to showers and baths as well. Italian children always take their baths before supper. An American mother might consider that a waste of clean clothes on young children who tend to be messy eaters. But an Italian mother is concerned only about the possible consequences of immersion after eating, consequences that are summed up by the Italian term "un accidente," which isn't a cold or a bit of indigestion, but something quite terrifying.

Fear of "un accidente" is also the reason why Italians never set foot outdoors with wet hair. Hair dryers are considered basic survival equipment, one of the first items to go into a suitcase. When children attend swimming lessons, parents must go along to help with the hair drying afterwards—not just for the girls with long hair, but even boys with crew cuts.

Then, there's another peculiarly Italian concern: fear of drafts of cool air. You'll find this out if you're on a stifling hot bus, and—like any American—you open a window. Some Italians will simply move away from the window. Others may give you a good scolding and shut it. They're worried they'll come down with "la cervicale," a common Italian ailment. It is more or less the equivalent of a stiff neck, which can affect Americans too, after sleeping in a strange position or looking up at the night sky. But for Italians, even the slightest breeze can apparently be the cause. That must be why you rarely see Italians without scarves around their necks at all times of year. These days, with air conditioning becoming more widespread, summer too is a time of risk.

It's easy for an American in Rome to wonder and laugh at what seem like Italian eccentricities. But perhaps Americans should pay attention to the things Italians notice when visiting the United States. Yes, they shiver in the polar temperatures of stores and restaurants—and wonder about the economic and environmental cost of keeping them that cold. They're horrified by the ever present ice cubes and astounded at the huge size of soft drink cups—and are shocked at all the obesity they see.

After all, the odd bits of Italian culture—fear of cold drinks, water, and drafts— are perhaps throwbacks to a time when people died relatively easily of pneumonia and other diseases, not so long ago in Italy. Italians can be forgiven for their eccentricities, which, after all, may be frustrating for an American but are basically harmless. The same can't be said for some of the things they notice about American culture.

**B.** *Write your finishing time:* _____ *Then turn to page 306 and answer the questions. Do not look back at the passage.*

**A.** *Write your starting time:* _____ *Then preview and read the passage.*

## The Importance of Civility

Orderly lines at the bus stop, polite greetings in shops, a respectful helping hand with a heavy bag. . . . What country is this? England, of course—a place many of us think of as a model for good manners and civilized behavior.

But some English people fear that may be changing. Countless stories in the media tell of vulgar behavior and many commentators have agreed with England's former Prime Minister, David Cameron, when he said: "People are rude to each other . . . public discourse is so bad mannered . . . civility is on a permanent and inevitable downward slide."

But fortunately, it seems that the media may have exaggerated. In day-to-day life, the British have not lost their good manners. This is the conclusion of a recent study by the Young Foundation. It reported that though many people expressed concern about the general state of affairs in Britain, most reported satisfaction with their own neighborhoods or towns. A large majority said they are usually treated with consideration and respect in their daily lives. They mentioned tolerance and politeness as reasons they liked living in Britain.

Furthermore, levels of trust have not fallen in the past decade, as many have claimed. A similar study in 1991 found that only 51 percent of the population believed that most people are trustworthy, but now, according to the Young Foundation, 65 percent feel this way. The rise in trust may be related to falling crime statistics and to the fact that people really are safer than they were ten years ago, in spite of the often melodramatic tone of the media.

According to the Young Foundation, civility is the most important factor in the way people feel about where they live. Think of your average day, of all the interactions in stores, on buses, or in the corridors at work or school. How do you feel when someone is rude? It sticks with you for hours. It darkens your mood and shortens your temper so that you're more likely to turn around and be rude to someone else. The fact that bad behavior tends to reproduce itself is well known. Studies of schoolyard relations, for example, have found that kids who are the victims of bullying are more likely to become bullies themselves.

The effects of good behavior have been studied less, so the findings of the Young Foundation are welcome. They have found, in fact, that civility is also contagious. If people are treated well, they're more likely to respond in the same way to others. This should not be surprising. Think of how you feel when someone smiles, makes a cheerful remark, or offers to help. It's like a beam of sunlight. Whatever your mood before, your load feels lighter, you're less alone, you want to smile.

But what exactly do we mean by civility? It's not just politeness, though that is part of the picture. Some young people seem to think that good manners are old-fashioned. Indeed, certain polite terms, such as *sir* or *madam,* can seem exotic to American ears (though perhaps not in the South). But many of the markers of good manners—*please, thank you, you're welcome,* and *excuse me*—still do wonders to oil the workings of daily relations.

Friendliness is also part of the picture. When you travel to a new country, your experience is colored by the way people react to you. You won't feel comfortable and you won't want to return to a place where the locals ignore you or treat you rudely.

We could say that respect for others lies at the heart of civility. Interestingly, the Young Foundation researchers found the most tolerance in the poorest and most diverse neighborhoods of London. They reported: "We observed how shoppers of a range of ethnicities queued [stood in line] patiently and stepped out of the way of prams [baby carriages] and elderly shoppers." As a shopkeeper in one of these neighborhoods commented: "We have to be polite because we're so different."

In affluent neighborhoods, on the other hand, the researchers found that "high levels of superficial civility . . . often hid deeper incivilities," including domestic violence and racism. On the whole, however, they concluded that racism in the U.K. was declining, and this has probably contributed to the improvement in civility. Certainly, the two are connected. Racism is a radical lack of respect for an entire group of people.

The pressures of modern life tend to undermine civility. It's harder to be decent when you're anxious and in a hurry. And then of course, there's the new technology, which has developed so fast we haven't had time to formulate acceptable standards of behavior. Still, it wouldn't take a degree in ethics to realize that a salesperson or clerk may be offended when you talk on the phone while paying. Or that an acquaintance may not enjoy chatting with you if you keep both ear buds in place.

Other kinds of problems arise from the use of alcohol and drugs, especially among young people. If you're out on a weekend evening in any English city (or, for that matter, on an American campus), you're likely to encounter loudly drunken groups of youths, and the next morning you'll see the mess they leave. When these young people go abroad, their behavior is no better. The police in many cities—from Estonia to Italy—have had to lock up young Brits and Americans for the night to keep them from harming themselves or others.

These problems need to be addressed. The Young Foundation report concludes that civility may not be in decline, but it could go that way all too easily. Perhaps we should look around at our own neighborhoods and ask ourselves what we can do to encourage civility at home. Families and schools are fundamental. So is the environment we live in. As the report recommends, we need public spaces that foster and reinforce positive interactions. We also need the people who are most visible to set good examples—in politics, sports, and in the media.

**B.** *Write your finishing time:* _____ *Then turn to page 307 and answer the questions. Do not look back at the passage.*

## EXERCISE 6

**A.** *Write your starting time:* _____ *Then preview and read the passage.*

### The Key to Efficiency: Work Less

Who is more productive at work—the employee who stays late at the office every evening and also comes in on Saturdays and Sundays, or the one who leaves regularly at 6:00 P.M. and rarely shows up on weekends? Many managers would say the first. Count up those additional hours, they'd say, and you'll get an equivalent amount of additional work.

Except that you won't. Productivity is not just about counting up hours; it's what's accomplished during those hours that matters. And since workers are humans, not machines, they get tired if they stay on the job too long. They become less efficient and they make mistakes.

Henry Ford recognized this fact in the early twentieth century when he reduced working hours in his factories. The work day was cut back from nine hours to eight, and the week from six days to five. Other industrialists at the time were shocked by these changes. They thought he was just giving in to the demands of workers and unions. But they soon changed their minds and reduced the hours in their factories, too, when they realized how much companies could gain that way.

In 1937, during the New Deal, the country adopted the 40-hour week as the standard for all workers who were paid by the hour. There was solid evidence by then in industrial research to prove that workers are more alert, healthy, productive, and safe in the short and the long run if they work no more than that (except for short-term exceptions of paid overtime).

But this standard has never been applied for "knowledge workers"—people in business, research, law, academics, and other professions. Since they work with their heads rather than their hands, it was—and still is—assumed that they don't tire out like factory workers. In certain professions, such as law and medicine, long hours have traditionally been part of the job. But over the past few decades, the practice has spread to many other professions, partly perhaps in imitation of the work ethic that seemed so successful in Silicon Valley. In companies like HP and Apple, bosses and employees alike dismissed the 40-hour week as old-fashioned and irrelevant. Everyone was expected to fit the pattern set by the early technology "geeks" of the 1980s like those at Macintosh who wore T-shirts that said: "Working 90 hours a week and loving it!"

Additional pressure has been felt by employees in many sectors due to the economic downturn in recent years. With the fear of losing their jobs ever present in their minds, they're afraid to say no to requests to stay late, work Saturdays, or skip vacations. Whatever the cost to their health, their relationships, or their families, they tend not to refuse or complain.

And the cost is considerable, first of all to health. A large study in 2011 involving more than 22,000 participants in seven developed countries including the United States, showed that working more than eight hours a day led to stress, higher blood pressure, and unhealthy eating—a combination that could cause serious health problems, including a 40-80 percent greater chance of heart disease.

As for the effects of long hours on relationships and families, they are not hard to imagine. Many marriages have disintegrated because of the strain of one or both partners regularly arriving home late and tired. To worsen the strain, companies now also expect employees to stay in touch electronically 24 hours a day, 7 days a week, so even when they've finally arrived home, they may be distracted by phone calls or emails. The employee under pressure may keep putting off a vacation, or take the vacation but ruin it for their partner or family because of the need to keep checking in with the office.

According to Tibor Scitovsky, professor emeritus of economics at Stanford University, the physical and mental absence from the home due to long working hours has profound effects, not only on the family, but on society as a whole. A shorter work week, he says, "would help make family ties stronger, reduce divorce rates, and increase quality parenting. The number of children home alone would fall, thereby improving school performance and stemming (lowering) the school dropout rate that makes so many of our youth today turn to drugs and crime because they are unemployable."

Ironically, there is plenty of evidence that long working days are not beneficial to companies either. As Ford recognized a century ago, people have their limits. In fact, studies have shown that knowledge workers reach their limits sooner than factory workers—in six hours instead of eight. After six hours of intense mental work, you may continue to sit in your office as your boss requires, but you are unlikely to accomplish much.

Indeed, if you are overtired, you are more likely to create problems than to solve them. This is especially true if you've been putting in long hours for weeks or months. If you're also not getting enough sleep, as is often the case, the situation can become critical. Research by the U.S. military has demonstrated that the loss of one hour of sleep per night for a week will lead to a mental state equivalent to drunkenness from alcohol. A recent Harvard study estimated that American companies lose $63 billion a year because of sleep deprivation.

Perhaps it's time to rethink our work ethic and the assumption that more hours worked equals more work done. A growing body of research suggests that, as Tony Schwarz writes, "the best way to get more done may be to spend more time doing less." Schwarz recommends taking time for "strategic renewal," by which he means time away from the office, not only physically but also mentally. This would involve taking breaks during the day for workouts at the gym or naps; sleeping more at night; taking longer, more frequent vacations; and, above all, turning off devices so the office cannot reach you. This is the way to boost productivity, improve creativity, and regain health.

**B.** *Write your finishing time: _____ Then turn to page 308 and answer the questions. Do not look back at the passage.*

# QUESTIONS For Unit 4

*Follow these steps for each exercise:*

1. *Check your answers with your teacher. Write your comprehension score (number of correct answers) in the progress chart.*

2. *Calculate your reading time: Finishing time – Starting time = Reading time: _____ Find your reading rate on page 263. Write it in the progress chart on page 264.*

3. *Re-read the passage and look for the answers to any questions you missed.*

4. *Go back through the passage again and underline the new vocabulary. Add any useful vocabulary to your notebook.*

## 1. The Perks of Reading Fiction

1. Which statement best expresses the overall idea of the passage?

   a. Reading fiction can help business people get ahead.
   b. Reading fiction is like having real experiences.
   c. Reading fiction is good for people in various ways.

2. Which of the following ideas is NOT mentioned in the passage?

   a. Students who read professional journals get ahead in their careers.
   b. Parents who read to their children are helping them in school.
   c. Students who read novels improve their language skills.

3. Researchers in Spain found that when you read a word associated with a smell, your brain

   a. acts as though you really smelled something.
   b. shows activity only in the language centers.
   c. performs better at school and at work.

4. The French studies looked at activity in the brain when

   a. children watched others playing sports and games.
   b. participants read about people making movements.
   c. researchers picked up a stick or kicked a ball.

5. What do Keith Oatley and his colleagues believe fiction can provide us?

   a. models for better behavior
   b. a representation of reality
   c. a realistic picture of the past

6. According to Oatley, people who read fiction can

   a. use computers better than those who don't read fiction.
   b. write stories better than those who don't read fiction.
   c. relate better to others than those who don't read fiction.

7. You can infer from the passage that successful business people

   a. don't have a clear understanding of people's emotions.
   b. may not always understand the emotions of others.
   c. are often concerned about how others will react emotionally.

8. Why does Oatley mention Aristotle?

   a. Because Aristotle was a great Greek writer of fiction.
   b. Because Aristotle made a similar argument in favor of fiction.
   c. Because Aristotle believed we should read history to understand the world.

## 2. Connection or Addiction?

1. Which statement best expresses the overall idea of the passage?

   a. Researchers believe that social media use can lead to addiction.
   b. For better or for worse, social media are an important part of students' lives.
   c. Recent years have seen dramatic changes in means of communication.

2. How did the University of Maryland students feel without social media?

   a. uncomfortable and alone
   b. worried about their families
   c. anxious about their grades

3. Dr. Larry Rosen thinks that Facebook users are often

   a. compulsive.
   b. addicted.
   c. narcissistic.

4. Which of the following can you infer from this passage?

   a. Young people often feel awkward with others.
   b. Some young people are unhappy at college.
   c. Many young people are anxious these days.

5. One consequence of social media may be that

   a. foreign students can more easily make new friends in the United States.
   b. young people make fewer new friends when they leave home.
   c. American students are more likely to make friends abroad.

6. Which of the following is NOT mentioned in the passage?

   a. Robert Huesca studied in Mexico City in 1980.
   b. He couldn't call home very often from there.
   c. He wishes he'd had Facebook back then.

7. Why does email tend to lower productivity?

   a. Because it interrupts and distracts workers.
   b. Because workers take too long to answer it.
   c. Because messages are long and confusing.

8. What does Dr. Rosen recommend?

   a. Students should stop using social media completely.
   b. Students should be careful about how and when they use social media.
   c. Students should use social media only on weekends and holidays.

### 3. Not Enough Nature

1. Which statement best expresses the overall idea of the passage?

    a. Children today should spend more time outdoors with nature.
    b. Children suffer from many physical and psychological problems.
    c. Children enjoy activities outdoors in green environments.

2. Which of the following is NOT mentioned in the passage?

    a. Traffic can be dangerous these days.
    b. Crime rates are lower than in the past.
    c. The risk of kidnapping is higher today.

3. Why are parents so worried about their children's safety?

    a. Because they constantly hear about crime from the media.
    b. Because they have seen bad things happen in their neighborhoods.
    c. Because they are too busy to watch their children all the time.

4. According to Richard Louv "electronic immersion"

    a. has a positive effect on human development.
    b. needs to be balanced by contact with nature.
    c. affects human abilities in a very negative way.

5. Which of the following can you infer from the passage?

    a. Compared with a generation ago, children now are less fit and happy.
    b. Compared with a generation ago, children now do poorly in school.
    c. Compared with a generation ago, children now have fewer pets.

6. The scientific studies of animals and humans

    a. differed in their conclusions about nature.
    b. contrasted with the views of nature lovers.
    c. came to similar conclusions about nature.

7. How does the passage suggest that crime rates might be lowered in a community?

    a. by creating a more green environment
    b. by helping people raise their incomes
    c. by making the streets safer for children

8. Which of the following is NOT mentioned in the passage?

    a. Playing in natural environments helps children become more creative.
    b. Playing in natural environments makes children better at solving problems.
    c. Playing in natural environments builds stronger bones in children.

### 4. Americans—at Home and in Rome

1. Which statement best expresses the overall idea of the passage?

    a. Italians worry more about their health than Americans.
    b. Cultures tend to vary widely from one country to another.
    c. Italians and Americans do many things differently.

2. Why don't many Americans want to try rabbit or horsemeat in Italy?

    a. Because they read and dream a lot about animals as children.

    b. Because they think rabbit and horsemeat are not healthy for you.

    c. Because they aren't served by Italian restaurants in America.

3. In the morning, most Italians

    a. have black coffee.

    b. never eat breakfast.

    c. have a light breakfast.

4. Which of the following can you infer from this passage?

    a. Many Italians enjoy drinks with ice in them.

    b. Many Americans like drinking very cold milk.

    c. Many Americans have milk and cookies for breakfast.

5. What do Italians think is a bad idea after lunch?

    a. taking a nap

    b. going swimming

    c. drinking a coffee

6. Which of the following is NOT mentioned in the passage?

    a. Italian children usually take baths before supper.

    b. Italians of all ages dry their hair after bathing.

    c. Many Italians have never learned how to swim.

7. According to Italians, "la cervicale" [a stiff neck] can be caused by

    a. sports or hard work.

    b. cool drafts or breezes.

    c. wearing a tight scarf.

8. Which of the following is NOT mentioned in the passage?

    a. Italians who visit the United States think the food is too expensive.

    b. Italians who visit the United States think places are too air conditioned.

    c. Italians who visit the United States think restaurants serve too much food.

## 5. The Importance of Civility

1. Which statement best expresses the overall idea of the passage?

    a. Civility is declining in modern England.

    b. Civility is an important value in modern society.

    c. The English are known for their good manners.

2. Media reports make the British seem

    a. ruder and more vulgar than they really are.

    b. more polite and civilized than they really are.

    c. about the same as they always have been.

3. According to the Young Foundation report, what do the British like most about their country?

    a. the low crime statistics
    b. the tolerance and politeness
    c. the traditions and lifestyle

4. Which of the following is NOT mentioned in the passage?

    a. The English generally trust each other more than in the past.
    b. The English are generally safer than in the past.
    c. The English are more likely to be rude than in the past.

5. The researchers found that good manners in one person

    a. tend to inspire good manners in others.
    b. does not necessarily lead to good manners in others.
    c. may cause a negative reaction in some people.

6. Which of the following can you infer from this passage?

    a. Wealthy people are more tolerant than the poor.
    b. Wealthy people are just as tolerant as the poor.
    c. Wealthy people tend to be less tolerant than the poor.

7. Which of the following is NOT mentioned in the passage?

    a. The stress of modern life can affect people's manners.
    b. Many people do not think of others when they use technology.
    c. Level of education tends to correlate to level to politeness.

8. The Young Foundation concludes that

    a. civility used to be an important value for many people.
    b. civility is still an important value, but it could easily decline.
    c. civility is losing its importance in the lives of many people.

## 6. The Key to Efficiency: Work Less

1. Which statement best expresses the overall idea of the passage?

    a. Working long hours is not good for workers or employers.
    b. The working day has become longer in recent decades.
    c. The physical and mental capacities of humans are limited.

2. How did Ford shock other industrialists in the early twentieth century?

    a. by allowing his workers to decide on their own hours
    b. by requiring workers to stay for additional hours
    c. by shortening the working hours in his factories

3. Which of the following can you infer from the passage?

    a. Employees of Silicon Valley companies rarely work long hours.
    b. The early technology workers were often obsessed with their work.
    c. Most technology workers do not have families and are not married.

4. Which of the following is NOT mentioned in the passage?

   a. Fear of unemployment may push employees to work more hours.
   b. Other companies imitate the work days of the tech companies.
   c. Most employees are able to resist requests to work longer hours.

5. Research has shown that heart disease can result from the stress of

   a. unemployment.
   b. long work days.
   c. a divorce.

6. What aspect of modern life increases the pressure on employees?

   a. the fact that communication with the office is always possible electronically
   b. the fact that values are changing among families and young people
   c. the fact that unemployment is higher than it was in the past

7. According to Tibor Scitovsky, a shorter work week would allow

   a. schools to help children perform better.
   b. companies to offer better jobs to young people.
   c. parents to take better care of their children.

8. Which of the following is NOT mentioned in the passage?

   a. If you don't get enough sleep, you can't think clearly.
   b. Eating poorly will affect your mental concentration.
   c. You can't think as well after six hours of mental effort.

# APPENDIX
# Frequently Used Words in English

\* Words included on the Academic Word List (A. Coxhead, 1998).

| | | | | | |
|---|---|---|---|---|---|
| abandon* | adult* | almost | appropriate* | attention | beer |
| able | advance | alone | approve | attitude* | before |
| abolish | advantage | along | approximately* | attract | beg |
| abortion | advent | already | arbitrary* | attractive | beginning |
| about | adventure | alter* | architecture | attribute* | behalf* |
| above | adverse | alternative* | area* | audience | behave |
| abroad | advertising | altogether | arena | authentic | behavior |
| absence | advice | alumnus | argue | author* | behind |
| absent | advocate* | always | arise | authority* | believe |
| absolutely | aesthetic | amazing | arm | automatically* | belong |
| absorb | affair | ambiguous* | army | autonomous | below |
| abstract* | affect* | ambition | around | available* | belt |
| absurd | affiliation | amend* | arouse | avenue | bend |
| abundance | affinity | amount | arrangement | average | benefit* |
| abuse | affirm | amplify | array | avoid | betray |
| academic* | afford | analogy* | arrest | await | bias* |
| accelerate | afraid | analysis* | arrive | award | big |
| accent | afternoon | ancestor | arrow | aware* | bill |
| accept | afterwards | ancient | art | away | billion |
| access n* | again | and | article | awesome | binary |
| accident | age | angle | articulate | awful | bind |
| accommodate* | agency | angry | artificial | awkward | biography |
| accompany* | agenda | animal | artist | axe | biology |
| accomplish | aggressive | anniversary | ascertain | axis | bird |
| accordingly | ago | announce | ascribe | baby | birth |
| account | agree | annual* | aside | back | birthday |
| accumulate* | agricultural | anonymous | ask | background | bit |
| accurate* | ahead | answer | aspect* | backward | bitter |
| accuse | aid* | anthropology | aspiration | badly | bizarre |
| achieve* | aim | anticipate* | assault | bag | black |
| acid | air | anxiety | assemble* | balance | blame |
| acknowledge* | aircraft | anybody | assertion | ball | blank |
| acquire* | airline | anymore | assessment* | ban | blend |
| across | airport | anyone | asset | band | blind |
| action | alarm | anything | assign* | bank | block |
| actually | album | anyway | assimilate | bar | blood |
| acute | alcohol | anywhere | assist* | bare | blow |
| adapt* | alert | apart | assistant | barrier | blue |
| add | algorithm | apartment | associate | basically | blur |
| addiction | alien | apparatus | assume* | basis | board |
| address | align | apparent* | assure* | bath | boast |
| adequate* | alike | appeal | athlete | battery | boat |
| adhere | alive | appear | atmosphere | battle | body |
| adjacent* | all | appetite | atom | be | boil |
| adjective | alleged | apple | attach* | beach | bold |
| adjust* | alliance | apply | attack | bear v | bond* |
| administration* | allocate* | appoint | attain* | beat | bone |
| admire | allow | appraisal | attempt | beauty | bonus |
| admit | allude | appreciate* | attend | become | book |
| adopt | ally | approach* | attendance | bed | boom |

| | | | | | |
|---|---|---|---|---|---|
| boost | cater | command | conversation* | curious | deploy |
| boot | cause | commence* | convert* | currency* | deposit |
| border | caution | comment* | convey | current | depression* |
| boring | cease* | commercial | conviction | curriculum | deprive |
| borrow | celebrate | commission* | convince* | curve | depth |
| boss | cell | commitment* | cook | customer | derive* |
| bother | cent | committee | cool | cut | descend |
| bottle | center | commodity* | cooperation* | cycle* | describe |
| bottom | century | common | coordinate* | daily | desert |
| boundary | ceremony | communication* | cope | damage | deserve |
| box | certain | community* | copy | dance | design* |
| boy | certificate | compact | copyright | dangerous | designate |
| bracket | chain | comprehensive* | core* | dare | desire |
| brain | chair | comprise* | corner | dark | desk |
| branch | chairman | compromise | corporate* | data* | desperate |
| brand | challenge* | compulsory | correct | database | despite* |
| breach | childhood | computer | correlation | date | destination |
| bread | chip | conceal | correspond* | datum | destroy |
| breadth | choose | concede | corruption | daughter | detach |
| break | chronic | conceive* | cost | day | detail |
| breakdown | church | concentrate* | costly | dead | detect* |
| breakfast | cigarette | concept* | council | deadline | determine |
| breast | cinema | concern | counsel | deal | devastating |
| breath | circle | concerned | count | dear | develop |
| breed | circuit | concert | counter | death | deviation* |
| bridge | circulate | concession | counterpart | debate* | device* |
| brief* | circumstance* | conclusion* | countless | debt | devise |
| bright | cite* | concrete | country | decade* | devote* |
| brilliant | citizen | condemn | countryside | decay | diagnose |
| bring | city | condition | county | decent | diagram |
| broad | civic | conduct* | couple* | decide | dialogue |
| broadcast | civil* | conference* | courage | declare | diameter |
| brother | claim | confidence | course | decline* | diary |
| brown | clarify* | configuration | court | decrease | dictate |
| budget | clash | confine* | courtesy | dedicated | dictionary |
| build | class | confirm* | cover | deduce* | die |
| bulk* | classic* | conflict* | cow | deem | diet |
| bunch | classification | conform* | crack | deep | different |
| burden | classroom | confront | craft | default | differentiate* |
| bureaucracy | clause* | confuse | crash | defeat | difficult |
| burn | clean | conjunction | crazy | defect | diffusion |
| burst | clear | connection | create | defend | dig |
| bury | clever | connotation | creature | deficit | digital |
| bus | click | contemporary* | credibility | define* | dignity |
| business | client | contend | credit* | definite* | dilemma |
| busy | climate | content | crew | degradation | dimension* |
| but | climb | contention | crime | degree | diminish* |
| button | coin | contest | crisis | delay | dinner |
| buy | coincide* | context* | criteria* | delegate | direct |
| cable | cold | continent | critical | deliberate | dirty |
| card | collaboration | contingent | critique | delicate | disability |
| care | collapse* | continual | crop | delight | disadvantage |
| career | colleague* | continuation | cross | deliver | disagree |
| carry | collection | continue | crowd | demand | disappear |
| cartoon | college | continuum | crucial* | democratic | disappoint |
| carve | colonial | contract* | crude | demographic | disaster |
| case | colony | contradiction* | cry | demonstrate* | discard |
| cash | color | contrary* | crystal | denial | discern |
| cast | column | contrast* | cue | denote* | discharge |
| casual | combat | contribute* | culminate | density | discipline |
| cat | combine | control | cult | deny* | disclose |
| catalogue | come | controversy* | culture* | department | discount |
| catalyst | comedy | convenient | cumulative | departure | discourage |
| catch | comfortable | convention* | cup | depend | discourse |
| category* | comic | convergence | cure | depict | discover |

discrepancy
discrete*
discrimination*
discursive
discuss
disease
disguise
dismiss
disorder
disparity
disperse
displace*
display*
dispose*
dispute
disrupt
dissertation
dissolve
distance
distinction*
distinguish
distort*
distract
distress
distribution*
district
disturb
divergence
diversity*
divide
divine
divorce
do
doctor
doctrine
document*
dog
dollar
domain*
domestic*
dominant*
donor
door
dose
double
doubt
down
dozen
draft*
drag
drama*
dramatic
draw
drawing
dream
dress
drink
drive
drop
drug
dry
dual
due
duration*
dust

duty
dynamic*
eager
ear
early
earn
earth
easily
east
easy
eat
echo
ecological
economic*
edge
editor*
education
effect
efficient
effort
egg
ego
either
elaborate
elderly
election
electrical
electronic
element*
elevated
elicit
eligible
eliminate*
elite
else
elsewhere
email
embark
embed
embody
embrace
emerge*
emergency
emission
emotional
emphasis*
empire
empirical*
employ
empower
empty
enable*
enact
encapsulate
enclose
encode
encompass
encounter*
encourage
end
endorse
endow
endure
enemy
energy

enforce*
engage
engender
engineering
enhance*
enjoy
enlarge
enlightenment
enormous*
enough
enquiry
enrich
enroll
ensue
ensure*
entail
enter
enterprise
entertain
entertainment
enthusiastic
entire
entitle
entity*
entrance
entrepreneur
entry
environment*
envisage
epic
epidemic
episode
equal*
equilibrium
equipment*
equity
equivalent*
era
erosion*
error*
escape
especially
essay
essential
establish*
estate*
estimate*
eternal
ethical*
ethnic*
evaluate*
even
evening
event
eventually*
ever
everybody
everyday
everyone
everything
everywhere
evidence*
evil
evoke
evolution

evolve*
exacerbate
exactly
exaggerate
examine
example
exceed*
excellent
exception
excess
exchange
exciting
exclude*
excuse
executive
exemplify
exercise
exert
exhaust
exhibit*
exist
exit
exotic
expand*
expect
expenditure
expense
experience
experiment
expert*
explain
explanation
explicit*
explode
exploit*
explore
explosion
export*
expose*
express
extent
external*
extinction
extra
extract*
extraordinary
extreme
eye
fabric
face
facet
facilitate*
facility
fact
factor*
factory
faculty
fade
fail
failure
fair
fairness
faith
fall
false

fame
familiar
family
famous
fan
fantasy
far
farm
fascinating
fashion
fast
fat
fate
father
fault
favorite
fear
feasible
feature*
federal*
fee*
feed
feedback
feel
fellow
female
feminist
festival
few
fiber
fiction
field
fierce
fig
fight
figure
file
fill
film
filter
final
finally
financial*
find
fine
finger
finish
finite*
fire
firm
firstly
fish
fit
fitness
fix
flag
flat
flaw
flee
flesh
flexible*
flight
float
flood
floor

flourish
flow
flower
fluctuation*
fluid
flux
fly
focus*
fold
folk
follow
food
foot
football
forbid
force
forefront
foreign
forest
forever
forge
forget
form
format*
former
formula*
forth
forthcoming*
fortunate
fortune
forum
forward
foster
foundation*
founded*
fraction
fragile
fragment
frame
framework*
frankly
free
freeze
frequently
fresh
friend
front
frontier
fruit
frustration
fuel
fulfill
full
fun
function*
fund*
fundamental*
funny
furniture
further
furthermore*
fusion
future
gain
gallery

| | | | | | |
|---|---|---|---|---|---|
| game | guess | hope | inadequate | install | join |
| gang | guest | horizon | inappropriate | instance* | joint |
| gap | guide | hormone | incapable | instant | jointly |
| garden | guideline* | horror | incentive* | instead | joke |
| gas | guilty | horse | inch | instinct | journal* |
| gate | gun | hospital | incidence* | institution* | journey |
| gather | guy | host | incident | instruction* | joy |
| gay | habit | host | incline* | instrument | judge |
| gaze | hair | hostile | include | insufficient | judicial |
| gender* | half | hot | income* | insurance | jump |
| gene | hall | hotel | incoming | intact | junior |
| general | hand | hour | incompatible | intake | jurisdiction |
| generate* | handbook | house | incomplete | integral* | just |
| generation* | handful | household | inconsistent | integrate* | justice |
| generic | handle | housing | incorporate* | integrity* | justify* |
| generous | hang | however | incorrect | intellectual | keen |
| genetic | happen | huge | increase | intelligent* | keep |
| genius | happy | human | incredible | intend | key |
| genre | hard | humor | incur | intense* | kick |
| gentle | hardware | hundred | indeed | interact* | kid |
| gentleman | harm | hunting | independent | interest | kill |
| genuine | harmony | hurt | index* | interface | kind |
| geography | harsh | husband | indicate* | interfere | king |
| geometry | hat | hybrid | indigenous | interior | kitchen |
| gesture | hate | hydrogen | indirect | intermediate* | knee |
| get | have | hypothesis* | individual* | internal* | knife |
| giant | hazard | ice | induce* | international | knock |
| gift | head | icon | indulge | interpersonal | know |
| girl | headline | idea | industry | interplay | lab |
| give | health | ideal | ineffective | interpretation* | label* |
| glad | healthcare | identical* | inequality | interrupt | labor* |
| glance | hear | identify* | inevitable* | intersection | laboratory |
| glass | heart | ideology* | infant | interval | lack |
| global* | heat | ignore* | infection | intervene* | ladder |
| go | heaven | ill | infer* | interview | lady |
| goal* | heavy | illegal | inferior | intimate | lake |
| god | height | illness | infinite | intriguing | land |
| gold | hell | illuminate | inflation | intrinsic* | landlord |
| good | help | illusion | influence | introduce | landscape |
| govern | hence* | illustrate* | informal | intuition | language |
| grab | here | image* | information | invade | large |
| grace | heritage | imagination | infrastructure* | invaluable | laser |
| grade* | hero | imbalance | ingredient | invariably | last |
| gradually | heterogeneous | imitate | inhabitant | invent | lasting |
| graduate | hidden | immediately | inherent* | inventory | late |
| grain | hide | immense | inherit | invest* | latter |
| grammar | hierarchy* | immerse | inhibit* | investigate* | laugh |
| grand | high | immigrant* | initial* | invisible | launch |
| grant* | highlight* | immune | initiate* | invite | law |
| graph | highly | impact* | injection | invoke* | lay |
| grasp | hill | imperative | injure* | involve* | layer* |
| grass | hinder | impetus | injustice | ion | lead |
| grateful | hint | implement* | inner | iron | league |
| gravity | hire | implication* | innocent | ironic | lean |
| great | history | implicit* | innovation* | irrational | learn |
| green | hit | imply* | input* | irregular | least |
| greet | hold | import | inquiry | irrelevant | leave |
| grid | hole | important | insert* | irrespective | lecture* |
| grip | holiday | impose* | inside | island | left |
| gross | holistic | impossible | insight* | isolate* | leg |
| ground | home | impression | insist | issue* | legacy |
| group | homogeneous | improve | insofar | item* | legal* |
| grow | homosexual | impulse | inspection* | jail | legend |
| guarantee* | honest | inability | inspire | jazz | legislation* |
| guard | honor | inaccurate | instability | job | legitimate |

| | | | | | |
|---|---|---|---|---|---|
| leisure | magazine | merit | multitude | number | outlook |
| lend | magic | message | murder | numerical | output* |
| length | magnetic | metal | muscle | numerous | outset |
| lens | magnitude | metaphor | museum | nurse | outside |
| less | mail | meter | music | nurture | outstanding |
| lesson | main | method* | mutual | obey | outweigh |
| let | mainstream | middle | mutually* | object | over |
| letter | maintain* | migration* | mystery | objective* | overall* |
| level | major* | mild | myth | obligation | overcome |
| liability | make | mile | naive | obscure | overlap* |
| liable | male | military* | naked | observe | overlook |
| liberal* | man | milk | name | obsession | overly |
| liberation | manage | million | narrative | obstacle | overseas* |
| liberty | mandate | mind | narrow | obtain* | oversee |
| library | manifest | mine | nasty | obvious* | overt |
| license* | manipulate* | mineral | national | occasion | overview |
| lie | manner | minimal* | native | occupy* | overwhelming |
| life | manual* | minimum* | nature | occur* | owe |
| lifestyle | manufacture | mining | near | ocean | own |
| lifetime | manuscript | minister | nearby | odd* | oxygen |
| lift | many | minor* | neat | off | pace |
| light | map | minority | necessary | offend | package |
| like | margin* | minute | neck | offer | page |
| likelihood | mark | mirror | need | office | pain |
| likewise* | market | mislead | negative* | offset* | paint |
| limb | marketing | miss | neglect | often | pair |
| limit | marketplace | mission | negotiate | oil | panel* |
| line | marriage | mistake | neighbor | okay | panic |
| linguistic | masculine | mix | neither | old | paper |
| link* | mask | mobile | nervous | omit | paradigm* |
| lip | mass | mode* | net | once | paradox |
| liquid | master | model | network* | ongoing* | paragraph |
| list | match | moderate | neutral* | online | parallel* |
| listen | mate | modern | never | only | parameter* |
| literacy | material | modest | nevertheless* | onset | parent |
| literal | mathematical | modify* | new | onwards | park |
| literature | matrix | module | news | open | parliament |
| little | matter | molecule | newspaper | opera | part |
| live | mature* | moment | next | operate | partial |
| load | maximum* | momentum | nice | opinion | participate* |
| loan | maybe | money | niche | opponent | particle |
| local | meal | monitor* | night | opportunity | particular |
| location* | mean | monopoly | noble | oppose | partly |
| lock | meaning | month | nobody | oppression | partner |
| locus | meanwhile | mood | node | opt | party |
| log | measure | moon | noise | optical | pass |
| logic* | meat | moral | nomination | optimal | passage |
| long | mechanism* | more | none | optimistic | passion |
| look | media* | moreover | nonetheless* | optimum | passive* |
| loop | mediate* | morning | norm* | option* | past |
| loose | medical* | mortality | normal* | optional | path |
| lose | medicine | most | north | oral | pathway |
| lot | medieval | mother | nose | order | patient |
| loud | medium* | motif | notable | ordinary | pattern |
| love | meet | motion | note | organ | pay |
| lovely | melt | motivation* | nothing | organic | peace |
| low | member | motor | notice | organization | peak |
| loyalty | memory | mount | notion* | orient* | peasant |
| luck | mental* | mountain | notorious | original | peculiar |
| lunch | mention | mouse | noun | other | peer |
| lung | mentor | mouth | novel | otherwise | pen |
| luxury | menu | move | now | outcome* | penalty |
| lyric | merchant | movie | nowadays | outer | penetrate |
| machine | mere | much | nowhere | outlet | pension |
| mad | merge | multiple | nuclear* | outline | people |

| | | | | | |
|---|---|---|---|---|---|
| perceive* | poor | priest | publish* | recommend | research* |
| percent* | pop | primary* | pull | reconcile | resemble |
| perfect | popular | prime* | pulse | reconstruct | resemble |
| performance | population | primitive | pump | record | reserve |
| perhaps | port | principal* | punish | recourse | resident* |
| period* | portfolio | principle* | pupil | recover* | residual |
| peripheral | portion* | print | purchase | recreation | resist |
| permanent | portray | prior* | pure | recruit | resolve* |
| permit | pose* | priority* | purpose | recur | resonance |
| perpetuate | posit | prise | pursue* | red | resort |
| persist* | position | prison | push | reduce | resource* |
| person | positive* | private | put | redundant | respect |
| personnel | possess | privilege | puzzle | refer | respond* |
| perspective* | possible | probably | qualify | reference | responsible |
| persuade | post | problem | qualitative* | refine* | rest |
| pertain | poster | procedure* | quality | reflect | restaurant |
| pertinent | postgraduate | proceed | quantity | reform | restore* |
| pervasive | pot | process* | quantum | refugee | restraint* |
| phase* | potential* | proclaim | quarter | refuse | restrict* |
| phenomenon* | pound | produce | query | regard | result |
| philosophy* | pour | professional* | quest | regardless* | resume |
| phone | poverty | profile | question | regime* | retail |
| photograph | power | profit | quick | region* | retain* |
| phrase | practical | profitable | quiet | register* | retention |
| physical* | practice | profound | quit | regular | rethink |
| physician | practitioner* | profoundly | quite | regulate* | retire |
| physics | pragmatic | program | quote* | reinforce* | retrieve |
| physiological | praise | progress | race | reiterate | return |
| piano | prayer | prohibit* | racial | reject* | reveal* |
| pick | precede* | project* | radiation | relate | revenue* |
| picture | precious | proliferation | radical* | relationship | reverse* |
| piece | precise* | prolonged | radio | relax | review |
| pig | preclude | prominent | radius | release* | revise* |
| pile | precursor | promise | rail | relevant* | revisit |
| pilot | predecessor | promote* | rain | reliable | revive |
| pioneer | predict* | prompt | raise | relief | revolutionary* |
| pipe | predominant* | prone | random* | religion | reward |
| pitch | prefer | pronounce | range* | reluctant* | rewrite |
| place | pregnant | proof | rank | rely* | rhetoric |
| placement | prejudice | propaganda | rape | remain | rhythm |
| plain | preliminary* | propagate | rapid | remark | rich |
| plan | premise | proper | rare | remarkable | rid |
| plane | premium | property | rate | remedy | ride |
| planet | preoccupation | proponent | rather | remember | ridiculous |
| plant | prepare | proportion* | rating | remind | right |
| plastic | prerequisite | propose | ratio* | remote | rigid* |
| plate | prescribe | prose | rational* | remove* | rigorous |
| platform | prescription | prospect* | raw | render | ring |
| plausible | presence | prosperity | ray | renew | rise |
| play | present | protect | reach | rent | risk |
| please | presentation | protein | reaction* | repair | ritual |
| plenty | preserve | protest | read | repeat | rival |
| plot | president | protocol* | ready | repertoire | river |
| pocket | press | prototype | real | replace | road |
| poem | pressure | proud | reality | replicate | robust |
| poetry | prestige | prove | realize | reply | rock |
| point | prestigious | provide | realm | report | role* |
| polar | presumably* | province | reason | represent | roll |
| pole | pretend | provoke | recall | repression | romantic |
| police | pretty | proximity | receipt | reprint | roof |
| policy* | prevail | psychological | receive | reproduce | room |
| political | prevent | pub | recent | reputation | root |
| poll | previous* | public | recipient | request | rotate |
| pollution | price | publication* | reciprocal | require* | rough |
| pool | pride | publicity | recognize | rescue | round |

| route* | seldom | silent | soul | stop | sure |
|---|---|---|---|---|---|
| routine | select* | silly | sound | storage | surface |
| row | self | silver | source* | store | surgery |
| ruin | sell | similar* | south | storey | surplus |
| rule | semantic | simple | sovereignty | storm | surprise |
| ruling | semester | simulation* | space | story | surround |
| run | seminar | simultaneous | span | straight | surroundings |
| rural | send | sin | spark | straightforward* | surveillance |
| rush | senior | sing | spatial | strain | survey* |
| sacred | sense | single | speak | strand | survive* |
| sacrifice | sentence | singular | special | strange | susceptible |
| sad | sentiment | sink | species | strategy* | suspect |
| safe | separate | sister | specific* | stream | suspend* |
| safeguard | sequence* | sit | specify* | street | sustain* |
| sake | series* | site* | spectacle | strength | swear |
| salary | serious | situation | spectrum | stress* | sweep |
| sale | serve | size | speculate | stretch | sweet |
| salt | session | sketch | speech | strict | swim |
| same | set | skill | speed | strike | swing |
| sample | settle | skin | spell | string | switch |
| sanction | settlement | skip | spend | strip | symbol* |
| sand | several | sky | sphere* | strive | symmetry |
| satellite | severe | slave | spin | stroke | sympathetic |
| satisfy | sex | sleep | spirit | strong | symptom |
| saturate | shade | slide | spiritual | structure* | syndrome |
| save | shadow | slight | spite | struggle | synthesis |
| say | shake | slip | split | student | system |
| scale | shallow | slope | sponsor | studio | table |
| scan | shame | slot | spontaneous | study | tackle |
| scandal | shape | slow | sport | stuff | tactic |
| scarce | share | small | spot | stupid | tag |
| scare | sharp | smart | spouse | style* | tail |
| scatter | shed | smell | spread | subject | tailor |
| scenario* | sheep | smile | spring | submit* | take |
| scene | sheer | smoke | square | subordinate* | tale |
| schedule* | sheet | smooth | stable* | subscribe | talent |
| scheme* | shelf | snow | staff | subsequent* | talk |
| scholar | shell | soap | stage | subsidy* | tall |
| school | shelter | social | stake | substance | tangible |
| science | shift* | society | stance | substantial | tank |
| scope* | shine | sociology | stand | substitute* | tap |
| score | ship | soft | standard | subtle | tape |
| scream | shirt | software | standpoint | succeed | target* |
| screen | shock | soil | star | successive* | task* |
| screening | shoe | solar | start | sudden | taste |
| script | shoot | soldier | state | suffer | tax |
| scrutiny | shop | sole* | static | sufficient* | taxation |
| sea | shore | solid | station | sugar | taxis |
| search | short | solidarity | statistic* | suggest | tea |
| season | shortage | solution | status* | suicide | teach |
| seat | shot | solve | statute | suit | team |
| second | shoulder | some | stay | suitable | tear |
| secondary | shout | somebody | steady | sum* | technical* |
| secret | show | somehow | steal | summary* | technique* |
| secretary | shrink | someone | steel | summer | technology* |
| section* | shut | something | stem | sun | teenager |
| sector* | sibling | sometimes | step | superficial | telephone |
| secular | sick | somewhat* | stereotype | superior | television |
| secure* | sickness | somewhere | stick | supermarket | tell |
| see | side | son | still | supervise | temperature |
| seed | sight | song | stimulate | supplement* | temporary* |
| seek* | sign | soon | stir | supply | tempt |
| seem | signal | sophisticated | stock | support | tend |
| segment | signature | sorry | stomach | suppose | tense* |
| seize | significant* | sort | stone | suppress | term |

terminal* token triumph universal victory welcome
terrain tolerance trivial university video welfare*
terrible tolerate troop unknown view well
territory tomorrow trouble unlikely viewpoint west
terror tone truck unnecessary vigorous wet
tertiary tongue true unpleasant village wheel
test tonight trust unprecedented violate* whereas*
testify too truth unpredictable violence while
testimony tool try unrealistic virtual* white
testing tooth tube unrelated virtue whole
text* top tuition unstable virus wide
textbook topic* tune unsuccessful visible* widespread
texture torture turn unusual vision* wife
thank total tutor unwilling visit wild
theater touch twenty update visual* willing
theme* tough twice uphold vital win
then tour twin upper vivid wind
theory* tower twist upset vocabulary window
therapy town type urban vocal wine
there toxic ugly urge voice wing
thereafter toy ultimate* urgent voltage winner
thereby* trace* unable usage volume* winter
therefore track unacceptable use voluntary* wipe
thermal trade unaware usual vote wire
thesis* tradition* uncertain utility vulnerable wisdom
thick traffic unchanged utterance wage wish
thin tragedy unclear utterly wait withdraw
thing tragic uncomfortable vacation wake witness
think trail uncommon vacuum walk woman
thorough train unconscious vague wall wonder
though training uncover valid* wander wood
thought trait underestimate value want word
thousand trajectory undergo* van war work
thread transaction undergraduate vanish ward workforce
threat transcend underground variable warm workplace
threaten transcript underlie* variance warn workshop
threshold transfer* underline variant warning world
thrive transform* undermine vary* warrant worldwide
through transition* underpin vast wash worry
throw translate understand vector waste worship
thrust transmit* undertake* vegetable watch worth
thus transparent undesirable vehicle* water worthwhile
ticket transportation* undoubtedly vein wave worthy
tide trap unemployment velocity wavelength wrap
tie trauma unequal venture way write
tight travel unexpected venue weak wrong
tightly treat unfair verb wealth yard
time treaty unfamiliar verbal weapon year
timing tree unfold verify wear yellow
tiny tremendous unfortunate verse weather yes
tip trend* unhappy version* weave yesterday
tired trial uniform* vertical web yet
tissue triangle unify* very website yield
title tribe union vessel wedding young
today trick unique* viable week youth
together trigger* unit vice weekend zero
toilet trip unite victim weigh zone

# Credits

**Notes**

# Notes

# Notes

# Notes

# Notes

# Notes

# Notes

# Notes

# Notes

# Notes